Networks and Imaging Systems in a Windowed Environment

Networks and Imaging Systems in a Windowed Environment

Marc R. D'Alleyrand, Ph.D.
Editor

BANTAM BOOKS
NEW YORK • TORONTO • LONDON • SYDNEY • AUCKLAND

NETWORKS AND IMAGING SYSTEMS IN A WINDOWED ENVIRONMENT
A Bantam Book / May 1993

ISBN 0-553-09245-6
Library of Congress Catalog Card Number 93-77093

Published simultaneously in the United States and Canada

Bantam Books are published by Bantam Books, Inc., a division of Bantam Double-
day Dell Publishing Group, Inc. Its trademark, consisting of the words "Bantam
Books" and the portrayal of a rooster, is Registered in U.S. Patent and Trademark
Office and in other countries. Marca Registrada, Bantam Books, Inc., 666 Fifth
Avenue, New York, New York 10103.

PRINTED IN THE UNITED STATES OF AMERICA

0   9   8   7   6   5   4   3   2   1

Contents

v

Part II   Planning and Design   117

Part III Implementation 253

Preface

The development of network technologies has made it possible to add imaging as a powerful tool to support the business process of an organization. With few exceptions, early image storage and retrieval systems (ISRS) were essentially stand-alone electronic filing cabinets, with a limited objective of mechanizing routine clerical operations. Assuming that documents were properly organized, these systems allowed users to store and retrieve information in a cost-effective manner. At that time, however, workstation processing power and operating systems limited their usefulness to single-task applications.

As communication and storage technologies developed, it became possible to design cost-effective centralized architectures where workstations could perform several tasks. Under that approach, the largest portion of the processing power, as well as system resources, was allocated to the central processor or processors, often a mainframe or a minicomputer.

The availability of inexpensive networkable environments, such as MS Windows, OS/2, and the Macintosh, allows redistribution of the workload to individual workstations with a reduced dependence on a mainframe. At the same time, progress in parallel processing architectures, adoption of portable software, and the penetration of standards in the data processing field are opening new opportunities for efficient use of the technology. Concomitantly, the principles of imaging system design can be expanded to handle all the other information formats covered by the concept of multimedia.

Fueled by the accelerated pace of technology development, the economics of imaging systems is faced with new issues. The rapid "commoditization" of low-cost software and hardware conflicts with the need to preserve existing investment in equipment and facilities. From a user point of view, imaging, which may have been perceived by some as a solution to all woes of information systems, is now a tool that needs to be integrated with the other tools in an organization to support its business needs.

It is the purpose of this book to present in a single work the discussion of design and implementation concepts made possible by the ready availability of multitasking (windowed) and communicating (networked) technologies, and to identify issues and solutions. As such it is a follow-up to two earlier works[1] that dealt with the why and how of imaging. This work focuses on the workstation as the physical interface between the organization and its information system and on the constraints that the use of imaged documents place on such an interface.

Additionally, this book is designed to be a guide to the selection, planning, design, and integration of image-based document storage and retrieval applications. The emphasis will be on printable/displayable text and graphics materials. However, its approach will be applicable to the emerging field of multimedia information systems, using video and voice in electronic document systems. The scope of this work is:

- The identification of the critical issues that are necessary to the efficient use of the technology in a multitasking environment.
- The description of the tools supporting that environment.

Networks and Imaging Systems in a Windowed Environment is written for the end users of document retrieval systems. The extension of electronic imaging beyond traditional document processing tasks makes it valuable as a vehicle for interdisciplinary development. Written with minimum technical terminology and from the point of view of the end user, this book will be of interest to designers of office systems, who need to understand the constraints of imaging systems; end users, who need a frame of reference to translate their needs into specifications; system planners and implementers, as well as support personnel, who need to understand the practical aspects of installed systems; students in the field, who need comprehensive treatment of specific applications of the technology. Because of its contents, this work also will likely be of interest to technical personnel involved one way or the other in the design and planning of imaging systems, as it will clarify some of the issues facing their clients.

Please note that throughout this book, the term data is often used to refer to machine-readable signals, and the term image to describe the digitized representation of a paper or microform document.

This book has been assembled with great care. However, because of the complexity of the field and the fact that there is no single or even best technical solution, there is no guarantee that a particular recommendation will work in a specific environment. Consequently, the contributors to this work, as well as this editor, cannot be held responsible or liable for any negative outcome of their writings. In addition, while occasional repetitions of subject matter between chapters have been avoided as much as possible, it has sometimes been necessary to reiterate earlier statements.

—Marc R. D'Alleyrand

NOTES

[1] D'Alleyrand, M. R., *Image Storage and Retrieval Systems* (New York: McGraw-Hill) 1989; M. R. D'Alleyrand, ed., *Handbook of Image Storage and Retrieval Systems* (New York: VanNostrand & Reinhold), 1992.

Part I

Introduction to Networks and Imaging Systems

1

Networks and Imaging Systems in the Business Process

Marc R. D'Alleyrand, Ph.D.

1.1   INTRODUCTION

All business activities are dependent on the exchange of some kind of information. Accuracy, completeness, and timeliness of processes supporting its transfer have become critical factors in economic survival. Two overlapping sets of mechanisms have proven to be essential to describe an information transfer process. The first one, which covers information capture, processing, storage, retrieval, and display, deals with the treatment of information by a given computer device. The second set, which governs the electronic connections between devices, ensures that information can be communicated between users of the computer system.

From a business standpoint, communications networks and processing systems have become strategic resources for any modern organization, with the ultimate objective to increase productivity and reduce operating costs. However, it is estimated that less than 10 percent of total volume of information flowing through organizations is treated by computers. The rest, primarily stored on paper or microforms, is still subject to manual processing.

Electronic document management systems (EDMS), often referred to in this work as imaging systems, allow the conversion of these paper- and microform-based documents to electronic images, which can then be processed by computer. This makes it possible to integrate documents and data about them into a uniform system. This integration, however, must often be done in the context of an existing computer system and of a network designed to handle the data necessary for the support of an organization's information needs. Because of the resources required for an efficient imaging system, the addition of imaging capabilities to existing computer and network installation cannot be merely the addition of another application. Handling and processing images requires much larger computing resources than traditional data. Consequently, achieving that integration demands a complete reassessment, and often redesign, of the existing computer and communications systems. To justify the costs involved, it will often be necessary to redesign the business process itself and reengineer the underlying workflow.

This book will identify the requirements of image-enabled systems, provide guidance for their selection and design, while supplying a methodology for reengineering the information transfer process necessary to support stated business objectives.

1.2　ORDERS OF MAGNITUDE AND OTHER CONSIDERATIONS

Quantitatively, documents in digital image representations are much larger data elements than in machine-readable formats. For instance, an average typewritten page is represented by a data stream of approximately 2,000 bytes in a word processing format, but some 50,000 bytes if handled as a compressed, bitonal electronic image. Even a blank page, which is represented by a few bytes as ASCII text, still requires several thousands of bytes in an image format. The implications for computer resources are obvious. From a storage standpoint, images of typewritten documents require at least ten times more storage capacity than the same document in a data format. And from a communication perspective, with everything else being equal, each page of text transmitted as an image may require ten times more time than if the document was in a data format.

At the same time, structural differences in data streams between image and machine-readable data create a host of problems for the communication system. For instance, while machine-readable data can often be transmitted as a succession of small digital packets, the same process for images would result in unacceptable transmission delays.

In addition, because images are an unpredictable assemblage of picture elements, their display for human utilization requires specialized graphic interfaces between the computer and its operator, thereby creating potential resource contention conflicts with other processing functions that may need to run concurrently with the imaging application. For instance, an image display may tie up all the memory available, thus preventing correct execution of supporting programs. It will be the purpose of specifically designed graphical user interfaces (GUIs) and supporting devices to optimize the resources necessary for an orderly functioning of an imaging system within specified operating conditions.

Therefore, an image-enabled system designed to meet specified levels of retrieval and response time performance will require a more powerful operating environment than its data-only counterpart. The industry has followed different approaches to solve that requirement, including using faster processors, new or enhanced operating systems, and new network architectures. In particular, the development of the client-server concept has allowed the dissociation of information retrieval from support tasks.

The following sections outline the history of some of these technological changes and review how they impact the design of an imaging system.

1.3 EVOLUTION OF NETWORKS

From a simplistic point of view, a computer network is a physical facility that allows communication between two points. Computer networks come in different sizes, ranging from very small, for the construction of computer devices, to very large, for information transfer. In either case, networks can be described in either a logical or a physical manner. Logical descriptions specify the information transfer process, in terms of data being exchanged, formats of the data stream, and signaling conventions. Physical descriptions cover the actual implementation of a given information flow and include the specification of the devices and their interconnections, or topologies, that will make that transfer possible.

For instance, in a token-ring topology, one of the major PC network arrangements currently in use, information is passed sequentially from one device to another along a closed loop. To ensure point-to-point communication, an addressing signal, or token, is used to identify the recipient of a given message so that the addressee station can capture the message, while others will ignore it. A logical description for such a network is a ring (see Figure 1.1), while a physical description is more like a star, in which all devices are connected to a central communication device, called a multiple access unit, to facilitate actual network operation (see Figure 1.2).

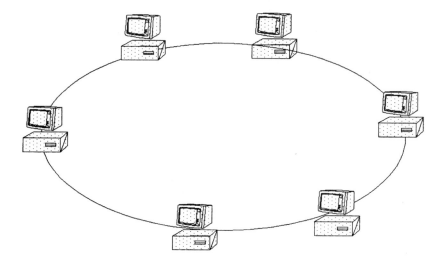

Figure 1.1   Logical representation of a token-ring network

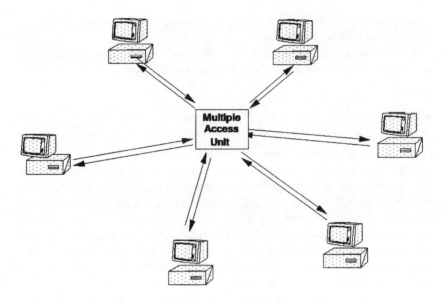

Figure 1.2   Physical configuration of a token-ring network

Initially, when the cost of computing equipment was extremely high, networks were information transfer links, designed for communication between a mainframe, which is a central processing machine, and terminals with limited processing capabilities. This was the time of the so-called "glass-house," referring to the physical environment containing the mainframe and its ancillary equipment. At that time, the cost of maintaining a computer installation, including hardware and software development, was such that it could only be justified in a centralized environment.

When the personal computer appeared and began to make local computing economically feasible, a second generation of networks appeared, in which individual processors could access high-cost peripherals, such as printers and storage devices. This device-sharing function was the original purpose of local area networks (LANs) and has remained in some organizations the sole purpose of networks.

In these two cases, most, if not all the intelligence necessary to direct information from one point to the other still resided in the processor itself. With the continuing expansion in personal computer processing capabilities, it became possible to migrate an increasing number of communication tasks to smaller machines, which allowed for the design of LANs, intelligent networks in which the computing resources required to support the information transfer process are distinct from those necessary for the support of information processing applications. This new generation of networks is characterized by a limitless ability to connect information providers, processors (restricted only by incompatibilities between computer and network architectures), communication hardware, software, and services.

An intriguing parallel to the development of LANs has been the technological change of the telecommunication marketplace. From a network theory point of view, data and telecommunication networks are two different forms of device linkage, with different design criteria to reflect different business requirements; one optimized for device sharing, the other for data transfer. The historical background of the two industries has resulted in different standards, but the ability to run both voice or data services on the same physical medium, whether wire or broadcasting channel, is bringing the two disciplines closer to each other. For instance, the compression standards for facsimile-based imaging systems are compatible with international telecommunication standards. One can foresee a near future in which the same information storage and retrieval services could be provided by either a data or a telecommunication network. This approach to networks is discussed in greater detail in Chapter 3.

1.4 EVOLUTION OF PROCESSORS

A computer can be described in terms of the speed at which it can process information, measured by the frequency of its clock, which is an internal synchronizing circuit; the amount of memory in which data can be stored for direct access by the processor; and the width of its data path, determined by the number of data elements that can be processed simultaneously. Initially, personal computers were powered by slow processors, with little main memory and a narrow data path. For instance, less than ten years ago, the PC-XT, the first microcomputer to use the DOS operating system, was running at less than 5MHz and had only 640KB of main memory, with an 8-bit data path. By comparison, one can now find machines on the market that run ten times faster, often have twenty times more memory, with a 32-bit data path, and which are still cheaper than the earlier machines. Machines running at 150MHz are beginning to appear in the marketplace with even more memory and a 64-bit data path. To give an idea of the importance of that data path in overall capability of a processor, Table 1.1 shows the number of distinct data elements that can be addressed individually in memory by machines with data paths

Table 1.1   Comparison between different data path widths

Data Path Width	Approximate Number of Addressable Data Elements	Approximate Number of Typewritten Pages	Approximate Length of Shelving (ft)
8	256	1/8	0
16	64,000	32	0
32	4,000,000,000	2,000,000	1,000
64	18,000,000,000,000,000,000	9,000,000,000,000	4,500,000,000,000

ranging from 8-bit to 64-bit. The third and fourth columns in that table are provided to place these numbers in perspective. They represent the number of pages of text that would be necessary to contain these addressable data elements, if they were typewritten on a page at 2,000 characters per page, and the length of shelving that would be necessary to store that paper.

Currently on the market there are several competing processing chips, each with its own set of features and capabilities. Intel xx86 series, RISC, SPARC, and DEC Alpha processors are designed to handle the large volumes of data required by imaging and network applications. However, taking advantage of their power could not happen without parallel progress in operating system sophistication.

1.5   EVOLUTION OF OPERATING SYSTEMS AND ENVIRONMENTS

The evolution in processing power made it possible to develop high-performance operating systems that provide more native functionalities. The early Disk Operating System (DOS) was designed to address a maximum of 640KB of memory, a limit based on the ability of the semiconductor industry to deliver high-capacity memories in a cost-effective manner. As a result, DOS was designed to support only character-based programs. In addition, DOS did not allow the processing of more than one application in memory at a time. This meant that users would have to exit (close) one task before starting another. In contrast, a mainframe installation could handle multitasking and graphical applications, which explains why early integrated imaging applications could not be implemented outside a mainframe environment.

Since then, progress in semiconductor technologies has made it possible to manufacture reliable multimegabyte capacity memories, making the 640KB limit of the operating system an artificially unacceptable restriction. This has created a demand for new operating systems and environments to support increasingly complex applications. Operating systems, including OS/2, NT, Macintosh, and UNIX, allow multitasking (windowing), which is simultaneous processing of different applications. New environments, such as MS Windows, allow the concurrent presence of different applications in memory, even though they still process applications one at a time, but appear to the user to occur simultaneously.

1.6   EVOLUTION OF USER INTERFACES

To maximize the benefits of data and imaging systems integration, it has been necessary to develop efficient modes of communication between the user and the computer systems and support the increasing number of functionalities found in imaging applications. A sampling of such functionalities is given in Figure 1.3.

By nature, imaging systems require a graphical user interface to display the image. Early imaging software allowed a coexistence between images of docu-

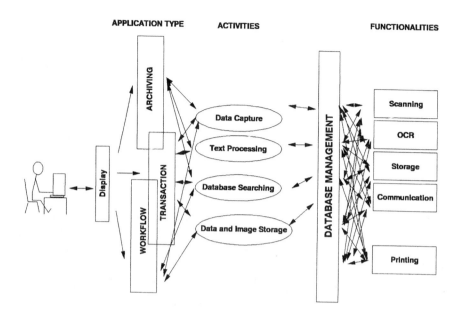

Figure 1.3   Sampling of functionalities found in imaging systems

ments and character-based information, such as file name or data entry screens. However, these early interfaces were not designed to increase "user friendliness," but rather to allow the display of images. In contrast, the purpose of conventional user interfaces, and more recently of graphical user interfaces (GUIs), is to increase productivity of the operator at the workstation and reduce the amount of learning.

In character-based systems, the user interfaces with the computer through a keyboard, either by entering a series of keystrokes on a command line or by selecting—again through the keyboard—entries in a menu or list of options. In many programs, recorded keystroke sequences, or macros, can be used to automate the performance of repeated commands or universal tasks, such as seeking a file or starting an application. However, the absence of standards, the difference in instruction sets between programs and perhaps the population of character-based users has prevented the wide acceptance of uniform keystroke sequences for these universal tasks. In addition, because of the sequential nature of keystrokes, character-based systems and the way they control screen displays have not been at all successful in competing with graphical interfaces to support concurrent applications.

In a graphical environment, the methods of interaction are much richer than under character-based conditions. Pointing devices, which can link a physical area on a computer screen with a data element, allow more powerful representation of data contents and instructions than a keystroke sequence; in particular, they allow the use of graphical metaphors to represent given activities and functions. The use of consistent information metaphors allows the system developer to isolate methods of access to a given system functionality from the actual processing tasks.

Because graphical metaphors are the most intuitive, graphical user interfaces have been highly successful in hiding from the user the commands necessary to execute a particular function. And because graphics allow nonsequential, two-dimensional representations, they make it possible to mimic the presence of simultaneous applications through the use of multiple "windows." While there are still differences between vendors, the trend toward similar "look-and-feel" GUIs allows the user to operate in a true (e.g., UNIX) or simulated (e.g., DOS) multitasking environment.

1.7   EVOLUTION OF NETWORKS

Initially, workstations did not have enough power to handle imaging applications on their own. Consequently, imaging networks were essentially centralized and controlled by a mainframe, which limited imaging systems to large installations. With more powerful workstations and lower costs, new architectures have become financially feasible. While the centralized (or file server) model is still used for applications that require a high level of control of data and the image base, distributed client-server and peer-to-peer architecture models have made great progress. These new networks are actually fueling and making possible a "downsizing" of installations, where applications are migrated from mainframe to smaller machines.

At the present time, there is a strong feeling that peer-to-peer architecture is not robust enough to support imaging networks. However, the combination of the increase in popularity and capability of workgroup computing software and the progress in network interoperability may well change the network landscape, to the point that both peer-to-peer and client-server will not only coexist in the same installation, but will support one another.

1.8   IMPLICATIONS FOR THE EVOLUTION OF IMAGING SYSTEMS

Technological progress that resulted in intelligent and cost-effective networks has also propelled the development of increasingly powerful imaging systems, with intelligence and a range of functionalities. Three different phases can be identified in this development.

In the first phase, imaging systems were functionally dedicated to the performance of specific tasks. Designed for centralized operation, their capabilities were essentially dependent on the size of the processor. In a mainframe environment, imaging systems could be designed as a complete replacement for paper-intensive operations. Several examples of monolithic imaging systems are still in operation in paper-intensive industries such as insurance and other financial applications. In the absence of a large processing capability, especially for PC-based systems, imaging was seen more as an electronic equivalent of—and with the same strategic importance as—manual filing, and its applications were limited to a replacement of paper documents by their digitized representation. During that phase, applications were cost justified essentially whenever a reduction of retrieval time from paper to electronic imaging meant an opportunity for headcount reduction in personnel. Most of the networks' activities were geared to the support of device sharing.

In the second phase, made possible by the development of intelligent networks, images could be communicated between workstations. However, because the level of resources necessary for image transfer outstripped the capabilities of early data networks, imaging systems most often developed independently from the rest of the computing industry. For instance, image database structures were optimized for the retrieval of the large data blocs, with little apparent concern for compatibility with other document systems such as word processing or computer output microfilm. In addition, because the nonerasable characteristics of early image storage media placed operational restrictions on storage device management, there was little integration between data and image systems.

The third phase, fueled by competition from other information technologies such as facsimile and electronic mail, progress in image processing such as optical character recognition (OCR), as well as further development in communication technologies, corresponds to the integration of imaging with other information facilities. This third phase is supported by the development of internetworks connectivity products and so-called open system technologies, which permit the transfer of information across different networks and platforms.

The design of third-phase imaging systems is facing a certain number of challenges:

- *Trivialization of imaging*   The fact that hardware has become inexpensive puts imaging applications within the reach of most businesses. At the same time, marketing hype makes it difficult to find out, without extensive testing, if an advertised feature is really as good as it sounds. For instance, one can now purchase a scanner for less than $1,000; one can also get one for $5,000, and even $50,000. A casual comparison may identify scanning speed as the major factor in price difference; however, other considerations, less easily quantifiable, need to be evaluated before a selection can be made. After all, how good are five $1,000 scanners producing the same throughput as a $5,000 scanner if, due to continuous production requirements, they all break down within a few days of operation, while the more expensive scanner would have been able to provide uninterrupted service for many years? Consequently, the challenge will be to convince the user that the underlying technical implementation difficulties should not be trivialized.

- *Increase in retrieval sophistication*   The growing demand for databases and indexing systems that can support the efficient retrieval of multimedia information in a platform-independent environment has deep implications for the application design and architecture of the information delivery system.

- *Cost justification*   Due to dropping costs in hardware and software packages, it becomes increasingly difficult to balance the initial relative low cost of off-the-shelf technical solutions with the hidden expenditures that may be necessary to customize such solutions for a specific business application.

- *Integration of imaging with other applications* The industry trend toward graphical interfaces for software has significant implications for the design and performance of imaging systems. On the one hand, the uniformity of the interface facilitates their integration with other applications; on the other, they will compete with these applications for memory and other computer resources. The way the integration is performed, and in particular the way the various programs share allocated resources, will result in dramatic differences in performance. In particular, a poorly designed integration may result in a total disruption of a network, with imaging preempting most of the available bandwidth during transmission.

1.9 IMPLICATIONS FOR WORKFLOW REENGINEERING

Workflow reengineering is the management process by which activities are rearranged to increase productivity and reduce operating costs. Because imaging captures information that was not available previously in a machine-processible form, it is a powerful tool in increasing computer control over an organization's information. Further, it makes it possible to combine tasks that previously may have been shared between manual and automated systems. This integration permits not only the automation of routine tasks, such as routing, data extraction, and the like, but also the insertion of quality controls, which could not have been cost justified in a paper-based environment. For instance, if the timing of document processing is as important as the actual actions taken, the imaging system can be designed to ensure that all documents are automatically date stamped at time of capture and that their processing is tracked throughout their life cycles, with exceptions to established procedures automatically flagged and reported.

But workflow reengineering cannot be done without consideration for existing systems. First, the demands of imaging on computer resources will require an analysis on whether imaging should be implemented as a new system or as an addition to an existing installation. Issues of protecting hardware and software investment will need to be raised in the context of the acquisition of more advanced equipment. In particular, it will be necessary to decide, very early in the system design, which activities of the imaging system will be available to which users. For instance, it may be more cost-effective for a service bureau to capture and index documents in a batch mode, keeping only retrieval operations in the main system. From a workflow reengineering standpoint, that may subsequently result in redistributing different workgroup activities that were previously performed concurrently in a manual environment.

One possible outcome of a workflow reengineering process that must not be overlooked is a shift in "ownership" of the documents and the information they contain. Because networked imaging systems make it possible to share information regardless of physical constraints, there will be a need for review and scrutiny of the security of the reengineered workflow.

1.10 CONCLUSION

The fact that networks are now indispensable to business operation is undeniable. As such, it is essential that the benefits of any functionality added to an existing operation be carefully evaluated before its implementation. There is little doubt that imaging technologies will in most cases enhance the business process. The questions surrounding their implementation will therefore often be how and when to integrate with an ongoing information system rather than whether it should be considered in the first place. The following chapters discuss the technical and business aspects of these issues.

2

Introduction to Networked Imaging Systems

Marc R. D'Alleyrand, Ph.D.

2.1 BACKGROUND

Regulatory requirements, traditional operating procedures, and the need to document and control large volumes of documents are resulting in an ever increasing demand for document storage. In turn, larger storage and longer retrieval times result in escalating costs. At the same time, the need for fast access to information is putting new requirements on document transmission systems. The issues to resolve are in the areas of:

- *Operations* Eliminate the operating difficulties associated with the unnecessary handling of vast amounts of paper.
- *Costs* Reduce the costs associated with the finding and retrieval of information in an expanding database and filing system, as well as costs resulting from printing and copying.
- *Security* Increase ease of access to authorized information in a way that still meets security and confidentiality requirements.
- *Dissemination* Ensure that the information is captured, processed, stored, displayed, and communicated under optimal conditions to the right people and in a timely manner.

Until a few years ago, the constraints of magnetic storage media made it impractical to accommodate information systems in which documents and machine-readable data were stored on the same medium. For instance, while personnel or financial data could be stored in a computer format, supporting documents related to that data had to be stored on either paper or microfilm. This plurality of media often proved inefficient, as it required two separate filing systems, one for documents (e.g., paper folders, microfilm rolls, microfiches) and one for the information about these documents (e.g., machine-readable computer reports and indices). In addition, nonmachine-readable documents could not be easily transmitted electronically, and access to them by different users often resulted in the creation of multiple copies.

The development of optical disk technology with its large storage capacity has made it practical to store both documents and information about them on the same medium in a digital form. This can be done regardless of content, be it machine-readable text, graphics, sound recordings, and images; and regardless of original format, be it paper, microform, tape, or other medium. To give an example: A high-density 5.25 inch diskette, with a storage capacity of 1.2 million bytes can store approximately 500 one-page typewritten memoranda in a machine-readable format. That same diskette cannot store the uncompressed image of one page. Even with most common compression schemes, such a disk would probably be able to store only ten to fifteen images of typewritten text, a number that rapidly decreases if the document contains shades of gray, such as in a photograph. By comparison, a 5.25 inch optical disk platter is capable of storing 20,000 pages, and a 12 inch platter up to 50,000 pages in a digitized image format.

Furthermore, because the storage process involves computer encoding, the information can be manipulated as computer data. In addition, digital signal processing is capable of electronic image enhancement, which means that it is possible to recover documents that under conventional optical means would be considered unusable. This is of specific importance when attempting to capture images of marginal material, such as poor carbon copies, poorly recorded microforms, or decaying paper with faded ink.

Optical disks make it possible to access, disseminate, and interpret document images in a manner similar to simple machine-readable material, especially in terms of security and encryption. That technology is of particular value to office correspondence, where documents, such as personnel files and other administrative materials, are created on paper in a nonmachine-legible format. Because it stores not only text but images, the digital format makes it possible to retrieve, disseminate, and display items such as facsimile signatures and handwritten marginalia in ways that were not possible before.

The combination of imaging and data processing in optical disk-based systems results in the following characteristics:

- *Immediacy*   Electronic capture of images eliminates the need for further manual processing of the original documents. Consequently, access to electronic images and updates is practically instantaneous, giving the ability to maintain files in a timely fashion.

- *Communication*   Because the electronic image is kept in a digitized form, it can be transmitted through data communication lines using well-known computer techniques. Encoding and standards might differ between systems, however, and will have to take into consideration the large amount of data being communicated. Nevertheless, the increased acceptance of protocols such as those recommended by the International Telegraph and Telephone Consultative Committee (CCITT) facilitates the design of compatible networks.

- *Image enhancement*   Image processing algorithms make it possible to detect edges of images and modify contrasts and thresholds, thereby reclaiming images that would have been unreadable in a microfilm environment. It is possible, for example, to strengthen the contrast in a blue carbon copy on a pink paper, an impossible task with microfilm.

- *Data extraction*   The development of affordable image processing software has made it possible to incorporate automatic data extraction in the imaging workflow and to integrate imaging into the business process. Because of the similarity of signals generated by an image scanner and an optical character reader (OCR), it is possible to process the image through an appropriate program that will identify and extract machine-readable characters in that image, thus enabling the capture of an image and extraction of the data that it contains at the same time.

- *Multimedia recording*   Electronic images are only one of the information elements that can be captured on optical disks. Other information elements, such as voice and music, can, once digitized, be added to the electronic records, making it possible to have an image stored with a verbal comment.

- *Hypermedia*   One capability offered by electronic imaging is called hypermedia, which is an arrangement of related documents where cross-referenced information can be accessed from any of the documents without having to leave the first document. Early examples of hypermedia, called hypertext, are well known, the simplest being a footnote or an explanation in the margin. What is important for information retrieval is that the cross-reference does not have to be textual any more. This makes it possible to thread a search not only through a series of references, but also through illustrative artifacts on a page. For instance, in a litigation support activity, a stain on a photograph can be directly shown by evoking its exhibit number.

These capabilities make the use of optical disks a strong contender in the information retrieval arena.

2.2   IMAGING SYSTEMS AS INFORMATION TRANSFER AGENTS

In less than five years, the development of document imaging systems seems to have followed two parallel although contradictory tracks.

1. In terms of size, document imaging systems have grown from stand-alone "electronic filing cabinets" to installations supporting mission critical applications.

2. In terms of relative importance in system design, their role has often been reduced from providing dedicated solutions to specific information control and processing problems to merely serving as efficient front-end data capture subsystems.

These tracks reflect two complementary perspectives of the same information delivery objective, which is to make information relevant to the conduct of business and available to the end users in a complete, accurate, timely, and cost-effective manner. In that context, document imaging ceases to be a miracle technology, capable of bringing instant cost reductions and productivity increases regardless of applications. On the contrary, it is increasingly evident that it is a very powerful tool, which, when fully and intelligently deployed, will enhance a business process. As a matter of fact, it can be shown that, when it is properly integrated in an organization workflow, it is an essential component and sometimes a critical one in the optimization of an organization's business process.

Given the fact that an estimated 80–90 percent of an organization's information has its source in a paper medium, document imaging is the fastest and least expensive method for inserting that information into an electronic medium. Consequently, that technology provides the needed front end to an integrated electronic data interchange (EDI) process.

2.3   INDUSTRY TRENDS

Current document imaging systems are the result of several converging technological trends. As such, they can incorporate the features of different legacies, ranging from records management to data processing and telecommunication.

Early document imaging systems essentially were implemented as electronic replacements for paper files. At that time, the only practical path to electronic document sharing was through a mainframe. The economics of computing, on the other hand, caused a segmentation of the imaging industry between stand-alone systems for simple storage and retrieval tasks and mainframe-based installations, which could deliver the processing power needed for more complex applications.

As mentioned earlier, the sustained increase in micro- and minicomputer power and the decrease in hardware and software development costs have contributed to cost-effective imaging applications outside the mainframe world. At the same time, progress in network technologies has made it possible to establish powerful information systems that do not need to rely on centralized processing.

Early document imaging systems can be classified in two groups:

1. Mainframe- (and to some extent mini- and midi-) based systems, where all resources including scanners, printers, and workstations are essentially peripherals connected to the mainframe, which holds the database and allows powerful multitasking functionalities. In these early systems, all the information processing power was concentrated in the mainframe.

2. Personal computer- (PC) based systems, which could be seen as a scaled-down version of the mainframe model, but with reduced capabilities, due to the limited processing power of their operating systems.

The structure of these two groups has traditionally been the result of technical as well as organizational politics and economics. Consequently, early on there was a wide gap between the computation-intensive requirements of workgroup applications, which only mainframes could support, and those of simple tasks such as word processing and spreadsheets, which could be easily accommodated at the PC level.

The competitive pressures of the hardware environment and the resulting production of increasingly powerful processors have built a bridge across that gap. The increase in processing power and storage capacity directly available to a PC has made it possible for microprocessors to begin supporting applications that only a few years ago required a mainframe, or at least a substantial mini or midi. In particular, the early selection criteria on what application could be efficiently designed for what platform (which were based on the maximum length of the basic instructions that could be processed by a given platform: 8-bit in the early PCs, 32-bits and over for minicomputers and mainframes) have somewhat disappeared with the advent of modern PCs capable of handling, sometimes with some "sleight-of-digit," 32-bit instructions. In addition, more efficient internal architecture and so-called cache memories can be used to smooth out inherent performance problems of lower-end systems. Now it is possible to port many mainframe-based, high-end applications to less expensive installations, thus enabling the implementation on local workstations of increasingly sophisticated and "power-hungry" applications. In addition, the increase of local processing power brought about the development of multitasking, or at least concurrent applications, a capability that previously had been available solely on mainframe installations.

At the same time, the development of network technologies has made the distribution of processing power along data utilization rather than resource lines possible, thus reducing the need to retain all information in a central mainframe. A major benefit of this development has been the ability to assign processors to specific tasks, such as file storage and printing, allowing for device sharing, thus making more processing power available to a user workstation.

These technological changes also have effected new challenges in imaging systems design, where the trade-offs needed to optimize performance involve the choice of architecture, underlying processing power of the supporting platform, and the relative importance of required functionalities for a given overall information delivery system.

While most of the earlier imaging systems implementations were essentially stand-alone installations, present systems are almost exclusively used in a network environment and may or may not be integrated in an overall data and information processing environment. An outgrowth of this is the adoption of a wide range of document imaging applications, where these technologies can be used as a mainstream rather than as so-called orphan technologies, to optimize operational and technical solutions for identified business process requirements.

The continued progress in workgroup computing also is presenting a new challenge to the imaging system designer. The proliferation of so-called personal document imaging systems (PDoc), with local mass storage capabilities, suddenly means imaging can be introduced at a much lower level of granularity in the overall information system, forcing at least a review, if not a reevaluation of the architecture and its image delivery capabilities.

2.4   THE ROLE OF IMAGING IN INFORMATION TRANSFER

Regardless of their capabilities, imaging systems are expected to preserve the integrity of the original documents. Therefore, the role of imaging, per se, is limited to accurate recording and storage and display in a computer processible format of documents. As such, it could have remained an electronic replacement for microforms. The capability to extract electronic data from captured images and include that data in a larger information base gives image-based systems a much larger business value than stand-alone systems. But one must be fully aware that the more sophisticated the information system, the smaller the contribution of the imaging system itself to the overall information transfer process.

In fact, the decreasing costs of imaging hardware and the modularization of the software that controls imaging functions are generating user preference for off-the-shelf, "plug-and-play" solutions. This trend may give the system designer a false sense of simplicity in system implementation, which is reinforced by the vendor promotional literature. This may actually have two different effects on imaging systems in particular and information systems in general:

1. The first, which is beneficial in the short term, relates to a reduction in design, development, and implementation costs of technical solutions.

2. The other, which may have long-term negative consequences, is the potential for "sclerosis" in systems design where only standard solutions, based on a limited number of products, are preferred to optimized implementations.

2.5   VARIOUS TYPES OF IMAGING SYSTEMS

Imaging systems fall into three main categories, corresponding to the role of the imaging function in the overall system. While there is a significant amount of overlap between the categories, that role cannot be dissociated from functions already supported by existing data processing installations. Specifically, transaction systems may use imaging to reduce the cost of data entry; business decision systems may use imaging to keep both documents and data about them organized; finally, archival systems will be used to reduce the cost of document retrieval.

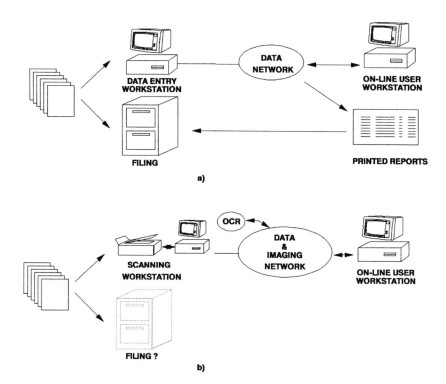

Figure 2.1   Using imaging as a front-end application

Front-End Applications

In traditional data processing systems (see Figure 2.1a), data from documents are captured on data entry workstations and, after processing, are made available to end users through a network. At the same time, supporting documents are filed and archived for future reference according to standard records management practices, which involve manual filing in the office followed by off-site archival storage.

In imaging systems (see Figure 2.1b), documents are captured on a scanning workstation, and the data they contain are either extracted through keyboarding from the displayed image or, if the document is amenable to automatic data extraction, extracted through optical character recognition or similar techniques. After processing, both data and supporting image are then made available to the end user through an image-capable network. Because the image of the document has been captured, it can be accessed in its electronic form, and there is no operational requirement to retain the original paper. However, other considerations may require that originals be archived, which will be done at off-site facilities.

Management Applications

Once documents and their contents are in an electronic form, they can be indexed and accessed in an orderly way, allowing for their systematic processing without loss of information. An increasingly important management application of imaging systems is associated with the management of the workflow throughout an organization, in which digitized documents are automatically moved electronically from workstation to workstation for processing according to established procedures. This ability to prescribe and control document progress electronically throughout an organization facilitates changes in document routing to accommodate different operational or business conditions, such as automatic escalation of unresolved issues or workload balancing. This new ability to manage the organizational workflow provides an opportunity to review an entire business process, which, in some cases, can lead to a complete redesign of existing data processing applications, with reported system maintenance cost reduction of better than 50 percent. This redesign process, sometimes called software rejuvenation, is discussed in more detail in Chapter 7.

Archiving Applications

Archiving imaging systems are found in situations where document retrieval time is an essential component of an organization's costs, or when speed of access is essential to organizational purpose. For instance, organizations involved in a regulated business may be required to collect large volumes of documents; at the same time, it may be critical to the organization that it be able to locate a small number of documents on a moment's notice. One example of such a situation is the chemical industry, where companies are required to keep track of all the chemicals and compounds utilized and of the hazards associated with their handling and storage for use in emergency situations. Another example, which is in fact an archival system application, is in customer services areas, where the ability to settle a question while in direct communication with a customer is a very efficient approach to cost reduction in postsales support.

2.6   TECHNOLOGICAL CONCERNS

The penetration of imaging systems into the information processing industry, and the resulting challenges and opportunities, are the outcome of various factors. The rapid pace of change of computer equipment, software, and services, both in cost and capabilities, continuously modifies the technological landscape. At the same time, these changes create serious difficulties in planning and selecting an optimal technical solution to a given information transfer requirement. For instance, previously discrete functionalities to manage information flow, which formerly would have been designed individually, are constantly being integrated into increasingly powerful devices and software packages. This creates a "pause-or-play" dilemma, well known to the designer of computer systems. One must choose between waiting for cheaper solutions, and absorb a continuing drain on organizational budgets, or implement existing and presumably more expensive options, and reap immediate financial benefits. The answer to this is that the best time for a new system is probably the present time, because no doubt there will always be more powerful systems with more features in the future. Waiting for them, however, will exact a higher toll on organizational resources than need be. A further twist in the decision-making process is the fact that, because imaging technology is moving so fast, there will be little opportunity to gather information on prior experience.

Simultaneously, the coinciding decline in equipment costs and increase in processing power make the selection of "the best" technical solutions to a given problem an increasingly difficult task. More often than not, the designer will have to settle for an optimized "better" technical solution, rather than the one and only best configuration. The following defines some of the issues facing a system designer.

- Intelligent workstations are becoming more proficient at performing local data processing tasks that were previously done on central mainframes. The question is whether to continue supporting a mainframe operation or adopt a "workgroup computing" philosophy, in which data processing is done at the workgroup level and then circulated in a "digested" form to all users of the overall information system.

- Low-cost multitasking environments enable intelligent workstations to perform local parallel processing of tasks, a capability that had been confined to mainframe installations. This raises issues of efficiency, distinct from the mainframe-workstation debate. One has to decide between concurrent task performance on the same workstation, as opposed to "assembly-line" processing on separate workstations, as in traditional situations.

- Specialized workstations dedicated to communication tasks allow the proliferation of distributed processing applications. This creates new design opportunities for system architecture—combining data capture, storage, processing, dissemination, retrieval, and use—that best support business requirements in terms of performance, cost, and competitive advantage.

- Inexpensive personal document imaging systems (PDocs) are replacing, in some cases, centralized image scanning and storage, trading off central control for desktop flexibility in imaging system design.

Economic considerations provide their own set of constraints: Business conditions may not be conducive to the adoption of a fully reengineered information system. In fact, earlier investments in hardware and software may have to be taken into consideration. These constraints may change an overall project from delivering an optimal system to simply providing a temporary solution "until things get better."

Political and individual factors further cloud the design of a document imaging system. Availability of a "technical champion"—assignment of project responsibility to a given organizational unit, personalities involved, and even the training and experience of the project team—will have a strong influence on the system design and the success of its implementation. For instance, the design of an image-based accounts payable system will likely be different if the project is led by the financial area or by the MIS area. The finance people may lean towards the use of PC-based solutions, with high emphasis on controls; on the other hand, the MIS department will likely be partial to a mainframe-supported design, with emphasis on power. Systems design may also be affected by the fact that self-taught computer professionals usually are more comfortable with "off-the-shelf" packages than with formal programming and analysis.

Fortunately, the current level of technology may provide the means to get around the risks associated with the "wrong" technical solutions. With the accelerated adoption of standards for information interchange and software design, one can hope that, sometime in the relatively near future, technical options compliant with standards will be interchangeable at minimum costs. For instance, if an increase in functionality requirements tasks an existing system, one may need only to change the processing platform, without having to rewrite the application programs. The early use of process simulation can already reduce the risks of such migration by identifying optimized alternatives.

2.7   IMPLICATIONS FOR SYSTEMS ARCHITECTURE

In this climate of constant change, the key to long-term stability of a given design will be the development of an approach that closely shadows the business needs of the organization. This can be achieved by a modular architecture, providing a value-added service consistent with the contribution of an organizational unit to the overall information flow. For instance, in an accounts payable application, the value added by imaging technologies may be limited to the receipt and verification of payment documents and for audits. There is no image-related value added for the actual processing of invoices. Consequently, the business rationale for changing data terminals to imaging terminals must be limited to those workstations assigned to material transaction verification, such as customer service.

Whereas the existing architecture may have had to deal with only a limited, well-defined set of devices and peripherals, the new architecture will have to support a wide variety of devices with increased throughput requirements and will need to be agile enough to adapt to rapid changes in business requirements.

2.8   A MULTILEVEL NETWORK FUNCTIONAL ARCHITECTURE

The design of an agile imaging system requires the resolution of a series of issues and problems unknown to the conventional machine-readable world. In particular, it will be necessary to know not only the volume of data traffic, but also to understand the nature and chronology of the various information processes involved.

For instance, not all imaging applications will involve a one-to-one relationship between document queries and image retrieval. In forms applications, where data are character strings in predetermined zones on the documents, the ratio between raster image size and forms contents in machine-readable form is often 100-to-1 and higher. In many of these applications, there may be a 10-to-1 probability that the machine-readable data will be sufficient to answer to an inquiry. Everything else being equal, the combination of these two factors will, without the benefit of a clear perception of business and retrieval requirements, yield designs with vastly different levels of performance. The lower end, found in many basic data LANs upgrades, will infrequently be involved with image retrieval; in fact, they may not be satisfactory for image display or printing if image retrieval is more than even a few percent of the total number of queries. Conversely, the higher end, corresponding to fully integrated imaging systems, will assume that all documents are to be retrieved as images, which may result in overdesign of the system.

Functional Factors Influencing Imaging Network Design

Efficient design requires the combination and optimization of various requirements, such as workflow and architecture definition requirements, indexing, database software, and a graphical user interface.

Workflow Requirements

Because imaging offers the ability to integrate documents and data about them in a uniform architecture, it is valuable to review and restructure the way information currently flows throughout an organization, and then, in the process of redesigning the underlying business process, reengineer the workflow.

Architecture Definition Requirements

The system architecture for networked imaging applications must be capable of supporting fast transfer of the large data packets representing digitized documents. The architecture also must be capable of supporting fast transfer of the large data packets representing digitized documents. The selected architecture probably will be based on a combination of the three common architecture models known as centralized, client-server, and peer-to-peer, which will reflect the kind and volume of data traffic.

To be complete, the architecture selection process must also involve the choice of physical and logical topology; protocols; operating systems; specification of connecting devices such as repeaters, bridges, routers, and gateways; cabling media; workstations; peripherals; mass storage; file-server platforms; and utility software.

The choice of architecture and supporting hardware and software will determine the maximum capabilities of an imaging system.

Indexing

Corresponding to the choice of the system architecture, which represents the "technical side" of an imaging network, indexing represents the "intellectual" side of the information transfer process. The word, by itself, has many meanings. In imaging systems, indexing refers to the machine-readable data stream assigned to a document for identification, storage, and retrieval purposes. One must realize that several indexing schemes coexist in an imaging system. Some are simple and transparent to the user, such as image location on a disk; others, such as document descriptors, are user-defined; still others, such as full text, are user-driven but automatically generated.

Because images are, in themselves, meaningless binary streams, the machine-readable data stream must be generated outside the image, either through keyboarding or by automatic data extraction.

The cost of indexing is, with document capture, the most expensive itemizable part of the operation of an imaging system.

Database Software

The database software used to fetch and display or print a document over the network links systems retrieval to network performance. Like indexing, many database software programs coexist on a network. Some, like the database that manages the distribution of documents on mass storage devices, are internal to the system and transparent to the user and optimized to speed up the physical access to the stored documents. Others, such as the image database retrieval software proper, are optimized to speed up the identification of relevant documents.

There are different types of image database software, the most popular meeting Structured Query Language (SQL) standards. However, these software may not provide efficient information retrieval in an imaging environment. It must be understood that retrieval in imaging networks involves a sequence of operations much more complex than for regular data, including storage and decompression delays. Consequently, it may be difficult to identify loss of degradation of performance as resulting from an overtaxed database or to other causes.

Graphical User Interface

Essential to the response of an imaging system is the graphical user interface, which must be compatible and coexist with the other programs on a user workstation. Because it competes for computer and memory resources, the choice of a GUI must not be taken for granted.

The Different Levels

Efficient imaging network architectures may be composed of several levels, involving different subnetworks, with each subnetwork optimized for the performance of specific tasks.

There are several accepted models that provide a formal description of the processes occurring in a network. Some, like the Open Systems Interconnection (OSI) standard, discussed in Chapter 3, divide the device-network interface into seven layers. Others, like IBM's System Network Architecture (SNA), provide specification for connections.

From a functional standpoint, a networked imaging system can be described in terms of four different functions: user interface, imaging and other user applications, information capture and control, and document storage and retrieval. These functions are supported in several places in a network. From the user point of view, they can be located in one of three levels: desktop, processor, or network.

Desktop Level

The desktop is the combination of the display screen, keyboard, and pointing devices that provide a functional interface between the user and the computer. It can be stand-alone or connected to a network. From a user point of view, as diagrammed in Figure 2.2, the configuration of the workstation is of no importance as long as it allows retrieval and processing of information in a timely, complete, easily readable, and accurate manner.

The minimum functionalities that must be provided at the desktop level include image-specific tasks (e.g., inquiry, retrieval, display, printing, storage) and nonimage-specific, which permit access to all the applications that are performed through that desktop.

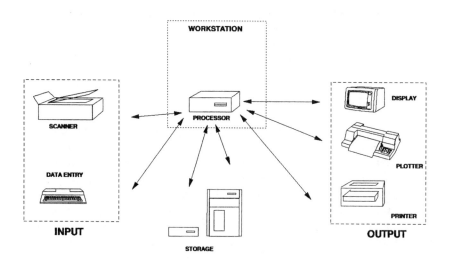

Figure 2.2   Basic components of an imaging system

Processor Level

The processor level is the functional interface between the desktop and the rest of the network system. The processor is designed to perform the tasks it can do locally, to forward through the network the tasks that must be performed by other processors, and to know the difference between the two.

While the desktop level is relatively easy to configure functionally, the configuration of the processor level requires a thorough understanding of the applications that must be run from the desktop so that the workload can be allocated between the user processor and other devices on the network. For instance, scanning can be performed in a distributed way, either locally or remotely, or centrally. Understanding the use of the digitized documents will facilitate the decision as to how the process should be carried out, and will help to achieve the optimization of the processor configuration.

Network Level

The network level corresponds to all the functionalities that are not processed locally. While the two other levels can conceivably, from a user perspective, be configured independently, the network level usually requires the contribution of network specialists to design and optimize this third level of functionalities.

2.9   IMPLICATIONS FOR USER INTERFACES

Because the desktop is the functional interface between the user and the computer system, it is also a bottleneck in the information transfer process. Graphical user interfaces and multimedia user interfaces (MUIs) are essential to minimize the impact of that bottleneck on desktop efficiency. Three functionalities must be supported by the interface: image display, commands access, and controls and management.

Image Display

The system display must meet a wide range of requirements, from high resolution for the scanned images, to the lower resolution for display of icons and commands in a windowed environment. Because each requirement corresponds to different demands on supporting hardware and software, it is important that the system design be compatible with the capabilities of the display. For instance, some document-intensive applications may require simultaneous display of a large number of scanned images, together with geometric graphics and machine-generated text. The GUI must be able to integrate all these requirements (multiple raster, vector, and character-based data) into a single display.

Commands Access

The issue here is the integration of user interaction with the system without interfering with ongoing processing of applications. Each GUI provides tools for exercising such interactions. However, the ways by which GUIs place calls to the system vary from system to system, and therefore the speed at which a given command is executed from the desktop depends on the particular GUI.

Controls and Management

This series of tasks corresponds to the display of system messages and programmed status reports. Depending on the nature of the messages, they may be character-based text or embedded with graphics to reflect a particular condition or attract attention.

GUIs require intensive computing resources. As such, they compete with the resource requirements of the imaging application itself. Consequently, the design of a networked imaging system must be done with due consideration for the potential conflicts in the local processor for access to the desktop.

2.10 STRUCTURE OF AN OPTICAL DISK SYSTEM

This section focuses on the physical components of an imaging system. As such, there will be some overlap with concepts already covered. However, the description that follows will now be device-bound, rather than information-bound. Consequently, the discussion of a given device such as a workstation performing several different functions, such as display and processing—functions kept separate in the past—is not a repetition of previous material but a reflection of the complexity of networked imaging systems.

All document imaging systems are an assembly of basic components, namely scanners, processors, storage, displays, and printers connected by communication links (see Figure 2.2). Basic imaging functions are as follows.

Document Capture

Documents are captured (input) into the system through a scanner that provides an electronic representation of the optical image of a document, which may be on paper or microform. The electronic representation of the image is initially in an analog form, which is then translated into a digital signal.

Processing

Processing incorporates several different functions, which cover acquisition, indexing, storage, retrieval, display, printing, and communication of images. Processing tasks are performed on one or several computers, which are loaded with software and processing boards specifically designed to handle quickly the large amount of data contained in an electronic image.

Most often, indexing, storage allocation, information retrieval, communication, and system management is handled in software. Hardware, on the other hand, usually handles computation-intensive operations, including data compression and decompression, format translation, image manipulation, and device interface between systems components. However, the rapid adoption by the marketplace of high-performance processors is making it possible to design systems in which tasks that were initially done in hardware, such as decompression and format conversion, can be executed in software at a lower cost.

Storage

The storage function is usually performed as a combination of magnetic (i.e., erasable) and optical (erasable and nonerasable) memories, where the magnetic memory is used as a scratch pad during the image capture process. It is also used to store indices to the image locations, as these need to be updated on a constant basis. The optical disk is used to store the permanent images. In systems using nonerasable disks, updating of an image is done by recording a new image on the optical disk, and amending the index on the magnetic disks to reflect the change. Optical disks can be kept in stand-alone drives or in what is called a jukebox, which is a device equipped with automated disk changers, thus allowing continued access to data. Depending on the number of workstations on the system and the frequency of access, a jukebox might include several drives working in tandem to meet needed response time.

Display

Display and printing devices are peripherals that make it possible to visualize and generate a physical representation of the digitized document. Later in the book, the major issues raised by the various models of GUIs, which ensure human-machine communication, are discussed. Because of the differences and limitations of the physical processes involved, there can be significant variations in overall performance and quality between displayed images and printed hard copies, as well as in outputs provided by different equipment.

In special applications, such as publishing, printing may be done on film or on other optical disks. A discussion of the application to microform production is provided in Chapter 16.

Communication

Communication tasks cover two different functions: One deals with the transfer of data within a given processor and between the processor and its associated peripherals; the other relates to data transfer between several processors. These

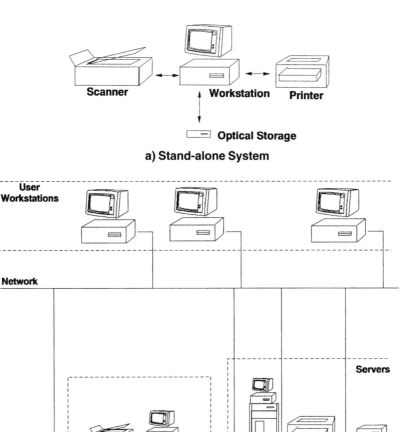

a) Stand-alone System

b) Networked System

Figure 2.3   Example of two typical configurations

functions are best described in terms of configuration, and two main configurations can be adopted for document imaging systems (see Figure 2.3).

In a stand-alone configuration, the processor controls document capture, storage, retrieval, and printing. Communications are purely internal to the system. In that configuration, which may be practical for very low use, tasks of document storage and document retrieval cannot be performed at the same time.

In a networked configuration, document capture, processing, and storage can be separated from retrieval, and multiple users can have access to the same image base. Consequently, storage and retrieval tasks can occur concurrently.

In the context of this chapter, communication devices are defined as the devices that interface the optical disk system with the outside world. In simple (stand-alone) systems, communication devices are limited to the interface that allows correct transfer of information between the optical disk storage and the printer or display. In more elaborate systems, communication devices allow the interconnection (networking) of several units for the purpose of sharing resources or information. A detailed discussion of the issues involved in the design of a networked imaging system is provided in the second part of this chapter.

2.11 EXAMPLES OF APPLICATIONS

Because optical disks make it possible to integrate data and images, they open processing opportunities that were previously impossible. For instance, in legal files applications, immediacy of image capture and availability of communication links allow attorneys to be immediately appraised of any change in an issue. And because these functions are computer driven, access can be controlled under well-established computer security procedures. Furthermore, if the information is collected in a standard form, it is possible to design the application from which data on the form can be extracted directly. This eliminates the need to keyboard standard data such as names and filing data, while retaining the ability to capture nonmachine-legible information such as signatures and similar information.

In regulatory and library applications, all documents can be integrated into a uniform display environment. In particular, word processing and imaged documents can be stored in the same database and retrieved under a consistent procedure.

With a detailed index, it becomes possible to eliminate filing, because the computer keeps track of the document automatically, and thus saves on clerical costs. The use of optical character recognition (OCR) algorithms can often simplify the task of indexing complex documents by extracting full text from imaged documents.

In applications related to transaction processing, the ability to provide multiple access to the same document can significantly shorten the overall processing time spent handling the document. If the system includes a jukebox, the index will automatically trigger the mounting of the appropriate disk and the performance of information retrieval.

Imaging can also be used as a front end to the preparation and use of interactive technical manuals, which can then be replicated on commercially available systems for dissemination.

2.12 DESIGN CONSIDERATIONS

Several considerations come into play when designing an optical disk application, and it is important that they be fully understood before a system is specified. In particular, because of the rapid evolution of technology, the relative importance of these considerations in design might vary within a short period of time. For instance, because hardware price performance ratio is increasing, the cost of hardware replacement is becoming a small factor in the overall system cost, forcing the designer to focus attention on design and conversion costs.

The first consideration is to ensure that information stored on optical disks is retrievable in a complete, accurate, and timely fashion. Because optical disks are not human-readable, it is essential that the procedures for collecting, recording, processing, storing, retrieving, displaying, and printing information guarantee the integrity of the information, an issue often referred to as the legality of optical disks. In most cases, if the procedures are well defined, and image capture is done in the due course of business, optical disks can conceivably replace microforms as a storage system, and the original documents can be discarded after recording. In other cases, the application might be such that optical disk systems serve an operational role, with the original documents kept for evidentiary purposes.

Other considerations are related to the need for all systems components to be compatible among themselves, and that they remain that way for the foreseeable future. Because of the lack of standards in the industry, compatibility might require selection of specialized interfaces to allow noncompatible machines to operate together and still maintain good performance levels. Of more importance is the concern that a particular component, or even a full system, will still be supported in a not too distant future. This consideration is usually handled through a cost-benefit analysis, where the overall system cost is established to provide a quick payback period. Because a conversion from one digital system to another can be done automatically, the cost of conversion is essentially a one-time charge. Under that condition, should there be a need to change the system, the replacement cost would not offset initial benefits.

In designing the overall system, answers to questions as to its size and the interconnection of its various functions will determine its overall architecture. The application of records management techniques that keep files to a minimum without sacrificing operational efficiency, in concert with a full understanding of the business requirements of the applications being supported, optimize the design for the current needs, and at the same time provide the opportunity to prepare for upgrades by embedding access points for future developments. Of particular importance is an assessment of growth requirements, so that the indexing system can absorb additional storage, such as linkage of additional jukeboxes, without loss in response time and other performance elements.

Related to the consideration of systems architecture is the issue of networking. While records management and workload studies can provide the data indicating the number of workstations to be used on the system, the question will be how to connect them. Of particular interest will be whether all stations should be equipped with a full complement of scanners, high-resolution displays, and printers, or whether device sharing will be acceptable. Attention will also have to be given to interaction with different systems. For instance, a personnel system might need the information that is in a payroll system, and there might be an operational value to having both systems share a common database. The same situation might involve a purchasing and accounts payable department. Different requirements will yield different types of networks, from fully centralized to fully distributed.

A last consideration before completing the design and selecting the hardware relates to conversion to the new system. In applications such as accounts payable, one might choose a day-forward system in which only new files are input into the system, using the argument that there is a low probability that older files will be accessed, and therefore there will be no financial benefit in bringing them into the system. In other situations, such as personnel, it is imperative to design retrospective systems, where all files are converted. Not doing so would prevent file integrity.

All these considerations directly influence the design of the database supporting the optical disk system and the nature of the indexing scheme to be used. For instance, if all the information/documents stored are composed of forms, the database can be built on a flat file design, with simple indexing. If, on the other hand, full-text documents are part of the document base, the database might require more complex features, including a relational structure; the indexing system might involve the capability of performing full-text searching. If conversion is involved, plans will have to be made as to the nature and compatibility of the conversion equipment and its integration with the equipment used for continued operation.

2.13 IMPLEMENTING AN OPTICAL DISK SYSTEM

The implementation of an optical disk system requires a well-orchestrated succession of steps, beginning with collecting baseline data. These data will enable the designer to size the project, to ensure that the design meets the expected level of performance. For instance, an initial study will be necessary to assess workload data so that the number of workstations is adequate and that the size of the processor is sufficient to handle the volume of transactions within acceptable response time. This might be done through a survey to identify core needs or those requirements that are essential to acceptable performance. An analysis of the current information flow will make it possible to determine the critical information path or the relationship between various functions, together with the identification of retrieval patterns and critical response times. The use of models and simulation can greatly improve the ability to specify the new system.

Once the baseline data have been collected and formally analyzed in a requirements analysis, the actual design can begin, starting with system and structure definition, and including functional requirements, hardware selection, and performance specifications. Of critical importance will be the design of a database structure consistent with the business needs of the organization and the selection of the database engine that will support it. Powerful design tools for efficient operation will include modeling and simulation.

The overall technical solution should then be submitted to various tests of acceptance, including budgetary value and admissibility of procurement procedures. Of importance to the design will be considerations of the life cycle of the proposed solution and whether the implementation will be conducted with in-house staff or through outside contractors.

Once the design has been finalized and accepted, its implementation will require installation planning, testing, and training, often with conversion serving as a prototype of operation. In the process, several issues will need to be resolved, including retraining or restaffing for the new system and the learning curve involved in implementing a new system. As found in the data processing field, it will take several months before trained users are able to articulate any requirements for enhancements, thus requiring system support beyond the initial startup period.

One of the most significant elements in the implementation of imaging systems is the cost of conversion and/or indexing for storage on optical disks. These costs can often be offset by savings from the elimination of filing tasks. In certain cases such as legal applications, such costs, which are already part of the legal file operating expenses in a manual environment, can be reduced through the use of OCR, which, in many cases, allows automatic extraction from the document.

Once the documents have been indexed, they can be arranged and displayed or printed at will, without having to physically handle the files. This gives, in a litigation support application for example, the ability to create, on demand, packages of documents that can be viewed either in a hypermedia/window fashion or distributed on paper, which need not be kept after the case has been settled.

Other facilities derived from the electronic image include the ability to receive and store directly facsimile transmissions as an integral part of the files and the ability to have several people working on the same file at various locations without risking a loss of file integrity.

2.14 CONCLUSION

Electronic imaging is a powerful tool for information retrieval and an efficient front end to an integrated information system. With a proper design, imaging systems can present significant cost advantage and additional benefits over manual and microfilm-based systems.

As indicated earlier, however, the adoption of a system should not be a trivial decision. Aside from the fact that implementation costs may be considerable, imaging systems represent a new way of doing business, and their acceptance may be an irreversible decision. Therefore, it may be beneficial to an organization to secure, either internally or through outside counsel, the necessary know-how to ensure success in implementation.

3

Imaging Networks

Marc R. D'Alleyrand, Ph.D.

3.1 INTRODUCTION

Imaging networks are computer-based information transfer facilities. There is no difference in principle between imaging and conventional computer (i.e., data-based) networks but for the channel capacity and nature of signals to be communicated. Therefore, all the fundamental principles of data network technologies apply to imaging networks . . . with a twist.

In a data-only local area network environment, the only intelligent intermediary between two user stations may be a processor called a file server that manages communication. In imaging systems, the complexity of transactions to be performed is such that relying on a single server would, in most but the simplest cases, result in unacceptably slow response times. Therefore, imaging systems will see the proliferation of auxiliary servers, dedicated (and optimized) to support specific functions such as scanning, document storage, printing, and faxing. These auxiliary servers, which are in fact equivalent to unattended workstations, are polled through the file server to effect a desired user-initiated function (e.g., storage or retrieval).

In addition, the support of image traffic requires many more computer resources than data communication. This results in the adoption of new architectures that maximize the capacity available to a given communication. One approach is to handle information storage and information retrieval separately, optimizing data flow between attended user workstations and unattended processing tasks performed in a background mode. A strategy for such an approach consists of using interconnected networks, each dedicated to support separate groups of tasks. Figure 3.1 shows a diagram of such an architecture, designed to preserve an existing investment in a data-only installation. In this example, the existing data network is image enabled by upgrading workstations to allow casual access to images, with imaging support provided by a separate service network. A dedicated network equipped with high-performance workstations handles all other imaging applications.

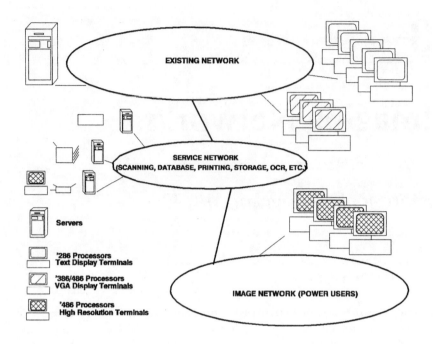

Figure 3.1   Diagram of a segmented network for imaging

The following is a primer on imaging networks. Its purpose is to stress the fact that imaging networks are complex systems, the planning of which should not be neglected. As such, it is designed to provide pointers for end users, but not to replace the advice of network professionals.

3.2   NETWORK FUNDAMENTALS

Networks exist in a variety of ways. In fact, the term network itself covers a general concept of electronic devices linked together to pass information and share resources. All imaging (and data) networks can be described in terms of physical and logical characteristics. The physical description, or structure, deals with the hardware components present on the network, and the cabling that ensures electrical continuity between them. The logical descriptions, or architecture, covers the rules governing data exchange between the various network components.

Network Architecture

From a workstation perspective, the network architecture determines the way that the workstation will exchange data with other devices. Two different types of architectures are prevalent for imaging systems: centralized and decentralized.

Centralized (or File-Server) Model

In this model, a workstation looks to a centralized processor for the files they need, the management of communication links, and device sharing. Centralized installations offer the maximum level of control, but require a powerful central processor, such as a mainframe. One of the weaknesses of centralized processing is that, in case of failure of the central processor, the whole network is inoperable.

Mainframe-based networks are good centralized examples. However, the presence of a mainframe in a network is not necessarily a sign of a centralized operation. In particular, image-enabled mainframe applications use either a centralized (with all processing under the control of the central machine) or a client-server model (see below), in which the mainframe appears only as a node on the network, providing files to imaging applications. A third alternative for mainframe operation is one where image capture and indexing is done on a separate installation, possibly in a service bureau, with the validated image database loaded on the central system. For all other cases, except the simplest installations, a client-server architecture will likely be the most efficient approach to imaging, as it balances the processing load among different servers, optimized for the particular workflow assigned to them.

Decentralized Model

In decentralized models, management of network functions and computer resources is shared between workstations. There are various way of effecting a decentralized operation.

Client-Server This is a very popular model, in which workstations look to different devices to provide required functionalities. A basic diagram showing the difference between file- and client-server models is given in Figure 3.2. While there are different interpretations in the industry as to what is a "real" client-server architecture, for the purpose of this book, it is defined as a network where workstations (clients) request functionalities from various devices (servers). In this simplified view, we do not concern ourselves with the fact that, in order to satisfy a workstation request, some of the servers may have to act themselves as clients of other devices. The advantage of client-server architectures is that workstations may still be able to perform some activities even if some of the servers are not operating.

Peer-to-Peer In a peer-to-peer architecture, resources attached to a given workstation are available to all the other workstations. One benefit of such an architecture is lower hardware costs. Drawbacks include response time, especially in a DOS environment, where requests to one workstation compete for processing time with applications running at that time on the target machine.

Defining a Network

Physically, a network is a collection of devices—some active (nodes), some inactive—linked by communication cables. A network is defined by its physical and logical features.

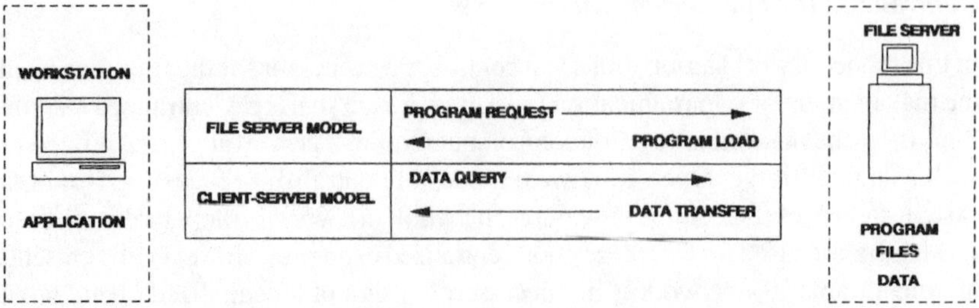

Figure 3.2   Comparison between client- and file-server relationships

Physical Characteristics

Type of Network   The type of network describes how information is passed to and resources are shared between users and the network. In broad terms, network types are labeled as local area networks (LANs), metropolitan area networks (MANs), and wide area networks (WANs) depending on their coverage. LANs use a single wiring medium (see below); MANs and WANs can use different media to connect different zones of the network.

Physical Topology   The physical topology describes the way cables run from device to device. It is often different from the way messages are constructed and passed from node to node, which is codified by protocols. Several physical topologies are used in the industry:

- *Daisy Chain (or Bus)* (see Figure 3.3a)   In this topology, devices are connected in sequence, with signals going from one device to the next. Correct data flow requires a terminating connector at each end of the chain. This topology yields the shortest cable length from device to device. Its main drawback is its vulnerability to failure. If one of the links is broken, transmission is interrupted for all the devices connected to that particular chain; and finding and isolating the defect can be time-consuming.
- *Ring* (see Figure 3.3b)   This topology is similar in principle to the daisy chain topology, but here cable path is looped and there is no terminating connector. The advantage over the daisy chain arrangement is that signals can be made to travel always in the same direction, facilitating data flow at higher speed than with a bus topology. The drawbacks are the same as for the linear daisy chain.
- *Star* (see Figure 3.3c)   Here all cables originate from central hubs and terminate at a device. While this arrangement requires a longer length of cable than a bus topology, it is easier to maintain, as failing connections can be easily identified and bypassed at the hub with limited disruption of network operation.

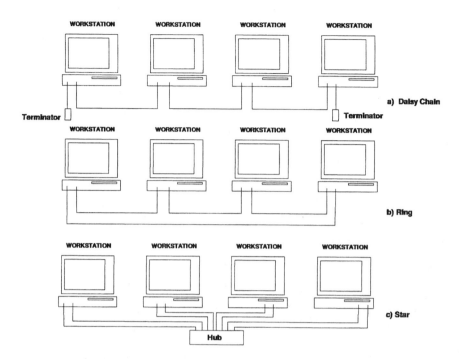

Figure 3.3   Different types of topologies

The choice of a physical topology has a direct impact on network installation cost, reliability, and maintenance. For imaging networks, operational benefits of flexibility, maintenance, and installation of star topologies more than offset the added cost of wiring hardware and additional cable lengths.

To keep data flow within limits consistent with constraints of the physical equipment used to carry and transmit data, it is often necessary to section a network into individual subnetworks, connected by one or more dedicated linking devices, which will be explained later on.

Network Protocols   Network protocols define the network's logical topology and how messages are encoded and interpreted when they pass from node to node. Three logical topologies have been codified by standards: Ethernet, token-ring, and ArcNet. While possibly simpler to install, ArcNet, a protocol initially developed by Data Point for connecting its proprietary hardware, is presently not favored for imaging networks due to its lower speed and logistics. This situation may change as new specifications will allow ArcNet topologies to run at similar or higher speed than the two other.

Protocols are sets of rules that initiate and maintain communications over a network. In particular, they specify data signal strength and format and dictate structure of data stream flow, structure and handling, and signaling speed. An effective way to describe protocols is to use the Open Systems Interconnection (OSI) model, which describes data communication in terms of seven successive

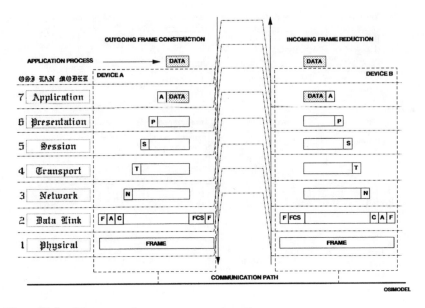

Figure 3.4　Diagram of a message construction

processes, from data transport over physical communication media to their interpretation and display. As outgoing data are processed through each layer, it is
provided with a header that contains pertinent information as to handling requirements until a complete formatted message, called a frame, is constructed and passed
to the communication channel. At the receiving end, the process is reversed, and
headers are progressively "peeled-off" until the initial data are released to the
receiving application. The process is diagrammed in Figure 3.4.[1] A brief description
of these layers is given below.

　　There are a variety of protocols in use on the marketplace, and most major ones
claim compatibility to the seven-layer Open Systems Interconnection (OSI) model.
Commercially available protocols can be assigned to three categories: lower-layer
protocols, higher-level protocols, and the top layer.

　　Lower-layer protocols specify cabling and connection methods (physical layer),
and access and control (data link layer). To that effect, they provide for establishing
links for device access, addressing, and error detection and correction of data
transmission; in particular, they specify the method under which devices communicate. The two most prevalent methods are:

- *Token passing*, in which a specified data stream (the token) runs through the
  network. Each device that needs to transmit will grab that token and attach
  the message together with the address of the destination device. All devices
  on the network read the data traffic, grabbing the messages that have their
  address and stripping them from the token, which then is released to the
  network for reuse.

- *Carrier sense*, in which all devices listen for a carrier, the signal that indicates that messages are on the network. If the device does not sense any traffic, it will begin transmitting. This may cause two devices to start transmitting at the same time, which may create a "collision" of data streams, detected by an increase in signal strength over a certain threshold. The protocol prescribes the actions that are taken by the network following a collision.

Several widely used lower-layer protocols, embodied in the Institute of Electrical and Electronic Engineers (IEEE) 802.X standards, relate to PC-based LANs:

- *IEEE 802.3* covers the carrier sense, multiple access, and collision detection (CSMA/CD) protocol often called Ethernet, even though the original Ethernet does not strictly adhere to that standard.
- *IEEE 802.4* (a bus architecture) and *IEEE 802.5* (a ring architecture) describe a token passing scheme, with various cabling arrangements. In particular, IEEE 802.5 describes the token-ring protocol used by IBM.
- *FDDI (Fiber Data Distributed Interface)* is an ANSI standard, describing a token passing scheme over optical fibers.
- *IEEE 802.6* relates to metropolitan area networks, using optical fiber cabling connecting LANs. Its importance for imaging is that it provides connectivity with telephone companies, offering services at multiples of 1.544MBits/second.

Higher-level protocols cover the functions described in the network (layer 3) and transport (layer 4) layers of the OSI model and handle the encoding of decisions as to the physical routing of the data on the network. Transmission Control Protocol/Internet Protocol (TCP/IP) and Internet Packet Exchange/Sequenced Packet Exchange (IPX/SPX) are examples of such higher-level protocols.

Depending on the vendors, the various functions of these higher protocols are performed at different levels in the OSI model, as exemplified in Table 3.1.[2] Consequently, two networks running Ethernet implementations may be incompatible at higher protocol levels, thus unable to exchange applications.

The top layers, in contrast to layers 1 to 4, which deal with the physical transfer of data to and from the network, the three remaining layers in the OSI model deal with their formatting.

- *The Session Layer* manages the dialog between two open systems to ensure that the data at both ends of the dialog are in a **form** meaningful to the receiving devices.
- *The Presentation Layer* manages the dialog between two open systems to ensure that the data at both ends of the dialog is meaningful **in content**, and is formatted (or translated, as the case may be) according to the requirements of the receiving device. This layer, which is responsible for the mapping of screen displays, is essential to the correct functioning of graphical user interfaces (GUIs).

Table 3.1   Comparison of IBM and Novell LAN NOS protocols

OSI	IBM				NOVELL Netware 386				
	OS/2 LAN SERVER	PC LAN			Original Novell	TCP/IP	OSI	IBM	Apple
APPLICATION	Application — Lan Server — Core Services	Application	Application Office Vision	Application FTP, TelNet SMTP		TCP/IP Appl.	OSI Appl.	IBM Appl.	
						NetWare Applications			
						NCP	NFS	SMB	AFP
PRESENTATION	Requester OS/2 Extended	NETBIOS	APPC/PC	NETBIOS	NetWare Core	NETWARE STREAM			
SESSION	APPC NETBIOS				Ortical (NCP)	NET BIOS	APPC	UNIX TLI	NAMED PIPES
TRANSPORT	(LU 6.2)	NETBIOS AND IPPC INTERFACE			Sequence Packet Exchange (SPX)	OSI Trnsprt	IBM SNA	TCP	NET- ATP
NETWORK	DIRECTLY TO 802.2 LOGICAL LINK CONTROL				Internet Packet Exchange (IPX)	OSI Netwrk	IBM or XNS	IP	BEUI
DATA LINK	LOGICAL LINK CONTROL MEDIA ACCESS CONTROL				Open Data Link Interface				
PHYSICAL	PHYSICAL 802.3, 802.5, PC LAN BROADBAND/BASEBAND				Physical				

(DOS PC LAN PROGRAM)

- *The Application Layer* defines and controls data transfer processes, from network operating system functions to application programs, including file sharing, electronic mail, database management, and other software.

Commonly Used Protocols   There is a tight relationship between protocols, the services they provide, and the applications they support. In particular, because different protocols operate at different levels of the OSI model, there may be incompatibility between a given protocol and applications with no linkage to a particular layer.

IBM-Specific Protocols: Because of the superiority of the IBM and IBM-compatible computer base, network protocols have been developed to support the specific communication needs of PC and mainframe installations.

Network Basic Input/Output System (NETBIOS), initially developed for the IBM world, establishes direct interfaces between network and application programs; supports services between network, transport, and session layers (layers 3, 4, and 5); and provides interface to the presentation or application layers (layers 6 or 7).

The implementation of NETBIOS protocols is highly vendor-dependent, with the support of communication from layers 1 to 5 implemented in a combination of firmware and software, shared between the network interface hardware and the host device. For instance, IBM token-ring adapter cards support only the physical and data link layers (layers 1 and 2); therefore, linkage to the NETBIOS protocol must be done through software emulation. Consequently, a "NETBIOS compatibility" feature may be misleading.

Nevertheless, the NETBIOS interface is an industry de facto standard for application-to-LAN interface. As such, its functioning is predictable, and calls to it receive the same response, regardless of actual protocol implementation. It is that implementation, most often done through emulation of the level 5 protocol and different transport and network layer protocols, that differentiates the major protocols that are found in imaging systems.

One of the weaknesses of NETBIOS is that it is not designed for remote communication, and therefore may be inefficient for most imaging systems spanning over several networks.

The Network Basic Extended User Interface (NETBEUI) is a memory resident program developed specifically for IBM token-ring networks implemented on PC machines. Its counterpart in the PS/2 environment is the IBM PC LAN Support Program, with which it communicates through the Data Link Control (DLC) protocol, a data link layer (layer 2) that is protocol-compatible with the IEEE 802.2 Logical Link Control (LLC) protocol.

The Logical Unit Type 6.2 (LU 6.2) is the protocol developed to support Advanced Program-to-Program Communication/PC (APPC/PC) strategy and information transfer between mainframes, minis, and PCs in a peer-to-peer architecture. Like NETBIOS, it provides network, transport, and session (layers 3, 4, and 5) services.

Named Pipes was developed for the OS/2 in a contiguous network application and is supported by MS-DOS. This protocol is more efficient than NETBIOS. While not technically a transport protocol, it serves the same functional purpose, connecting applications on different machines.

Systems Network Architecture (SNA) is a proprietary architecture developed by IBM to ensure reliable and error-free connectivity between devices supporting that architecture. What distinguishes SNA from other architectures is that its focus is on standardization of communication between nodes in a single architecture; the others focus on standardization of interface in a multiple architecture environment. Although OSI and SNA models have the same number of layers, they are not compatible, as shown in Figure 3.5. Historically, IBM has been able, by focusing on communication rather than on interface, to maintain forward compatibility and upgradability. However, this operational advantage may not be sufficient to offset the price advantage of PC-based, client-server types of LANs, which incur the maintenance cost of a mainframe operation.

Non-IBM-Specific Protocols: Like the IBM-specific protocols, they operate between the data link and session layers (layers 2 and 5), but they are incompatible and cannot communicate.

The Transmission Control Protocol/Internet Protocol (TCP/IP) was designed to connect dissimilar computers over dissimilar networks. Consequently, it is the protocol of choice for heterogeneous installations composed of PC workstations, minicomputers, and mainframes, running under a variety of operating systems. In addition, because most of the major network operating systems vendors provide

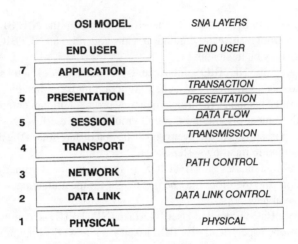

Figure 3.5   Comparisons between OSI and SNA layers

implementation schemes for TCP/IP, that protocol is a prime contender for complex imaging systems, even though full internetwork connectivity may require some fine-tuning between different vendor implementations.

TCP/IP is in fact the combination of a reliable, connection-oriented protocol (TCP) that guarantees that data packets will be transmitted in the proper order and error-free between two remote stations (or processes) and the Internet (IP) protocol, which supports routing in a way similar to XNS's IDP protocol (see below). TCP/IP also includes the three generic application protocols needed for interoperability, covering file transfer (FTP), mail transfer (SMTP), and terminal emulation program.

With the appropriate device drivers, TCP/IP can run on any combination of physical and data link layers (layer 1 and 2). As such it can run on token-ring as well as Ethernet for imaging applications.

The Network File System (NFS) is not a standard protocol per se, but it is of interest for windowed imaging systems because it provides PCs with multiple access to UNIX computers, which can then be used as file servers. NFS is a commercial product developed by Sun Microsystems to expand the capabilities of TCP/IP. It does so by defining two additional protocols. The first, Remote Procedure Calls (RPC), executes file-oriented commands at the session layer (layer 3) level on remote nodes and passing parameters, such as directories and file names. The second, Extended Data Representation (XDR), operates at the presentation layer (layer 6) to normalize data representation among a variety of otherwise incompatible vendors.

The Xerox Network Service (XNS) is a Xerox product developed for Ethernet networks. It provides several classes of services covering the application, session, transport, and network layers (layers 7, 5, 4, and 3).

In particular, at the network layer, it supports the Internet Datagram Protocol (IDP), which encapsulates data with a header that contains data destination based on the application and sends the completed packet on the network. At the receiving end, the packet is stripped from its header and stored for future use. XNS also supports in the same network layer the Routing Information Protocol (RIP), which maintains routing tables in an internetwork. XNS provides the model for 3Com, Banyan, and Novell Network products.

Novell SPX/IPX are two transport protocols commercialized by Novell and are essentially equivalent to XNS. NetWare's Sequenced Packet Exchange (SPX) and Internet Packet Exchange (IPX) directly span from the session to the network layer (layer 5 to 3). Like TCP/IP, they can work on different topologies and network implementations.

Application to Internetworking and Interoperability Generally, imaging networks involve heterogeneous networks. Even when imaging is introduced as an agent of change for the purpose of business redesign and workflow reengineering, protection of the existing investment often drives the need to function across multiple networks and platforms. Most of the interoperability will be ensured through compatible protocols operating at the network layer (layer 3). The only notable exception to this is the APPC/PC protocol, which is designed specifically for the IBM SNA environment.

Interoperability is determined by the ability of two protocols, or two different implementations of the same protocol, to exist on the same internetwork. To enable the coexistence of different protocols, the most common approach is the implementation of parallel protocol "stacks." However, because of the unlimited way in which protocols can be implemented, interoperability needs to be tested, using specialized programs called network analyzers, which can trap and read data packets to identify their components.

Connecting to Remote Networks Connection to remote networks is one area of interoperability where the two disciplines and technologies of digital data and communication networks must coexist. This is done through gateways (see below).

Operational Characteristics

Protocols implementation is done through groups of computer programs and routines, called operating systems. Three types of operating systems must coexist and be compatible on a network for proper functioning.

Network Operating Systems A network operating system (NOS) is a group of programs that ensures that all network components run in an integrated fashion. In particular, it maintains the logical addresses of alls nodes on the network and manages the services to provide and facilitate user access to network resources. For imaging applications, the NOS should reside on a dedicated processor, called the file server. There are basically two categories of NOS:

- *DOS-Based* This type of NOS is mentioned here for the sake of completeness. Usable for simple device-sharing networks, it is not recommended for imaging applications. Because DOS is not designed to handle multiple tasks or to handle simultaneous users, DOS-based NOSs support the concurrent functions necessary for network operation by intercepting requests, buffering them, and sharing processing time between users. Consequently, the type of network-oriented function calls, such as setting and redirecting devices, requires additional network operating software to function properly. Therefore, DOS cannot be used in full-featured imaging systems.

- *Non-DOS-Based*   Several NOSs are available in this category, including Novell NetWare, Banyan's Vine, OS/2, MS-LAN Manager, and UNIX. To allow interaction with users, these network operating systems, which are loaded on the file server, must be able to accept requests from their workstations, which, but for mainframe installations, have their own operating systems. Consequently, there must be compatibility between the NOS and workstation operating system; this is currently happening with DOS computers. In the case of UNIX, there may be a need to reconcile workstation and server "flavors" of a UNIX operating system.

While there is a growing interest on the marketplace for Apple Computer's NOS, its consideration is outside the scope of this work.

The key features that characterize a network operating system include hardware independence, support for multiple servers, and connection with similar networks; it must provide management functions, such as backup, security, fault tolerance and performance monitoring, security and access, and user interface.

Two other operating systems must also be considered in conjunction with an NOS to ensure proper functioning of the entire network.

Host (Server Platform) Operating System   This group of programs allows the server to support the NOS and any other application that may reside on the file server. The host operating system provides the basic computer functionalities at the workstation level, including connection with attached input/output devices. Several host systems can be used in conjunction with a given NOS to ensure complete operation of the network. For instance, Novell uses a proprietary server operating system that supports only NetWare. Others, such as UNIX, can support several different NOSs, including:

- *MS-DOS (Versions 3.1 and higher)*   A single-user, single-tasking operating system, MS-DOS now supports the device and file sharing capabilities necessary for network operations, including security through file access control, file locking, and byte-range locking. This operating system is not designed, however, to handle the type of transaction volumes that will be required by larger networks. To support multitasking to manage the network, it may be desirable that the host runs under Windows 3.x rather than under MS-DOS alone.

- *OS/2*   This is a single-user, multitasking operating system that provides more flexibility than MS-DOS. (There is no general agreement as to whether the Windows environment has the same performance.) While it is not recommended that a host be used as a workstation, the ability to accommodate multiple sessions facilitates the handling of network management tasks independently from the network traffic.

- *UNIX*   UNIX is a multiuser, multitasking operating system, which is therefore well adapted to the high level of simultaneous transactions of larger imaging systems. Unlike MS-DOS and OS/2, there are various versions (flavors) of UNIX on the market, and, consequently, there may be issues of optimization between a given UNIX version and its supporting platform.

- *Apple*   Apple-based operating systems and Apple platforms, such as the Macintosh, share the functionalities of UNIX installations, and therefore constitute good potential platforms for imaging systems. However, there is not sufficient history on the market for large "Apple"-only document imaging systems. Rather, Apple networks are found as interoperable with other LANs.

Workstation Operating System   This is the operating system that supports the user workstation. It must be able to support both the file services provided by the network, as well as the other user applications. In particular, it must be able to pass instructions to, and understand commands from, the file server. To that effect, a copy of applicable subsets of the NOS must be present on each installed workstation. Therefore, restrictions as to the choice of workstation and server operating systems are the same.

An operating system for pen computers is mentioned here for the purpose of completeness, but is outside the scope of this book. Pen computer products with commercial applications in the document imaging field are still, by and large, in a developmental state.

Often, compatibility between the NOS, server, and user workstation operating systems is dependent on vendor strategy. Table 3.2 shows a comparison of the features of various major vendor offerings.[3]

Network Components

Regardless of its physical and logical description, a network is an assembly of devices connected by cables. These components are, from a workstation looking to the rest of the network:

- the workstation itself
- an interface linking the workstation to the rest of the network
- a cabling scheme
- a series of servers, which are processors dedicated to perform specified file-handling functions within a given network
- processors dedicated to linking different networks

Table 3.2   Features of Major NOS Offerings

Features	Banyan VINES	IBM LAN Serv.	Novell NW/386	3COM 3+
Server OS	UNIX	OS/2 EE	Proprietary	OS/2
NOS	VINES 4.x	LAN Serv.	NetW.386	LAN Mngr.
User OS	MS-DOS, OS/2, Macintosh, UNIX	PC DOS, OS/2	MS-DOS, OS/2, Macintosh	MS-DOS, OS/2, Macintosh
Server CPU	80386, 68000	80286, 80386	80386, Others	80286, 80386
TCP/IP Support	Yes	No	Yes	Yes
Mainframe Con.	DEC, IBM	IBM	DEC, IBM	DEC, IBM
Conn./Serv.	No Limit	254	250	254

The Workstation

Imaging workstations are described in detail in Chapter 4. What is important to know at this point is that, in a windowed environment, imaging will likely coexist with other programs, some local (i.e., residing on the workstation hard disk) such as personal productivity tools, some either local or remote (i.e., residing on the local hard disk or delivered through the network) such as spreadsheets and word processing, and some remote (i.e., residing only on the network) such as the bulk of imaging applications or electronic mail. Demands on computer resources (which impact on choice of workstation) depend on the anticipated distributed workflow between local and remote applications. Consequently, deciding on the workstation for an image-enabled system should not be done without consideration of the network architecture.

For the purpose of this discussion, i.e., selection, they can be assigned, in increasing order of complexity and costs to three levels of performance, which are discussed below.

Depending on the application, the selected workstation may include scanners, optical storage drive, and printers for local document access. There is a subtle difference, explained below, between a networked workstation with local capabilities and the stand-alone imaging systems that are becoming known as "personal imaging systems," which can be upgraded to run on a network.

In addition, integrated imaging devices that combine scanning, storage, document processing, and printing are making their appearance on the marketplace. Currently, they are primarily designed for personal use, and their inclusion in this discussion is prompted by the issues of compatibility with the rest of the imaging network.

Low-Performance Workstations   These are units that are not used in imaging-intensive applications, and in which their users only need casual access to the image database. Low-performance workstations can run on 80386-class processors, with at least 4MB of RAM to handle the windowing environment. Some early 80286 machines may not have room to add the necessary RAM and, in order to preserve that older investment, one would need to use such machines under DOS rather than under a windowed environment, which would mean of course the loss of windowed, i.e., multitasking, capabilities. There are still some imaging software on the market that can display scanned images on such processors, but before investing in such a solution, one should assess the incremental cost of replacing aging 80286 machines with 80386 or 80486 workstations against the operational issues resulting from running dissimilar systems. One should also bear in mind that, through reengineering, it may not be necessary to make a one-to-one replacement.

Whatever the workstation, it should be equipped, whenever possible, with a video accelerator board to speed up the display of images. In addition, the workstation must be able to decompress image bitstreams, either through a decompression board or through software. While hardware decompression is often faster, the cost of a decompression card may not be justified in a low-performance workstation. In all cases, it is essential that there be compatibility between image formats and display capabilities.

In many cases, a VGA monitor may be adequate for the display of the decompressed images. It should, however, be noted that the VGA format does not display a full page (8.5" × 11") format and, without zooming, may not be of a high enough resolution to show the finer details of scanned documents. Consequently, one should select display software that provides panning (to see the entire image) and zooming (to see the finer details). Most decompression board drivers and decompression software offer these capabilities with varied ease of use.

High-Performance Workstations These workstations are intended to support a fair amount of imaging applications, while supporting other needs on the network. With the price of hardware and software declining, these workstations should be based on at least 80486-class processors, with a minimum of 8MB of RAM. An increasing number of imaging systems offer RISC- or 68040-based processors, in particular in support of UNIX and Apple-based systems.

These workstations should all be equipped with accelerator cards and again, depending on the application, perform image decompression either in hardware or software.

Displays should be at least on large screen (at least super VGA); and, because of the color capabilities of windowed GUIs, it may be advisable to use color monitors, whose incremental cost will be more than offset by increased productivity.

Dedicated Workstations These are workstations that are fully reserved for imaging applications, principally for quality control of scanned images and intensive document processing, as in insurance claims handling. These machines need the same level of performance that the high-performance machines do, but here the critical element is not the processing platform as much as the quality of the display. In most cases, given the fact that most scanned images are still black and white, the display will likely be a high-resolution, large-screen "paper white" monitor.

In multimedia applications, it may be desirable to use a color monitor, but this will probably require the use of color-capable image capture and printing, additional storage space, and appropriate software. It is obvious that a color imaging network also will require a good business case to justify the significant extra cost involved—at least for the next few years.

Workstations and Local Input/Output Imaging Devices   Sometimes it is necessary, or convenient, to provide local scanning, mass storage, or a printing facility. If these local devices are connected directly to the workstation and not to the network, they should be sized for a single-user workload. They should not, even if the workstation is running in a multitasking environment, be available to the rest of the network, because of the potential impact on the workstation or the network performance. If the data or services provided by these local devices need to be shared with other workstations, these devices should be selected so that they can be directly connected to the network, which makes them logically and physically distinct from the workstation concept.

However, great care should be taken to ensure that this arrangement does not result in a degradation in network performance. A much better alternative for all but the simplest networks is to configure these devices as dedicated servers, with the additional hardware costs fully offset by the benefits derived from maintaining network performance.

Personal Imaging Workstations   Personal imaging workstations are stand-alone processors connected to local scanning, mass storage, document processing, and printing facilities. With the drop in hardware and software costs, many of these workstations also offer faxing and OCR capabilities. Because these configurations can be upgraded to network operation by the simple addition of an NIC to the processor, they present an easy entry point into an imaging environment.

Their selection, however, should be made with consideration of the fact that these systems are tightly integrated. Consequently, their connection to the network may require resolution of conflict between their native software and operating settings and the other applications running on the network. In particular, these installations are optimized for "personal" size files, and may not be easily scaled up for larger installations. Because they use imaging and indexing formats that are largely proprietary, it may be difficult to protect software and image capture investments. Nevertheless, these personal systems may well be sufficient for small departmental applications.

"Combo" Workstations   These recently introduced workstations provide, under PC control and within the same device, all digitizing functions associated with scanning, storage, and printing. In addition, they can function as a personal digital copier and send/receive fax machines. Because the documents handled by these machines are essentially in a fax Group 3 format, they cannot be readily integrated without prior format conversion with the rest of the imaging network. However, their low cost makes them attractive as personal imaging systems in which throughput for capturing or printing is less than ten pages per minute.

Diskless Workstations Special consideration must be given to diskless workstations. A diskless workstation has the same processing power as a regular workstation, but does not have any local storage capability; all files are kept on the appropriate server on the network and downloaded on demand. One benefit of this arrangement is higher security. The drawbacks include the need to use specially configured and more expensive NICs—the cost of which may offset the savings on disk drives—higher network traffic, and reduced flexibility in using the workstation for applications that are not normally kept on the network. Consequently, while there may be some specific applications for such an arrangement, diskless devices are not recommended as a general workstation on an imaging network.

The Network Interface

The connection between a workstation and a network is made through circuit boards, called network adapter cards (NACs) or network interface cards (NICs). Their purpose is to convert between parallel data streams used in the workstation and serial data flow in the network, and to perform media access control (MAC) and management according to the network protocol (refer to the earlier discussion of the various protocols). An increasing number of workstations on the market, especially portable units, have built-in network interfaces. While this arrangement saves space on the machine and allows the insertion of portable machines, it also restricts the choice of network to which these machines can be connected.

The Cabling Scheme

The physical link to the network is made through a connector that must match the connectors placed on the cables carrying the network signals. Depending on the type of installation and on the preexistence of a network, the choice of card may dictate the choice of cables (for new installations) or vice versa.

There are two components to the wiring scheme: the wiring medium, more or less specified by industry and international standards; and the connecting hardware, which may or may not be proprietary. For instance, connecting hardware for IBM Token-Ring and Ethernet installations running the same type of wire will be different.

The wiring medium, or cable, determines the nature and maximum speed of signals that can be exchanged without irrecoverable signal distortion. Current standards recognize the wiring media specified below:

Twisted Pair (Shielded [10BaseT] and Unshielded [UTP]) These two variations of a common cabling medium used by the telephone companies can carry signals with acceptable attenuation over a distance of up to 100 meters, at a frequency of up to 16MHz with special communication techniques.

Coaxial Cables (Thin [10Base2] or Thick [10Base5]) These two types of wiring can carry baseband signals with acceptable attenuation over 200 and 500 meters, at frequencies over 100MHz. They have a much higher resistance to electromagnetic noise than unshielded twisted pair cables.

Different topologies call for different cabling specifications, which should be found imprinted on the exterior of the cable. For instance, a thin Ethernet cable should be identified as RG-58/A-AU (or compliant with IEEE 802.3 specification) while ArcNet will call for an identical looking cable labeled as RG-62/A-AU.

The wiring medium should not be considered independently from its terminating hardware or connector. Twisted pair cables usually require so-called RJ-45 connectors, an 8-pin modular connector similar (but larger in size) to the RJ-11 device used in telephone instruments. Most coaxial cables use BNC and T connectors which, for reliability purposes, should be compliant with UG-274 military specification. Cables used in token-ring installations require proprietary connectors, which vary with the type of device they are attached to.

Fiber Optic Cables   Depending on the conditions of manufacturing and the type of modulation, these cables can carry signals at even higher frequencies over 3,500 meters without objectionable attenuations. Here, more than with copper cables, connectors must be selected and installed with great care.

Other Cabling Schemes   There are several proposed standards for mixed media cables, such as fiber over copper, designed to support a variety of equipment configurations. While these schemes have definite operational advantages, they should be considered with caution until the standards are finalized to avoid the operational problems of interfacing noncompliant installations with standard networks.

The advent of infrared communication links is equivalent to the establishment of virtual cable capabilities. However, it may take some time until this type of "cabling" can be widely used in imaging systems, and discussion on this subject is outside the scope of this work.

The Servers

Imaging systems normally use dedicated combined processors and storage devices called servers to manage traffic between workstations and between workstations and shared devices. While there are designs on the market that allow workstations to also manage traffic flow on the network, these are not practical for imaging applications. Under these conditions, there is a minimum of one server, usually called the file server or network server. Other processors are used to perform background tasks.

The File Server   This server is essential to the operation of an imaging network. Its role is to orchestrate the execution of workstation requests for network resources and files, while ensuring the integrity and security of the information transfer process. In smaller systems, the file server also contains the index to the image database. There is no organic distinction between a server and a workstation; the difference is in software loaded on the file server and in the size and quality of the components. Because of the volume of data that will transmit through the file server, they are usually more powerful than user workstations, with large amounts of memory and disk space. They also often use advanced time-saving caching techniques.

One file server growing in popularity is called PC-X server, running under X Windows. While still in its infancy, its progress should be followed, as it may become a key to efficient imaging networks. The difference between a conventional and a PC-X server is more a software than a hardware issue. Because X Windows is a platform- and operating system-independent protocol, it can run on PC as well as UNIX platforms. In particular, PC-X server software can run DOS or MS Windows applications.

A new breed of server, called superserver, is appearing on the market. A generally accepted definition of superservers is that of a processor that provides a minimum of 16MB of RAM with at least 2GB of storage. In that same category are multiprocessors and multibus machines. Superservers provide a minimum of 32-bit data path. Multiprocessor/multibus devices offer capacity and scalability capabilities that are not possible with single processors, while the 32-bit and above bus enables a high level of performance. In addition, superservers offer built-in fault tolerance, data integrity, and error recovery. Superservers may be considered as devices that support all the other servers mentioned below. While this may be operationally attractive, it also introduces a single point of failure in the network design.

Print Server Print servers are processors designed to buffer large-size images being printed. Sometimes a luxury in data-only networks, especially with the newer printers that have large built-in storage, they are generally a necessity in imaging installations where the amount of data that needs to be buffered is beyond printer memory capacity.

Document Server Document servers are used to control and manage access to optical disk jukeboxes. These devices are used in lieu of direct file-server access, when the load on the server from file access results in unacceptable performance degradation.

Scanning Server These servers are sometimes used to centralize the output of scanners until documents have passed quality control. Here again, the need for a scanning server is determined by load considerations.

Data Extraction and Processing (OCR) Server In many applications, data are extracted from imaged documents through optical character recognition (OCR) and similar image-processing techniques. These operations are computation intensive. It is often practical to conduct them in the background on a dedicated machine.

Communication Servers These are servers that handle data traffic over modems, as opposed to workstation traffic. Such servers include:

- *Fax Servers* These are devices that store fax communications. While fax documents are essentially images, there are several reasons to keep fax traffic separate from other imaging applications. First, most commercial fax documents are transmitted with a CCITT Group 3 data compression algorithm, incompatible with CCITT Group 4 compression schemes, the most common for document imaging systems. Their conversion to Group 4 requires additional processing, as well as their indexing to integrate them into the rest of the document system. This is best done outside the main document server.

- *Asynchronous Communication (Network Modem) Servers* These servers are actually pools of data modems and allow workstations to communicate through telephone lines. Because they operate at modem speed, they are usually too slow for imaging applications. They can, however, be useful for the emergency transmission of isolated images. One such application might be the need to send a one-page contract with signature for incorporation into a document to a workstation that would not have access to a fax modem.

Intranetwork Connections

As indicated earlier, the simplest logical topologies connect nodes (workstations and servers) in either a daisy chain or a ring. However, in many cases, it is necessary to insert devices between nodes to ensure proper network operation.

Hubs (or Concentrators) A hub is essentially a device to which all nodes on the network are connected, providing electrical and physical connection to the network (see Figure 3.6). There are various types of hubs: Some are simple patch panels, which are used to provide a clean physical wiring; others have a microprocessor on board that is designed to control access to each of the nodes and, in case of failure, can automatically bypass them. These intelligent hubs run under their own software and can perform network management functions that would normally be handled by the file server.

A particular type of intelligent hub, called a multiple access unit (MAU), is a required component of IBM Token-Ring topologies, and provides connectivity to as many as four or eight devices per MAU.

The recent appearance of switched hubs, which allow devices on the network to have access to entire channel capacity rather than sharing it with other applications, may have a profound impact on imaging network design.

Repeaters Electrical signals become distorted during their travel along copper wires. The maximum distance allowed before a signal is considered to be too distorted to be accurately recognizable is determined by standards. For instance, in a token-ring topology, the maximum cable length between devices running on UTP wiring at 16MBits is 200 feet. Repeaters are devices that connect two cable segments, taking degraded input and regenerating new signals in the proper shape and strength. Consequently, they can be used to increase the reach of a network. However, because the regeneration is not perfect, that reach is still limited. For instance, IEEE 802.3 standards (so-called Ethernet protocols) specify a maximum

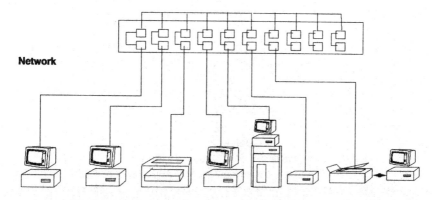

Figure 3.6   Diagram of a hub

cable length of 500 feet; by using repeaters, the physical distance between two nodes can be extended to 3,000 feet. Some models can be used to interconnect cables with different media and thus can provide cabling flexibility between heterogeneous NICs.

Internetwork Connections

In but the simplest cases, image-enabled networks need to be partitioned into several subnetworks, as shown in Figure 3.1. Even when this is not an initial operating requirement, imaging system designers must be prepared for the fact that, as imaging traffic increases, the need to balance the load on the network may force them to partition the network into linked clusters of users, organized according to file-sharing requirements. Several devices are used to ensure communication between networks.

Bridges Bridges are microprocessors that combine the features of a repeater with those associated with directing data traffic according to the network destination of a data stream. The bridge reads the network address of each data packet and routes it to the appropriate cable link. The industry distinguishes between local and remote bridges, depending on whether there is a need for one (local) or two (remote) devices to connect two different networks. Depending on the sophistication of the bridge, updating device addresses can be manual or automated.

Bridges, like repeaters, are protocol-independent, and are used to link different networks using the same protocol, regardless of their cabling schemes, which are handled by the repeater. There are different bridge software algorithms on the market that determine the best path between network segments and, in case of failure, reroute data traffic. Some are compliant with IEEE standards, but do not support remote bridges and therefore are not appropriate for networks connected through communication lines. In such cases, one needs to use algorithms specifically designed for remote bridges, such as the IBM source routing and the protocol transparent routing algorithms.

Routers   While bridges need to know the address of a communication, routers are used to address specific network segments and establish the shortest path according to either static or dynamic algorithms, which take into consideration various factors such as transmission costs and traffic loads. Contrary to bridges, routers only handle data streams with the "proper" address and ignore the others, providing a level of safety between network sections. An important distinction between bridges and routers is that bridges are protocol-independent, and routers are not. For instance, a router for TCP/IP will ignore all messages under SPX/IPX.

Brouters   Brouters are products that combine the protocol independence of the bridge with the data discrimination of routers. This allows for the design of effective handling of heterogenous networks, because the brouter will address incoming data stream to the network with a compatible protocol.

Gateways   Gateways are devices that allow interconnection between networks operating under different protocols by repackaging each frame in a data stream. As such, gateways allow the exchange and integration of data between mainframes and PCs and other networks, such as electronic mail. They are essential to the integration of an imaging network with the business process data flow.

Because each of these devices operates at different levels of the OSI model (see Figure 3.7,[4] which summarizes the relationship between them), not all may be necessary to a given installation. The only device that is indispensable is the NIC. Repeaters, bridges, routers, and brouters are not needed for small installations. However, when the imaging network is to be linked with a mainframe, it is necessary to use a gateway, regardless of the size of the imaging operation.

Layer	*Functions*	*Linking Device*
7 Application	Applications move files, emulate terminals, and generate other traffic	Gateway
6 Presentation	Programs format data and convert characters	Gateway
5 Session	Programs negotiate and establish connections between nodes	Gateway
4 Transport	Programs ensure end-to-end delivery	None
3 Network	Programs route packets across multiple inter-LAN links	Router
2 Data Link	Firmware transfers packets or frames	Bridge
1 Physical	Firmware sequences packets or frames for transmission	Repeater

Figure 3.7   Relationship of internetwork devices with the OSI model

3.3 SELECTING AN IMAGING NETWORK

The selection of an imaging network can be done either from a network or from a user perspective. Both have advantages and drawbacks. A network approach tends to maximize the use of an existing data network investment and therefore may lead to constraints in the types of applications that the imaging system may have to support in the future. A workstation approach, on the other hand, provides a better support of business needs, but may inflate requirements. For instance, it is always tempting to have the best and most efficient hardware: Large-screen, high-resolution color monitors always have a greater appeal than monochrome VGA displays, and, as an end user, it is easy to find a rationale for needing the former. However, not everybody *really* needs the latest hardware, and a network-based approach may quickly put a pragmatic limit to otherwise unrestrained "business" requirements.

The most prudent approach to the selection of an imaging system is dictated by the fact that, regardless of the origin of an imaging project, its adoption will change an organization's culture and the way it conducts its business. Consequently, it makes more sense to take an iterative approach, in which a bottom-up design of the new installation, seen from the user point of view, is matched against top-down considerations of the constraints placed by the existing environment. Starting with a top-down methodology carries the risk that an inordinate share of old methodologies are recycled and embedded in the new system.

Once the network has been designed from the bottom up, a full design review should take place, in which:

1. The requirements are matched against the existing resources.
2. The costs of migrating from an existing installation to the proposed system (upgrading workstations, installation of new servers, relocating and rewiring users) are tabulated and compared to the benefits that were projected in the initial project cost justification.

If the costs are on budget, the proposed network should be adopted without attempting to reduce its costs. It should always be understood that like—and probably more than—all computer systems, imaging networks suffer from the so-called "highway effect," where, by the time the system is in place, user needs may have already exhausted provisions for growth that were incorporated in the design. Therefore, there is no long-term operational benefit in attempting to reduce startup costs, because future demands on resources may sooner than later force a costly upgrade of the initial system.

It is when projected costs exceed anticipated benefits that trade-offs, beginning with users' requirements, should be considered, with the selection process reiterated until the project costs fall within acceptable limits.

Conducting a Needs Assessment Survey

The selection of an imaging network appropriate to an organization's business requirements is dictated by the expected data traffic, which should be defined in terms of:

- Volume of files to be captured, processed, and retrieved at any given time, and definition of their life cycle
- Number of users that are expected to use the imaging network at any given time
- Other applications that are available to the end user. In particular, will users want to have access to electronic mail and fax services? In a windowed environment, in particular, these services need to be integrated with the workflow, and the user workstation must be configured to accept the additional processing load.

Therefore, the objective of the survey will be to answer the following questions:

1. *Who* will need some kind of access to imaged documents and in what volume? This will determine the kind of workstation that is necessary to service the different users. For instance, users with critical, ad hoc needs will require powerful machines that can download large documents and process them locally, without tying up network resources. In contrast, users with predictive requirements, such as forms processing, can be accommodated with less powerful workstations under scheduled workflow management, which will administer the actual routing of documents. Selection of a workstation should involve not only choice of processor, but also monitor display and storage of the image files beyond the processor internal hard disk. Separating storage and workstation selections may result in loss of overall performance.

2. *What* type of document will be accessed? The answer to this question will provide guidance as to the structure and organization of the collection of stored documents. For instance, unstructured documents may lead to the adoption of physical grouping of similar documents to facilitate retrieval and a powerful indexing system to reduce search time. On the other hand, structured documents in a transaction processing application may be accommodated by a simple chronological arrangement, with simple document number indexing.

3. *Where* will the different users be located? The answer to this question will determine the kind of network topology that will provide faster access to the documents. In fact, the best, or at least a reasonable answer, may be difficult to determine, because user locations usually reflect more established relationships than defined by business rationale. Because of the cost of cabling and interface devices, the difference between optimized and unoptimized topologies can be substantial. A good guiding principle may be to organize

the network around operational clusters, the topology of which can be simply engineered.

4. *Why* will the documents be needed? This question will help to determine the nature and volume of document transit, and thus assist in selecting the network operating system that provides the best support of business objectives and the network security controls necessary to ensure integrity of the database system. Here the issue is not so much one of preventing access to sensitive information, which can be resolved more effectively through network security and software access functions, but one of guarding against uncontrolled changes leading to corrupted information kept on the network. This is a very important and often underestimated requirement when designing imaging systems, because a significant amount of stored documents may be indexed solely through their subject matter, and their detailed contents may be available only through browsing. Not knowing why someone needs a given document, regardless of access right, may lead to inflated estimates of requirements for system support.

5. *When* will the documents be needed? This question will determine the number, types, and capacity of servers that must be provided. For instance, nontime-critical retrievals of scheduled applications may be accommodated with a combination of off-line, near-line, and on-line storage, with a rotation between the two, thus lowering the capacity of a document server. For instance, a vital records application may anticipate a peak in retrieval of birth records for three-, five-, twenty-, and sixty-year-olds corresponding to the main events in an individual life. On that basis, it is possible to periodically rotate birth records between off-line (on the storage shelves) for low probability of demand, to on-line (in a jukebox) for high probability, leaving the rest of the network to process new records. The rare off-year requests can then be handled in a near-line fashion, using an auxiliary drive to read the records retrieved on demand from the storage shelves.

6. *How* will the documents be used? This last question will determine the need for concurrent applications and the nature of desirable graphical user interfaces. For instance, some existing applications may come with their own user interface, optimized for the particular equipment and software configuration. The need for concurrent access to different programs may limit the choices of operating systems and user interfaces or result in contention for resources.

As already emphasized, an imaging network must support stated business objectives. Therefore, a survey for the purpose of needs assessment should closely match a business and workflow requirement study. When there is an opportunity to conduct the three at the same time, as in the case of a workflow reengineering project, it is a good practice to integrate and reconcile these three aspects, either electronically using a configuration management software, or manually with a worksheet such as the one shown in Figure 3.8.[5]

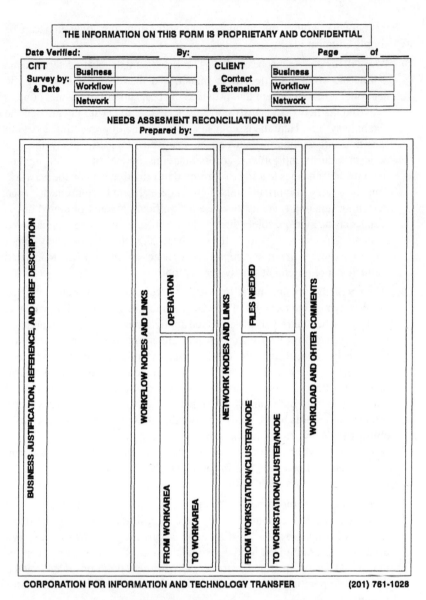

CORPORATION FOR INFORMATION AND TECHNOLOGY TRANSFER   (201) 761-1028

Figure 3.8   Example of integrated needs assessment survey

Selecting a Workstation

The technical decision elements for various types of workstations that can be used have been already described. In addition to these elements, selection criteria include cost and reliability and compatibility of parts with the installed base. In particular, interface boards should be compatible from machine to machine to facilitate maintenance and inventory. It is also important to determine the compression method (in hardware or in software) and the quality of the display screen.

As indicated earlier, 386 machines usually are sufficient for low-level work-stations. High-level installations with high-resolution monitors for dedicated workstations will require more powerful machines. In fact, the incremental cost between a 386 and a 486 processor is so low that it may be advisable to standardize over 486 platforms. For enterprise-wide capabilities, UNIX capable installations are often preferred, as their initial costs will be more than offset by their flexibility. To accommodate image handling, the processor should have a minimum of 8MB, and a minimum of 120MB of hard disk storage for storing both application programs and downloading/caching images during high-volume retrieval activities.

Other workstations, such as "combos," should be considered only for specific and well-understood situations.

Selecting a Document Grouping Structure

Establishing a structure for a document grouping is an activity entirely different from the design of a database management system (DBMS). While the latter is responsible for the tracking and retrieval of information, the former determines for a given DBMS the efficiency of the retrieval process itself. For instance, an index-based DBMS will work much more efficiently if the records in the database are arranged alphabetically than if they are unsorted.

In the case of imaging, where access to documents stored in optical jukeboxes constitutes a significant time delay in the retrieval process, the organization of the document base is a major factor in the overall efficiency and acceptance of an imaging system. In addition, because the network load associated with the image data stream is significant, it is necessary that the volume of image traffic be kept to a minimum, or network performance will deteriorate rapidly. Therefore, organizing the collection base to reduce both length and frequency of document travel is essential to the design of an efficient imaging network. This is particularly important when building image capabilities into an existing network, where the system designer will be tempted to upgrade the nodes that are in place to handle images, without realizing that the current topology has become replete with potential imaging bottlenecks.

The selection of the document collection structure should be consistent with sound records management principles as they apply to active records. These can be summarized as follows:

- Whenever possible, segregate and store records according to a commonality of usage. For instance, keep documents generated and used within a work-group on the same storage medium and as close as possible to the workgroup itself. There is no technical reason why mass storage cannot be distributed throughout a network, and the resulting incremental hardware costs should be weighed against cost of lower performance due to network congestion.

- Establish a records maintenance and disposition schedule so that documents can be removed from active storage once their expected level of activity has fallen to such a degree that it is no longer cost-justifiable to keep them on line.

- Whenever possible, organize documents according to their commonality of processing requirements; for example, keep together documents to be submitted to OCR or forms extraction.

Once segregation of records has been performed according to the above criteria and other operational considerations, it is possible to put them in the order they will be needed and perform any document processing that does not require operator intervention in a background mode.

Selecting a Network Topology

The end user should be able to make valid choices up to this point without having any significant network experience. From now on, however, it is recommended that the rest of the selection process be made with the advice of a professional in network design, implementation, and testing.

There is no such thing as the best topology, but any choice should take into consideration the following elements:

- The scope of the proposed imaging project
- The cost of establishing and connecting new dedicated imaging networks compared to the cost of adding image capabilities to existing installations
- The projected growth of the imaging system

For small, stand-alone departmental size projects, it may be sufficient to select a single LAN, with a daisy chain topology. For centralized imaging systems involving a mainframe, a token-ring topology may be recommended. For larger systems or systems with large document processing requirements, a composite topology may be most appropriate, as shown in Figure 3.1, with one network dedicated to image processing and connected to all the other networks.

The selection of a topology should not be done without consideration of the protocols and NOS that will run on that topology. However, in this writer's opinion, image capture, quality control, and indexing functions should be kept on sub-networks separate from image retrieval and other applications in all but the simplest installations.

Selecting Operating Systems and Protocols

The selection of the NOS and the operating system will have the most impact on the value of the imaging network to the organization. It is, therefore, probably the most important design choice to be made by the system designer. Even in composite installations, it is easier to manage homogeneous networks running under the same NOS and protocols. However, existing data networks and applications may limit the options available.

Here again, there is probably no such thing as the best NOS and protocols. Operation pragmatism may play an equal or even bigger role than technical superiority of a particular design solution. That said, the following should be considered, everything else being equal. First, because of the amount of traffic required to support imaging applications, DOS-based solutions will become progressively less attractive as the size of the installation grows. The time it takes before a given system becomes unsatisfactory will vary with the type of usage, and it may be difficult to establish it precisely in an ongoing installation. What probably will happen is that performance on a spartan budget-based network will progressively deteriorate as users are added to the network, to the point that it will be wiser politically to upgrade the network than to keep to a low budget.

In this writer's opinion, the network should initially be designed for a configuration corresponding to the highest realistic level of service, with all the "basic" services in place. While this approach will result in higher up-front expenditures, it will also provide a longer system life and eliminate the costs of transition associated with systems designed to support only present demands.

While the use of a subnetwork will reduce traffic on a given segment, DOS-based solutions often become inefficient when more than 50 workstations are concurrently processing imaging applications.

LAN NOS Selection Criteria

Five elements are most important in the selection of an NOS for imaging applications.

Compatibility with the OSI Model   Because it is likely that an imaging network will interact with other information utilities, compatibility with the OSI model will facilitate bridging between different installations and ensure long-term interoperability. This criterion is important in the context of progressive adoption of the concept of electronic data interchange (EDI) and electronic commerce (EC) in all industries.

Hardware Independence   Because of the competitive hardware marketplace, and the fact that most hardware procurement will be based on price, it is essential that the NOS be supported by a large variety of vendors.

Multiple Server Support   Because imaging networks use dedicated processors to perform specific imaging and database tasks, it is critical that the NOS support communication between multiple servers, such as those dedicated to mass storage, printing and faxing, and communication.

Network Management   Because of the difference in performance and complexity of the network, the NOS must be able to support shared resources and powerful network management utilities, in addition to the minimum requirements of managing users, performing backup, and the like.

Capacity for Growth   Because expansion of an imaging system will quickly absorb network capacity and resources, the NOS must be selected in such a way that it supports graceful migration to larger installations.

Other selection criteria, including ease of installation and maintenance, are consistent with the requirements of conventional data systems.

Network Operating System

Processing resources necessary to manage a large number of workstations in a high-volume operation requires powerful multitasking software. In all but specialized cases, imaging networks should be UNIX-based, with the caveat that not all UNIX implementations are similar. However, such a solution will ensure a reasonable portability of applications between platforms and facilitate growth.

For smaller, departmental installations, involving fewer than 50 workstations running imaging at the same time, PC-based NOS, offered by Novell, 3Com, and Banyan, are usable.

For workgroup applications, one should also look at using software products, such as those offered by Microsoft (MS WorkGroup for Windows), Lotus Notes (LN:DI), Artisoft, and Novell that are designed to work in a peer-to-peer architecture. It should be noted that these products have NOS functionalities that may conflict with other NOSs, and may not easily integrate with a larger network.

Host (Platform) Operating Systems

For single-site networks, the host operating system needs only to be the same as the NOS. However, if the imaging network is likely to be part of a larger entity, the host operating system should be UNIX-based.

Workstation Operating Systems

The workstation operating system, which may require a multitasking environment such as MS Windows, should be selected to match the anticipated workload. With an appropriately configured workstation, dedicated, simple office document imaging applications can be accommodated satisfactorily with a DOS or OS/2 operating system. Other applications, such as those found in engineering, may require a UNIX operating system just to run existing programs, thus forcing imaging to run on the same operating system.

Selecting Servers

As indicated earlier, there is no intrinsic hardware difference between a server and a workstation, except for the fact that servers need to be—and usually are—more powerful than the workstations they support.

File Servers

For imaging applications running under DOS it is not recommended to use less than 80486 processors, preferably 486DX class machines, with a minimum of 8MB

Table 3.3   Comparison between mass storage devices

Drive Type	Transfer Rate
IDE	1.4KB
SCSI-2	10–20MB
ESDI	20MB

of RAM and 1.2GB of hard disk. While smaller storage may be sufficient for a while, the savings realized from installing a smaller configured server will be more than offset by the cost of an eventual upgrade.

In some installations, there may be some benefit in considering the use of superservers. However, a decision to use a superserver should be taken with full understanding that such machines may cost four to five times as much as a regular server, and they require trained staff for maintenance.

Servers are often customized to meet specific operating conditions. Consequently, particular consideration should be given to the selection of devices that will be attached to the processor, as they may influence the choice, or at least the configuration, of the server itself. In particular, special attention should be given to mass storage, the type of which will depend on various considerations, including:

- Performance, which depends on the trade-off between capacity, type of interface (such as IDE and SCSI), interface controller card, and device drivers, all appraised in the context of processor bus architecture and interface format. While there may be, for instance, an improvement in response time with larger disks, that benefit may be lost if the bus architecture (or the network) does not allow fast enough transfer rates. Usually, 32-bit, SCSI-2 drives provide the best cost trade-off for imaging applications. In contrast, as shown in Table 3.3, IDE drives are much too slow for use on network servers (even if they are much cheaper).

- Physical requirements, from form factor to power consumption. Larger drives, when configured internally to a server, may occupy more than one drive bay.

- Compatibility between drives and the network operating system. For instance, it is easier to interface an SCSI-2 drive than an ESDI. One should always check compatibility between drive, drive controller, and operating software, down to the level of software settings.

Display screens suitable for server use must be capable of displaying graphics. However, potential conflicts with network software should limit their choice to VGA monochrome monitors.

Other Servers

As indicated earlier, there is little difference in principle between file and other device servers. As with dedicated processors, their selection can follow a similar methodology, with a few exceptions, as noted. In some cases the services provided are delivered in a peer-to-peer fashion, using workstations as a server. Note that there may be a performance penalty to this potentially less expensive solution to full-server installations.

Image (Document) Servers   These are devices that store active images. In peer-to-peer arrangements, they are directly attached to the workstation; in client servers, they are separate. Most image servers store and retrieve documents on optical disks, arranged in a jukebox. Depending on the size of the installation, the jukebox may be directly attached to the file server.

Backup and archiving units can also be used in a server configuration.

Print Servers   Like the image server, printers can be attached to a workstation and be accessible to the network in a peer-to-peer fashion; or, they can have their own servers. An emerging breed of printers is composed of devices with built-in processors, which allow them to act as digital copiers and fax output machines.

Selecting a Windowed Environment

The issue in a windowed environment is not so much the graphical user interface at the workstation, but the compatibility between the various GUIs required by concurrent applications and their level of performance with the workstation configuration. It should be noted that with new products constantly being introduced on the market, the choice of environment may be more difficult and more irrelevant to an optimum solution. Competition forces differences between products to become more and more elusive. A detailed discussion of the subject is given in Chapter 12.

3.4   OTHER REQUIREMENTS

The preceding discussion focused on the selection of a network configuration that best supports an organization's needs. Provisions should also be made for requirements that are not directly related to the imaging and other business applications, but that are necessary to ensure proper and responsible network behavior.

Network Management Software

Network management software are series of programs designed to identify device failures and reallocate resources to accommodate changing operational conditions. These programs monitor data traffic as seen from the device on which they are loaded, most often on the network file server, and the responses that a particular device gives to specific instructions. Effective use of network management software requires significant technical know-how, and it is unlikely that end users will exploit them. However, these programs are essential to the diagnostics of network incompatibilities and to the optimization of the entire installation. They should, therefore, be included in the budget of the imaging system. Depending on the complexity of the software, their cost can range between $1,000 and $100,000 and above, thereby impacting significantly on the technical solution.

Network Simulation

Given the variety of options in topologies, hardware, and software, it may be difficult to identify an optimum technical solution that will work well in a wide range of operating conditions. This can be verified through modeling, and there are a variety of network simulation programs on the market. Such packages can save a significant amount of money by helping to identify an optimum configuration. In particular, they can be very effective in defining the document storage configuration that provides the fastest response time. They are, however, expensive. Consequently, a trade-off analysis should be made as to the benefit of acquiring such a tool to monitor and test service delivery effectiveness against having a consulting firm conduct audits of the new network.

Configuration Management and Version Control

Configuration management and version control are two aspects of the same problem, which is to ensure that all the network components and its database are properly identified and controlled. Configuration management is essentially a hardware and software inventory activity and should be conducted by the personnel responsible for network maintenance. Lack of configuration management may result in an inability to identify the cause of failure; for example, the information regarding the actual release number of a particular software may not be available.

Version control is a historical inventory of documents in the database. Without it, it may not be possible to maintain up-to-date work packages in the context of frequent revisions to the type of multiformat documents found in imaging systems. Here again, a trade-off analysis should be made to determine the value of such tools, as their costs will be added to the total cost of the imaging project.

Workflow Management

Workflow management is actually the establishment of document static and dynamic routing schemes to meet prescribed business objectives. Workflow management programs are similar to those used for simulation, but the difference in functionalities available to the end users makes them a distinct class of tools.

Static (i.e., procedural) workflow can be established either through programming or through the use of workflow software; dynamic (ad hoc) workflow is done through workflow software. Because changes in workflow may generate different workload patterns on the network, it is desirable that they be analyzed for possible impact on network traffic and fine-tuning.

3.4   CONCLUSION

The selection and design of a particular network configuration is a complex undertaking. In fact, deciding on the optimal technical solutions is becoming increasingly difficult; decrease in hardware costs, the appearance of new technologies such as new bus design or processors to increase workstation capabilities, new software packages providing off-the-shelf functionalities can suddenly turn an initially unacceptable option into a desirable choice. However, it should always be remembered that adoption of unproven technologies is sometimes a recipe for disaster. In that context, a sound approach to implementing an imaging system may well be the one that integrates business justification with technical conservatism.

NOTES

[1] Adapted from Thomas C. Bartree, *ISDN, DECnet and SNA Communications* (Indianapolis: Howard W. Sams & Co.), 1989.

[2] Adapted from Thomas W. Madron, *Local Area Networks, the Next Generation,* 2d ed. (New York: John Wiley & Sons), 1990.

[3] Ibid.

[4] Adapted from Frank J. Derfler, *PC Magazine Guide to Connectivity* (New York: Ziff-Davis), 1991.

[5] Courtesy of the Corporation for Information and Technology Transfer.

4

User Perspective of Imaging Systems

Marc R. D'Alleyrand, Ph.D.

4.1 INTRODUCTION: THE BUSINESS CASE

An imaging system is a tool used to enhance the transfer of information. Its value is directly related to the ease with which it can be integrated into an organization's business activities. More specifically, its value is determined by its contribution to the design of cost-effective information storage and retrieval systems, or to the streamlining of an existing workflow.

Information life cycles are similar in image and data systems; therefore, it is relatively easy to design integration schemes that merge needed information regardless of form or medium. But imaged documents are represented by much larger data streams than purely machine-readable information, thereby restricting system designers to three choices, which correspond to three levels of system design:

1. Design an image system separate from the existing data processing installation. This approach is equivalent to the creation of an electronic file cabinet. Its business justification is limited to applications where storage and retrieval comprise the major portion of the business, and where integrating imaging with the rest of the organization's information flow would not reduce overall costs or increase productivity.

2. Add the capability of accessing image information to an existing data system. This approach, called "image enabling," involves either a system redesign to handle the added processing load from the imaging applications or performance trade-offs for the overall system.

3. Embed imaging in a totally redesigned workflow environment, fully consistent with business requirements. The business justification for this approach

of "integrated imaging" is found in downsizing or rightsizing efforts, aimed at increasing productivity and reducing costs. It will probably involve preliminary workflow reengineering and business process redesign.

The correct approach should be made after assessing management considerations, rather than technical requirements. Factors to consider are relative costs, anticipated benefits, conversion and systems design efforts, and competitive or strategic opportunities. These combined elements will determine the nature of the interactions between end users and the imaging systems implemented through a workstation. This workstation is a combination of connected physical (hardware) and logical (software) components, which provide, at a minimum, access to and display of document images and data about them. From a user standpoint, the paramount advantage of such systems over data-only methods is that access can be integrated with access to related information, be it other documents or information processing applications.

For instance, the value of an accounts payable imaging system is not so much that it can store and retrieve invoices, but that it can display all documents related to a particular procurement, from purchase request to contract to material receipt. And it can do this whether the documents have been generated in different parts of the organization or outside the organization. Similarly, in a legal environment, the value of an imaging system is to see that it becomes increasingly cost-effective to retrieve information and display that information in disparate documents.

Access to any system feature, service, or capability requires the use of necessarily limited processing, storage, or communication resources. Therefore, the value of an imaging system to a given user requires that the system deliver the needed information more efficiently and at a cheaper cost than competing methods. The commercial availability of a wide range of imaging systems components provides the user with the flexibility necessary to meet most, if not all, operating requirements in a given business environment. But each application is different, and the design of a specific system may require customization of a standard system design, in which individual components are selected and optimized to yield the highest level of performance. It is the purpose of this chapter to identify these various components from the user's perspective and describe how they are integrated in a networked imaging system in a windowed environment.

4.2 THE COMPONENTS

In a windowed environment, all imaging activities of interest at any given time to a user—ranging from document capture to retrieval, as well as access to and performance of nonimaging applications—are displayed on a computer terminal in windows, which are delineated screen areas that can be overlaid at will. Each active window can be maximized (contents displayed) or minimized (represented by a small icon), with no effect on actual processing. Depending on the system configuration and the supporting operating system, multiple applications processing may or may not occur in parallel. For instance, the UNIX, OS/2, and Windows NT operating systems are designed for multiprocessing (i.e., concurrent); DOS-based systems are not. A windowed environment such as MS Windows gives the illusion of multitasking by keeping all open tasks in memory, even though only one task can run at a time. Manual steps of opening and closing files, as well as dynamic allocation of computer resources for the execution of different tasks, are done under program control.

From a user perspective, therefore, an imaging system in a windowed environment can be represented on a display screen. Access is provided by opening an appropriate window. The universally accepted method for accessing or launching the applications is to select the icon representing the application and validate that selection with a pointing device such as a mouse or a light pen. The display screen is always attached to a workstation, and so, from the user point of view, the workstation is equivalent to the desktop. As such, a workstation can be seen as an information processing facility, connecting information and underlying data through a set of functionalities (see Figure 4.1). It is in fact a complex combination of hardware and software that connects input, output, and storage devices (Figure 4.2) either directly, for stand-alone systems (Figure 4.3), or through communication links in a networked or shared resources environment. As shown in Figure 4.4, the resources available to a networked workstation are provided by specialized devices called servers (file, print, fax, etc.), which are designed to perform specific services, such as file storage, retrieval, and printing, in an optimized way for the entire network. In many cases, the resources necessary to deliver all the requested functionalities require the additional use of workstations dedicated to the performance of tasks such as scanning, printing, and telecommunication.

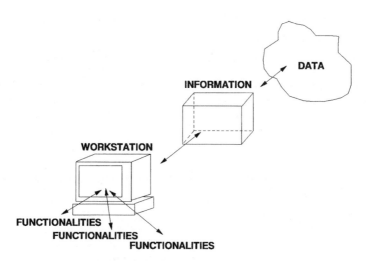

Figure 4.1   User perspective of an imaging system

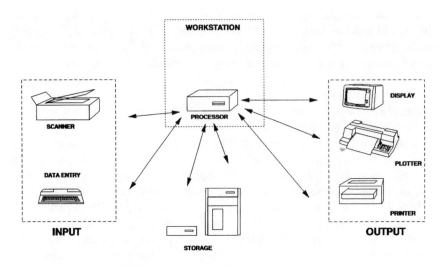

Figure 4.2   Workstation functionalities from a user perspective

4.3   THE WORKSTATION

A workstation is engineered to give the user access to the digital world. Depending on the architecture of the imaging system, workstations support one or more of the following:

- Control the operation of external imaging devices, such as scanners and printers
- Execute queries to the imaging database, and/or launch programs related to the imaging applications
- Format the data stream representing the retrieved images and display them to the user

Many functions can be implemented in different ways; therefore, there is no such thing as a "standard" imaging platform. Image decompression, for instance,

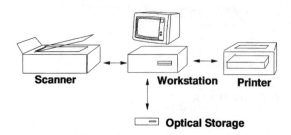

Figure 4.3   Stand-alone workstation

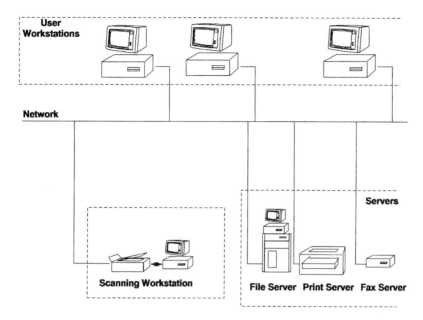

Figure 4.4   Networked workstations

which is necessary for examination of images on a computer screen, can be achieved either in hardware or software. The hardware solution is implemented by the insertion of an appropriate decompression board in the workstation. However, the choice of decompression board may in some cases be dictated by the compression method, which is usually proprietary. Similar compatibility considerations apply to the selection of all the imaging system peripherals.

The next section identifies the major components found in all workstations and discusses them in the context of imaging applications.

The Desktop

For a user, in a windowed environment the workstation (or desktop) is the "window" to the world that can incorporate three levels of imaging systems:

1. Level I, or stand-alone: All image-related activities, including capture, storage, retrieval, and processing are performed at the workstation, which directly controls the storage devices as well as related applications.

2. Level II, or departmental: At this level, all functionalities are provided through a network, which supports various workstations through different dedicated servers.

3. Level III, or enterprise-wide: At Level III, the workstation has access to several heterogeneous networks throughout an organization, supporting different platforms and functioning under different operating systems.

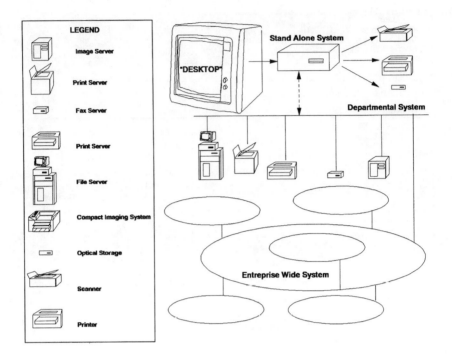

Figure 4.5   User view from the desktop

The distinction between these levels is somewhat arbitrary, and there may be a significant overlap between them. Figure 4.5 outlines the concept of the desktop as a "window to the world."

System Unit

The system unit is the heart of the workstation. It contains the basic elements necessary to process information. Structurally, the system unit is mounted on a physical card, called a motherboard, which is composed of several superimposed conductive traces, separated by an electrically insulating glue. It can be described in terms of a central processing unit (CPU), random access memory (RAM), and an input/output (I/O) bus.

Central Processing Unit

The CPU is the element essential to the overall performance of the workstation, as well as its compatibility with the rest of the imaging system. It is primarily characterized by the architecture of its integrated circuit (the processing chip) and its operating (clock) speed. There are various implementations of the same architecture on the market, corresponding to different speeds and performances. One, the Intel 80386 processor (the so-called 386 chip), exists in at least in two versions (386SX and 386DX), which run at 20MHz or 25MHz for the 386SX and 30MHz for the 386DX. At 33MHz, an Intel 80486 processor (the 486 chip) has been reported to be at least 50 percent better than a 386 chip running at the same speed. By comparison, the architecture of the 486 chip allows a 50-to-1 and 10-to-1 performance increase ratio respectively when compared to the early PC-XT, which had an Intel 8088 running at 4.7MHz, and the PC-AT, with an Intel 80286 (286 CPU) running at 8MHz.

Higher speed is not the only characteristic of the newer chips. For instance, the 386 chip has a 32-bit processing capability and can address up to 4GB of internal memory, while the 286 can address only 16MB. In addition, the 386 has internal memory management and, under specific conditions, can run several DOS applications concurrently. The 486 is an enhanced version of the 386, with an improved architecture and, in certain models (486DX), an integrated math coprocessor to speed up performance. It is still possible to find software that allow limited imaging applications on a 286-based machine, but it is only a matter of time until support for such applications disappears.

Other chip manufacturers have created CPUs whose architectures can compete with the 386/486 set. Two of these are the SPARC, initially designed by Sun Microsystems and now offered in over 50 configurations by different vendors; and the RISC, which includes the 68000 series by Motorola used on Mac machines. New RISC designs, like the forthcoming alpha chip from DEC, will have a 64-bit data path and will be capable of running at a minimum of 100MHz.

Given the capabilities and the decreasing costs of new chips, it is advisable to design any new imaging applications on workstations powered by at least a 386 processor or by one of the competing architectures.

Random Access Memory

RAM stores programs and data for execution and supplies data to the processor. Different memory organization schemes, including page, interleaved, and cache, are used to reduce or eliminate idle processing time that may result from inability of the memory to accept or supply data to the processor in a timely fashion. Cache memory is the most efficient and most complex method of the three and may require a separate device, called a cache controller, to manage data traffic in and out of memory. Similar considerations concerning the use of cache memory enter into the design of 80X86, SPARC, and RISC chips.

Some processors, such as the 486 chip, offer a fast access internal cache, limited at this time to fewer than 10KB. Depending on the processor's addressing capabilities, much larger external caches may be added; in fact, as will be discussed later on, caching is an efficient method to increase not only CPU performance but also reduce waiting time between images during retrieval from digital storage.

Depending on the processor, different cache memory organizations can be embedded in the design of the motherboard to improve speed. For instance, with a 486 processor, the cache may be arranged either as direct map or set-associative. Both divide the memory into blocks, but the first assigns only one cache location per block, while the second assigns multiple locations. The result is simpler implementation for direct mapping, but at the cost of potential problems for multitasking operations. The set-associative method is better for multitasking, but more complex to fine-tune. In tests reported by *PC Magazine,*[1] a 64KB, 4-locations set-associative cache was found to be equivalent to a 256KB mapped implementation in a 486 environment.

Another factor that affects the performance of the cache, and consequently the overall response time of an imaging system, is the so-called "write policy" that governs the kinds of data that will be written to cache. The simplest, called "write-through," operates only on read data and ignores data to be written to memory. A more complex policy, called "posted" or "buffered write-through," reads and writes information only during CPU cycles that do not require access to memory. The most complex write policy, called "write-back" cache, tracks all transactions. The resulting improvement in performance is at the price of more expensive motherboards.

Because images are displayed in an uncompressed form, a significant amount of RAM is necessary to retain both the retrieved image and the supporting operating and application software. In addition, because fast paging and display of retrieved images are often desirable features in imaging systems, it is recommended that a good trade-off analysis be conducted to determine what's more important: high performance or the cost of sophisticated motherboards and associated devices.

Input/Output Bus

The I/O bus is the data link between the CPU and devices, be they memory or other components. Different bus designs exist to support different chips. All I/O buses are characterized by their width, or data path, corresponding to the number of data streams that can travel simultaneously through the bus. For PC devices, several different bus architectures are currently in competition: the 16-bit (i.e., 16 1-bit data streams) Industry Standard Architecture (ISA) bus, the 32-bit Extended Industry Standard Architecture (EISA), and the IBM proprietary Micro Channel Architecture (MCA) bus. Depending on the motherboard design, more than one bus may coexist, with a 32-bit I/O bus dedicated to CPU and memory traffic and a 16-bit I/O bus dedicated to communication with external devices, which, by nature, may not be able to accept 32-bit signals. Other bus designs and architectures exist for non-PC-compatible machines or are being proposed to increase input/output interactions.

The Associate Processors

Often, it is possible to have some of the lower-level processing necessary to the entire imaging functions done by associate processors. These are auxiliary devices or software algorithms that operate on the data flow initiated by the main unit. This makes it possible to reserve CPU resources for the management of the user-system interaction and enhance overall systems response. Among the tasks that can be delegated to associate processors are:

Compression/Decompression The representation of images requires large data streams. Image display and printing, as well as processing for enhancement or data extraction, must occur within the total bitstream. However, whenever imaging properties of the bitstream are not involved, it is advantageous to reduce the demand on computer resources through data compression of images.

Compression takes place at the scanning level, while decompression occurs at the display, printing, and data extraction devices. Data compression/decompression can be performed either in hardware or software, according to one of many algorithms, some standard, some not.

Most document imaging applications are based on the recommendations of the Comité Consultatif Internationale de Télégraphique et Téléphonique (CCITT), Group 3 for analog fax transmission and Group IV for all-digital communications. Newer standards are being adopted to integrate multimedia material, such as the Joint Photographic Engineering Group (JPEG) and Motion Picture Engineering Group (MPEG). In addition, specialized standards have been developed to handle high-quality images, such as medical X-rays.

Most imaging systems currently use CCITT Group 4 and/or CCITT Group 3, for integrated fax capabilities. Usually, CCITT Group 4 algorithms yield compression ratios of about 10-to-1 for standard office documents, corresponding to approximately a 50KB data stream. However, in the case of poor-quality documents, the "compressed" bitstream may actually be longer than the original signal.

Compression in hardware is usually faster than in software. As a result, imaging systems use a compression board directly on the scanning device to reduce traffic to the rest of the system. These boards also recognize poor-quality documents, in which case they transmit the original signal rather than an expanded bitstream. But, because there are several ways of implementing the CCITT recommendations, compression boards are proprietary, and images compressed with a compression board from one manufacturer may not be readable with a decompression board from another.

Also, most boards perform additional tasks. For instance, a decompression board will also provide data extraction, which, while financially attractive, is, without a software "patch," operationally unworkable for lack of compatibility. This fact narrows the flexibility of the system designer. This is the case when trying to integrate Group 4 (scanned) and Group 3 (faxed) documents in the same database. Often, an intermediary conversion step between the two compression schemes must take place before the two can be accessed in a seamless fashion.

On the decompression side, depending on the quality of the image, choices must be made between hardware and software solutions. Decompression in hardware is faster, but it also requires a decompression board at each workstation, which means users will lean toward buying one of the fast decompression software packages on the market. Such software are also often capable of reading different compression algorithms, thus eliminating the issue of proprietary compression. If throughput is not a concern, as is the case with inexpensive hand-held scanners, software may be used for both compression and decompression.

Accelerators and Coprocessors These are hardware devices specifically designed to perform the computation-intensive signal processing operations associated with image display and formatting, such as on-screen image scaling. The two are similar in nature, but accelerators are not programmable and optimized for a given task, and coprocessors are more versatile. Accelerators may be integrated with other boards to enhance existing applications or sold separately with a set of software tools and development libraries for integration with the rest of the system. Here again, issues of compatibility must be taken into consideration before choosing such devices.

Graphic applications can be served by specially designed accelerators. However, their selection requires a knowledge of the type of graphic data to be processed. For low-end documents applications, an 8-bit card may be sufficient; for high-end work, and artwork involving color photographs, a more expensive 24-bit graphic accelerator is necessary.

Disk Caching Controller These devices are cache memories specifically designed to accelerate the read/write cycle from hard disk by storing and often managing data on an intermediary bank of RAM chips. As such, disk caching controllers can also reduce the CPU management load, freeing it for other tasks, such as database searching.

Video Boards Video boards operate directly on workstation monitors and are critical to high-speed display in a windowed environment. The display of an 8.5" × 11" 8-bit color or gray scale document displayed at an SVGA resolution of 1,024 × 768 pixels requires a minimum of some 60MB of storage for "instant" replay. Without these boards and the additional memory they carry, the painting of the screen would be extremely slow. In addition, video boards running at their own screen refresh signals are essential for the elimination of screen flicker, a troublesome by-product, if not corrected, of large-screen displays. The effectiveness of a video board is dependent on its associated software (driver), and, in some cases, it is beneficial to use a separately purchased driver.

Device Interface The selection of an appropriate device interface can also reduce the load of the main CPU. For instance, Small Computer Systems Interface (SCSI), a multitasking link that is the most commonly used in the imaging industry, efficiently manages printers and external storage and, by performing input/output functions, reduces the CPU load. In addition, because one interface can manage several devices, it facilitates device sharing, provided the equipment manufacturers are using the same version of the interface.

Image Processing Boards These devices are associate processors that perform data extraction from the scanned image. Of course, these tasks can be performed in software, but having a dedicated board perform OCR, form extraction, and other similar data processing chores increases throughput by freeing CPU time. Note, though, that many of these image processing boards do not have an independent processor, requiring either a multitasking or batch operating environment.

Installing associate processors requires changing the configuration of the main CPU to reallocate some of its resources. Depending on the platform, the card, and its accompanying software, such reallocation, which involves changing memory, disk space, and input/output addresses, may or may not be automatic. In addition, the number of free and available slots on the computer chassis may create space limitations. Finally, any field installation should be done with the customary precautions, including backing up data, protecting against electrostatic charges, recording configuration, and securing legal copies of all software.

The selection of associate processors should be based on performance comparisons, conducted under conditions similar to the intended applications. That means if the imaging system is used to review vast amounts of documents, it is advisable to select a board that provides a high screen-paint speed, as opposed to one that provides high linear-drawing velocity: The two may not perform the same way.

The Rest of the Hardware

To a user on a network, the "rest of the hardware" includes all the devices that are linked to the system unit, directly or indirectly. They include peripherals that may be under the control of the system unit programs, have their own software, or operate under a combination of both. For instance, high-performance displays may combine a device called a video graphic adapter (VGA) on the motherboard with another circuit called a video accelerator directly attached to the monitor hardware. Consequently, imaging systems are an assembly of components, which have to be carefully selected not only for their impact on performance, but also for their compatibility with other devices in the system. To that end, while most imaging vendors provide an array of peripherals that are compatible with their systems, the user must be aware that so-called "shrink-wrapped" configurations, especially for lower-cost systems, may not be optimized for the application or may not work with other devices. For example, decompression boards for different monitors may not be interchangeable.

The rest of the hardware also includes devices that may be available to the user through the network, such as print and scan servers.

Monitors

Monitors are probably the most obvious and underestimated component of imaging systems, especially in a windowed environment. Monitors are usually under the control of the local workstation, although there are an increasing number of enterprise operations in which one workstation shares control of a remote monitor through network communication, allowing interactive graphical conferencing sessions. A monitor should, in fact, never be considered alone, but with two other components: a display adapter and a video driver software. Two factors should influence the selection of a monitor; one deals with image quality, the other with overall performance.

Image quality is essentially monitor-dependent. Monitors are graphic devices for image viewing; therefore, screen resolution needs to be as high as possible. Depending on the technology, the number of individual horizontally and vertically addressable picture elements (pixels) on most imaging systems screens range from 640×480 for VGA monitors, to $1,280 \times 1,024$ and higher for high-resolution screens. Document applications usually deal with monochrome images, and monochrome monitors have been traditionally sufficient for most applications; VGA is usually used in lower-end systems, and high-resolution monitors are used for quality display. However, in a windowed environment, monochrome monitors are not as effective as color devices and have comparatively higher resolution. The number of colors that can be incorporated in a color monitor is in part dictated by the video driver software and the amount of video memory available to store imaging information at time of display. The driver software, which translates the image bitstream into electronic signals to actuate the cathode ray tube (CRT) in the monitor, must be able to operate at the speed of the CPU. Video memory limits the number of colors and shades that can be displayed by a given monitor. For instance, a monochrome tube dedicated to imaging with approximately one million addressable pixels without gray shades (i.e., running at one-bit-per-pixel) needs only 100KB of video memory. A color tube running the standard 16-colors Windows palette may require 1MB of memory, which is stored in RAM.

The performance of an imaging system is determined, from a user point of view, by the time it takes to display an image on the screen. This depends on a variety of factors independent from the display subsystem. Access to and retrieval from storage, obsolete drivers, and display adapters are, along with image decompression, among the most influential factors in system response time. For instance, the difference between poorly and well-selected video components may result in a 10-to-1 decrease in the time needed to display an image. This is an important factor, because of the volume of data that must be "painted" on the monitor screen, moved to the monitor, and "refreshed" to eliminate screen flicker. Depending on the manufacturer, three methods are used to speed up the display process, using frame buffers, accelerator cards, and coprocessing. Frame buffers are standard with all monitors, while accelerators and coprocessors must be ordered separately. Accelerator cards are often used to boost lower-performance machines. For instance, an accelerator card on a 20Mhz PC can, under certain conditions, outrun a frame buffer configuration on a 33Mhz machine. Coprocessors are similar to accelerators, but have the advantage, at an added cost, of being programmable, which is not in general a requirement for a document imaging system, but may be needed for other applications running on the same machine.

An alternate method to increase performance is being tested in the imaging industry. It involves the use, on specially designed motherboards, of video bus designs and topologies to connect directly the display to the CPU, thus increasing the data path between the two devices.

Table 4.1   Scanner selection criteria

Selection Criteria	Unit	Comments
Resolution	dots per inch (dpi)	200–300 for document applications; 1,000 and over for fine arts
Page Size	inches or cm.	Depending on target application, from office document to engineering drawings
Dynamic Range	bits per pixel	1 for document applications; up to 24 for gray scale and color work
Speed	pages per min (ppm)	Low-volume machines: 2–8; Medium- to high-speed machines: 10–60
Number of Sides	side	Depending on construction, single or dual
Color/Mono		Depending on construction
Compression	compression	Most are CCITT G4; fax is CCITT G3
File Format	format	Most are TIFF-compatible
Interface	interface	Most are SCSI
Cost	$	Range from $500 to $50,000 and more

Scanners

Scanners can be attached either to a user workstation as a convenience device, shared on a network, or operated in a centralized fashion. In some low-volume installations, they also can double as fax machines.

Scanners come in a variety of shapes and offer varying degrees of performance, from hand-held low-volume instruments, suitable for insertion of small scanned images in a primarily text document, to desktop and self-standing machines for medium- to high-volume imaging applications. Depending on construction, they can have automatic feed, scan in black and white or color, on single- or dual-sided documents in a variety of sizes. A summary of scanner selection criteria is given in Table 4.1.

In a workgroup environment, scanners are attached to a given workstation (see Figure 4.6a), and images can be sent through the network to other workstations. In a shared configuration, they have their own processors and appear as a node on the network (see Figure 4.6b). In a centralized architecture, a scanner usually is part of an imaging service network (see Figure 4.6c).

In all three cases, provisions should be made for quality control of the captured image before storage. In the workgroup and shared conditions, quality control should probably be done at the same time as image capture, so that errors can be rectified immediately. In the case of central scanning, which involves the use of expensive equipment, quality control and error correction should be done in a batch mode to minimize downtime at the scanning station.

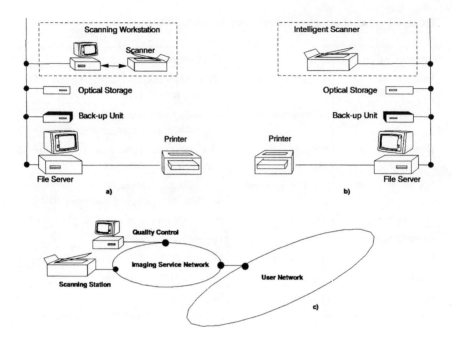

Figure 4.6   Various scanner configurations

Printers

Like scanners, printers can be attached to a workstation, shared as a node on a network, or stand as a centralized print server. However, because printing is a "simple" output operation, there is no need for a separate printing network.

Because of their slowness, impact printers are not usable in most imaging applications, even though it is possible to write device drivers for printing raster images on dot-matrix printers.

Currently on the market there are several types of printers that can be used for imaging, some of them designed specifically for color imaging applications. Table 4.2 summarizes some of the selection criteria for imaging printers. Of great importance is the amount of RAM that is available in the printer; too little RAM, and the images will need to be printed in segments, slowing down the process. For imaging applications, minimum memory should be 4MB of RAM; for high-speed and color printing installations, this number should be much higher.

Printer RAM does not take the place of whatever memory is needed by the processor. In particular, if the printer is part of a print server, the server itself will have its own memory and fast storage to intercept and buffer images being sent to printing.

Particular attention should be given to the use of what are called "calligraphic" printers, which have stored printer language instructions such as PostScript or TrueType to print text in a highly flexible manner. These printers bring no real benefit for imaging applications, and the system should be designed in such a way

Table 4.2 Summary of printer selection criteria

Selection Criteria	Unit	Comments
Type		Laser, Ink Jet, Thermal, Dye, Sublimation, Bubble
Resolution	dots per inch (dpi)	200–300 for document applications; 1,000 and over for fine arts
Memory	MB	Depending on application, up to 16MB
Page Size	inches or cm.	Depending on target application, from office document to engineering drawings
Dynamic Range	bits per pixel	1 for document applications; up to 24 for gray scale and color work
Speed	pages per min (ppm)	Low-volume machines: 2–8; Medium- to high-speed machines: 10–60
Number of Sides	side	Depending on construction, single or dual
Color/Mono		Depending on construction
Decompression	algorithm	Either on-board or through software. Most are CCITT G4; some accept G3.
File Format	format	Most are TIFF-compatible
Interface	interface	Most are SCSI
Cost	$	Range from $500 to $50,000 and more

that the calligraphic features are disabled during the printing of nontextual graphics. Failure to do so would slow the printing process to a virtual halt.

Storage

From the desktop perspective, storage of images and other data can be placed in a hierarchy that trades off speed for capacity and media price (see Figure 4.7). To simplify: At the top is the RAM, the most expensive per MB and the fastest. It holds images at time of display and performs other related operations. Under it is magnetic storage represented by hard disks in various configurations, from fixed to removable, with typical access time of 10 minutes. Further down, and somewhat overlapping, are the optical disks, also in various configurations. These include "floptical" which have the same form factor as 3.5" magnetic disks, but store about 15 times more information; and the single 5.25" optical, WORM or rewritable, which stores about 1GB (1,000 megabytes), with a raw access time of 50 minutes, some 50 percent of the capacity of the 2GB hard drive capacity that is becoming commonly available on PC workstations. Finally, there is the 1 terabyte (1,000 gigabytes) and over optical disk jukeboxes and optical tapes. At the base, at least

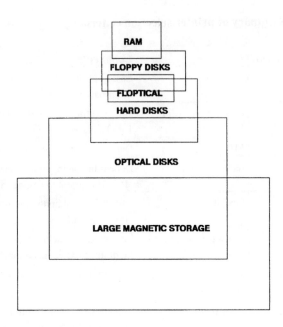

Figure 4.7   Hierarchy of storage

for now, are the various forms of magnetic tape arrangements with similar storage capacities, but at a slower access rate due to the sequential nature of tape readout.

Selection of the proper storage medium should be, from the user point of view, a nonissue, as long as access to the documents is provided in a timely fashion. For the system designer, combining intelligent caching schemes and shuffling data from slower to faster storage can hide sluggish access time. For instance, a well-engineered staging of multiple-page document images may provide the same performance as if the documents were all kept in RAM. Similar design decisions may allow the seamless integration of imaging with the rest of the network.

Software

In the design of an imaging network, imaging packages themselves may be not as important as their ability to work in harmony with the rest of the system, both hardware and software.

To reach this harmony, the system designer needs to be able to link various programs and ensure their compatibility with operating hardware requirements. To facilitate such integration, the system designer will want to use (clone) proven computer programs and routines. This will channel the selection of imaging network building blocks to the vendors that offer the largest and richest libraries of application software and tools.

From a user perspective, software can be organized in a hierarchy of purpose, from presentation, to application, database management, and data/document repository administration. However, performance of the imaging system will be judged on how successfully the database management and the data/document storage administration interact to provide the fastest information retrieval for the application and present the results to the user in the most efficient and "pleasing" manner.

In fact, depending on the level of integration of the imaging system with the rest of an organization's information system, there will be four interacting categories of software.

Imaging Dedicated Software

This category includes programs to drive the scanner, summarily index and store the image either on hard or optical disk, perform simple retrieval, and display and print retrieved images. These programs are loaded on the processors that drive the individual devices and are activated from the appropriate workstation.

Image Processing Software

This category corresponds to data (OCR) and forms extraction packages, which usually operate in a batch mode, and as such do not directly present performance problems for the "line" image applications. Computation-intensive operations require that they usually be loaded on a dedicated processor.

Application Dedicated Software

Software in this category deal with more advanced indexing and information retrieval, as well as package applications such as spreadsheets and word processing. Depending on the nature of the packages, they may be loaded on separate servers and downloaded to the workstation or loaded as stand-alone programs on the workstation itself. Either case has advantages and drawbacks as far as performance, compatibility, and contention for workstation resources.

Network Management and Workflow Software

This category of software deals with the management of the information transfer process and involves the full range of integration issues, from operating system to supporting platform. They usually are loaded on the file server, with portions loaded on individual workstations.

From a user perspective, access to the different software may or may not be needed. For instance, users in a large system may not need (or wish) to know how images are created, as long as they are available. At the same time, the staff may capture and index documents on a subnetwork dedicated to image services, without concern as to their utilization. This mutual ignorance may last until overload on the network begins to slow down response time.

It is the responsibility of the users, as well as of the designer, to ensure that the entire document flow is compatible with business requirements. After all, it takes only some 100 concurrent image transaction pages on a given network segment running conventional Ethernet to start creating problems: Without caching or other network optimization techniques, five ten-page documents "blindly" retrieved and printed are sufficient to result in an unacceptable level of performance on that network segment.

4.3   CONCLUSION

The user perspective often hides the technical complexity of meeting required operating conditions. Consequently, while functional specifications may often be adequately described by educated users, the choice of technical solutions must be left to technical experts. It is, of course, expected that sophisticated and even some nonsophisticated users may be tempted, through well-orchestrated marketing, to bypass the use of unbiased advisors and adopt one of the many "off-the-shelf" solutions. That approach may be effective for a small installation. It will not be a responsible strategy for larger systems, where the difficulties of choice are compounded with the problems of integrating the selected system with the rest of the information network.

NOTES

[1] *PC Magazine*, July 1992, p. 122.

5

Considerations for Network Imaging Hardware

Marc R. D'Alleyrand, Ph.D.

5.1 INTRODUCTION

This chapter is designed to give the user some practical advice for selecting imaging hardware. It is not intended to be a selection guide, but rather to provide elements of "sanity check." Because there is so much hardware and software on the market, today's selection is likely to be challenged tomorrow; underlying principles, however, may not.

5.2 SCANNERS

Scanners are the entry points for digitized documents, and, as such, their selection is critical to the success of an image-enabled network. Criteria depend not only on features, but also on utilization. For instance, fast scanners may be necessary for a centralized environment, but unjustified for desktop, distributed input. And, because scanners are attended by operating personnel, ergonomics and ease of use, such as a larger capacity of an automatic feeder, and controls, such as automatic contrast, also play an important part in a procurement decision.

Scanners should always be selected in conjunction with consideration for display and printing, as there will be a need for matching input and ouput quality. For instance, there is no demonstrated value to using a high-quality scanner if the printers are of lower quality. In addition, scanners designed for higher quality or

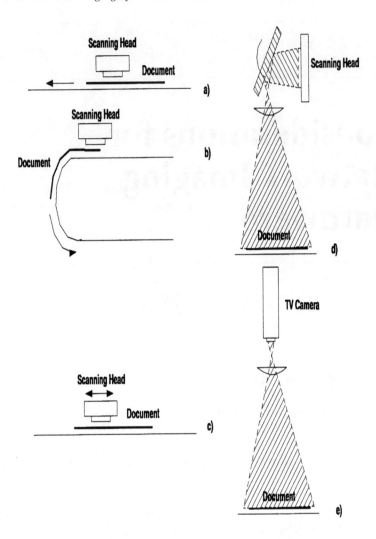

Figure 5.1   Different types of scanners

color will generate larger bitstreams, which require larger storage and, for equal performance, faster networks.

Regardless of the technical features, such as resolution, depth of digitization (or number of bits-per-pixel) scanning speed, there are structural differences between scanners that are essential to an efficient operation.

Transport Mechanism—Paper Scanners

There are essentially three types of transports. In the first, the documents move past the scanning array; in the second, the scanning array moves past the document being scanned; and in the third, both are stationary (see Figure 5.1).

Moving the Document

These provide the fastest type of scanners, and at the same time a theoretically better image, because the scanning array, being stationary, is less subject to vibrations and thus is less likely to generate scanning artifacts. Several types of scanners are on the market, with either straight (Figure 5.1a) or folded document paths (Figure 5.1b). Some scanners have two scanning heads for dual-sided scanning. Both require resubmitting misfed pages to the scanner, with the folded path providing somewhat easier handling, because the document input and output are in close proximity. However, folded path machines are more susceptible to jams and accept a more limited range of document size and paper weight than straight path equipment.

Moving the Scanning Head

Scanners of this type (Figure 5.1c) are typically slower than the previous class of scanners, but are also cheaper. Most of them use the same mechanical arrangements as copiers. In fact, many of these devices can be used, and are used, as digital copiers. Because the document is stationary, rescanning for contrast adjustment, for instance, does not require document refeeding. This type of scanners includes hand-held devices, which may, in a pinch, be made compatible with their full-size cousins, but they are slow, and are not recommended for full-scale imaging applciations. In particular, they do not allow the scanning of a full 8.5" width in a single pass. However, many of these devices provide, through software, a "stitching" mechanism that makes it possible to reconstruct a complete document. This, and other utilities such as OCR, makes it possible to use hand-held scanners in occasional situations where response time is not an overriding factor and where a dedicated scanner may not be justified.

Stationary Scanners

These scanners are characterized by a scanning head that sits well above the document plane, in a configuration similar to a photographic enlarger. Because of the distance between the scanning head and the document plane, they can be used to image three-dimensional objects. There are basically two types of such scanners: In one, a rotating mirror causes the image of the document to pass in front of the scannning head (Figure 5.1d); in the other, the scanning head is actually a television camera (Figure 5.1e). In their present configuration, these scanners are inherently slow, as they are designed only for manual feed. In addition, with the current document plane, image sharpness is not as good as with the other types of scanners. These limitations may be eliminated with different designs.

When attempting to integrate stationary scanners with an imaging network, it is essential to verify compatibility of data stream with the compression and file formats used for the rest of the system.

Scanners—Microforms

Microform scanners are incorporated in imaging networks to digitize documents stored on microforms without having to go through an intermediary paper print. They are similar in principle to paper scanners, but are specifically designed to accommodate the optical qualities of microforms. In addition, mechanical considerations require that the scanning head be fixed to minimize the effects of vibrations on the overall resolution.

Usually, commercial scanners are dedicated to one type of microform, roll (16- and 35mm) or card (microfiche or aperture cards). Because film scanning is rarely an ad hoc operation, involving quality control and often intensive batch indexing, film scanners are generally installed on dedicated networks so that they can run in background without impacting the rest of the installation.

Characteristics of Scanners

Regardless of the technical construction of the scanner, its selection will be based essentially on format (paper, photographs, microforms), speed, size of document, and capability to handle double-sided scanning. All commercial document scanners now on the market probably are CCITT. Additional requirements will include resolution (with 300 dpi a minimum industry standard for most document imaging applications), color, and continuous-tone capabilities.

Scanner Adjuncts

Image Enhancement

Many documents, such as carbon copies and shipping documents, are of poor quality and cannot be directly accommodated by a uniform threshold setting and one-bit-per-pixel encoding, as provided by many scanners. There is at least one device on the market, manufactured by Image Processing Technologies, that can be added to most scanners to adjust threshold dynamically so that the digitization is optimized throughout the whole document area.

OCR

OCR devices, which allow for the extraction of text from raster images, are now becoming desirable, if not necessary, to full-featured imaging systems. While optical character recognition can be done either in hardware or software, the conversion time is longer than image capture. Consequently, OCR operations often require a separate processor, often actually an OCR server; or, to save on hardware costs, be performed in background on a specially equipped scanning workstation during periods when the scanner is inactive.

Forms Extraction

Forms extraction is another image processing methodology in which lines of printed forms are electronically removed from the image, which reduces the storage requirements for the remaining bitstream and increases recognition of the text on the form. There are different algorithms on the market, characterized by the way they handle overlaps between text and form boundaries. There is one company at least, Visionshape, that has incorporated forms extraction with a high-speed scanner.

Fax Machines as Scanning Devices

The importance of fax communication, and the fact that fax machines are actually scanner-printer combinations, makes their use for standard document capture very intriguing. Several considerations must be looked into, however, before attempting to build an imaging network based exclusively on fax service.

First, commerical fax scanners are slow machines, as they are designed to run on regular telephone lines. In addition, the CCITT Group 3 compression algorithm used for commercial fax is not compatible with the CCITT Group 4 algorithm, which is the standard for digital document systems. And while there are conversion methods from one to the other, the difference in error correction schemes, which are at the heart of the difference between the two, and the limited resolution of the fax format, places significant constraints on the quality of the stored images. Nevertheless, fax machines are inexpensive!

5.3   PRINTERS

Printers and Print Servers

Under the proper configuration, all users on a network can have access to all printers attached to a given workstation or to a server. However, printing imaged documents through a workstation, as is done in a peer-to-peer architecture, will slow down any job that happens to be running on that workstation at that time.

The print server alleviates that problem. The print server, which can control several printers, writes incoming jobs in a "print spool" directory on a dedicated large-capacity hard disk. When the job is completed, the server selects a printer that matches the job requirements (e.g., paper size, compatibility with data format) and queues the job for printing as soon as the printer is available. To reduce the network traffic, the print server, the storage hard disk, and the printer or printers, apear as being the same node.

A recent breed of printers, specifically designed for network operation, include all the processing necessary to handle the job. These printers are designed for higher volumes than most desktop printers. While some of them may be configured for only one type of network, they are significantly faster, have large memory on board, and incorporate printing enhancements. Consequently, they should be chosen with the proper interface.

There are also specialized devices on the market that can be used as servers without the need for a dedicated workstation. These devices, which are about the size of a videotape cassette without keyboard or monitor, are preprogrammed to run on specific network operating systems, and, using that system print-server software, manage the print-queue function. However, because these devices do not have a hard disk, they also do not have the internal capacity to handle imaging applications.

Different Types of Imaging Printers

The vast majority of imaging printers use a laser engine. This section briefly describes other types of competing print engines. The selection criteria used to determine the best adapted solution include print speed requirements, acceptable resolution and quality, printing medium (e.g., paper or transparency), color, and cost. While color is still not a big requirement in most office document applications, it is only a matter of time before it becomes so, especially if the imaging is integrated in an industry such as advertising, where color is important to the business, or in applications such as production of high-quality reports, where color is already used to enhance the appearance of a document.

One of the selection criteria for imaging printers is their ability to handle PostScript internally, so that they can be used for "text" as well as image printing. The issue of "mixed" format printing is discussed in more detail later in this chapter.

Inkjet Printers

These devices are the least expensive for imaging applications and, because their output quality is acceptable, they are used in lieu of a true color laser process, which, at the present time, exists only on stand-alone digital copiers.

Inkjet printers work by forcing a spray out of one or several print heads, through either piezzo electric vibrations or heat. Different types of print heads exist on the market; single-head devices are used for black-and-white printers, and multiple heads are used for color printing. Resolution is at least 300 dpi for black-and-white material, and they are comparatively slow, with typical output speeds of three pages per minute in black and white; color takes up to several minutes per page. Most printers can use a variety of output media and format. Drawbacks of the process are that images may smear, and the ink may dry in the print cartridge.

A process similar to inkjet, called phase change, uses melted wax that, once sprayed and cooled, is pressed into the printed medium. This process is slower than inkjet, and the print easily cracks if folded.

LaserJet Printers

These are the most common, high-quality printers on the market, and most of them offer a minimum of 300 dpi resolution for black-and-white printing. Because of the way laser printers work, and depending on the print driver, that resolution may drop significantly when printing continuous-tone materials. Speed is typically eight pages per minute for desktop machines, and up to thirty double-sided pages per minute and more for high-volume machines. To increase productivity, some of the higher-end printers have their own processor and storage on board. Like the inkjet, laser printers can print on a variety of media.

Thermal Printers

Thermal printers are relatively low-cost color printers. Early printers used three different colors of wax, transferred from a roll of acetate to the printing medium in three successive passes. The resulting potential registration problem between colors is being eliminated by the use of solid wax sticks that, once melted, are sprayed in one pass. The major drawback of such devices is that the resulting image is highly sensitive to folding and bending of the paper substrate. Resolution is in the 300 dpi range, and they can print at the speed of about one minute per page.

Dye Sublimation Printers

The dye sublimation process is similar to wax transfer in that it uses a color transfer medium, but, instead of full sheets, the process uses interspersed color blocks of a compound, which, when heated, release a gaseous dye that is absorbed by a specially coated paper. This type of printer is the most expensive, providing the highest quality of continuous-tone output using 4" × 5" material. Their resolution is typically 300 dpi, and their speed is in the range of five minutes per image.

Color Laser Printers

At the present time there are no networkable true color laser printers. However, through "sneakernet" it is possible to use a digital color copier. The price of the unit—over $50,000—puts it outside the cost justification range of most business applications.

Printers and Plotters

When dealing with images that contain geometric graphics, such as engineering drawings or line illustrations, it is sometimes preferable to output the document in a vector format through a plotter, rather than as a raster image.

Plotters are drawing output devices, and as such are faster than raster for line work, but slower in situations requiring detailed dot-to-dot type of drawing construction, such as textual materials where each character has to be scribed separately. There are hardware and software devices on the market that are designed to perform raster-to-vector conversion into a format, such as IGES or CGM, appropriate for plotter handling. However, unless there is a significant business interest in this type of graphics, like in engineering and architecture industry, raster printers are likely to be preferred.

Network Printing Issues

A major concern is matching the printer to the network interface. When using a printer on the network, as opposed to attached to a workstation, it is essential that the network "knows" the status of that device, not only in terms of jobs being queued, but also in terms of actual operation. Without the capability to identify device failures remotely, a jam or out-of-paper condition will result in delays to correct that malfunction.

Some of the newer and more expensive printers provide facilities to interrogate the print engine and therefore give the network management system the ability to detect print failures. However, there is no standard protocol at the present time to ensure transportability of diagnostics across a heterogeneous network. In particular, the many platform-dependent printer languages will, without additional software overhead, limit the network ability to send any print job to any printer.

There are efforts under way to establish an industry network printer protocol. Such a protocol will allow bidirectional communication between printers, PCs, and networks. The protocol would also provide for automatic adjustment of operating parameters (such as identification of which printer is available with the proper paper size), provide remote job control (such as start and stop job and number of pages printed), and control printed document processing (such as duplexing and collating).

Raster, PostScript, TrueType, and Other Printing

When dealing with textual material in machine-readable form, it is often more expedient to separate content from form. PostScript and TrueType are two different font description languages, which, once downloaded to a suitable printer, allow for the automatic configuration of the printed document, including on-the-fly font and character height changes.

In addition, most textual documents have embedded formatting instructions, some proprietary such as the ones used in word processing, some others standardized such as the standard generalized markup language (SGML), which can be used to create composite documents that mix text and graphics.

As far as the printer is concerned, it does not matter what signal it receives, as long as it can interpret it. It will print the document—eventually! From a network system perspective, it is a different story. A poorly configured printer or a poorly formatted document may seriously degrade network performance. As a matter of fact, if poorly implemented, printing services may be the weakest element of an imaging network.

5.4   DOCUMENT STORAGE

To meet different operational requirements, documents are stored in different areas and on different media on a network, with each storage presenting its own characteristics.

Hard Disks

Whether at the scanning or the user workstation or on the server, hard disks are used to store images in a read-write mode. Hard disks, either single or in arrays, should be selected in concert with the processor architecture, controller cards, driver software, and data path, all of which should be optimized for the operating system and network operating system, and the number of other devices already installed.

Optical Disks

Because of their high intrinsic storage capacity, optical disks are at the heart of imaging systems. Their inherently slower response makes them better adapted for document storage than for file servers. However, with the advent of read-write optical disks, and progress in drive design, competition between the two media, at least for desktop storage, is increasing.

There are few differences in principle between single drive and automatic changers (jukeboxes), but driver incompatibilities may prevent upgrading from single- to multiple-platter installation. Also, because there is no real standard in place for optical disk beyond CD ROMs, disks recorded on one drive may not be readable on another.

Optical disk systems come in many flavors, including CD ROMs, write-once read-many (WORM), and rewritable, each with its own sets of drivers and installation requirements. In operation, single platters are usually attached to one workstation or sometimes the file server, if traffic is not too heavy. It is recommended that jukeboxes be installed on a dedicated processor connected to the network, which is often dubbed image or document server.

Tape Storage

Tape storage is used essentially to back up. There are several formats that are acceptable for imaging applications, from high-density DAT tape to optical tape. Capacity ranges from over 2GB for a DAT tape to 1 terabyte for optical tape. While there is a need for such a capacity in imaging systems, there is only one vendor at this time for optical tape. Consequently, most installations requiring high backup capacity should use automated tape jukeboxes.

5.5   CONCLUSION

Imaging hardware is essentially a dynamic commodity, and, as such, any technical solution will "technically" be obsolete by the time it has been implemented; new devices will have been introduced, new ways of solving similar problems will have been shown effective. However, what is important to remember is that the purpose of the system is to solve a business solution, not to set a technical record.

Consequently, once a solution has been found to work, it should be implemented, without remorse or hesitation. But, to protect one's options, including those necessary to adapt to "unforeseen conditions," it will be advisable to carefully design the architecture of the network and of the imaging system so that technological changes can be made, if required, without having to "reengineer" the entire system.

6

Display Selection for Document Imaging in Windowed Environments

Thomas T. van Overbeek

Cornerstone Technology

Editor's Notes

While the majority of office documents are still black and white and are scanned that way, most monitors used in windowed environments are color. This chapter discusses the various trade-offs between the higher resolution of monochrome monitors and the more attractive color screens. Because of the differences in performance, it may be useful to select high-resolution black-and-white monitors for dedicated imaging applications, such as scanning and quality control, and adopt high-resolution color monitors for document retrieval, even if the main beneficiaries will be nonimaging applications.

It will be important to note that the number of manufacturers of high-quality cathode ray tubes, the heart of imaging displays, is very small, probably less than ten worldwide. Consequently, most commercial displays can be associated with tube families, to which individual constructors have added some proprietary circuitry. In addition, the same display may be found in different products under different names. When comparing displays, it will be advisable to identify the source of the various display components.

6.1   OVERVIEW: DISPLAY REQUIREMENTS IN WINDOWED ENVIRONMENTS

Document imaging systems are usually purchased to improve productivity, but they also make unique demands on workstation hardware and software in two areas that are major determinants of productivity and user acceptance: display readability and display speed. This chapter discusses what makes a good display for document imaging, how to make the right choice for your application, and how windows impact the choice of display.[*]

A typical office document has 25 times as many dots (pixels) that create the image on the page as does a normal PC (VGA) display, so it's not surprising that normal PC displays are very difficult to read when used for document imaging. Document imaging users normally read from the screen for longer periods than users of other applications, which exacerbates eye fatigue problems caused by poor display quality. For these reasons, VGA-type PC displays are inadequate for all but occasional document imaging use. Large-screen, high-resolution, high-performance color and grayscale display subsystems designed for the specific needs of document imaging alleviate these problems and are used in the vast majority of document imaging systems.

Windowed user interfaces, while simplifying the user interface, require acceleration hardware in the display controller to prevent degradation of image display speed. Consequently, the other impact of windows in document imaging is increased user preference for color displays. Special care must be taken to select appropriate color monitors for document imaging due to the generally lower display quality of color displays compared to large-screen grayscale displays.

In addition to windows acceleration, the other major variable that determines display speed is the speed with which image data can be decompressed and displayed. Image retrieval performance depends on the hardware and/or software decompression mechanism and the speed of the system CPU. Various display, decompression, and windows acceleration solutions also are discussed in this chapter.

6.2   IMAGE READABILITY

CRT display quality is the critical factor that determines document image readability and, therefore, the productivity and user acceptance of the document imaging system.

---

[*]   In this chapter "windows" with a lowercase w refers to both Microsoft Windows and IBM's OS/2 Presentation Manager; "Windows" with a capital W refers exclusively to Microsoft Windows.

Research on Readability and Eye Fatigue

Research and empirical evidence indicate that reading from standard PC CRTs (VGA) is approximately one-third slower than reading from a high-resolution grayscale display or paper; additionally, CRT workers report eyestrain, fatigue, and muscular strain. A recent study by the Steelcase Corporation of U.S. office workers found that eyestrain was the most frequently reported health related complaint. Both eyestrain and reading speed have an obvious adverse impact on productivity and are particularly important problems for users of DIP systems.

The IBM/Gould Study

The CRTs in wide use today on PCs (VGA, EGA, and MDA) are very similar in that they all display 24 lines of text, have screen refresh rates of about 60 times per second (hertz), and display a total of about 300,000 pixels. A number of studies have found that reading from this type of CRT is significantly slower than reading from paper.

In their 1987 article, "Reading Is Slower from CRT Displays Than from Paper: Attempts to Isolate a Single Variable Solution," authors Gould, Alfaro, Barnes, et al., of the IBM Research Center, conducted an experiment in which twenty-four people were asked to proofread from excerpts of magazine and newspaper articles displayed on an IBM 3277 CRT and perform the identical task from paper hard copy. The researchers took pains to remove as many variables as possible between the text presented on paper and the CRT screen. The text for both paper and screen was formatted identically with 23 lines vertically and 62–65 characters per line.

The participants read at an average speed of 205 words per minute from paper as compared with 159 words per minute from the CRT screen, or 29 percent faster reading from paper (see Figure 6.1a). An experiment conducted by Professors Muter and Kruk of the University of Toronto yielded similar results.

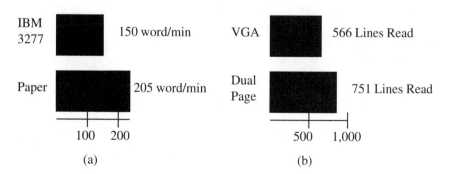

Figure 6.1   Reading speed bar graph

The Sheedy Study

In 1991, Dr. James Sheedy, a member of the School of Optometry at the University of California at Berkeley, conducted an experiment in which subjects were asked to read from both an IBM VGA display and a large-screen (19") grayscale display subsystem designed for document imaging. The VGA display had an addressable resolution of 640×480 (307,000 pixels), and the large screen $1,600 \times 1,280$ (2,050,000 pixels). The large-screen display used a controller that provided 4 bits of gray (sixteen shades of gray). Subjects were asked to read from the *Adventures of Sherlock Holmes* for 30-minute periods, after which the amount of material read was recorded and any symptoms logged.

Dr. Sheedy's study found that when reading from the large-screen display, subjects read 33 percent faster than from the VGA display (see Figure 6.1b). Furthermore, complaints of eyestrain and muscle fatigue were two-thirds lower when subjects read from the large-screen display. Research has found that users of small-screen 60Hz CRTs suffer from many more symptoms of visual stress than workers who do not use CRTs. Another study by Dr. Sheedy found that 70 percent of CRT users reported one or more of the symptoms listed below:

Headaches

Near blurred vision

Slowness in focusing (distant to near and back)

Double vision

Eyestrain (sore eyes or eye fatigue)

Glare (light) sensitivity

Eye irritation (burning, dryness, redness)

Neck and shoulder pain

Back pain

Research and common sense clearly indicate that CRT display quality is a major determinant of user fatigue, eyestrain, reading speeds, and, therefore, productivity and user acceptance of the system. The selection of displays of appropriate quality for the imaging application should be carefully considered when implementing a document image processing system.

Display Factors Affecting Readability and Eye Fatigue

To achieve the productivity potential of document imaging systems, system users should work on displays that are as close as possible to the display quality of office documents. "Paper-like" display subsystems and high-resolution color display subsystems designed to optimize document image processing display performance are available at a reasonable cost thanks to advances in CRT and semiconductor design. These subsystems are characterized by large, bright, clear, black-and-white or color screens with more stable screen images than typical CRTs. The typical small-screen CRT, when compared to a typical office document, has one-twentieth the resolution, one-eighth the brightness, has lower contrast, is one-third the size, and flickers. Obviously, there's room for improvement.

There are five major display subsystem design factors that influence CRT display quality: resolution, scale to gray, refresh rate, brightness, and screen size. This section explains how typical office documents, standard small-screen CRT, and paper-like display subsystems compare in these five areas.

Resolution

The Webster's *Ninth New Collegiate Dictionary* defines resolution as "the process or capability of making distinguishable the individual parts of an object, closely adjacent optical images, or sources of light." There are a number of variables that contribute to this broad definition of resolution as it relates to computer displays. The most important are: the number of addressable pixels (this is what is commonly referred to when the term "resolution" is used), dot size (dot pitch), and contrast.

CRT and document images are composed of dots called pixels (short for picture element), arranged to display letters or pictures. Addressable pixels are the dots the computer can control (address) to create an image on the CRT screen. In general, more addressable pixels in a given area yield better image quality. The difference between the number of pixels in a typical office document (about 8.4 million pixels at 300 dpi) and a typical small-screen CRT (about 300,000 pixels) explains much of the difference in image quality between paper and CRT screens.

The number of addressable pixels is usually expressed in two ways: dpi (dots per inch) and as a set of numbers (for instance 640×480) that describe the number of pixels in the horizontal axis first and the vertical axis second. For example, a CRT with 640×480 resolution has 640 pixels per line and 480 lines of pixels. The 640×480 display in this example has about 60 addressable pixels per inch (dpi). For document image processing, in which scanned images with a variety of font styles and sizes must be read from the CRT, higher pixel densities in the 120 dpi range have become standard. This translates into a resolution of 1,600 by 1,200 on a 19" (diagonal), two-page CRT.

Table 6.1 compares the number of pixels horizontally and vertically; the corresponding pixel density or dots per inch (dpi) for the commonly used 14" VGA monitor; a SuperVGA 17"; a large-screen paper-like display subsystem; and laser printed paper documents.

The paper-like display example has two to three times the pixel density of VGA, the most popular small-screen 60Hz type monitor, and displays 6.5 to 10 times as many pixels, making it much closer in resolution to paper than typical CRTs.

Spot Size and Dot Pitch (Pixel Size) These quantities are important determinants of resolution. Pixel size is called "dot size" on grayscale monitors and "dot pitch" on color monitors. A large number of addressable pixels doesn't necessarily result in better image quality, for example, when the dots are so large that they

Table 6.1　Range of display resolution

	H. Pixels × V. Pixels	*dpi*	*Total Pixels*
Typical 14" VGA color display	640 × 480	57	307, 200
SuperVGA 17" (XGA)	1,024 × 768	96	786,432
large-screen grayscale two-page display	1,600 × 1,200	120	2,480,000
Typical office laser printed document (8.5" × 11")	Printed document	300	8,415,000

overlap one another. In general, CRTs with smaller dot size and pitch have a sharper, more focused display.

In color monitors, each pixel is comprised of a triad of red, green, and blue dots. These primary colors are mixed to achieve the desired pixel color. The dot pitch of a color monitor is determined by the size of the holes in the metal plate, called a "shadow mask, just behind the screen." A dot pitch of .28mm or smaller is recommended for color displays used for document imaging.

Contrast　Contrast is a measure of a ratio between dark and clear areas on the display screen; higher contrast is usually better. The major culprit responsible for reducing contrast on CRTs is ambient light reflected from the surface of the CRT. One simple (and free) way to improve CRT contrast is to reduce the amount of ambient light in the office by turning down lights or removing fluorescent tubes from fixtures. This has the same effect as dimming the lights in a movie theater.

The use of nonglare or antireflective panels is a very important factor in improving contrast. There are a number of products that are commonly used on lower-resolution monitors to reduce glare, including fabric mesh panels and mechanical and chemical etching. However, these products are not suitable for high-resolution displays used for document imaging because they also degrade focus. It is strongly recommended that glass antireflective panels, also referred to as OCLI panels, be used for document imaging systems. OCLI significantly enhances contrast without degrading focus.

Display Enhancing Techniques: Scale to Gray

Scale to gray is really part of the resolution discussion, but it's an important enough advancement in display technology that it deserves separate mention. Scale to gray is a technique that enhances the display of scanned document images; it can double their resolution.

The effect of scale to gray appears in two primary ways: first, medium-sized characters become much clearer and focused; second, very small characters, which are unreadable without scale to gray, become readable.

Whenever documents are scanned at one resolution and displayed at another, a process called scaling must take place to accommodate the resolution of the

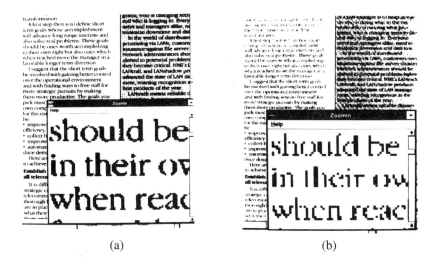

(a)   (b)

Figure 6.2   Document with and without scale to gray

document image to the resolution of the display. For instance, if a document is scanned at 300 dpi and displayed at 100 dpi, each block of 9 pixels in the document must be scaled down to 1 on the display.

Scale to gray works so well because unlike other scaling techniques, all the pixel information in a scanned document (300 dpi in our example) is used when it is displayed at a lower resolution. It works by using gray pixels of varying intensities to fill in the jagged edges of characters in scanned document images (see Figure 6.2). The gray levels correspond to the proportion of black-and-white pixels in the block on the edge of the character being scaled. For instance, in a 9-pixel block, if 4 were black and 5 white and scaled to 1, a gray intensity of 4/9th black would be displayed. Scale to gray's biggest impact is on characters in the 8 to 10 point size range, exactly the size characters found in most business documents.

Software-based scale to gray has been around for some time but seldom used because it is a computationally intensive scaling technique that usually results in very slow image retrieval speeds when implemented in software. Cornerstone Technology, a manufacturer of display subsystems for document imaging, has developed the first chip with scale to gray in hardware called ImageAccel. ImageAccel provides the display improvements of scale to gray without the usual performance degradation.

Manufacturers of displays for DIP make similar claims about the superiority of their products, and many of these products have similar specifications. In actual practice, however, there are vastly different levels of display clarity and image retrieval performance. Scale to gray is an example of a technology that must be seen to be appreciated. A good rule when selecting DIP displays for your system is to have end users extensively evaluate display alternatives.

Screen Refresh Rate (Vertical Rate)

Refresh rate refers to the number of times per second the image on the CRT screen is rewritten or refreshed and is expressed in hertz (Hz), which means events per second. Refresh rate influences three critical aspects of CRT image quality: flicker, resolution, and brightness. Like resolution, a variable to which it is very closely tied, the higher the refresh rate, the better.

An image on a CRT is generated by an electron beam scanning the inside of the CRT tube. The beam is turned on to create dots (pixels) which form the images on the screen. Perhaps the most significant difference between images on paper and images displayed on CRTs is that images on CRTs must be constantly refreshed because the phosphor immediately begins to fade after it is excited by the electron beam. This can result in screen flicker if the screen is not refreshed quickly enough.

The major ergonomic problem posed by low refresh rates is flicker. It is one of the major contributors to user eyestrain and fatigue, particularly for users of document imaging systems who spend a large portion of the day reading scanned document images from CRTs. Fast refresh rates reduce flicker.

The refresh rate at which flicker is detectable is called the critical flicker frequency (CFF). The CFF is dependent upon a number of variables including screen brightness and size. Fundamentally, the more light emitted by the display, the higher the threshold of detectable flicker will be. In general, screen refresh rates of 60Hz to 65Hz or below will result in noticeable flicker. Research indicates that, subconsciously, the eye detects flicker at refresh rates as high as 100Hz, which is much higher than the CFF. Since flicker results from the screen being repeatedly turned on and off, the eye is constantly trying to adjust to changes in brightness. This is a major cause of fatigue by users of small-screen 50–60Hz CRTs. Increasing refresh rates beyond the CFF is an important factor in reducing CRT worker fatigue; high-quality paper-like CRTs now have screen refresh rates above 70Hz (see Table 6.2).

There is some confusion on the subject of refresh rates caused by claims of display manufacturers that quote maximum refresh rates and resolution for their products without revealing that you can't get both at the same time! Make sure to ask for the refresh rate at your desired resolution.

Table 6.2   Refresh rate of commonly used CRTs vs. paper

Format	Screen Refresh Ratio
IBM Green CRT	50Hz
VGA	60Hz
Large Screen	76Hz
Paper	N.A. (100Hz)*

*100Hz is the frequency at which researchers believe that the human eye can no longer detect flicker.

Brightness

Everyone has had the experience of struggling to read in poor light, and a bright, crisp screen is essential if it is to be easily read. Typically, the ambient lighting in offices is much brighter than the CRT, so bright CRTs are important because there are a number of benefits to having the brightness of the CRT and the office environment similar.

Bright CRTs improve display contrast that improves readability by reducing the difference in brightness between the screen and ambient light. A large difference in brightness between the CRT and ambient light in the office causes user fatigue because every time the eye moves away from the CRT—to look at reference material, for instance—the eye must adjust to the new light level. One simple way to alleviate this problem is to reduce the brightness of the office; another is to use a bright paper-like display.

Color displays are usually less bright than grayscale displays, because color monitors require a "shadow mask," which is a metal plate between the screen and the electron gun that manages the red, green, and blue signals. Trinitron monitors use stretched metal wires called an arpeture grill to perform the same function. This metal plate reduces the amount of light color monitors can emit. Special consideration must be given to ambient light levels and monitor placement if color displays are selected for an imaging system.

Screen Size

Perhaps the most obvious difference between information displayed on paper and small-screen 24-line CRTs is the size of the display area (see Table 6.3). United States documents typically display 55 or so lines of text; popular small-screen CRTs display only 24 lines, or less than half a page. Viewing only half a page is a problem because it forces the user to "scroll" text on the screen to see the 50 percent not displayed, which wastes time and is very cumbersome if document images are viewed for any extended period.

Large-screen CRTs usually come in 17", 19", and 21" sizes. The 19" or 21" sizes are required to display one or two full pages of 8.5" × 11" documents. Displays of this size are commonly referred to as "dual-page" displays. Large-screen CRTs are an obvious advantage for users who have to read images of page-size documents from CRT screens.

Table 6.3   Display size

Medium	*Percent of Page Visible*
8.5" × 11" Paper	100%
13" VGA CRT	36%
Large-screen Display	200%

When imaging is not the full-time task of the user or the documents are smaller than a page, 17" color monitors have become popular for document imaging. The 17" form factor is a compromise between screen size and screen performance necessitated by the existing limit of 78KHz as the horizontal rate of commonly available color monitors. The 78KHz does not provide enough bandwidth to have 120 dpi and 70+Hz screen refresh rates on a 19" monitor at the same time. However, by reducing the size to 17", 120 dpi and 70Hz refresh can be achieved within the limitations of the 78KHz horizontal rate. The 78KHz bandwidth limitation should be lifted in the near future by display manufacturers, but currently, 120 dpi, 19" form factor, and 70+Hz screen refresh rates cannot be achieved at the same time with 78KHz color monitors.

VGA Problems

The most popular display used on PCs today is VGA (video graphics adapter). VGA is a display standard introduced by IBM in 1987. Although adequate for normal PC applications such as word processing and spreadsheets, the poor image quality of VGA is not acceptable at image retrieval stations where documents must be read and processed. Not only are documents difficult or impossible to read, users often report complaints of fatigue, eyestrain, and assorted muscular disorders. Productivity is also affected by having to zoom and scroll documents frequently.

6.3   DISPLAY PERFORMANCE

After display quality, the speed with which the workstation can retrieve and display document images is the most important determinant of productivity. This is sometimes referred to as the "flip rate." One second or less to display a new page has become a benchmark of user acceptability. The two major variables determining display speed are: how quickly the document image is scaled and decompressed, and the performance of the display controller under windows.

Document Image Scaling and Decompression Alternatives

Document images are compressed after they are scanned to reduce storage space requirements and improve network performance. Before being displayed, they must be decompressed and scaled. The compression technique universally used (CCITT, Group 3 and 4) basically works by removing the white space in documents. An 8.5" × 11" document scanned in at 300 dpi would require 1MB of storage uncompressed; compressed this document would require 25KB to 30KB. CCITT Group 3 and 4 is also the standard for fax documents. Compression takes place at the scan station and decompression at the retrieval workstation.

Scaling

Scaling is the process by which a document image scanned at one resolution (usually 200–400 dpi) is displayed on a monitor at lower (usually 100–150 dpi) resolution. Typical scanning resolutions range from 200–400 dpi. Display resolutions range from 70 dpi on a standard VGA monitor, to 150 dpi on a high-resolution monochrome large-screen monitor; therefore, the number of pixels displayed on the monitor must be reduced from the scanned image.

Scaling technique has a major impact both on display speed and image quality. In the latter case, it determines the smoothness of the edges of characters displayed in document images. Display speed, on the other hand, is affected by the complexity of the scaling technique. There are two popular scaling techniques: decimation and scale to gray (see Figure 6.3).

Decimation scaling is the most simple form of scaling. Using this technique, pixels from the scanned image are selected at a fixed interval. For example, scaling by a factor of 3 (300 dpi scanned to 100 dpi displayed) results in every third pixel on every third line being "picked" and copied to the display. The remaining pixels are discarded. Because 8 out of the original 9 pixels are discarded, decimation scaling results in jagged character display, but good performance.

Formerly, decimation was the standard scaling technique, but it has been superseded by scale to gray because of the display quality improvements it affords. Scale to gray produces dramatic improvements because it is the only scaling technique that preserves all of the original scanned document image. In a scaled-to-gray image, pixels on the edges of characters are a shade of gray rather than black or white. Pixel blocks are analyzed to determine the proportion of black-and-white pixels. Gray pixels that most accurately represent the proportion of black-to-white pixels in the original pixel block are then displayed. These grays are used to "fill in" the jagged edges of fonts. The human eye is a very effective integrator; it "wants" to see straight lines in "*L*s" and curves in "*a*s." These gray pixels help the

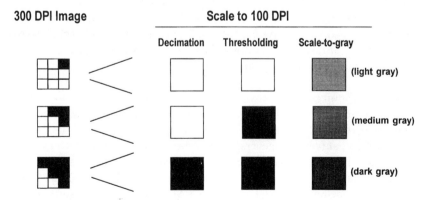

Figure 6.3   Scaling techniques

eye smooth lines in images resulting in much sharper and clearer font display. Scale to gray can effectively double the perceived resolution and is therefore a very important determinant of document image readability on a color monitor.

To take advantage of scale to gray, the display controller must be capable of displaying shades of gray. For document imaging, 16 grayscales is normal (4 bits). Some grayscale display controllers have 256 shades of gray (8 bits), which is desirable for displaying photographs but unnecessary for document images.

Decimation scaling provides the best performance, but the worst display quality, whereas scale to gray provides the best display quality but can limit system performance unless it is supported in hardware. Scale to gray is the most cost-effective way to improve display quality, and because display controller hardware designed specifically to improve performance is now available, scale to gray is becoming the standard scaling technique.

Scaling and Decompression Solution

The right hardware and/or software decompression solution is critical to achieve both high-quality image display and fast retrieval performance. There are three commonly used alternatives to decompress and scale document images at the workstation: dedicated decompression boards, software, and multifunction imaging controllers.

Dedicated Decompression Boards   When document imaging was first done on PCs in 1985, CPUs were of the 8088 and 80286 variety, and 8MHz was state of the art. As a result, trying to decompress document images without hardware assist resulted in painfully slow decompression, as long as 15 seconds per page! Companies like Kofax and Xionics developed decompression boards that dramatically improved decompression performance. These boards were expensive ($1,500 to $2,500) but were the only way to get acceptable page flip rates.

By 1992, one of the standard CPUs was a 25MHz 486DX. As a result, dedicated decompression boards are almost never used at retrieval workstations because of their high cost and because system CPUs have become powerful enough so that decompression can take place in software. Today, if you want to maximize retrieval workstation performance, invest in a faster CPU.

Software Decompression   Software decompression has become the most popular way to decompress document images at the workstation due to low cost and the improving performance of system CPUs. Decompression software varies widely in performance, although in general, software-only decompression solutions are slower than either dedicated decompression boards or multifunction imaging controllers. Make sure to evaluate the performance of the software you choose with samples of the documents you intend to image. Most decompression software uses decimation scaling, although some use scale to gray. Software-based scale to gray may yield unacceptably slow display performance.

Multifunction Imaging Controllers Multifunction imaging controllers combine a high-resolution display controller with specific functionality for document imaging and windows acceleration. These controllers are designed to share the workload with the 80×86 CPU. In general, the 80×86 architecture is efficient at functions that require memory management, table look-up, or very flexible algorithms, but not efficient at some tasks important for document imaging such as moving large amounts of data from main memory to the screen, image scaling, and rotation. As just stated, multifunction imaging controllers are designed to share the workload with the 80×86 CPU, delegating to the CPU what it does well and letting the display controller perform the document imaging specific functions. In this way, multifunction imaging controllers allow users to take advantage of increasing performance and the decreasing cost of the 80×86 architecture, which means combining low cost with very fast image retrieval performance using scale to gray.

Windows and Document Image Processing Display Performance

Microsoft Windows and OS/2 Presentation Manager have become standard user interfaces for document image processing systems. But, while Windows makes things easier for the user it makes things harder for the computer because it places a burden on display subsystem performance. This can be overcome, however, with display hardware designed for DIP systems. In general, some sort of acceleration hardware on the display controller board is necessary to achieve acceptable performance if Windows is part of your imaging system.

Methods of Windows Acceleration

There are three classes of display controllers with windows acceleration commonly available:

1. VGA (+) accelerators provide improved Windows performance in normal PC applications, but have limited resolution and low refresh rates due to VGA architectural constraints. These products are generally limited to $1,024 \times 768$ resolution at acceptable refresh rates. No document imaging assists are available. VGA displays are used only at workstations where document images are viewed infrequently.

2. TIGA coprocessors were originally designed for CAD applications and provide good image retrieval performance. They provide good resolution, refresh rates, and color support, but are expensive and provide no support for specific document imaging functions like rotation and scale to gray.

3. Multifunction imaging controllers, designed for document imaging, combine windows acceleration with display control and document imaging functionality. These boards are designed to deal with the performance

bottlenecks specific to document imaging—specifically, how to move large amounts of data from main memory to the screen. They also provide support for image decompression and scale to gray. Multifunction imaging controllers have the fastest flip rates if used with 25MHz 386 or faster CPUs.

The performance of these windows accelerators varies widely in document imaging applications because this process involves a number of functions, some irrelevant to document imaging and some critical. Therefore, it is necessary to evaluate performance with each application and not depend on windows performance benchmarks designed to measure performance in general-purpose applications.

The Cost of Slow Image Flip Rate

Slow image flip rates reduce productivity. Dollars lost to slow flip rates vary by application and are a function of the frequency with which the worker "flips" images and the percentage of time the worker is viewing and flipping images. For example: A personnel manager needs to fill a number of open positions. He or she begins by reviewing résumés that have been scanned into an imaging system and is able to review each résumé page in approximately fifteen seconds. With a subsecond flip rate, a total of four résumé pages per minute can be viewed. Now, assume the image flip rate is increased to five seconds: This means the manager can review only three pages per minute (15 seconds to review + 5 seconds to flip = 20 seconds per page.) The result is a 25 percent productivity loss.

Let's further assume this personnel manager represents a $32,500 burdened cost to the company. The standard work year is 1,840 hours; therefore, the hourly cost to the company is $17.65. As shown, a five-second flip rate results in a 25 percent productivity loss. If the manager spends only 30 percent of the time viewing résumés, an annual loss of $2,435 can be attributed to slow image flip rate (see Figure 6.4).

$25,000 Salary - $32,500 Burdened Cost
1840 Hours Per Year
25% Productivity Impact

% Time Viewing	Lost Hrs/Yr	Lost Dollars	5 Years
10	46	$ 810	$ 4,050
30	138	$ 2,435	$ 12,175
50	230	$ 4,060	$ 20,300
100	460	$ 8,120	$ 40,600

Figure 6.4   Cost of slow image flip rate

6.4 SELECTING THE RIGHT DISPLAY

Everything from VGA to 3-million pixel 24" grayscale displays is used for document image processing. There is no one right display solution for document imaging, but selecting a display with inadequate quality and performance can have a major adverse impact on productivity and user acceptance of the system. The right choice for any system depends on the following factors:

- The proportion of the day users will spend viewing document images. The more time users spend in front of the display, the more important display quality, screen size, and display performance are.

- Whether color is critical to the design of the software or is required for use in other applications. Color displays are both more expensive and have poorer display quality than grayscale. If you don't need color, use a grayscale display.

- The quality of source documents. Poor-quality source documents require good-quality displays in order to be readable. Scale to gray helps improve the readability of poor-quality source documents.

- The size of source documents. If source documents are smaller than a normal page, a smaller (and less expensive) monitor is usually sufficient.

- User preference. Most people have strong preconceptions about displays that change after they use an imaging system. Be sure to have system users carefully evaluate displays *before* a purchase decision is made.

Displays for Dedicated Document Imaging Systems

By far the most widely used display for document imaging systems is a 19" 120 dpi grayscale monitor. The two leading suppliers are Cornerstone Technology and IBM. Approximately 80 percent of retrieval workstations in large document imaging systems use displays of this description. These displays are popular because they provide excellent quality, a screen large enough to view two document pages at once, and are reasonably priced. Because users of dedicated document imaging systems usually spend all of their days in front of the display, good image readability and high performance are particularly important for productivity and user acceptance.

Document Imaging in a Mixed Application Environment

"Shrink-wrapped" document imaging software products, such as Keyfile, have been designed to manage workflow or automate paper processes. Additionally, popular business software platforms (Lotus Notes, for example) are now incorporating document imaging capability into their offerings. These new products will be used to "image enable" existing applications, which will make document imaging a much more common capability on networked business PCs. If imaging is a significant part of the workload, normal VGA displays may not be adequate.

The following list offers guidelines for selecting displays for image-enabled Windows applications:

VGA, 640 × 480	very occasional image use
SuperVGA, 1,024 × 768	daily light image use
1,280 × 1,024	1–2 hours per day image use
1,600 × 1,200	more than 4 hours image use

Impact of Windows on Display Selection

Today, Windows, rather than IBM hardware standards, defines applications software compatibility with display hardware. While hardware display standards such as VGA can be important for compatibility with DOS applications, users are assured that any display products desirable for document image processing that are Windows-compatible will run and display their Windows applications.

Windows creates a host of new demands on display performance, especially for document image processing. Hardware-based acceleration is a must for the management of document images in Windows environments. However, users must be careful to select an accelerator that doesn't compromise image readability factors. Some accelerator products are unable to provide the high-resolution and high refresh rates desirable for document imaging.

Color or Grayscale

Very high quality grayscale display subsystems designed for document image processing have been around for some time and are the standard for dedicated high-volume document workstations where document images are accessed frequently. However, improvements in color monitor design, scale-to-gray technology, and the availability of cost-effective high-resolution color subsystems designed for document image processing have made color a reasonable choice for some imaging applications.* In addition, the image enabling of existing applications used with color displays, the use of color in the design of many document imaging applications using workflow concepts, and the almost universal adoption of windowed environments as the front end to imaging applications have been powerful influences in the use of color displays for document imaging.

---

* When contrasting the advantages of color and grayscale displays, it is assumed that the addressable resolutions and size are similar; this is not a comparison of VGA with 19" grayscale displays.

Compared to large-screen color displays, large-screen grayscale displays are brighter, have much better image clarity, and have the bandwidth to support 70+Hz refresh rates on 19" 120 dpi displays. They are also about 60 percent the cost of a color monitor of similar size. Grayscale displays are ideal solutions for:

- Users who spend a large part of their days reading scanned documents.
- Users who must view complex document images, such as those containing small type, shaded areas, handwriting, or diagrams.
- Users who view images of poor-quality source documents, such as bills of lading or fax input.

Today's better color displays with resolutions of 100 dpi or better (with scale to gray) have adequate document image display quality for many applications. It is better to use color when the following conditions exist:

- Mixed applications are used under Windows where document imaging is not the full-time task.
- The document imaging application has color designed into it (workflow, for example).
- Color images or photographs need to be viewed.
- A color interface is being retained, such as in IBM 3278 mainframe applications.

The number of colors the display system should support also must be determined. Although the VGA standard of 16 colors is adequate for some everyday applications, better color is becoming important to users. Support for 256 colors is essential for many desktop publishing and graphics applications. At a minimum, a color display controller used for document imaging should be able to display 16 colors and 16 shades of gray.

Screen Size

A productive Windows display system needs to be large enough to accommodate several windows, each of reasonable size, as well as the document image. The recently introduced class of 17", 78KHz monitors is becoming popular for occasional users of document imaging. These displays are appropriate solutions for users who generally view one document image and a small menu or have two or fewer windows open simultaneously. They offer a cost-effective solution in a form factor that is ideal for today's work areas.

Full-time document imaging users find that 19"–21" monitors are important if they need to view two document images side by side, need to view multiple windows (such as a document image and a 3278 window), or are using applications that require a large screen (desktop publishing or big spreadsheets).

In addition to screen size, users must consider how much of the screen is actually usable. Many larger-screen monitors lose focus around the edges. Edge focus may not be as important for applications where center screen is the focal point (such as

CAD), but it is absolutely critical for document imaging applications, where the most important part of the image is often displayed on the outer edges of the monitor.

6.5   SUMMARY

To achieve user acceptance and productivity, two factors are essential in the selection of displays for imaging systems: display readability and display speed. To repeat, the more time that system users spend viewing the system, the more important these factors are.

As noted, most purchasers of new document imaging systems have strong preconceptions about what type of displays they want to use with their imaging systems, and these displays may or may not be appropriate for the system. It is strongly recommended that imaging system managers delay any final purchases until after a thorough two-week trial of the display(s) with the intended application is performed.

Part II

Planning and Design

7

Planning an Imaging System: Workflow Redesign

Marc R. D'Alleyrand, Ph.D.

7.1 INTRODUCTION

The selection of a technical solution that links the user to the imaging network depends essentially on four strategic decisions, diagrammed in Figure 7.1. These decisions involve:

- The system architecture, which defines where data are stored; it must reflect operational requirements, while optimizing data transfer between users.
- The data organization and identification method, which is a determining factor in the operating costs of an imaging system, both for document capture and information retrieval.
- The platform selection.
- The indexing and data structure, which determines the efficiency of the retrieval process.

Each of these strategic decisions usually is the result of operational, financial, and sometimes political and pragmatic trade-offs. Therefore, there rarely will be a single valid technical solution. More often than not, there will be "better" solutions in a given user environment.

When imaging technologies are added to the panoply of options, choices that best fit required trade-offs will often need to be reconsidered:

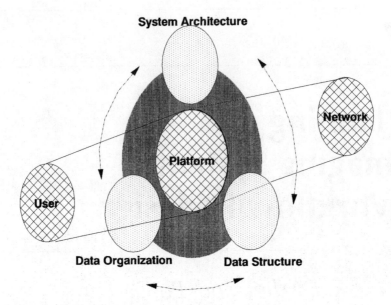

Figure 7.1　Strategic decision elements for an imaging system network

- Methods and processes, from the creation of a data dictionary to the standardization of hardware and supporting software, may now have to differentiate between data- and image-based information.
- Standards for architecture and supporting indexing methodology will need to accommodate information in a different medium and format.
- Heretofore interoperable (i.e., compatible) platforms for workstations, file servers, operating systems, and human interface may now perform at different levels of competence, requiring a complete reworking of the network.

7.2　GUIDELINES FOR SELECTION OF A NETWORKED IMAGING SYSTEM

In many cases, it is possible to adapt methods developed for data-only systems, such as structured analysis, to the implementation of an imaging system. However, because the information contained in images can be represented either in a logical or a physical manner, the methodology may have to be applied to different information flows, the results of which would need to be reconciled.

System Architecture

As indicated earlier, system architectures present both physical and logical aspects; the former is defined by the flow of information in that system and where electronic processing of data takes place, the latter by the electrical connection between devices.

The potential complexity of networked installations may dictate that another architecture, based on ownership of data as well as on nature of processing, be defined. In that context, there are three major types of architectures:

1. *Centralized*: Data ownership is on one machine and all processing is done on that central installation. This is the traditional "mainframe" environment, in which concern for data security and control is an overriding factor. (Currently, the market share of this architecture is under strong attack due to downsizing and cost reduction efforts.)

2. *Decentralized*: Each user retains ownership of his or her data, even while sharing information with other users; all processing is done at the user workstations. This is more the domain of peer-to-peer networks. Until recently this was not advisable for most imaging systems, because of the potential for lower overall performance. However, this situation may change with the growing interest in personal imaging workstations, which may reduce the drain on remote workstation resources.

3. *Distributed*: Users can process data, but do not gain ownership of the data, even after they have processed them. This approach, which was made possible by the rapid drop in hardware prices and increase in software capabilities, is characterized by the "client-server" model.

Operationally, the distinction between these three models is hazy, as information sharing may require data processing outside user control for purposes such as ensuring integrity of the information flow, thus blurring the issue of information ownership. This is the case with client-server architectures, where a particular workstation may change its role from client to server according to the type of transaction.

Data Organization

Architectures are selected to provide optimized system efficiency. Data organizations are selected to provide fastest retrieval. From a design standpoint, architecture deals with the physical location of data elements, while organization is concerned with their logical relationships. However, the two concerns are related and influence each other. In particular, in distributed architectures, data organization plays an essential role in the overall performance of the system. Depending on the task, one structure may be more appropriate than another.

From a user point of view, the primary concern is the selection of "application" data structures, which reflect information retrieval requirements. Once these structures have been defined (either flat, hierarchical, relational, or object-oriented), they freeze the path to information retrieval. At that time, the imaging system can take over the responsibility of maintaining relationships between various data structures to ensure efficient processing, even if this implies internal translation from a "user-oriented" structure to a "machine-oriented" organization.

Platform Selection

A platform is a hardware/software solution on which a given system is run. Depending on design and requirements, platform selection may be as much a matter of personal preference as a technical solution. In some cases, the imaging application may require a specific platform because it is the only one that can support anticipated information processing; in others, the choice is more a matter of tradition.

What is critical to keep in mind is that the current trends towards interoperability reduce the risk that a particular platform choice will not work at all in a given environment. Furthermore, appropriate architectures can ensure concurrent operation of different platforms. Consequently, with hardware costs decreasing rapidly, economic considerations are becoming major factors in platform selections.

Indexing and Data Identification

In this book, the word "indexing" refers to the activity of assigning an identifying term to describe a characteristic of a document's contents. An index also is a list of terms that makes it possible to retrieve a document through its contents. As such, the word "index" has a radically different meaning from that of database management programs, in which a list of pointers contains information about the location of the records in a database file.

While architecture and platform determine the initial cost of a system, the choice of an indexing methodology will probably be the most significant strategic decision in terms of operating costs, because document retrievability will be dependent on the quality of the indexing process. To be sure, documents can be captured and indexed at low cost through an assigned document number, but that inexpensive capture will result in an expensive search if retrieval also requires contents access.

Several methods for indexing are possible, ranging from the assignment of keywords to the use of full-text searching. While the latter is often used in automated indexing systems to reduce the cost of setting up a data architecture, it is helpful only if the document has been translated into a machine-readable form through the use of OCR techniques. In addition to the various issues of index quality that may be raised by such a technique, it is of little value if the document is in an image format, which requires the assignment of a content descriptor by a human operator. Furthermore, full-text searching can be used only for explicit terms, although new search techniques based on artificial intelligence software, such as query-by-example, are progressively reducing the importance of that issue.

Integration of the Strategic Decisions

To ensure optimum system performance, it is essential that these four decisions, system architecture, data organization, platform, and structure, be integrated as tightly as possible during the system design. Economic considerations resulting from decreasing costs for equipment and off-the-shelf software will tend to reduce the relative importance of technology and enhance the value of efficient process design.

The successful outcome of these decisions presupposes that the system design is congruent with organizational objectives. However, as indicated in an earlier chapter, the implementation of an imaging system usually profoundly changes the way an organization transacts its business. The preliminary conduct of a workflow redesign effort will provide the operational parameters necessary to reach organizational objectives with the new system.

7.3   BASIC PRINCIPLES AND OBJECTIVES OF WORKFLOW REDESIGN

Introduction

As already stated, imaging changes the way an organization conducts its business. As a result, it is likely that the existing information processing infrastructure will need to be modified. In fact, because the changes will probably be significant, the adoption of imaging provides an opportunity to take a fresh look at that infrastructure and investigate how it can be optimized. Three situations will be the prime targets for that review:

1. The existing data system is a collection of nonintegrated programs, developed over the years without periodic review for efficiency.

2. The maintenance costs of the existing data system are high, as a result of older programs that do not take advantage of more recent operating systems releases.

3. The demands that imaging would place on the existing system cannot be accommodated with the current computer resources.

Workflow redesign can provide sound methodology tools to diagnose inefficiencies and identify remedies. Depending on the complexity of the existing processing tasks and the need to protect the software investment, these remedies will range from software "rejuvenation" and integration, to replacement with commercial packages.

Redesigning makes it possible to effect major changes in the way information is processed in an organization by automating tasks, while at the same time reducing operating costs and increasing productivity. They may include the following:

- Automatic assignment and routing of documents according to preestablished procedures.
- Elimination of redundant efforts in document creation, filing, and retrieval.
- Concurrent document processing.
- Integration through networking of all organizational information.

Changes in enabling technologies will spur the acceptance of workflow redesign as they make cost-effective task integration a reality. These technologies, essentially cost-effective imaging systems and integrated data networks, enable the exchange of information between previously incompatible formats.

Document imaging simultaneously offers the opportunity to review the cost-effectiveness of information throughout an organization and thus identifies opportunities for cost savings. Document imaging can eliminate duplicate documents, extract data from those documents through optical character recognition (OCR), and make it possible to view documents side by side with related data, and, through networking, consolidate and/or eliminate information processing tasks.

Workflow redesign affects two separate components of the information flow:

1. A physical one, following the tangible flow of documents. In manual systems, this is the so-called back-office operation, which handles both information-bearing documents, such as bills and invoices, purchase orders, and shipping memos; and secondary materials, containing information derived from the primary documents, such as financial reports.

2. A logical component, which corresponds to the actual flow of information contained in these documents and supports the business process itself.

From an information management standpoint, these two components must often be considered separately. In manual and traditional automated systems, this is a necessary state of affairs, because of the substantial difference between documents and the information they contain. In fact, once information has been extracted from a physical source document, it can be processed in the logical stream independent from the source document. This leads to the well-documented dual streams of "paper" and "data" processing. The first deals with the manual (or increasingly computer-assisted) capture of data contained in paper documents and the disposition of the paper media; the other, with the computer processing of the extracted data. In imaging systems, both streams can be combined and brought back under a single computer-based umbrella, thus eliminating the inefficiencies associated with the maintenance of two parallel systems.

Objectives of Workflow Redesign

The traditional objectives of a workflow redesign are enhancement of organizational productivity, reduction of operating costs, and increase in competitiveness in the marketplace. These objectives are the same as those of imaging in a network environment, and, therefore, workflow redesign methodology provides the functional specifications for such systems.

Achieving these objectives will require changing the information flow to support a redesigned operation and consolidating different information systems into a unified architecture. In the process of changing the information flow throughout the organization, redesign also provides the opportunity to change the focus from storage to retrieval. As such, it will help to determine the "right" size of the information processing support facility that will be necessary for meeting business requirements.

The technology can be used in a modular fashion; therefore, it will not always be necessary to implement large systems, as would be the case with a mainframe installation. Rather, if the redesign is based on a sound architecture, the redesigned system will be able to grow in an incremental fashion in concert with business needs.

The Redesign Process

The redesign process requires a consistent comparison of present and proposed systems. The following elements are necessary for a solid analysis and technical solution:

- Objectively compare information transfer processes.
- Identify redesign options in compatible terms between the two systems.
- Design a coherent transition mechanism necessary for continuity of business operations.
- Build justification models based on comparable cost elements.

Following a consistent analysis methodology will ensure that the proposed system will operate satisfactorily on a network, especially if it involves a multi-departmental environment. This is particularly the case for a client-server environment, where the imaging/document server is operating essentially as a data repository without any clear relationship between information collected and business needs. Without a methodology to describe how data are captured, stored, retrieved, and used, it will be difficult to identify conflicting needs, goals, and departmental objectives.

A complete workflow analysis should:

- Assess the strengths and weaknesses of the existing information system in terms of its value to the business needs of the organization.
- Determine which information paths can be optimized to reduce the cost of information transfer.
- Identify the operational information requirements, such as workloads, data to be retrieved, users and suppliers of information, and needed response time.

Redesign projects vary greatly in magnitude and complexity. There usually are three levels of efforts, ranging from simple "facilitator" to complete process redesign, which may involve a variety of organizational processes. In fact, in most instances, different workflows may be necessary to represent a given activity. For instance, the definition of a manufacturing process will require at least five different but related workflows, describing sales and ordering, machining and assembly of mechanical parts, inventory control, system maintenance, and accounts payable.

In each of these workflows, each step is definable by the information that it receives from and releases to its environment and by the operations that it performs. Therefore, a workflow can be seen not only as a representation of a succession of operational steps, but also as the representation of an information transfer process, which can be described in two successive operations:

1. The first step deals with the optimization of the information flow itself, by determining data architectures and implementation procedures that ensure availability of needed information in a timely, accurate, complete, and cost-effective manner. The outcome of this step, which requires the optimization of both the physical and logical models, will be a set of functional specifications that must be met by the redesigned system.

2. The second step identifies the technical solution or solutions that will support information requirements and meet the functional specifications set above.

The state of the market indicates that commercial hardware and software products will be able to meet requirements with no or little development effort. Consequently, the major effort of a workflow redesign should be directed at methodology rather than technical solutions.

7.4   THE REDESIGN PROCESS

On the surface, workflow redesign is business application-specific. The history and legacy of an existing system and the differences in business objectives make a "standard" approach to workflow redesign seem like a utopian proposition. Furthermore, different industries may appear to require entirely separate approaches, just because they are different. For instance, a service and a manufacturing organization may seem disparate when viewed from a redesign methodology standpoint: A service business delivers intangible products; a manufacturing business produces tangible goods. However, because the redesign process (Figure 7.2[1]) deals with optimizing information flow, methodology differences will probably be limited to implementation. The methodology for the design of the logical model will apply to both the service and manufacturing environments. Similarly, the physical model will apply to the product being handled. In the service organization, it will represent the status of the service product; in manufacturing, the status of the material goods. In either case, workflow redesign will be directed at the delivery of better and more cost-effective products.

Present System Analysis

The analysis of the existing system establishes an operational baseline, against which the redesigned system will be measured. In short, that analysis is a statement of "where we are now." That analysis must:

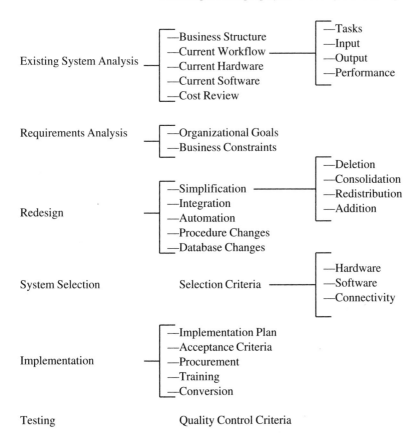

Figure 7.2   Components of a workflow redesign process

- Document the present organizational structure and business drivers.
- Identify the installed system architecture, hardware, and software base.
- Determine the existing cost structure.

The actual analysis of the current workflow should focus on the identification of tasks being performed, input and output data and products, and workload and response time for each task. An efficient way to keep track of the tasks is to conduct the analysis using a work breakdown structure (WBS), which is briefly explained below. The result of the analysis will be a snapshot of the operation to be redesigned, placed in the context of organizational constraints.

The data necessary to the analysis usually is recorded on some kind of questionnaire. For large and complex redesign projects, it may be desirable to use machine-readable forms, to enable a more comprehensive data collection than would be possible with manual forms and to facilitate data extraction.

Identification of Required Changes

Once the required changes have been identified, the existing system can be mapped into the proposed redesigned operation. Without that mapping, it is impossible to ensure that all existing tasks have been accounted for in the new system. This step results in the generation of a requirements analysis, which spells out what is expected of the system. As such, it answers the question, "where do we want to go?" without concern as to how the requirements will be met.

A requirements analysis must clearly spell out which organizational goals the redesign system will support and identify the current business constraints that it will address. The identification of required changes should be organized around the tasks that need to be performed in the redesigned system. These tasks will be based on the list of tasks in the present system, but expanded to meet organizational objectives and associated production requirements.

Tasks

For purposes of this discussion, redesigned tasks are assigned to one of what we call the "must-may-may-not-do lists." For the sake of consistency, the redesigned tasks should be described through a work breakdown structure, cross-referenced with those identified in the present system.

"Must-Do" List

The "must-do" list corresponds to information that needs to be transferred because it is essential for the conduct of business. This information flow is the backbone of the redesigned workplace, and any disruption of this flow will seriously impact upon the organization's ability to perform. Included in the "must-do" list is the maintenance of an uninterrupted stream of information about cash flow, invoices, inventories, and production. Very often this type of information is already available in a conventional computerized data processing environment. The redesign process, especially in an imaging environment, will make it necessary to review whether the information already collected meets long-term business needs or will have to be reformatted for more efficient use.

"May-Do" List

"May-do" items are optional requirements that support the "must-do" activities, which either enhance the use of the information or facilitate its processing. Their absence from the redesign plan or the interruption of their delivery may create some tolerable operational problems, with some negative cost implications. For instance, the selection of ergonomic workstations does not in itself improve information flow, but it has an indirect positive effect on the workflow. Consequently, the adoption of optional requirements will depend on a cost-benefits analysis.

"May-Not-Do" List

"May-not-do" requirements correspond to items in the present system that are to be eliminated, either because they will cease to be necessary or useful in the new system due to the redesign process or because they are already redundant. A large proportion of these "may-not-do" items are processing tasks that generate a multitude of reports that can be consolidated or contain information already available elsewhere.

Performance

Various factors determine performance requirements, the most common of which include volume and response time of the tasks and transactions that must be accommodated in the redesigned system. Response time usually is easy to compute and specify; volume, however, is not. Volume must support three different operating modes: maintenance of the current level of service, growth resulting from the impact of redesign, and growth resulting from changing market conditions. While it may be tempting to "guess" at growth factors, guessing wrong may result in long-term performance problems.

7.5 SYSTEM REDESIGN

Designing the new system first involves taking an accounting of all the items already noted and translating them into the new system by one of the following methods: addition, deletion, consolidation, or redistribution.

Addition

The addition of tasks represents the creation of new tasks that have no counterpart in the present system. Additions usually occur when new functionalities are made possible by the infusion of technology or when the deletion of tasks results in a breakdown of the information flow. For instance, in an insurance application, the consolidation of claims receipt and policy substantiation may result in the elimination of independent verification. To maintain the integrity of the claims process would require the addition of a separate substantiation.

At first glance, the addition of tasks may appear to contradict the purpose of redesign, but these new tasks are in general automated, and thus can be completed at a fraction of the corresponding cost in the present system. In this example, independent verification could be done automatically, and its results provided by a summary report to an auditor.

Deletion

Deletion corresponds to the handling of the "may-not" list. Deletion of these items from the new system must be done after verification either that the data they used will be obsolete or that they will still be accessible for the remaining tasks that would need them. Usually, deletion of tasks corresponds to the elimination of noninformation-bearing tasks, such as the creation of redundant reports.

Consolidation

Consolidation covers tasks that through the use of technologies can be performed at one workstation, instead of in different areas. Consolidation usually occurs whenever the performance of related tasks requires the same level of skills. For instance, in an insurance application, the capture of a claim and verification that the claimant's policy is current require the same level of assessment. The display of an existing policy at the time of claim capture combines two look-ups into one.

The effectiveness of consolidation depends on the precision of the information description standards developed as part of the redesign targets, which results in the identification of similarities in information capture, processing, and use. Consolidation may be either simply geographical, when more powerful tools allow for a reduction of unit cost, or involve streamlining of the overall process.

Another example of consolidation is an accounts payable application in which a manual procedure physically matches purchase orders against actual invoices and receipts. Imaging can streamline the process by automating matching, thus allowing for expedited processing and payment of invoices.

Task consolidation must be scrutinized and validated, however, for though it offers great opportunities for savings through simplification of the workflow, it may also eliminate the protection of checks and balances characteristic of more traditional systems. It is incumbent upon the designer of the redesigned system to set up computerized procedures to reinstate any required safeguards.

Redistribution

Redistribution describes the breakdown of activities into individual tasks, which can be performed more efficiently through mechanization. Redistribution in general occurs when the initial activity called for a wide variety of skills that results in the underutilization of personnel during some portion of the activity cycle. An example of redistribution is the segregation of scanning from quality control in an image capture operation. Note that redistribution in one area results in consolidation in another.

7.6 SELECTION OF A TECHNICAL SOLUTION

In principle, workflow redesign is technology-independent. While this is true for the logical model, this may not be the case for the physical model. In particular, the ability to combine tasks is contingent on the availability of devices capable of meeting stated operating requirements and constraints. For instance, a redesigned workflow using optical character recognition (OCR) to extract data from scanned documents can be effective only if the precision of the OCR device is sufficient. If it is not, then the redesigned workflow may require the use of a concurrent manual data entry path or ignore OCR technology altogether.

The existing network infrastructure places constraints on the number of options for a technical solution. The cost and time required to replace existing equipment may be politically high enough to eliminate a "best" solution in favor of a "serviceable" one. Therefore, before going any further into the process, the redesigned system should review not only an acceptable technical solution, but also the existing investment and migration costs associated with conversion to the redesigned system.

The choice of a technical solution involves the specification of hardware, software, and connectivity requirements. Of particular importance is the establishment of selection criteria to be used for the actual selection of systems components.

An important aspect of the technological solution is its ability to protect the redesigned system against technological obsolescence. One approach to this issue is the selection of a technical solution that can be amortized quickly so that equipment can be replaced early by more modern devices without reduction in cost benefits.

7.7 IMPLEMENTATION

Implementation covers the translation of systems design into technical specifications: the selection, procurement, and installation of equipment. Depending on the business objectives, implementation may or may not include conversion of data from the old to the new system. While a detailed discussion of these activities is beyond the scope of this book, they must be at least peripherally considered as part of the redesign process because it is only at implementation that undetected design flaws become apparent. Major components of the implementation phase are outlined below.

Design of the Implementation Plan

The implementation plan is a key element of the redesign project because it will provide the references necessary for monitoring progress. The plan should include—at a minimum—a project timetable with milestones and a budget plan keyed to these milestones so that the project can be managed in a cost-effective manner.

Determination of Acceptance Criteria

Acceptance criteria are necessary for determining whether performance divergence between the design and the implementation is acceptable or not. Although these criteria may have been drafted during the design process, their finalization cannot occur before the completion of a technical solution.

Procurement

Procurement of goods and services is considered part of the implementation phase, once selection criteria and project budgets have been finalized. Depending on the circumstances, procurement constraints may require revision of both the implementation timetable and budgets.

Training

Even though training represents a significant portion of the implementation budget, it is often overlooked or underestimated during the planning of a workflow redesign. Training may be done in a variety of ways, ranging from "on-the-job" situations to classroom settings. The most effective training method for a given situation depends on many factors, including the availability of qualified instructors and the amount of training needed by the staff. Remember, there is a trade-off between cost of training and cost of startup to bring the redesigned system to full production level.

Conversion

Conversion activities concern the translation of data used in the present system to a format acceptable in the redesigned environment. Depending on the differences between present and proposed system, conversion may involve either a simple recopying of data from one system to the other or a complete change in format and medium. When implementing an imaging system, conversion involves a change in medium and format. Like training, provisions for conversion are often neglected, sometimes caused by a lack of understanding of the issues, sometimes by a desire to make a project financially more attractive.

In so-called "day-one" or "forward" systems, which handle only new materials, conversion is kept to a minimum, but this is at the expense of having to run the redesigned operation in parallel with a minimum level of "old" services until older materials have been retired.

Under certain circumstances, it is possible to use conversion as an opportunity for staff training. One such approach is to begin conversion before the system has been fully implemented and use the staff to do the conversion. In this way, staff can learn the new system without the risk of damaging "live documents." The probability of retrieval of older documents is small; therefore, the risks to the organization caused by staff errors during training are kept to a minimum.

7.8 VERIFYING THE REDESIGN

As workflow redesign modifies the business process, there usually is no reliable precedent in the organization to predict what effect the changes will have on the reengineered operation. Using modeling and simulation techniques reduces the risk that the proposed changes are of poor design.

Workflow Simulation

Modeling for imaging network applications provides a formal method to describe a particular system, including topologies, relationships, and capabilities of the systems components, such as input/output rates and data distribution. A simulation reports on the behaviors of the underlying model, based on the application of computation rules that are pertinent to the data being examined. This allows the system designer to project the impact of changes in hardware topology or capabilities.

There are several modeling and simulation tools on the market, each offering different functionalities and levels of complexity. Most of these tools were not originally designed for imaging and usually reflect their manufacturing, process control, or telecommunication heritage.

At the present time, all commercial tools provide graphical representations of the physical topology of an imaging network. The simplest ones deal only with the flow of documents, basically displaying routing schemes and determining out-of-bound performance conditions. For instance, a simple imaging network modeling and simulation package may display an apparently correct installation (Figure 7.3a), while simulation, shown in Figure 7.3b, may reveal that, under the contem-

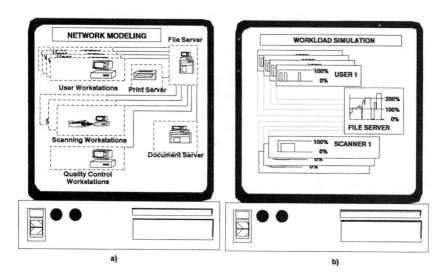

Figure 7.3   Modeling and simulation of an imaging network

plated workloads and equipment performance characteristics, the file server will be overloaded.

More sophisticated packages will feed back output data in order to compute actual performance. In the example diagrammed above, a more sophisticated software would, for instance, allocate network bandwidth according to the various active devices traffic and adjust their individual contribution to the overall data flow so that the file server never operates at more than 100 percent capacity.

Top-of-the-line packages accept external input, such as actual network traffic, which then can be compared to predicted performance and in case of a discrepancy, provide a diagnostic tool for the identification of systems problems.

Planning an Imaging Network

A first and immediate application of modeling is in the planning of a new system to verify that the selected components can perform efficiently. In that type of application, simulation identifies bottlenecks—where devices are idled by upstream congestion. In some cases, simulation may distinguish between structural and operational bottlenecks, where delays are not the result of underperforming hardware, but reflect inadequate staging of the workflow. For instance, an apparent low throughput in document scanning may not be due to internal scanning performance degradation, but to the fact that there has been no provision made for adjusting the difference between scanning and quality control time. A simple solution for such a situation is to have the scanning function start earlier than the quality control.

Workflow Control

Simulation models also are useful to ascertain control of the redesigned workflow. Data used to model the imaging system are rarely based on historical data, but instead are usually derived from industry estimates. Because this data is used to justify the cost of the redesigned system, it is imperative that it be reassessed in a postimplementation verification. Feeding actual data into the model will quickly provide an accurate view of whether the system as implemented will meet its performance objectives. This is of particular value in systems where the simulation model is integrated with the data flow and production data are captured automatically, as it can sound an early warning when operational conditions in the imaging system may have a negative impact on the overall network performance.

System Maintenance

Simulation also can help to maintain performance by predicting the impact that changes in an operational imaging system can have on the overall network performance. "What-if" scenarios also can be played to identify problem areas. For instance, the production of a high-volume imaging conversion system may be strongly dependent on an even data flow over the network. Data flow obviously is affected by absenteeism; therefore, it is important for the system manager to understand the relative impact on workflow of an absent staff member. This will allow for the implementation of corrective measures before the situation starts to deteriorate.

Running the model also is beneficial when contemplating systems upgrade, and it is necessary to evaluate whether the proposed change will generate benefits commensurate with the associated cost of the upgrade. The model may show that there is no difference in the number of transactions that a user can physically adjudicate if the system runs on 30MHz or 60MHz processors, thus making an equipment upgrade unnecessary from that standpoint.

Network Simulation

Network models are, by nature, less probabilistic than workflow constructs, so naturally they require different modeling techniques. For instance, while there is a physical limit to a system buffer, there is seldom such a constraint in a workflow model: If the backlog is too large, documents may be piled up outside their designated containers, but the workflow system will not likely stop for that reason.

In addition, because of the variety of devices and topologies that can be used on a network, commercial communication simulation packages provide many more tools than for workflow simulation. Currently, object-oriented packages designed to consolidate both telecommunication and local area network simulation are appearing on the market. In particular, there are efforts to import data provided by network analyzers into a simulation package to provide them with a real-time "what-if" capability.

7.9   STRATEGIC DECISIONS FOR WORKFLOW REDESIGN

The impact of workflow redesign on the way business is conducted and the fact that its consequences may be irreversible require that system design decisions be considered strategically rather than simply as technical solutions. Specifically, this implies that the manner in which the above targets is addressed be analyzed from a business implications perspective.

Adoption of Standards

The adoption of standards is essential to workflow redesign. In fact, it is probably the most necessary and frustrating requirement of redesign. On the one hand, the imaging industry is too young to have really "mature" standards; on the other, redesign cannot be done without a stable standard base.

There are two types of standards. The first, "internal," deals with the terminology used throughout the organization and is directed at removing inefficiencies due to a lack of uniform data structure. Due to the fact that information will flow throughout the workplace, it is essential that it be constantly referred to in the same manner regardless of its use. Selection of a uniform terminology is a complex task. Terms must be unique and specific to their context. For instance, the term record may mean an entry in a database or a full document; failure to have a precise definition for that word in the context of the information system may lead to confusion.

The second type of standard is external and refers to those adopted or endorsed by professional organizations, based on the appropriate international standards. This problem of standards is accentuated when images are transmitted. The need to define an image, its position on a printed page, and its method of encoding for efficient storage and transmission has created a large number of incompatible formats. In spite of standardization efforts, such as from the International Organization for Standardization (ISO) and Computer-aided Acquisition and Logistic Support (CALS), there is still a wide variety of "incompatible compliant" formats. Translators, which are programs or devices that convert from one format to another, do not entirely resolve the management issues of accepting these machine-readable data because of the resulting processing delays. (A list of the most important standards, in particular those that are applicable to imaging, can be obtained from the Association of Information and Image Management [AIIM].)

It is important to note that some external standards may have direct influence on the adoption of internal standards. For instance, the word "basic," which in ISO-8613 is the standard for office documents in electronic format, refers to specific vendor-supported functionalities; it should not be used in an internal standard to mean a "simple" format.

Data Capture

Initially, data capture does not appear to be a strategic decision. However, to choose a method that does not take into consideration the format in which data are available to the reengineered system may result in unnecessary additional conversion and processing costs. In addition, from a strategic point of view, the selection of the wrong data capture method will freeze the upward capability of the reengineered system. It is therefore essential that the selection be made with a thorough understanding of the organization's business objectives and the nature of information that will support these objectives.

Three basic methods of data capture are available. The first is data entry, the process of transcribing from paper documents; the second is acceptance of machine-readable data; the third consists of extracting machine-readable data directly from documents. The advantages and drawbacks of these methods are summarized in Table 7.1.

Data extraction, in conjunction with imaging, is at the present time the most versatile method for data acquisition. The fact that it allows simultaneous capture of both structured and nonstructured information makes it possible to design a flexible information system which can adapt to changing business conditions. Once the redesign of the information flow has been completed, new types of data may

Table 7.1   Advantages and drawbacks of data capture methods

Method	Advantages	Drawbacks	Comments
Data Entry	Flexibility Low-cost entry	Error rate Labor-intensive	Still recommended for difficult documents
Machine-Readable	High-speed reliability	Requires standardization	Long-term trends favor this method
Data Extraction (OCR)	Simplicity Low-cost capture	Requires good- quality documents	Allows for the capture of both structured and unstructured data

be added to that flow without significantly impacting the workflow. For instance, in the purchasing example, capturing handwritten notes from conversations with vendors may be an afterthought. In a traditional data system, this capture would require significant additional costs of transcription. In an imaging environment, it is only an additional page to scan.

Other benefits can be derived from imaging. From a cost standpoint, it is cheaper to enter data from scanned documents than from paper, even if the quality of documents does not allow for automated data collection. Operationally, the software necessary to handle the retrieval of images is similar to the software designed to retrieve other nontextual data, such as live video and voice. Thus, a system reengineered to accept image capture can be easily adapted to other media, which is a prudent strategy in view of the dynamics of the computerized multimedia document marketplace.

Indexing

The selection of an indexing methodology that balances the cost of data identification with the cost of information retrieval is of strategic importance for the long-term cost-effectiveness of the information system. Indexing is a relatively expensive, one-time expense which can be projected with a high degree of precision once the indexing criteria have been specified. In contrast, retrieval costs depend on the speed of access to the data. The lower the level of indexing, the higher the retrieval costs; however, this cost is spread over the number of retrievals. Therefore, a high level of indexing may still be cost justified in a highly active retrieval system because the initial unit cost of indexing has been more than offset by the reduction in retrieval costs (see Figure 7.4). Justifying the cost of an indexing process redesign then becomes an issue of "pay now" vs. "pay later."

The selection of an indexing system will determine how information is retrieved. Its choice therefore is essential. Two aspects of indexing must be considered. One deals with indexing for storage and defines an item so that it is uniquely identified in a database. The second aspect is indexing from a retrieval standpoint and describes an item so that it can be uniquely retrieved from the same database. In

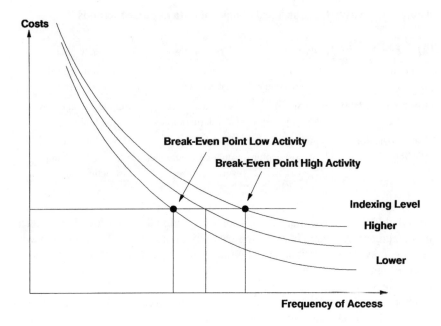

Figure 7.4   Comparison between retrieval and indexing costs

order for data to be consistently accessed and used, these two requirements must be reconciled. In the earlier procurement example, identifying a purchase order by its number is a very efficient method for storage, but practically useless for retrieval by anything else than that number. The challenge, therefore, is to define the minimum amount of detail at the input end that will result in the maximum retrievability of the information. Indexing requirements *must* be reconciled with data collection capabilities so that the overall cost of data capture and identification is minimized. For instance, the full accessibility to the contents of a document provided by imaging techniques simplifies the need for indexing, as it may be sufficient to retrieve some of the data through browsing of the scanned images. Under those conditions, incompletely recorded purchasing transactions may still be retrieved if similar transactions are kept together. A cost-effective method may then be to use a combination of indexing and browsing, with a "first" level of indexing giving quick access to a group of transactions and the exact item then located through browsing.

This combination of direct access and browsing is the most important characteristic of retrievability in an imaging environment. The strategic decision will be to decide how many of the retrieval requirements will be met through direct access and how many through browsing. An empiric rule, often called the "80/20" rule, predicts that 80 percent of the information requested in a system probably can be achieved by 20 percent of direct indexing.

Information Retrieval

Clearly specified retrieval requirements have a long-term impact on the ability of the reengineered system to support organizational objectives, which is why they are so strategically important. In fact, the ability to retrieve information in a cost-effective, accurate, and timely manner over the life cycle of the system is the ultimate validation of the redesign process. This requirement implies that the formulation of retrieval needs must shadow and/or anticipate the long-term business objectives of the organization. Therefore, redesign solutions will be based on the answers to questions such as: What do people really need to know, now and in the future, in order to conduct their business? What information is and/or will be necessary to the business as a whole and to departments as unique entities of the whole?

To answer these and similar questions, it may be worthwhile to visualize information flow as composed of three related data streams in both the present and the reengineered information systems: A tactical stream carries the information necessary to conduct the current business; a strategic stream carries the information necessary for the long-term survival of the organization; and a support stream handles the information necessary to the operation of the information system itself. These three data streams will intersect at discrete information nodes whenever they use the same data.

From a strategic standpoint, the definition of retrieval needs will dictate not only the type of data to be collected and stored, but their organization and allocation among the information nodes. From a redesign standpoint, the challenge will be to develop a cost-effective retrieval system, which supports the existing business yet is flexible enough to adapt to future business requirements.

The early selection of a database design to support these three different data streams is crucial. As with indexing, a larger initial investment in a sophisticated database design may result in better long-term information retrievability than would be possible with a less complex structure. For instance, the immediate needs of a relational design may not be initially evident, but future requirements may make the use of a simpler hierarchical design that is impractical in the long run. Such considerations are of great importance when imaging is considered as part of a redesign solution. Image-capable database systems have requirements that are unknown in numerical data-only systems.

Processing System

The processing system is the complex link between data storage and information retrieval. It includes mainstream processes, which generate the information necessary to conduct of business and support tasks. These processes, which range from user interface to system security, are essential to the long-term survival of the system itself.

Strategic considerations should first relate to the extended support of the retrieval requirements and the database design, which should have been selected prior to the consideration of processing needs. This involves the selection of a system architecture, platform, and operating system. Depending on the retrieval requirements, the architecture may be centralized or distributed, stand-alone or networked; depending on the application and volume of data to be exchanged, the platform may be a PC, a mini, or a mainframe, and with or without communication to other installations. Finally, depending on the operating requirements, the operating system should be selected from among one of the few standard systems.

The industry trend in processing systems is to integrate modular solutions. This means lower redesign costs through the use of commercial off-the-shelf solutions and long-term system flexibility and adaptability for growth thanks to the interchangeability of modules.

The Data Networking Environment

This consideration has been left for the end of this chapter not because it is the least important but because it is the one that should be handled when all the other issues have been settled. However, especially when imaging is implemented as an enhancement to an existing data system, constraints of the operational environment may strongly influence the redesign process.

Deciding on the new network environment often involves choosing between "enhancing" an existing configuration through the addition of a separate image-capable network, or replacing the current system in place, with its concomitant requirement to redesign and/or upgrade the supporting databases and application programs.

7.10 CONCLUSION: REDESIGN AND THE ORGANIZATIONAL STRUCTURE

Once the redesign system has been defined, it is necessary to verify that the organization is better served by the new information flow. Generally, it becomes clear that the benefits from workflow redesign cannot be achieved without a redesign of the organization itself along the new information streams.

As a result, the adoption of a redesigned workflow may result in a reassignment of responsibilities, dispensing with some and creating others. The success of that reorganization will depend on the optimization of stated information needs and the ability to staff corresponding "information-keeper" positions. Restructuring may result in the elimination of intermediate job titles, and possibly require that lower-level employees assume additional responsibilities. At the same time, senior managers may need to better understand the details of the tasks and positions reporting to them, thus extending the financial implications of redesign beyond operational considerations. Clearly, workflow redesign should also be considered as a tool to implement management as well as process changes.

NOTES

[1] D'Alleyrand, Marc, *Workflow in Imaging Systems* (Silver Springs, MD: AIIM), 1992.

8

Justifying a Networked Imaging System

Marc R. D'Alleyrand, Ph.D.

8.1 INTRODUCTION: THE JUSTIFICATION PROCESS

Justifying the implementation of an imaging system is a critical activity. After all, the proposed system will change the organization's way of conducting its business, and this change involves a certain level of risk. It is therefore necessary that management be given all the facts so that it can evaluate objectively the risk/reward ratio in the context of other investment/savings opportunities. Consequently, a credible justification must:

- Demonstrate how the new system will improve the financial value of the organization.

- Present an accurate comparison of *all* costs and benefits between the existing and proposed environments through the project life cycle.

- Provide continuity and consistency in cost and benefits tracking between both systems.

- Use established methods for determining present and future costs, and present an acceptable evaluation of anticipated benefits, whether directly or indirectly quantifiable.

8.2 LIMITATIONS OF TRADITIONAL JUSTIFICATION MODELS

Traditional justification models using financial indicators such as return on invest-ment (ROI) and payback periods have been developed to justify productivity in mechanized production environments. Consequently, they do not always recognize *all* costs and benefits, and thus tend to distort the financial justification of most information transfer systems where tasks are not repetitive in nature.

These justification models are built on the theory that capital expenditures for the purpose of automating the workplace will result in an increase in productivity and/or cost reduction equivalent to a generation of revenues. Expenditures in information systems are seen, therefore, as an opportunity that can be ranked, from an investment point of view, with other business opportunities available to an organization, ranging from purchasing of securities to mergers and acquisitions.

The financial indicators traditionally used to evaluate the use of capital in these "investment" models, such as payback period and net present value (NPV), discussed later in this chapter, apply to models where costs and benefits of the system can be linked directly to the implementation of the information system. These models work well in environments where benefits such as increase in productivity and cost reduction are directly measurable. Their application to "operational" models, whose costs and benefits are not directly quantifiable, requires more sophisticated models, where a reasonable monetary value can be assigned to nonmeasurable benefits, which can then be incorporated in a financially acceptable model.

It is important to note that the reason a given financial model is ill-adapted to cost justify document imaging systems, is often because that particular model does not fully or accurately capture expenses and revenues, thus providing erroneous calculations for the corresponding financial indicators. It must also be understood that these indicators are the only accepted tools for the evaluation of financial investments. Consequently, the challenge of cost justification is to develop a methodology that ensures objective accounting of costs and benefits.

Such a methodology and the creation of accurate financial models is already a significant task in the justification of traditional office automation. It is even more so in the case of imaging, because imaging involves both a change of process and information products, the value of which may be unrelated to the project itself, thus making a reconciliation of costs a sometimes difficult exercise. In fact, as often happens in workflow redesign projects, cost justification might be driven more by the benefits derived from new functionalities than by direct cost savings and increases in productivity.

8.3 DEFINING A JUSTIFICATION MODEL FOR IMAGING APPLICATIONS

Regardless of the type of imaging network being proposed, the justification model should be consistent with the organization's accounting and budgeting procedures.

In that context, it will have to accommodate "hard" and "soft" figures that can be projected from the new way of doing business.

Determining the Cost Structure

The first priority is to harmonize the various cost structures of the operational units that will be affected by the imaging system. This harmonization must be done objectively, regardless of prior budgetary practices.

Integrating imaging with the existing network no doubt will involve department consolidations; therefore, establishing a true comparison of cost structure "before" and "after" often requires the consolidation of different budgets into a single cost or profit center. Table 8.1 gives a limited example of such a consolidation of two personnel budgets. The revised column facilitates the comparison between budgets.

This mapping of budget lines into a uniform format is an effective device to ensure consistent reporting, regardless of the individual budgets. In this way, *all* current and projected expenses through the life cycle of the project are included. A chart of accounts, which is a list of all valid types of expenses in an organization's budgeting system, can serve that purpose. A simple example of such a chart is given in Table 8.2, where entries for the budget of the present system (column 1) have been complemented by other items to provide the revised system (column 2) so that it can accommodate present and future categories of costs and revenues.

The use of such a chart reduces the possibility that current expenses are forgotten in the evaluation of savings, or that new costs are omitted because there is no corresponding entry in the current operational budget. As an example, the current budget does not account for maintenance, but the new system will require this type of expense. Once the new chart of accounts has been drawn, it should be used for all future budget planning activities. From now on, we will deal with consolidated budget projects.

Building a Financial Justification Model

Two financial models can be used to record the results of the justification:

1. A traditional model, which, starting from expected returns, looks at the investment value of the proposed project.

2. An opportunity model, which, starting from specified investment objectives, determines a ceiling of system costs, and from there provides the reference for a system configuration which will provide results consistent with the investment objectives.

Table 8.3 outlines the two models. The traditional model is easier to put in place, but its acceptance may require several attempts to meet financial objectives, because the cost of the configuration is determined only after a technical solution has been finalized.

In contrast, the opportunity model can provide a quick path to project approval, as it starts from an agreed upon set of financial objectives. As long as a technical

Table 8.1   Example of cost structure consolidation

COST STRUCTURE DEPARTMENT A (PRESENT BUDGET)			
OPERATING EXPENSES	*Present*	*Revised*	*Comments*
PERSONNEL			
Salaries Exempt	40,000	40,000	No change
Salaries Nonexempt	N/A	0	Add budget line
Overtime	N/A	0	Add budget line
Personnel Benefits	15,000	15,000	No change

COST STRUCTURE DEPARTMENT B (PRESENT BUDGET)			
OPERATING EXPENSES	*Present*	*Revised*	*Comments*
PERSONNEL			
Salaries Exempt	N/A	0	Add budget line
Salaries Nonexempt	60,000	60,000	No change
Overtime	25,000	25,000	No change
Personnel Benefits	35,000	35,000	No change

CONSOLIDATED COST STRUCTURE (PRESENT BUDGET)	
OPERATING EXPENSES	*Present*
PERSONNEL	
Salaries Exempt	60,000
Salaries Nonexempt	60,000
Overtime	25,000
Personnel Benefits	50,000

solution can be found that meets the maximum investment level, constraints there will be no roadblock to approval.

Cost Components of a Financial Justification

Both models require the determination of the same cost elements. The following shows how this is done with a traditional model. This is an example of the type of data that is often found in a cost justification. Their actual nature and amount should always be determined in concert with the organization's financial managers.

Increases in Revenues

Increases in revenues can come from several sources, as summarized in Table 8.4.

Table 8.2   Simplified chart of accounts

Operating Expenses	Present System (1)	Revised System (2)
PERSONNEL		
Salaries Exempt	X	X
Salaries Nonexempt	X	X
Overtime	X	X
Personnel Benefits	X	X
T&E		
Travel	X	X
Company Meetings	X	X
Meal Allowance	X	X
COMMUNICATIONS		
Telephone	X	X
Postage	X	X
Freight	X	X
SUPPLIES	X	X
OFFICE SERVICES		
Office Temporaries	X	X
Secretarial Pool	X	X
Messengers	X	X
PROFESSIONAL SERVICES		
Legal Fees		X
Consultant Fees		X
Other Fees		
RENTAL COSTS		
Rental of Premises		X
Rental of Computer Equipment		X
Rental of Office Equipment	X	X
UTILITIES	X	X
MAINTENANCE		
Equipment Maintenance		X
Facility Maintenance		X

Table 8.2 (continued)   Simplified chart of accounts

Operating Expenses	Present System (1)	Revised System (2)
CAPITAL EXPENDITURES		x
DEPRECIATION		x
REAL ESTATE TAXES		x
LEASEHOLD		x
TUITION AND SEMINARS	x	x
EXPENSE CREDITS		x
CORPORATE ALLOCATION	x	x

Table 8.3   Components in a document imaging system justification

Justification Element	Description	Formula
I. REVENUE INCREASES		
I.1 Cost Reduction	Reduction in current budget line items	Add
I.2 Enhanced Revenues	Increase in productivity or efficiency	Add
I.3 Intangible Benefits	Nondirectly quantifiable benefits and new business opportunities	Add
II. ANNUAL COSTS	All operating costs, as identified from the chart of accounts	Subtract
III. NET CASH FLOW	Balance between I.1 and I.2	Difference
Traditional Model		
IV. SYSTEM COSTS	Capital and operating costs associated with selected technical solution	Subtract previous difference
V. INVESTMENT VALUE	As required, IRR, ROI, and/or NPV	Compute investment value
Opportunity Model		
VI. MAXIMUM INVESTMENT	Value of investment that provides the same net cash flow	Compute investment value
VII. CORRESPONDING CONFIGURATION	Capital cost of the system that can be procured under the limit set by IV	Compute cost of system

Table 8.4   Sampling of cost savings opportunities

Categories of Costs	*Examples of Cost Elements*
Personnel Costs	Salaries
	Benefits
	Overtime
	Meal allowance
	Office space
	Travel
	Supervision
Rental of Premises	Reduction of file space
	Office maintenance
	Utilities
	Real estate taxes
Supplies	Office supplies
	Photocopying
Communications	Telephone and facsimile machine(s)
Other Business Expenses	Equipment maintenance
	Equipment rental
	Security

Note: Some of these savings may be offset by similar costs for the proposed system.

Cost Reduction   The first opportunity to increase revenues comes as a result of the reduction in operating costs. These costs should be established in the context of a workflow redesign process and include the following major elements:

- Personnel: These costs include not only the salaries and benefits of employees, but also the cost of initial training and ongoing education necessary to maintain their new skills.
- Rental of premises: Integrating imaging with an existing network often makes it possible to reduce the physical space necessary to an operation. However, no savings should be accounted for if the new system does not result in actual reduction of allocated lease expenses.
- Supplies: The elimination of paper documents and photocopying is often an underestimated source of reduced costs.
- Maintenance: This corresponds mainly to savings that result from the reduction of hardware maintenance costs, such as those following the elimination of a mainframe through downsizing, which is made possible by the adoption of the imaging system.

- Depreciation: This corresponds mainly to the disposition of equipment, usually less than five years old. Therefore, actual computation of depreciation savings may or may not occur depending on the age of the equipment being disposed.

Cost reduction assessments require an understanding of the relationship between direct costs (on which the system user has full control, such as personnel and supplies), and indirect costs (such as allocated rent and utilities charges, upon which the end user rarely has any authority).

Enhanced Revenues   While technically not exactly revenue items, the second opportunity for networked imaging systems to increase revenues results from the following:

- Increase in productivity: This increase is defined as the ability to produce more goods or services with the current level of staffing but reduce the time it takes to perform a given task. An increase in productivity is sometimes seen as a form of cost savings, but we recommend that, for practical reasons, it be considered as enhanced revenues.
- Increase in efficiency: This is defined as the ability to generate additional revenues by optimizing a process: Make the most of opportunities, do away with idle equipment waiting for information, etc. Quantification of an increase in efficiency should be done through computer simulation.

When assessing the benefits derived from a new way of doing business, be honest. Don't consider opportunities that in all likelihood won't occur. For example, don't count as savings the performance of tasks that should not be done in the first place—they do not support the organization's business objectives. Second, accept the fact that the new system may not be able to deliver the anticipated benefits. To account for this, prorate your expected benefits by your estimated probability of occurrence. For instance, if there is a consensus that the proposed system has a 10 percent chance of generating $100,000 of new revenues, you should probably quantify that benefit at $10,000.

The quantification of added revenues must be made in two steps:

1. Initial quantification: Use the same business assumptions as those used for the cost reduction component.
2. Additional quantification of "incremental" gains: This results from the new way of doing business in the context of new business conditions.

By following these steps, it is possible to isolate the improvement of the core business as a result of cost reduction from the business risks associated with a new opportunity. As a further safeguard against overly optimistic evaluation, you may want to consider additional benefits as the result of a separate business entity.

Intangible Benefits and Added Value   Added value and intangible benefits differ from cost reduction and enhanced revenue justification by the fact that they deal with projections of what the new "business order" will allow the organization to do. Be aware that in this area it is very easy to overestimate revenues. Among the major categories of intangible benefits and added value are:

- Internal Operation, which includes: improved access to information, reduction of response time, and lower cost of internal controls.
- External Operation, which includes: better product recognition and improved customer service.
- Development of new markets, the creation of different products, or better customer service.

Value-added assumptions must be scrutinized carefully whenever they relate to new services for which there is no prior company experience. Capabilities that the organization would not pay for in the first place should not be included.

Quantifying the financial value of added benefits, which usually requires additional research, should be done through sensitivity analysis. For instance, an assessment of the value of better customer service may be done through quantification of statistical studies of the relationship between sales and customer satisfaction.

Offsetting Costs

The costs incurred to adopt the document imaging system will offset the savings and benefits in three categories: initial setup costs, ongoing operating costs, and transition costs.

Initial Setup Costs   These include the cost of recabling and the replacement of network devices to upgrade for imaging operation. These costs *must* be included even if they can be considered as part of "basic network services" provided by an MIS department.

Initial costs cover expenditures beginning at the time when planning starts in earnest (sometimes referred to as "when the pencil hits the paper") and ending when the system is turned over to the client. These costs—summarized in Table 8.5— include:

- Project preparation up to the approval of an overall project budget.
- System procurement costs, including design, hardware and software acquisition, whether off-the-shelf or developed specifically for the project; integration and documentation.
- Implementation of the system, including the cost of changes in the organizational structure due to workflow reengineering.

It is *essential* that all initial costs be clearly identified, quantified, and discussed with the project financial advisor, so that the proper tax categorizations be made. For instance, a poorly planned or documented software development effort may be considered as an operating expense, rather than capital investment, thus impacting the outcome of the financial justification.

Table 8.5   Initial systems costs

Cost Categories	Description
1. PREPARATION COSTS	Covers all project-related expenditures from project approval to the issuance of procurement documents, including justification, planning, systems design, creation of bidding documents, and selection of vendors.
2. SYSTEMS COSTS	Refers to expenditures necessary to implement the project plan as per the justification model.
2.1 Hardware	Relates to the purchase of equipment and utility programs necessary to the implementation of the document imaging system.
2.2 Software	Refers to "unbundled" costs of off-the-shelf programs, distinct from the utilities provided with the hardware.
2.3 Development	Covers the cost of writing integration and application software necessary for a harmonious system operation, including implementation, testing, and documentation of all software.
2.4 Implementation	Corresponds to one-time expenditures associated with bringing the new system up to operational status, including facility improvement, delivery to the site, testing the new system as installed, expenses resulting from any workplace/workflow reengineering—moving, relocating, and rewiring of other operations, and training.

Ongoing Operating Costs   These costs should include any expenses that may be "inflicted" on other users who may have to upgrade their own installations to remain compatible with the new level of service.

Ongoing costs also are those associated with the actual operation of the proposed system. They can be classified in two categories: operating and long-term support (see Table 8.6).

- Operating costs include the recurring costs of day-to-day operation that can be easily predicted; and nonrecurring costs, such as parts replacement, which cannot be easily quantified. Do not underestimate the demand of an imaging system on telecommunication lines or on supplies, especially if growth in service is planned.

- Long-term support costs go beyond maintenance, which should be accounted for as part of the operating budget discussed above. They include expenditures that are necessary to the long-term survival of the system, but that do not result

Table 8.6   Ongoing costs

Cost Categories	Description
1. OPERATING COSTS	
1.1. Recurring	
1.1.1. Personnel	Personnel directly affected by the system
1.1.2. Communications	Cost of use and rental of telephone lines
1.1.3. Supplies	Includes optical media and tapes
1.1.4. Office Services	Cost of external personnel support
1.1.5. Rental of Premises	Monthly cost of premises
1.1.6. Rental of Equipment	Lease/rental equipment
1.1.7. Utilities	Utilities to run the system
1.1.8. Equipment Maintenance	Cost of hardware/software maintenance
1.1.9. Facilities Maintenance	Cleaning and other similar services
1.1.10. Depreciation	Associated with capital expenditures
1.1.11. Real Estate Taxes	Pass-along charge for leased premises
1.2. Nonrecurring Costs	
1.2.1. Installation	Freight and moving costs
1.2.2. Repairs	Estimated cost of on-call repairs
1.2.3. Reserve	Estimated cost of incidental expenses
1.2.4. Site Visits	Includes travel to evaluate system
2. LONG-TERM SUPPORT	
2.1. Upgrade	Estimated over the life of the system
2.2. Retraining	Estimated over the life of the system

in increased performance or benefits such as periodic upgrades that may involve temporary disruption of service or staff retraining to maintain skills necessary to keep the new system running.

Such costs, even though they may not be directly linked to the proper functioning of the proposed system, should at least be quantified and assessed.

You may want to replace the projection of future costs with a sensitivity analysis of the aggregate of all your other costs. If that analysis shows a very thin margin for error, it may indicate a hidden problem in the overall project. Here again, your financial advisor should provide guidance.

Transition Costs   Transition costs include not only conversion, but retraining of staff, and, in the case of reduction in work force, costs associated with lay-offs, even if these costs are charged to a separate budget.

Transition costs cover one-time expenditures to bring the existing environment into the proposed system. They differ from nonrecurring costs by the fact that they

Table 8.7   Transition costs

Cost Categories	Description
1. CONSULTING	Surveys, design, training
2. CONVERSION	Service bureaus or staff, supplies and equipment directly assigned to conversion, as opposed to day-to-day operation
3. TRAINING	For systems operation and new procedures
4. RESTAFFING	Covers the cost of staff reallocation, including cost of termination

essentially represent staff and services expenses rather than equipment. As such, they are somewhat discretionary. The four major sources of transition costs are consulting, conversion, training, and restaffing (see Table 8.7).

- Consulting covers the cost of consultants retained to design the proposed system, write specifications, and other similar activities. Depending on the conditions, these costs may be bundled with the cost of hardware.

- Conversion costs represent the costs associated with the change of database and medium. Depending on the conversion method (in-house vs. service bureau) and the volume of files to be converted (backfiles vs. new files), these costs will fluctuate markedly.

- Training associated with the new system is composed of two parts: One is the cost of time spent by company personnel on learning new skills, which would otherwise have been spent on actual work. The second part relates to the training in new procedures. It should be noted that vendor training will seldom deal with issues other than system startup, thus requiring additional expenses. One way of estimating any additional "hidden" training expenses is to compute the cost of partially idle staff during the transition period from installation to full operation, often called the "ramp-up" period.

- Restaffing, when significant reengineering is involved, is a combination of retraining and restaffing, transfers, lay-offs, and new hires. These costs are usually determined through formulas, which are best handled by human resources personnel once the technical solution has been finalized.

Depending on the nature of the project and applicable tax laws, some of these costs may be treated as operating costs or capital investments. Again, guidance on this should come from your financial advisor.

8.4   LIFE-CYCLE JUSTIFICATION

Expenditures and the benefits derived from the new system obviously do not occur all at once. Because of the money value of time, when each of them occurs may

Table 8.8   Timing of costs and benefits

Cost/Benefits Categories	Initial	Ongoing	Transition
1. COSTS			
Preparation	x		
Systems	x	x	x
Operating		x	x
Long-Term Support		x	
Transition			x
2. BENEFITS			
Cost Reduction		x	
Enhanced Revenues		x	
Intangible Benefits		x	

strongly influence the net cash flow generated by the system. Table 8.8 shows a simplified time classification for the major benefits and expenses.

Project Justification and Project Survival

The approval of a project initially does not guarantee continued support throughout its life cycle. In fact, continued support cannot be dissociated from an organization's budget cycle. Technological investments, which may have been initially attractive, subsequently may be challenged under future adverse budgetary conditions before they have had the opportunity to prove themselves. Consequently, it is imperative that the project be organized so that its long-term survival is insulated from the vagaries of funding levels. The larger the project, the more important this concern. Its resolution implies a modular project development approach, with each module designed to achieve a specific autonomous goal that is achievable within a budget cycle.

Under these conditions, it is possible to implement a "leap-and-hold" strategy, where the survival of an operational module is not at the mercy of the support of follow-up modules.

8.5   EXAMPLES OF COST JUSTIFICATION ACTIVITIES

To credibly justify the implementation of a document imaging system, three components must be detailed:

1. Operational, which compares procedures and workflows between the present and proposed system.

2. Technical, which specifies the equipment and other considerations that are necessary to support the system.

3. Financial, which provides the economic rationale for adopting the proposed system.

It is the responsibility of the project manager to ensure that all three components are developed in harmony. In particular, the project manager must see to:

- The early creation of a cohesive project team composed of users, financial advisors, and technical experts.
- The preparation and implementation of a project plan that is endorsed by the project team.
- The continued support from senior management for the project as a whole.

Management will not support a project that does not demonstrate congruence with the organization's operational and financial objectives. To engage this support, it is a good idea to:

- Define the document imaging application in terms of scope, needs, and expected results.
- Identify an initial project team composed of individuals familiar with the current operation, with the financial environment, and with document imaging technologies.
- Conduct an initial assessment of the magnitude of the project to identify potential areas of cost savings and productivity increases, as well as operational and other benefits.
- After discussion with the advisory team, prepare a summary of findings for submission to management that outlines issues, technical solution, costs-benefits analysis, and a preliminary project plan and budget.

Once management support has been secured and the project budget has been approved, repeat the previous steps in greater depth. Specifically:

- Refine the project scope to identify primary and secondary organizational units that are directly (primary) and indirectly (secondary) affected by the project.
- Reassemble and/or enlarge the project team, whose members are able to dedicate the time called for in the preliminary project budget. Part of the project team should be a group specifically responsible for any workflow reengineering.
- Review initial assessments to obtain precise operational data for accurate quantification of costs and benefits. Use any available surveys and current budgets, supplemented by industry statistics. When precise data do not exist or may not be directly available, develop with the help of the financial advisors indirect quantification methods.

- On a periodic basis, meet with the project team to ensure that the project design meets users' operational requirements, that the proposed solution is technically feasible, and that the cost and benefits of the proposed system are identified and quantified in a satisfactory manner. At the same time, keep management informed of progress, using the preliminary project plan as a benchmark.

- Translate costs and benefits into financial terms compatible with organizational policies and prepare a detailed project justification.

Chronology of the Justification Process

Once approval in principle has been granted by management, it is time to develop a practical chronology for the justification process. Such a chronology is outlined below and summarized in Table 8.9.

Project Charter

A project charter establishes the project scope, boundaries, and operational and financial expectations of the project. It identifies the departments involved and tasks or functions that are the targets of the project. This must be done with the concurrence and endorsement of senior management. An example of a project charter is given in Figure 8.1.

Application Specification

Application specification expands the project charter to provide operational requirements. It is a relatively short document, which includes:

- statement of objectives
- outline of constraints
- outline of project budget
- timetable and milestones

This document, which should be reviewed and endorsed by all parties involved, should be detailed enough to serve as a basis for policy and strategic decisions by the project team.

Vital Statistics Surveys

Many of these statistics may already have been collected and analyzed for the purpose of workflow redesign. They relate to operating data in each department concerned, including:

Table 8.9   Summary of project chronology

Activities	Purpose	Responsibilities
I. Application Specifications	Sets project scope and boundaries	Project Manager; Endorsement by Senior Management
II. Project Charter	Provides the project plan of action	Project Manager; Endorsement by Operating Units
II.1. Statement of Objectives	Defines result targets	Operating Units
II.2. Technical Solution	Defines technical process and system architecture	Technical Advisor
II.3. Project Budget	Defines the project financial envelope	Financial Advisor
II.4. Timetable	Specifies milestones	Project Manager
III. Collection of Statistics		
III.1. Volume Surveys	Determination of equipment needs	Operating Units
III.2. Workflow Surveys	Determination of personnel savings	Project Manager and Operating Units
III.3. Operating Budget	Cost savings	Financial Advisor
III.4. Organizational Charts	Workflow reengineering	Project Manager
III.5. Floor Plans	Space utilization	Project Manager and Operating Units
III.6. Equipment List	Determination of equipment needs	Operating Units and Technical Advisor
III.7. Staffing Rosters and Job Descriptions	Reorganization	Project Manager and Personnel
IV. Project Costing	Costing of technical project implementation	Project Manager and Technical Advisor
V. Cost-Benefit Analysis	Determination of financial indicators	Project Manager and Financial Advisor
VI. Preparation of Justification Document	Project approval	Project Team

- Data necessary for sizing the project: workload and volume of documents handled, workflow diagrams and analysis, and operating budgets for all departments concerned
- Data necessary for operational justification: organizational charts, floor plans, and equipment lists
- Data necessary for planning the system: staffing rosters and job descriptions

Samples of simple forms that can be used to collect data on workload, workflow, and equipment are shown in Figures 8.2, 8.3, and 8.4. These sample forms should be expanded or modified to reflect local requirements.

DOCUMENT IMAGING SYSTEM PROJECT CHARTER	
Object	*Comments*
1. Purpose of the Project	a) Reduce the cost of transaction processing in the Accounts Payable area.
	b) Improve relations with our suppliers.
	c) Improve cash management effectiveness.
2. Scope	Link Purchasing, Accounts Payable, and Receiving through an image database for prompt expediting of transactions.
3. Departments Concerned	Finance, Purchasing, Receiving, Personnel, Facilities
4. Expected Results	Payment based on purchase order within 24 hours after approval of material receipt.
5. Expected Performance	Return on investment: 35% Time frame: 6 months Maximum budget: $150.00

Figure 8.1   Sample of project charter

Determination of Costs and Benefits

To determine costs and benefits over the life of the project you will need to quantify the various financial factors in a uniform manner.

Establishing a Financial Frame of Reference

The financial frame of reference provides the infrastructure for the cost comparison. It will usually involve:

- Securing the organization's account chart and the budgets of all departments concerned with the project, as discussed previously.
- Establishing a common list of accounts for all these departments.
- Combining all budgets into one consolidated budget.
- Reconciling cost accounting methods between all departments, including handling of corporate allocations and other charges.

Determining Technical Costs and Benefits

Technical cost elements include items such as leasehold improvement, hardware, software, and conversion costs. They should then be tabulated for each year of the project life cycle to obtain:

WORKLOAD SURVEY FORM: _____ of____				
WORKSTATION NAME: _____				
Document Title	*Peak Volume*	*Min. Volume*	*Average*	*Proc. Time*
1				
2				
3				
4				
5				
6				
7				
8				
9				
10				
COMMENTS:				
REVIEWED BY: DATE:				

Figure 8.2   Sample of workload survey form

- capital investment
- operating profits or loss for that year as a result of the proposed system

A methodology for computing these costs is given below, and Table 8.10 shows the results of these activities for a hypothetical case where two successive capital investments ($100,000 at initiation of project and $25,000 the following year) generated a total operating profit of $339,000 over ten years.

Once the operating profits have been established, you can compute the appropriate financial indicators, described in detail at the end of this chapter. For this you will need to:

- Expand your operating profits table to show annual depreciation, taxes, net income, and cash flows.
- Compute the financial indicators required by the justification.

Manually, the computation of financial indicators is a tedious process. It is, therefore, recommended that either a financial electronic calculator or computerized spreadsheet program be used; or, even better, ask your financial advisor to help once you have determined the annual accumulated cash flows.

Table 8.11 gives an example of such a schedule, based on the operating profit table. In this example, the computation gives an internal rate of return (IRR) of 52 percent, and a payback period of approximately two years, results which are typical of a good imaging application.

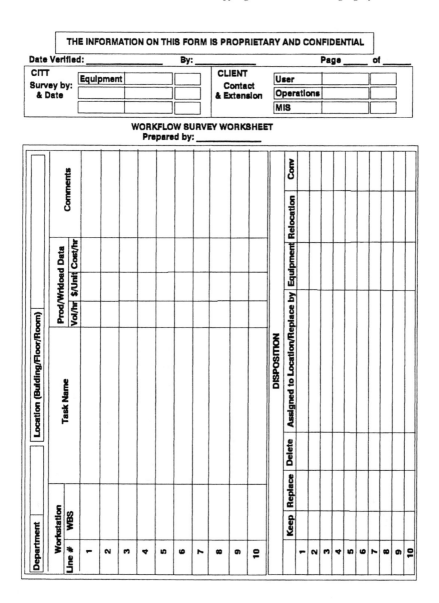

Figure 8.3   Sample of workflow survey form

Preparation of the Justification Document

Once the financial indicators have been computed and found to be in line with the organization's guidelines for capital investments, the formal justification document can be prepared. Depending on the organization's practices, the justification may be a simple document, which accompanies the project charter with a detailed cash flow analysis.

THE INFORMATION ON THIS FORM IS PROPRIETARY AND CONFIDENTIAL

Date Verified: _____ By: _____ Page _____ of _____

CITT Survey by: & Date — Equipment

CLIENT Contact & Extension — User / Operations / MIS

EQUIPMENT SURVEY
Prepared by: _____

Department | Location (Building/Floor/Room) | Workstation Ref. # | Function | Floor Ref. | Description Name/Model | Purchase Price | Book Value | Connectivity Requirements

1 2 3 4 5 6 7 8 9 10

DISPOSITION | Keep | Replace | Assigned to Location/Replace by | Discard | Cost Equ. | Cost Reloc | Salvage

1 2 3 4 5 6 7 8 9 10

Figure 8.4   Sample of equipment survey form

8.6   METHODOLOGY FOR SELECTION OF NETWORK DOCUMENT IMAGING APPLICATIONS IN A COMPETITIVE ENVIRONMENT

The plan to image enable an existing network or install an entirely new installation often must compete for funding with other projects. To avoid fruitless proposal

Table 8.10   Example of a cost/benefit justification table

Year	Capital	Operating Profit/(Loss)
0	($100.00)	
1	($25.00)	$15.00
2		$25.00
3		$15.00
4		$30.00
5		$33.00
6		$36.03
7		$39.90
8		$43.90
9		$48.30
10		$53.10
TOTAL	($125.00)	$339.60

writing, it is imperative to select early on in the project the application that has the highest probability of attracting management support.

A quick determination of the most "marketable" application can be achieved by analyzing how well the contemplated application matches a profile of the organization's objectives. The assessment begins by recognizing those objectives that are of the greatest concern. For instance:

- reduction of operating costs
- increase in productivity
- generation of strategic benefits
- functional reorganization

Obviously, the relative importance to the organization of these objectives will change from time to time according to economic and operational imperatives. However, once you have identified objectives of interest, you can rank them in order of importance to the organization at the time of justification. You can also assign a weight that reflects the relevance of each application being considered for each individual objective. The combination of ranking and weights then can be used to select from among competing applications the ones that most closely match organizational requirements at the time. A simple weighing method, defined in Table 8.12, shows how such an analysis can be conducted. In this example, three competing applications are being compared.

Table 8.11   Example of capital project schedule

Year	Capital	Operating Profit/(Loss)	Depreciation	Cash Flow	Tax @ 50%	Net Income	Depreciation	Net Cash Flow	Accumulated Cash Flow (8)
(0)	(1)	(2)	(3)	(3)=(2)+(1)	(4)=-.5*(3)	(5)=(3)+(4)	(6)=(3)	(7)=(5)+(6)	
0	($100.00)			($100.00)	$50.00	($50.00)	$0.00	($50.00)	($50.00)
1	($25.00)	$15.00	$20.00	($10.00)	$5.00	($5.00)	$20.00	$15.00	($35.00)
2		$25.00	$25.00	$25.00	($12.50)	$12.50	$25.00	$37.50	$2.50
3		$15.00	$25.00	$15.00	($7.50)	$7.50	$25.00	$32.50	$35.00
4		$30.00	$25.00	$30.00	($15.00)	$15.00	$25.00	$40.00	$75.00
5		$33.00	$25.00	$33.00	($16.50)	$16.50	$25.00	$41.50	$116.50
6		$36.30	$5.00	$36.30	($18.20)	$18.20	$5.00	$23.20	$139.70
7		$39.90		$39.90	($20.00)	$20.00	$0.00	$20.00	$159.60
8		$43.90		$43.90	($22.00)	$22.00	$0.00	$22.00	$181.60
9		$48.30		$48.30	($24.20)	$24.20	$0.00	$24.20	$205.70
10		$53.10		$53.10	($26.60)	$26.60	$0.00	$26.60	$232.30
TOTAL	($125.00)	$339.60	$125.00	$214.60	($107.30)	$107.30	$125.00	$232.30	
	IRR = 52%				NPV = $296.40				Payback = 2 years

Ranking Method

The ranking method used in Table 8.12 can be adapted to other circumstances. It is organized as follows:

1. Set up a table and list vertically the objectives to be met; list horizontally the competing applications.

2. Assign to each objective a factor from 1 (lowest) to 4 (highest), which reflects its present importance to management at the time. In this example, cost reduction has the highest priority, strategic value the lowest.

3. Assign, for each imaging project under consideration, a numerical value for each of these objectives to represent the relevance of the project to the particular objective. In this example, Application 1 has little bearing on reorganization, but a high impact on cost reduction.

Table 8.12   Preliminary ranking of imaging applications

		Application 1		Application 2		Application 3	
	Weight	*Rank*	*Value*	*Rank*	*Value*	*Rank*	*Value*
Cost Reduction	4	4	16	1	4	2	8
Productivity Increase	3	3	9	2	6	4	12
Strategic Benefits	1	2	2	3	3	3	3
Reorganization	2	1	2	4	8	1	2
TOTAL			29		21		25

4. Compute a relative value to the organization of each objective for a given application by multiplying the objective weight by its corresponding ranking factor for that application.

5. Add all the values for each application on the total line. The highest total identifies the imaging application that most closely matches organizational objectives, and therefore—everything else being equal—the highest chance of being accepted by management. In this example, Application 2 has the highest score and should be given first priority for the justification effort.

8.7   CONCLUSION

Cost justifying an imaging system should not be considered as a trivial exercise. The implementation of such systems may be irreversible; therefore, cost justification must be as objective as possible. The challenge will be to ensure that any cost comparison to existing systems bears on similar factors, or, if they do not, that there is a credible methodology in place to yield a reasonable assumption of the magnitude of costs involved.

The successful justification begins with the establishment of compatible financial models between the existing and proposed operations and not by the selection of an attractive technical solution.

9

Image-LAN Enabling and Integrating LAN-Based Imaging Systems with Existing Mainframe Applications

Peter Dolshun

Sigma Imaging Systems

Marc R. D'Alleyrand, Ph.D.

9.1 INTRODUCTION

In most systems, the issues of data ownership, usage, and custody are at the heart of information flow strategy decisions. The resolution of these issues supplies the rationale for funding existing operations, the cost justification of new projects, and, more importantly perhaps, for the political support to achieve change. In that respect, workflow redesign focuses not only on operational perspectives, such as transaction volumes and database integrity, but also on the identification of access rights. In particular, consolidation of tasks is one of the many processes where the issue of data ownership must be well understood.

For instance, does an accounting department have "ownership" of the data that go into a general ledger because that department is the only one empowered to make entries in accounting records? Conversely, does this department then only have custody of the supporting documents because they do not generate them? And does a budgeting department have ownership of reports that they prepared from accounting data, when, through network and dynamic data exchange linkage between programs, the underlying figures can be automatically adjusted and replaced in the report itself, possibly not only invalidating earlier analysis, but creating discrepancies between data and conclusions without the knowledge of the reporting party?

In earlier data systems, such issues could be easily resolved by providing different access rights to different users, assuming for instance, that "writing" privileges are equivalent to ownership. This simple approach might resolve the ownership issue for initial entries, but it does not settle the case of derivative documents, generated as composites from different sources. From that standpoint, image enabling an existing network is a complex operation, because, at the same time that the system brings together data and images, it merges the two hierarchies of data ownership based on automated and manual systems.

The difficulties in assigning responsibilities for data ownership and access are exacerbated when dealing with the integration of a mainframe operation with an imaging network. Here, however, even though the technical obstacles may be significant, they are predictable and well defined. In fact, they may be considered minor when compared with the issue of potential loss of total control over database and system architecture resulting from the integration of the two systems.

This section describes the issues to be addressed in managing the integration of a distributed LAN-based imaging system with a mainframe-based transaction processing application. Making the proper selection of an implementation approach has deep-rooted strategic implications that can save (or lose) a substantial investment in scarce capital, personnel, and other corporate resources already invested in the mainframe environment. Doubtless, an LAN-based imaging integration *can* yield a more flexible, better performing, and more cost-effective operation than a centralized mainframe imaging application, but final benefits depend on the quality of the integration effort.

Mainframe application design and maintenance methodologies are well known; however, the changes necessary to integrate such applications with an LAN-based, client-server application may prove to be somewhat of a challenge. This chapter focuses on some of the details that must be faced in order to reduce the difficulty associated with the planning and implementation of the integration.

9.2   CURRENT TRENDS AND CHALLENGES

Integrating existing mainframe systems with newer LAN and workstation technologies goes hand-in-hand with the migration of small mainframe-based applications toward less expensive and more user friendly local area network departmental systems. LAN-based systems are already cost-effective, and reductions or outright freezes on new mainframe project budgets has further accelerated this movement.

Thus, the interest in distributed LAN-based imaging systems and their associated integration tools is also extremely intense.

Technological problems still exist that prevent the conversion of very large-scale, high-volume transaction processing applications to a local area network environment. This will be a mainframe stronghold for a long time to come, especially in the largest corporate installations. Mature, sophisticated mainframe platforms still excel in areas of centralized control of massive data stores and high availability for hundreds or thousands of simultaneous users. So, while the desire is there to move in the direction of inexpensive, distributed PC platforms, the conversion of large applications that must support hundreds of users will take place only when the LAN environment is as reliable, secure, and as easily controlled as the mainframe side of the shop. But, more powerful hardware and more production-capable software (system operating software, network operating systems, and applications) are now available, and client-server software development techniques are maturing, so the trend to resist new mainframe development will continue in parallel with the growth of networked workstation systems.

In addition, risks associated with major changes to core business applications are a major deterrent to decentralization, unless there are overriding strategic or economic considerations. Furthermore, the political issues associated with loss of status in MIS departments as a result of potential large-scale downsizing, may create obstacles in securing investments for systems that may ultimately migrate from the mainframe.

Under these conditions, it may be risky to attempt the integration of imaging systems directly with host applications, as it may actually result in a destabilization of mission critical transaction processing operations. The use of LAN-based imaging solutions does not present these difficulties and provides a perfect fit for this kind of environment. Existing applications do not have to be impacted at all in order to take advantage of today's latest document imaging systems technologies and the associated benefits. MIS management can take a low-risk strategy by providing a more flexible, transparent "add-on" solution with an LAN-based imaging system. By carefully defining the integration requirements, the existing base of mainframe applications (which may work perfectly well) requires very few changes.

For some companies with a heavy investment in mainframe applications, imaging implemented on workstations may also be their first exposure to a large-scale LAN implementation that does not require that they first redesign their existing operation. In fact, the resulting installation of the LAN/WAN/workstation facilities allows the enterprise to initially take advantage of imaging capabilities and simultaneously open the door to new application possibilities. In this way the imaging system, which typically has a comparatively short payback period, justifies its existence and also paves the way for a more powerful future; and, through workflow redesign, it enhances the benefits of the new networked infrastructure.

9.3   IMPACT ON TRADITIONAL TRANSACTION PROCESSING OPERATIONS

Preserving existing systems during the transition to LAN-based imaging systems also benefits the user community, because it reduces the extent of workforce retraining. In many LAN-based image-enabling applications, the imaging system can coexist with the mainframe to support its simplest function: replacement of paper with the automatically controlled delivery of electronic document images.

Another advantage of the adoption of LAN-based imaging as opposed to mainframe installation is the fact that, typically, very few companies would install imaging systems throughout an organization without preliminary testing. Instead, small pilots are installed for evaluation and expanded if successful. This "scaling up" approach, which can be very expensive for centralized, mainframe-based systems, is much easier to put in place with an LAN installation, as it can be more easily scaled up to accommodate high production volumes by simply configuring additional servers and workstations as needed.

The impact of an imaging system installation will be felt throughout the enterprise; therefore, comprehensive, long-term planning is essential to prevent costly mistakes later on. For example, the lack of standardization across departmental implementations will create communications problems once the desire to access document images throughout the company is realized.

The software chosen must be able to handle protocol and data format conversions. Lack of a standard platform also leads to complex interoperability issues (which the enterprise must be willing to support). Certainly, interoperability between different systems is feasible, but it is advisable to keep the number of different platforms to a minimum to reduce the cost of maintaining heterogeneous installations.

It may take years to go from planning to implementation of a successful large-scale imaging operation; therefore, the challenges should not be underestimated. It is worthwhile to attempt a simplified initial implementation strategy in order to ensure early success. Most imaging systems tend to be analyzed and designed in terms of departmental business requirements, which makes sense, because individual departments are usually divided by lines of business, and each is held accountable for its productivity.

Each department processes a well-defined subset of the organization's total transaction workload. Under these conditions, departmental users are best able to assess how the introduction of a new imaging technology will affect their day-to-day operations, and their needs must be the major guidelines for proper design and installation of the new systems. Positive user feedback early in the design and evaluation phase, as with any application, is crucial for initial acceptance.

9.4 MOVING FROM LOW- TO HIGH-VOLUME TRANSACTION PROCESSING

Although the applications may be identical, low- and high-volume processing present structural differences, an important concept that is explained throughout this section.

Low-Volume Transaction Processing

The type of operation that characterizes low-volume processing, such as would be found in a typical pilot installation, can be described in the following manner:

- The tasks are not mission critical.
- The system is often used in a departmental environment.
- The tasks performed relate to one type of work.
- These tasks are self-contained, and involve only a few people whose skills may be sufficient to run the application without additional training.
- The operation is well insulated from the rest of the organization and requires minimal external support.

These low-volume operations are often conceived as proof-of-concept rather than as part of an integrated design, and thus have few, or no interface with the rest of the organization or dependencies on other external systems. Consequently, they may be difficult to expand or use elsewhere, as the system's functions may be too specialized or restrictive.

High-Volume Transaction Processing

By contrast, high-volume transaction systems are designed to operate on a company-wide basis. Their characteristics include:

- Ability to simultaneously handle many complex and different transaction types.
- Workstations are geographically dispersed.
- Efficient use of imaging requires a complex image data storage hierarchy, which itself may be distributed.
- The system reaches almost all departments in the organization, regardless of responsibilities.
- Installation and maintenance of the enterprise system requires training and acquisition of new technical skills for a significant portion of the staff.

- The imaging system is based on a combination of core processing capabilities with standard interface and custom applications to accommodate departmental needs.
- The system is tightly integrated with existing internal and external installations.

Matching Imaging System Features with Mainframe Requirements

Choosing the imaging system that matches a given mainframe-based installation depends on the nature of functions being supported. The recognition of transaction types and processing requirements is essential to that determination, because the performance of imaging applications as implemented will depend on constraints defined by the type of transaction being processed.

Some transactions are relatively simple (single-step data entry); others can be very complex (multiple steps, multiple departments completing different portions of the entire transactions at different times). Because of this, target operator processing rates may be different for each step in the workflow. The timing requirements of the mainframe system being integrated (batch vs. on-line, multiple data capture and processing cycles, reporting and audit trail processing dependencies, batch and backup processing windows) are other major factors to consider. One size of imaging system may not fit all unless it is flexible enough to accommodate all of the organization's processing needs.

During the design and planning stages, transaction profiles should be examined and understood in terms of their image throughput needs. Different departments will have unique configuration requirements.

Examples of Transaction Types and Processing

Imaging network requirements are dependent on the response time necessary to support the business process and the volume of data to be retained on line, as exemplified in Table 9.1. Typical examples are as follows:

- Applications requiring high-volume local server capacity, fast image retrieval and display are characteristic of: customer service telephone inquiries, priority insurance claims processing (i.e., Medicare claims processing), single-step (simple), "heads-down" data entry.
- Applications requiring access to multiple mainframe applications, and for which image display performance is still very important, including: multistep (complex) data entry, health care claims processing, transaction correction and reprocessing applications.
- Applications where fast image display is not critical, but workstation capacity and power are needed to access multiple mainframe and PC applications (such as spreadsheets and word processors) at the same time. These include:

Table 9.1   Processes volume and speed requirements

	Server Capacity	*Retrieval Speed*	*Display Speed*
Telephone Inquiries	High	High	High
Insurance Claims	Medium	Medium (if under workflow control)	Medium
Correspondence	Low	Low	Low

automobile insurance claim processing, insurance policy and contract underwriting, customer service correspondence processing, auditing.

At the same time, mainframe application access requirements will vary. Heads-down data entry applications typically require a single host session. Complex transactions may require access to many host applications and databases simultaneously in order to resolve a complex customer service inquiry, for example.

Since document images usually participate as information stores in many different kinds of organizational transactions, the new system must integrate and optimize interdepartmental workflows and routing capabilities, often under different retrieval operating conditions. The software should be configurable to minimize customizing programming to enable these features, because the underlying transactions, performance requirements, and organizations can change frequently, regardless of the complexity of the underlying business requirements.

Measuring Results

In any image-enabling project, the measure of its success, let alone its justification, will be increase in user productivity, quantified for instance by operator's response time. The speed at which a randomly selected document image can be retrieved from anywhere in the organization will range from slow transaction response requirements (e.g., overnight audit project) to fast (e.g., customer service telephone inquiries requiring document verification).

Performance depends on a variety of factors, the most important of which is probably the design of document storage hierarchy, which is the automatic staging of work in anticipation of its retrieval by the operator in order to minimize response time. The following discusses some of these aspects from the mainframe perspective.

Document Image Caching, Routing, and Staging in a High-Volume Environment

Caching of work in progress is the most effective method to increase productivity. Assuming that a hierarchy of storage has been adopted, the main design issue becomes the definition of a document allocation scheme on local servers for departmental processing.

Table 9.2   Example of processing stream in an image-enabled operation

1. **Document Receipt:** Documents are received at the mail room. They are opened, date/time stamped, and sorted by line of business.

2. **Preparation:** Line of Business documents are prepped (staples are removed, tears are repaired, etc.) and batched (counted and assigned control numbers).

3. **Document Capture:** Documents are processed with high-speed scanners, which create digitized images. In the LAN-based configuration, each scanner is controlled by its own CPU (a PC) with some hard disk storage to hold the scanned images. As each document is scanned, attributes can be assigned automatically by the scanner software. These attributes (an incremented control number, a date and time stamp, or from a bar code found on the paper document) can be set manually by the operator, or automatically.

4. **Quality Control:** The scanner controllers, attached to the LAN with network adapters, can release the document images into the network and route them to an appropriate quality control workstation, which, in case of error, can delete the rejected document and send a message to the holder of the paper original to rescan it.

5. **Distribution:** Once the images have passed the quality control sep, they are routed to their destination, determined by the attributes of each document. The imaging system software can be configured to always send one copy of each document to servers attached to optical storage devices (to accommodate archival requirements) and simultaneously send another copy to the appropriate departmental servers as work in progress.

6. **Mainframe Monitoring and Control of Image Placement:** The mainframe application does not need to know where the images are stored. Workflow software and the document database will maintain a directory of scanned documents, which may span several destination servers, established to hold specific subsets of work types known to the mainframe applications. The same workflow software will usually control the image placement throughout its life cycle and control the local server cache size, according to the number of devices attached and the volume of work being processed, thereby optimizing resources to ensure peak productivity.

In most high-volume installations, documents to be processed are received in a central mail room and sorted by line of business. In image-enabled installations, the documents are then scanned at one or more locations (usually close to the mail room operations). A typical sequence of events looks like the one displayed in Table 9.2.

Staging document images from archival storage complements the caching of newly scanned work. Response time for archive retrieval (from optical disk jukeboxes), whether channel-attached to the mainframe or server-attached on the LAN, takes anywhere from a few seconds to several minutes; a platter mount for an off-site disk not resident in a jukebox may require an overnight delay. The way to maximize productivity is to minimize this response time through intelligent staging to hard disks on local servers. The definition and anticipation of the data is required to complete a transaction before the operator attempts to begin processing. This includes the document image, of course, but it also implies that the images are stored where the work is to be processed. How can this be done?

Given the wide variety of individual transaction types that an enterprise must execute, it is usually organized along lines of processing work and further subdivided by lines of business. For example, a health insurance carrier must divide the claims processing area into data entry, suspension processing, audit, and customer service departments. Within these, each department is split further by type of claim (medical, dental, prescription, etc.). This is usually done because each resulting division (dental data entry, for example) may require specialized operator skill sets for transaction completion. Mainframe application operators are usually aggregated locally along these lines.

For instance, distributed systems must be configured to contain locally all the data required to process specialized transactions. Since the departmental organization is well defined in terms of the type of work it performs, document images with the corresponding attributes can be placed electronically (under system control) where and when they are needed.

Once work is staged and processed, it must be deleted to provide space for new images. This may be done immediately after the transaction has been acknowledged as completed. For data entry operations, the decision is simple: Delete the document image immediately after keying and verification is completed; the imaging system can perform this automatically. The deletion decision can also depend upon the status of the transaction as determined by the mainframe application, in which case, the application must somehow communicate with the local departmental system and indicate that it is safe to delete a document. This is usually true of multistep transactions where the document image must stay resident until the mainframe application finalizes the unit of work. Productivity would be substantially slower if operators had to constantly mount optical disks for document image retrievals from the archive only. Local caching within departmental systems is the way to maximize throughput. Alternatively, a time-triggered process executing on the server can delete image objects based on a simplified criterion, such as last referenced date.

The management of this staging and deletion process is not as difficult as this description first seems. Normal transaction processing generally requires that the oldest work has priority and must be processed first. Many operations require that the day's receipts must be processed in a predetermined time interval in order to prevent a backlog.

9.5 PRODUCTIVITY FACTORS

Productivity increases associated with image-enabled mainframe applications depend on user acceptance of distributed imaging systems, as well as on technical parameters.

Human Factors

Human factors begin with the commitment from the top down to the use of the new system to enhance long-term business objectives. Failure to do so prevents efficient communication between users and systems planners, and places obstacles in the path of management support. This may have disastrous consequences because, like an airplane taking off, there is a point-of-no-return in the development cycle of an image-enabled system.

Technical Factors

Productivity is a prime user acceptance criterion driven not only by savings and profit motives, but also by industry regulations and legislative directives. The new imaging system must provide enhanced productivity in order to be considered a success. Transaction processing cycles must be at least as short and quick as existing applications. Given the large storage requirements for document images, this is an extremely complex technical challenge: how to rapidly present document images to terminal operators. This is accomplished through the use of operator workstations configured with enough memory and processing power to enable the caching of images at the workstations. Typically, the minimum configuration is a 386SX-class machine loaded with a minimum of 8MB RAM, but 486-class machines loaded with 16MB or more will become common as the cost of this hardware continues to decrease.

High-performance image presentation is much more difficult to support from a centralized mainframe application. Expensive mainframe DASD must be used, CPU cycles are much more costly, and network bandwidth is typically optimized to transmit short bursts of small 3270 data packets. By distributing the image-handling application over LAN servers and intelligent workstations, image services can be delivered in "parallel processing" fashion. Departmental installations can be individually configured and tuned according to the type of transaction being processed locally. Mainframe performance degradation is avoided as the demand for image storage and throughput increases. The aggregate physical imaging system hardware foundation is cheaper to scale-up with LAN-based implementations, and avoids these kinds of bottlenecks.

9.6   ISSUES IN IMPLEMENTING IMAGE ENABLING

Workflow Control

A transaction's complexity determines the corresponding complexity of the workflow, but the mapping does not necessarily have to mimic what exists currently in the paper environment.

Many organizations initially configure the imaging system one way and then implement workflow redesign changes later once the system is in place and the operational staff has been fully trained. With intelligent workstation capabilities and access to multiple applications, an operator can be retrained to do in one step what may have taken several steps in the past. The intelligent workstation is a powerful operator tool that can now consolidate transaction solution data from widely dispersed sources.

Workflow Control—Mainframe or LAN

With images residing on LAN-connected servers, data transmitted from the mainframe transaction processing systems can be used to control the placement and status of locally resident document images. The synchronization mode of mainframe and LAN processes depends in part on whether the transaction processing system is batch-oriented or on line, and on how complex the transaction is. Synchronization is more complex where many steps are involved in completing the transaction, especially if each step requires an operator possessing a different skill set.

Indexing and Referencing Document Images

One of the critical decisions in image enabling a mainframe through a network is the location of the index to images. The problem is less technical as it involves strategic data management appraisal.

Indexing on the mainframe has the advantage of continuing the integrity of controls that characterize the mainframe. Its drawback is that it forces additional network traffic; in addition, as users migrate to multimedia applications at their workstations, centralized indexing may increase maintenance requirements to ensure compatibility. These issues may be difficult to handle with existing staff.

Local indexing offers more flexibility and is likely to reduce network traffic. At the same time, it raises the issues of cross-referencing document identifiers to the mainframe applications and maintenance of indexing standards.

System Administration and Management Issues

Integrating imaging with a mainframe also requires a review, from the imaging system point of view, of a host of items that probably were already resolved in the mainframe system. These include:

- Integration of remote diagnostics and alerts for all imaging operation problems, such as device failure. While some of these alerts may not be of interest to the mainframe, it is essential that their definition be compatible with those already in place. For instance, while it may be unlikely that a failed scanner that runs on its own network and under its own server control would be of interest to the mainframe, at some point in the future, fax machines and scanners may be the same input device, and the fax machine may be directed by the mainframe. Therefore, it is advisable that error messages be harmonized now to facilitate downstream maintenance.

- Configuration management and control, to ensure accurate cross-referencing between documents in image form, index, and their ASCII representation if any. This is especially important when documents with the same ASCII text are represented with images with handwritten annotations that reflect different versions of the same document.

- Security, from the point of view of access to both the installation and to the information contained in the system.

- Hardware and software management, to ensure compatibility in upgrades and maintenance.

- Archive management, to keep on-line storage requirements to a minimum and ensure proper disposition of obsolete records.

- Software distribution, to ensure—especially in a heterogenous environment—that all upgrades are performed in a uniform manner.

In addition, close attention should be given to training and the coordination of staff development programs related to imaging systems, including users, operators, and systems administrators.

Implications of Future Technologies

The continued progress in hardware technologies, supported by increasingly accepted standards—including faster processors, fiber optics, width, multiprocessing, parallel processing servers, 32-bit operating systems, 64-bit processors, RAID, and Windows accelerators—will facilitate the integration of high-performance imaging systems with mainframes, but at the same time, create additional pressure for downsizing.

These developments will persist in raising the issues of compatibility, cost, reliability, redundancy, and data integrity. Of primary importance will be the preservation of the various audit trails in the context of a changing technological environment.

Checklist of Technical Issues

To facilitate integration of imaging with the existing mainframe, it is often useful to develop a checklist to consolidate the technical requirements of the mainframe operation and to query the proposed technical solutions to these issues. An example of such a checklist, which covers some of the "obvious and always forgotten" issues in system integration is given in Table 9.3.

Standardized Integration Tools: Imaging and Mainframe Applications Working Together

Modern mainframe architecture provides tools to integrate imaging with existing applications, thereby eliminating the concerns about security and an audit trail that early file transfer protocols created.

Table 9.3   Example of checklist of technical issues

1. **Intersystem dependencies**

   Integration with multiple mainframe applications

   Interdepartmental routing of work

   Consistency of processing cycles with business needs

2. **Provision for growth**

3. **Provisions for scanning and archival operations**

   Turnaround requirements

   Capacity planning to avoid backlogs, day and night shift operations

   Processing "windows" and system dependencies

   High-volume print requirements

4. **Backup and recovery from component failure**

   Procedures

   Component redundancy

   Software

   Hardware

   Network

   Operational errors

5. **Data integrity procedures and controls**

   Procedures

   Audit trail

   Data security and privacy

6. **Workflow management**

   Procedures dealing with bottlenecks

   Escalation of system problems

   Peak vs. average workloads system design

   Workflow control

   Manual intervention

   Automated control

7. **File sharing**

   Remote connectivity

8. **Education**

   Senior management

   Users

   Operators

9. **Miscellaneous**

   Facilities preparation

Many of these tools are platform-dependent on the mainframe side. The use of off-the-shelf packages for the network side facilitates the integration.

LU 6.2 and APPC

LU (Logical Unit) 6.2 is the underlying System Network Architecture (SNA) protocol suite that allows program-to-program communications across hardware and operating system platforms. APPC (Advanced Program-to-Program Communication) technically is the set of APIs that allow developers to code "conversations" between programs using the SNA network infrastructure. In this way programmers can build applications that cross platform boundaries without having to worry about lower-level communications details that are platform-dependent. A workstation can talk to a server process or a mainframe application using the same conversational verbs and rules. Mainframe applications, in turn, can activate server and workstation programs in an as-needed connect and disconnect basis.

APPC programming can be used to transmit local server processing statistics to a remote mainframe MIS reporting application, for example. As document images move electronically through different worksteps on the LAN, statistics for the rate of processing (to monitor productivity bottlenecks) can be easily collected and summarized.

Server processes can also converse with other servers, whether local or remote in the SNA network, using the same APPC syntax. The use of this standardized communication protocol for sophisticated control of the imaging system and related processes is the key to building powerful LAN-based imaging systems. It allows for the complex coupling of diverse applications on different platforms in many locations.

APPN

Complementing APPC, which is already a well-established product, is the recently announced APPN (Advanced Program-to-Program Network) support, which now makes it easier for an enterprise to program, implement, and support LU 6.2 functions into applications without as much concern for network addressing details.

Front-End Tools and Workstation Issues

As stated, imaging systems must deliver at least the same productivity as existing systems, subjective and qualitative savings notwithstanding. The workstation configuration is a key technical design issue; hardware power overkill can be very wasteful and costly, stretching the expected payback period out to unacceptable time frames. Completing technical homework in advance and shopping around can really pay off here. Recurring issues in the planning for system design and implementation include consideration of performance when replacing 3270 terminals with workstations capable of running up to five 3270-emulation windows.

Windowed Workstations vs. Dumb 3270 Terminals

Operator acceptance of the new environment usually is very favorable. A "when am I going to have an imaging workstation" attitude develops, especially when the new system installation is accompanied by upgraded facilities and ergonomics improvements.

A windowed environment, because it is user-configurable, has the advantage over the 3270s of visual ergonomics. The availability of multitasking environments gives access to multiple applications and multiple transactions simultaneously, especially when assisted with front-end tools such as EASEL.

There are tools that allow a direct link to the mainframe screen. For instance, the IBM product known as EHLLAPI (Emulator High-Level Language Application Programming Interface) allows a developer to build links between a PC-based program and 3270 emulation screens. However, this API requires a significant amount of training, and its output is difficult to support; if a host application changes, so must the EHLLAPI mapping code. Also, EHLLAPI programming techniques are usually dependent on the anticipation of mainframe protocol behaviors (i.e., acknowledgments in the form of "not busy, you can send or receive data now"). Other more user-friendly tool sets are coming on the market to speed prototyping and development time.

In fact, protocols such as Windows DDE make it possible, with the proper workstation software and programming, to preserve a user interface while changing the attached mainframe applications, to the point where it is possible to substitute host systems without requiring any operator retraining.

Be aware, however, that there may be only a minimum productivity increase when developing front-end using interprocess communication protocols. A case in point is DDE (dynamic data exchange), defined for use in Windows and OS/2 environments, which in complex applications may be costly to develop and support without resulting in any significant productivity increase.

Image Retrieval Considerations

The mainframe/LAN imaging configuration provides a simple model for document storage hierarchy. The work-in-process document images are stored on a local server magnetic disk to optimize workstation throughput until departmental transactions have been completed. The lifetime of the magnetic copy is usually very short; a corporation's daily mail receipts are typically entered within 24 hours.

For long-term archival needs, where legal requirements may dictate that the document image be retained for a long period of time (2–10 years), optical storage is the answer. Although microfilm is still cheap and suitable for many archival needs, as optical storage becomes more inexpensive and offers continual increases in storage density, the benefits of electronic access from remote workstations— document sharing, rapid retrieval, high-quality images, prevention of document loss, improved and highly controlled security—make optical storage the preferred method.

This model makes it possible to design an image-enabled system and to specify type and location of media, size of workstation memory and workstation hard disk, nature and location and size of servers' hard disks, mass storage devices, and optical disk jukebox (with mounted, unmounted, and resident platters, and unmounted and nonresident platters), as well as other mass storage modalities such as RAID arrays and backup tapes.

Other Considerations

Other considerations include the handling of remote site image retrieval, WAN integration with imaging capabilities, and high-volume printing. The solution, which is application-dependent, hinges on the strategy adopted for mainframe-image integration, which includes the choice to incorporate either local or main-frame indexing. The applications can be programmed to run either on the mainframe or from the local workstation, either using all necessary local and remote network resources or the mainframe as a node on that network or on the mainframe.

Image enabling requires a review of existing configurations and the applicability of monitoring and reporting tools, system administration, and integration with the existing network attached to the mainframe. In particular, there will be questions regarding:

- Methods of communicating (addressing) with departmental servers and work-stations.
- Benefits of local LAN vs. WAN requirements or bridged LANs.
- Geographical dispersement bandwidth considerations, and contention with imaging traffic in various topologies, such as the 16MB token-ring.
- LAN image location and storage management.
- Loose vs. tight applications coupling.
- Mainframe batch processing control.
- Impact of imaging in 3270 traffic and response on the LAN.

LAN/WAN Integration for Dispersed Geographic Sites

While there are numerous tools now available to perform integration with existing mainframe-based systems, the real potential lies in enhancing these systems to provide a tighter coupling with the LAN-resident imaging systems. Workload management based on transaction processing rates and attributes and sophisticated linear programming techniques may be implemented in the centralized mainframe application in order to more efficiently control the placement of images on LAN servers in anticipation of their use by a certain department or even a particular workstation. This requires a combination of mainframe integration and client-server–based programming techniques. It can provide maximum productivity by caching images locally in anticipation of their need. In this way, image retrieval response from local hard disks takes seconds, instead of jukebox/optical platter retrievals, which can take hours depending on the status of the platter and the volume of pending requests.

Backup and Recovery

Backing up an image-enabled system is not a trivial issue. Beyond the physical backup of the stored images, done by disk mirroring or off-time replication, there are issues of synchronization with the mainframe applications that must be resolved. While there are several tried and true mechanisms for ensuring rapid recovery in traditional mainframe applications, the integration of a similar level of data integrity for the LAN-based system may have to be developed internally.

In particular, the inability to recover quickly from individual server failures can cause major system problems.

Recovery time must be as quick as possible to ensure critical and high-availability operations. The adoption of advanced LAN-based imaging software with "failsafe" processing, where a single departmental server failure will not affect any workstation processing, is one way of achieving this goal. Other solutions may lie in the choice of the topology of the network itself: Bridges and intelligent hubs make it possible to bypass failed devices; additional protection can be implemented through the use of RAID disk arrays and fault-tolerant server architectures.

Whereas a downsized application is independent of any mainframe processes, even though the data is being accessed, an imaging system integrated with a mainframe application brings a new set of problems. The two applications can be processing units of work independently or dependently. When there is transaction dependency between the applications, this implies that the two applications are synchronized. For example, the scanning of a new image and the creation of its associated index information on the LAN is usually followed by the transmission of this information as "initial inventory."

The systems must therefore maintain their synchronization for accurate processing of transactions, reporting on work in progress, etc. The two systems can easily get out of sync if one of them loses critical production data (i.e., a server crash or mainframe database loss in the middle of the day). Both applications may possess backward and forward recovery facilities, but recovery may require an additional step before resuming production work: verification of synchronization.

Additional Consideration When Downsizing

Downsizing efforts (or, more accurately, right-sizing) are often considered in parallel with the implementation of imaging systems in a mainframe environment. When this occurs, several conflicting considerations must be taken into account.

In traditional mainframe environments, the CPU performs processing for all terminals. Traffic to users is limited essentially to characters, fields, and print files, and the heavy data traffic involving transfer between storage and CPU is done on dedicated channels. In a downsizing environment, that traffic appears on the general network, claiming its share of bandwidth. Considering that a mainframe may communicate at 4.5MB per second—about 50 percent of the bandwidth of an Ethernet channel—this is sufficient to choke any attempt to run imaging applications on the same network.

The solution to acceptable service requires reducing traffic on a given network segment or increasing available bandwidth or both. Techniques include data compression, increasing the number of file servers, use of different indexing techniques, and network architecture redesign. As indicated earlier, the use of simulation of the proposed installation is essential.

9.7   CONCLUSION: OUTLINE OF IMPLEMENTATION STRATEGY

The following provides a model for the implementation of an image-enabled mainframe system:

1. Complete feasibility studies and functional specifications.

2. Identify and resolve interface issues between the mainframe and imaging network.

3. Complete technical specification.

4. Select imaging system vendor or in-house development team.

5. Prepare facilities.

6. Install network, server, and workstation infrastructure (hardware and software).

7. Train departmental users and imaging system support personnel.

8. Complete user acceptance testing and sign-off.

9. Convert from paper and microfilm to high-volume scanning, archiving, and retrieval operations.

10. Migrate to imaging systems by Line of Business, associated with corresponding mainframe application, using terminal emulation and image display at the workstation.

11. Upgrade to enhanced workstation capabilities.

12. Upgrade from loosely-coupled to tightly-coupled applications integration.

10

Imaging Data Structure and Indexing

Dan Truesdell

Excalibur Technologies

Editor's Notes

The focus of this chapter is document imaging, but the principles are not limited to business files and related materials. Storage, retrieval, and management of a generalized document, which incorporates the various types of multimedia recording now accessible from the desktop, can be accommodated with the same methodologies because standardization reduces the problems of incompatibility between formats.

The only real difference with conventional office material is the computer encoding of the multimedia information, the nature of the data capture devices, and the device user interfaces. As a matter of fact, the addition of voice annotation and color photographs to imaging systems has already crossed the traditional "office document" boundaries, with media-capable PCs for the generalized document playing the same role as the graphic workstation plays for imaged documents.

The major nontechnical difficulty that must be resolved when dealing with a generalized document is that of describing the contents of that document. Limiting its scope to images, this chapter discusses some of the immediate issues involved when the contents cannot be interpreted directly in machine-readable form.

10.1 COMPUTER IMAGES

Recorded computer images must consist only of numbers—that is all that computers can really "think" about. The numbers describe the actions some piece of hardware must perform in order to physically manifest the image. The action might be to strike a pin onto an inked printer ribbon, or it might be to control the combination and intensity of three scanning electron beams to produce the correct mixture of red, green, and blue pixels on a computer display.

Because there are more ways to create images than the two examples above, computer image formats range from the quite simple to the utterly complex. It would be impractical to list all known formats in detail, but it is possible to elaborate on some of them generally.

Binary

Binary are bitonal (black and white only) images, such as printed text or pen and ink drawings. Each 1 or 0 in the image data bitstream corresponds to either a black or white pixel in the output image pattern. Gray can be emulated by scattering different proportions of black dots into the darker and lighter regions of the image (see Figure 10.1a).

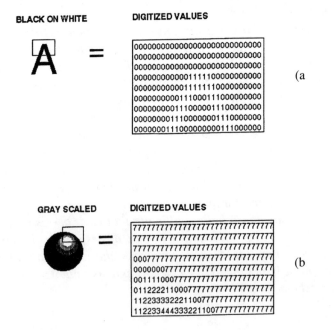

Figure 10.1   Picture of letter A and shaded ball showing relationship of binary and gray-scaled data value to the printed page

Grayscale

Grayscale images are integer pixel values stored in columns and rows, each of which corresponds to a brightness level in the output image. Integer values can range from 2 bits (4 shades of gray) to 32 bits (billions of shades of gray), which may seem excessive except when scientific instruments are involved (see Figure 10.1b).

Color

Color images are made up of codes that control the proportions of red, green, and blue light intensity seen by the eye at each pixel location. The codes can be arbitrary predefined codes like the 16 EGA colors of an IBM PC; or 32-bit codes, 24 bits of which make up the 8-bit numbers directly corresponding to red, green, and blue, with another 8 bits used for special overlay codes.

Video

Video images are streams of grayscaled or color TV, computer animation, etc. One second of animation may require 30 or more frames of still images displayed one after the other. Standard (NTSC) video signal coding uses a low ratio compression known as YUV, which is then converted to red, green, and blue intensities by television electronics. Someday, the high definition TV standards now in competition may replace the current poor standard, but it will probably be a gradual adaptation.

10.2 COMPRESSED IMAGE FORMATS

Compression is extremely important for network environments, because there is a limited bandwidth for data transmission between processing nodes and vast amounts of data storage necessary for images files. The ideal setup is when all compression occurs at the point of image creation and all decompression occurs at the point of display or usage (see Figure 10.2). Any time that image files must be stored to disk or transferred across the network, they should be in a compressed form.

It may be tempting to centralize the compression and decompression processing on a single server, especially if specialized hardware must be employed. But while this may seem to save in hardware costs, it definitely will cost in time. For more than a few users, network traffic will become overwhelming. The servers also may become overwhelmed if too many simultaneous decompressions are attempted. Most servers can allow only limited hardware interfaces to be accessed simultaneously anyway, and multiple clients would have to wait in queues.

Networks offer the advantage of distributed processing, which can make a cluster of cheap single-user computers better able to perform than a much more expensive multiuser computer.

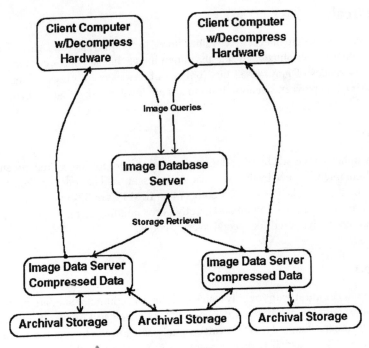

Figure 10.2   Decompression of images on a network. The image data remains compressed until received by CLIENT for hardware decompression and presentation so that network traffic can be minimized.

Plotter/Vector Descriptors

A vast amount of work goes into developing better and faster methods of compression. Early forms of image compression are still with us today in the form of vector graphics and plotters. A set of instructions with parameters determines where pixels should be created in the output stream; therefore, no bit-for-bit storage or transmission is necessary. If a circle is to be drawn using a plotter, it can accept a relatively small amount of numbers that describes the operation ARC, the radius of the arc, starting angle, ending angle, and so on. Of course, not all resulting circles are smaller in pixel size than total size of the plotter language statements that must describe them. But the probability of overall compression is high enough for it to be effective.

Many desktop publishing and CAD systems store images as sets of operation statements that are executed in sequence, thus decompressing the stored codes into a picture. Usually, only line art and text are described in this manner, but in some cases very complex three-dimensional drawings can be rendered. One drawback of this method is that it is extremely difficult to automate the compression phase.

Compressed Binary

Compressed binary images are bitonal images that have been described by codes that a software or hardware process can decompress into binary bitmap patterns. CCITT Group 3 and 4 are popular binary compression standards; bit-for-bit compression techniques are used in fax machines. The CCITT Group 3 and 4 compressions are designed specifically for black lines or text on white paper; Group 3 is simplest but allows for the compression of one row of bits at once; Group 3-2D; Group 4 allows for two-dimensional compression, but demands more computation and tolerates fewer errors in data transmission. Faxes can often be read when only a few lines become garbled, but if large sections become garbled, the fax business would not last very long.

Compressed Grayscale and Color

These gray images have been described by codes which can then be processed to expand back into the original (or similar) image. JPEG is an example of this kind of compression. Depending on the source of color data, there are many methods of compressing color codes. One interesting method is to use fractal mathematics; another is to compress separately the red, green, and blue values with JPEG or as several planes of binary images, each of which is then reduced to CCITT bitonal compression codes.

Grayscale and color compression is more difficult, but in many cases the separation of the codes into planes of bits allows the use of CCITT or other simpler bit compression techniques. Also, the quality of shading or color rendering can be sacrificed to gain better compression ratios. The human eye is very easily fooled and is tolerant of minor distortion. However, in scientific and many legal, or archival, concerns, the loss of data is not permissible. JPEG is a current standard of gray or color compression that allows for image quality that is inversely proportional to the compression ratio.

Compressed Video

Obviously, combinations of the above types might be used as subcompressions of a video supercompression. The vastness of the logistic problems and data size involved with video compression makes it one of the remaining challenges of computer science. A format called MPEG is a modified form of JPEG that makes use of deltas between video frames to enhance compression ratios.

Video compression techniques can rely on the tendency of animation sequences to consist of largely unchanging areas or objects in the images. In some cases, the entire image may move completely, but yet have areas that are identical to previous sequences, only slightly and predictably offset in space. Therefore, only the deltas, or differences between frames, must be described in order to recreate the full animation. This, of course, assumes that sufficient transmission bandwidth and processing capability exists to attain the necessary effect in real time. Moving images are not pleasing to the brain unless they closely match the motion effects of real life. Usually, the cheapest solutions are jerky or display lower-resolution, unrealistic colors.

10.3 IMAGE STORAGE AND RETRIEVAL

Images are generally stored in computers on magnetic disk as files or in databases as BLOb entries. A good storage management system also allows extended storage on high-capacity devices such as WORM disks, DAT tapes, and distributed network servers. Regardless of the methods used to store data, however, the question becomes how to retrieve it again.

How do humans usually organize their papers anyway? Each individual has a favorite method, ranging from simply haphazardly stuffing things into closets, boxes, and sacks, to elaborate business filing systems consisting of file rooms, cabinets, drawers, folders, tabs, color-coded page separators, clerks, check-out logs, and so on.

Many businesses and individuals have been successful at organizing things in these ways for many centuries, and some people seem uncomfortable unless the computer interface resembles real life, so perhaps it is best not to reinvent the wheel. Therefore, often the basic paradigm for file cabinets should be adhered to for image or document databases. The following data organization outline can serve as a model:

FILE WORLD	(A planet strewn with FILE PALACES)
FILE PALACE	(A structure full of FILE ROOMS)
FILE ROOM	(A structure full of CABINETS)
CABINET	(A structure full of DRAWERS)
DRAWER	(A structure full of FOLDERS)
FOLDER	(A structure full of DOCUMENTS)
DOCUMENT	(A structure full of BOOKLETS)
BOOKLET	(A structure full of PAGES)
PAGE	(The actual IMAGE itself)

The FILE WORLD is the total available computational and storage resources that can be accessed by the business using wide area and local area networks combined. Information transfers may be relatively slow, data may require user access security, and only a rough data storage indexing can be globally available.

The FILE PALACE can be thought of as the accessible resources for the total local area network. An example is a computer network consisting of a few dozen workstations connected by Ethernet, each storing a few gigabytes of information on line. Information transfers may be very fast, and larger, more detailed indices of data storage can be maintained.

The FILE ROOM is a single organized database accessible by a single server on the network (even though the data and processing components within may still be sprinkled about on other nodes). Complete content indexing can be achieved at this level, as long as the total data storage is within the "natural" addressing range of the computer system.

The CABINET, DRAWER through BOOKLET levels are merely conveniences that allow for hierarchical organizations. Labels, icons, numeric coding systems, and other schemes can be implemented in their places. All that is intended is a convenient way of browsing through the various sublevels of the database and a method of mapping actual computer files to the components of the hierarchies. Many simpler, nonnetworked image systems deal only with the DRAWER, FOLDER, and DOCUMENT levels.

The PAGE level is the actual "electronic paper" itself. It may be a word processor document page or a scanned photograph image or even a full-color three-hour video. Depending on the nature of the object, there may be other definable components within the PAGE. There may be posted note insets, text panels, photos, hypertext links, redlining overlays, etc., according to the nature of the business and other integrated products.

The complexity of such a system is obvious, and the methods used to index the data and superstructures become an important issue. Here are several ideas:

1. Remember the names or index IDs of stored data files: The user must be able to associate a name with the contents of an image. This is fine for small numbers of images but depends on fallible human memory for retrieval. The memory task is taxed further if the files being accessed are in a complex computer network. The data may have a name like:

```
superdog:/jukebox1/images/automobiles/antiques/jaguar1956.tif
```

2. Three-by-five-inch card descriptions and name or ID of data files: A computerized (or real) card catalog index of descriptions can be kept by the user. The user must read each "card" and then refer to a name or access ID. This might work well for precategorized descriptions in which only a few dozen or hundreds of index cards need be searched at any given time. Otherwise, it is similar to the infamous British museum method, which is to simply compare a sample insect to thousands of cataloged insects, without regard to time or fatigue, that evokes the scorn of so many software engineers.

3. Structured database and indices: The use of SQL or other database access methods can be used for a database of index cards structured by author, source, content descriptors, dates, or other information. The advantages are obvious, but this method necessitates a laborious setup and ever vigilant upkeep. If the user is careful to enter all the information accurately and maintains the updates religiously, then a wide range of programs can share in the automated retrieval of stored images. (The SQL and database software itself usually do not directly display or process images.)

4. Image pattern indices: A pattern recognition program can extract image components for use in a content-based retrieval method. Similar images are

used as "clues" to retrieve the stored images. Fingerprints, mug shots, automatic part sorting, and a few other applications benefit from this kind of indexing.

5. Image key scene indices: Once the extreme difficulty of recognizing objects from image components is accomplished, the recognized image patterns can be described in a symbolic manner, such as: "contains one lion, ten zebra, three wildebeest," in order to produce the descriptions needed by the index card or SQL methods. Although simplistic descriptions could be generated by computer software, human intervention would probably still be necessary for sophisticated descriptions such as, "frogs piloting lovely lily pads peacefully across a glass smooth pond."

6. OCR plus content-based retrieval: Optical character recognition can be used to convert the text portions of the images into ASCII text directly for index card or SQL methods. OCR tends to fail some percentage of the time (up to 50 percent), so that extensive human repair might be necessary. If the cost of repairing OCR data is too high, then a fuzzy keyword search method might be used rather than SQL. This method cannot automatically describe all documents, since many may contain no text at all or relate poorly to the images, but as long as they are grouped with documents that pertain to them, they still may be accessible by relative browsing.

7. Hypertext object linkage: The MAC environment uses mouse pointers and buttons to explore the databases of objects. Each object presents several possible ways to reach other objects via menu buttons or hotspots. Multimedia and hypertext databases are currently created and maintained by great effort. Many forms of hypertext linkages can be added automatically, however, using pattern recognition or other correlative methods.

8. Multimedia mania: The current rage of authoring systems that allows voyaging into CD ROM and other large databases can be augmented with simultaneous signal, voice, video, and text content indexing. The world of virtual reality has dipped into some of this technology by integrating human motion information into the data access and video processing subsystems.

9. Giant databases: The interface and usage of a fully functional multimedia database would be reminiscent of Isaac Asimov's Foundation series and his concept of the Encyclopedia Galactica. Eventually, an entire planet is devoted to the creation and maintenance of the encyclopedia. It contains all the knowledge of all civilizations strewn across a federation of many planets. Surely the indexing methodologies employed would have to be very sophisticated to locate any specific piece of information amongst the googaplexes of possible pieces (see Figure 10.3).

Our own real civilization has a similar desire to record enormous amounts of information, and already the quantities are beyond current abilities to properly index it—with any methods. One consideration involved designing a system that could index the contents of warehouses full of crates of paper documents. The documents contain various typewritten material, handwriting, signatures, rubber

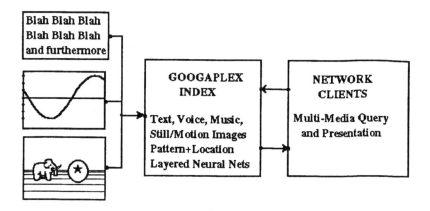

Figure 10.3   The wish to simultaneously index text, signal, and vision data for a content-based multimedia database.

stamp impressions, pictures, preprinted forms, coffee stains, and so forth. Some of the crates were stored according to some rule of order, and some just filled haphazardly with piles of documents. In addition, any indexing that requires forktrucks or cranes can only be dismally laborious.

In addition to warehouses of old documents, there are millions of miles of magnetic tapes storing NASA and military satellite telemetry. The FBI has at least 25,000,000 sets of 10 individual fingerprints, thousands of wiretap transcripts, and dossiers on millions of humans, criminal or otherwise. The CIA and other intelligence agencies record huge quantities of real-time global communications, far beyond what they could ever hope to process. Other countries have similarly vast quantities of such data. There is a human genome project with its "billion letter word" describing the molecular compression codes that expand into baby humans.

Electronic Document Filing

It's a dirty job, but somebody's got to do it. The components for scanning, storing, and indexing paper documents already exist and can be purchased off the shelf. Few of those components are completely integrated, since the technologies are relatively immature, but in time the technologies will converge. The following sequence is an example scenario based on a real, working document image system (see Figure 10.4):

1. A stack of legal documents is placed into a document scanner.
2. A computer operator selects a hierarchical database location in the form of CABINET, DRAWER, FOLDER, and DOCUMENT BASE name, then presses the ADD PAGES button.
3. The documents are scanned as binary images into the computer's memory.

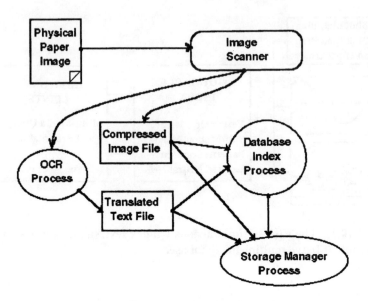

Figure 10.4   Typical flow of document images through scanner, OCR process, indexing process, and storage management

4. The images are passed to an optical character recognition process that produces an ASCII text file for each image (with inevitable mistakes and all).

5. The document images are compressed into CCITT Group 4, and both the compressed images and the text files are written to disk via a storage management subsystem and labeled according to the location selected within CABINETS, DRAWERS, etc.

6. The text files are "learned" by a neural net-like system that can associate the patterns of text in each document to the document's text and image files storage key.

7. At a different terminal, a legal analyst enters a clue into the computer such as "State of Ohio vs. Mr. Hyde" and presses SEARCH CONTENT button.

8. A few seconds later, the computer displays the correct document, even though Mr. Hyde was spelled incorrectly because of an OCR error and came out "Mr. 11yde." The neural net forgives many of the errors that normally would incapacitate a database query language. And, rather than looking at a text file with garbled words, the exact image of the original document is viewed, pictures and all, allowing direct human pattern recognition to read the document flawlessly.

That is an electronic filing system. It removes the necessity of reproducing multiple copies of paper documents, laborious filing and storage, and reduces the even more laborious and frantic searching for misfiled documents. Of course, there may be legal requirements to store real documents in real file cabinets, so probably a true "paperless office" is not possible yet. But, this type of system might pay for the lives of a few trees with a few kilowatts of electrical power.

In practice, the storage of 15,000 black-and-white documents requires the use of almost a gigabyte (1 billion characters) of disk. Most of the space is used to store the image files, but approximately 10 percent is used to store the text and index files. The storage requirements for grayscale and color images might involve an order of magnitude or more storage.

Electronic Image Filing

A similar method of image storage involves pictures rather than written text. Although there are prototypes for such systems, the following is an imaginary scenario for the sequence:

1. A digitizing camera system snaps color photographs of a criminal for use as "mug shots" and stores the images into the computer's memory.

2. A neural net processes the image by separating the colors into shades of RED, GREEN, and BLUE and finding the shape or pattern relationships in the proportions between them. Rather than just learning the whole face as a gestalt, the neural net learns small pieces of the facial features, such as parts of the eyes, parts of the nose, etc. The pattern relationships are associated to the "mug shot" identity database key.

3. The image file is compressed using JPEG or a fractal compression method and stored in a hard disk and to an archival CD.

4. Years later, an investigator isolates the eyes and mouth from a bank robbery recording from the CCTV camera in the bank. The face of the alleged criminal is obscured by a ski mask and only the mouth and eyes are visible.

5. The eye and mouth subimages are entered as "clues" to the computer system and the "SEARCH CONTENT" button is pressed.

6. A few seconds later the computer displays the mug shot pictures of several possible criminals whose eyes and mouth closely match those in the bank robbery recording. The criminal records of each, from several cities, are also displayed along with the pictures. The human investigator can then use his or her own animal intelligence to further discriminate between the possible candidates.

10.4 IMAGE/DOCUMENT DATABASE INDEX DESIGN

How can image databases be structured to accommodate such usage? Much of what is described in the examples of image or document databases can be accomplished with standard relational or hierarchical database management systems. There are many missing parts, however. Standard databases consist of typed fields for each

PALACE	ROOM	CABINET	DRAWER	FOLDER	DOCUMENT	BOOKLET	PAGE
TajMahal	Teak	Gargoyle	J758	12	1	2	357
TajMahal	Teak	Jelly Bean	S005	59	12	37	29
TajMahal	Ebony	Kokomo	M031	44	1	1	34

a)

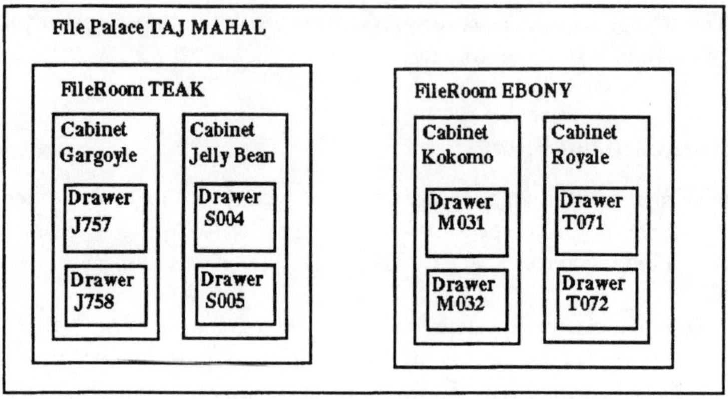

b)

Figure 10.5   Comparison of relational database method of (a) hierarchically organizing image storage to (b) a physically hierarchical database

item of information stored in them. Typically, there are date fields, number fields, Boolean (true or false) fields, and character string fields. Many databases also support a "BLOb" field as well, which can serve to store image data (see Figure 10.5).

In addition to the structure of a database, there must be an access method (or many) in order to retrieve the structured information. SQL is a well-known method for submitting information requests. It works by allowing English-like queries to reference specific ranges of field content combinations. For example, the English translation of an SQL statement might request:

```
"Return all records from the bugs_database where the bug
size is less than 100 and the number of legs is greater
than 20, or where the bug is hairy."
```

Everything is fine, so far. For all data that can be organized in nice little fields, which competent computer operators maintain accurately, a logical access method language can be constructed to retrieve the data. The problem arises when the data is not structured in fields, is too complex to describe in a concise manner, or is too filled with errors to ever be organized successfully. Imagine trying to build an SQL statement from:

```
"Return all records from the image_database where there
are pictures of little pink fairies dancing around
polka-dotted mushrooms in a forest that sort of reminds
me of Robin Hood."
```

Currently, fingerprint databases suffer from this. Instead of a simple SQL statement, the following laborious effort is required:

1. Examine the details of a latent or unidentified fingerprint according to prescribed gross and minutiae methods. Note such things as whether or not a whorl pattern or loop pattern exists, or whether a delta exists on the right or left of center. Count ridges and pinpoint various forks or endpoints of lines.

2. Transcribe the detailed observations into a format that can be accepted by the central fingerprint bureau computers, which perform the initial database look-up.

3. Use a human expert to examine the 100, 1,000, or more fingerprints that are returned, again with detail-for-detail pattern matching.

Research into completely computerized methods for fingerprint recognition systems is in progress and may soon replace this method completely. In place of any kind of detailed query formatting the investigator will simply input an image of an unknown fingerprint into a computer and the rest will be automatic. SQL will not be used directly for the query, and only dossier information or BLObs of fingerprint images will be accessed via SQL in a database. Some additional processing and indexing will have to be used to perform storage and retrieval. The processing might go as follows:

1. Perform image enhancement algorithms to improve contrast or edge regularity of fingerprint ridge patterns.

2. Create directional or linear subfeatures from fingerprint image. Recognize groups of subfeatures as significant features in a coarse index, which then assigns access to some of many detailed indices. (Neural nets or statistical mathematics might be used for these pattern recognition operations.) Use final features as an N-dimensional key into a relational database to retrieve the most closely similar fingerprints on file.

3. Use a human expert to check the reliability of this otherwise automatic fingerprint database, refining process step 2 until eventually the human expert may no longer be required.

In many respects, the above example is similar to the mug shot example. In fact, there may be only a few areas in step 2 where a domain-specific optimization might be in order; otherwise, the identical process would work.

10.5 INDEXING MOVING IMAGES

Some aspects of motion video make indexing more effective than with still images. The fact that objects move draws attention to them and separates them from the background. In fact, this also allows a special kind of compression to be performed. It is possible to imagine a process where a full-motion video is processed frame by frame and converted to a sequence of simpler "cartoon-like" frames that simply describe the contents of each frame with placeholder images made of stick-men, stick-cars, stick-trees, etc. Corresponding indices that denote the frame locations of each stick-object would then allow storage and retrieval in simple ways.

An alternative method might take advantage of the current practice of supplying a "closed caption" band simultaneous with TV video and audio bands. The closed caption data could be converted to text and used as a content-addressing base for the associated video and audio frames. Thus, the "deaf" and "blind" computer might understand the dialog and narrative portions of a movie, at least.

10.6 ADVANCED IMAGE DATABASES

An endeavor to provide artificial intelligence capable of image or scene understanding may be somewhat beyond today's technology. This would require that both pattern-recognition efforts and expert-reasoning efforts be coordinated into an integrated system. This kind of work can be illustrated in microcosm by describing the problems in making fault-tolerant optical character recognition systems.

OCR usually segregates typeface letters from the noisy background of a document image and then attempts to classify the character using a database of font-specific pictures of characters (or abstracted features of the characters). Some of the most common faults are distinguishing the number "1" from the letter "l" or the number "0" from the letter "O." Many other problems occur because of characters touching or being printed poorly, etc.

Humans can overcome errors in type by contextually examining the words or sentences around the errors in order to correctly guess the right character. Although a few OCR systems can "spell check" their way out of a few problems, it is not very effective in general. The context at the word level is probably too small, and it may require examining the meanings of the sentences or the whole document before full accurate interpretation of a single fault can be done.

Computers are (so far) failures at understanding the meanings of any words that are not simple logical instructions. Humans have the added experience of emotion and history from which to extend their contextual understandings of "meanings." Computers are too finite, and programming is too difficult. Pitifully small amounts of "meaning" can be comprehended by the average computer until both memory capacity and programming techniques are enhanced several orders of magnitude.

The probable impracticality of "image understanding" as an indexing method for image databases means that humans will have to be satisfied with something a little more clunky. Until a future day, probably it is less fanciful to improve the interface between computers and humans in order to make use of human abilities to understand images.

Typing in a long description of contents or features about a group of images is cumbersome and wearisome to most people. Invoking a mouse- or voice-operated icon choice system might aid humans a little, at least until carpal tunnel syndrome or throat soreness interferes.

10.7 INDEX DATA STRUCTURES

The key components of image database elements are:

- Image data
- Structured control information
- Structured control information access indices
- Unstructured text description data
- Unstructured text description content indices
- Format information

These data elements are necessary to both storage and retrieval and can be found in most of the commercially available database management systems.

Image Data

The image name or location descriptions can be any of the following forms. All that is necessary is that a unique identifier be available in order to refer to a specific image and some indication of its type, in case there are mixtures of image formats stored in a single database. For instance, TIFF files can be signified by typing TIF, JPEG compressed files can be JPG, and run length encoded files can be signified by RLC.

Since there may also be a mixture of storage techniques, the system should allow for types of storage. LOCAL means somewhere on the local computer's disk; RDBMS means somewhere in a relational database BLOb; REMOTE means somewhere on the network; and STOMAN means somewhere known only to a centralized storage management system.

```
[LOCAL]  [TIF] /users/joe/images/racecar.pic
[REMOTE] [RLC] bozo:/archive/images/compressed/foobar.img
[RDBMS]  [JPG] big_data_base:image_table:#000001
[STOMAN] [TIF] central_archives:ALQ-51237
```

It may be important that any actual locations specified by image identifiers be easily changed. If an indirect identifier that seldom changes refers to an entry in a database of names that can easily be changed when the image data itself has been moved, then centralized storage management can be implemented. Many indices or views of the data can remain intact without regard to rapid changes in physical storage locations.

Of course, there may be user access codes for security purposes and many other details that allow for integration with other software products. This design refrains from addressing those concerns to preserve relative simplicity.

Structured Control Information

The control information refers to typical fields of structured data as might be found in any SQL database:

```
Submitter: Tom Pinkyfinger
EDN: 0150340-26
Date: August 15, 1979
Subject: Aircraft Wing Design Engineering Change Notice
Status: Unclassified
Comments: Filed with FAA Panam Flight #443 Accident Report
```

Structured Control Information Access Indices

SQL statements can be used with indexing to speed up the searches or references to control information. Paradoxically, this will also result in much larger storage requirements and could be a maintenance headache.

Unstructured Text Descriptions Data

Text descriptions can be any of several forms, ranging from human narratives or written descriptions about each image to automatically created OCR text which strips only readable text from each image with hopes that someone else already did the describing. For instance, a human may write the following:

```
"Detail of left 737 wing. Inset shows servo lead screw
bulkhead bracket. Also shows hydraulic relay rack in
isomorphic projection. Possible knowledge of problem
well in advance of accident . . ."
```

An OCR process may instead produce (errors shown):

```
"Boeing ECN 150340-2G Pdge 12 of 23 Subasscnnbly
Schematie of Left 3rd spar Hydraulics valve rclay mount.
Approved by: [-3['' |ads]/EDN737-1503 40mill //'s& SERVO
SCR=YY RETRACTION NOTCH 30mill See Ii\sct . . ."
```

Unstructured Text Description Content Indices

In both the human- and OCR-produced text description examples just given, there may have been sufficient information with which to produce keyword indices. Of course, the human may have been more specific and less prone to severe spelling errors. Also, the human may have been more biased and written only what seemed relevant at the time. More objective information may have been obtained from an OCR operation, allowing some unknown future reference to be possible. In any case, the OCR example is only useful when images contain printed text data, or very, very neatly rendered handprinted text. Actually, a combination of both would work even better, so that any special information that humans added to the OCRed text descriptions would allow more relevant searches.

In any event, SQL alone does not do full-text retrieval very effectively, so that some other supplemental indexing and searching methods must be used if content-based retrieval is desired. There is a standard syntax known as SFQL (Standard FullText Query Language), but it does not define which underlying retrieval methods may actually be used, only the syntax of the queries.

The use of "concepts" is a popular form of content-based indexing. A human knowledge engineer must set up the concept relationships and corresponding weight charts in advance of actual indexing. A simple example of concept indexing is the following: One picture shows several men playing frisbee with dogs; another depicts contestants engaged in Olympic archery. Concepts include: animals, people, sports, tools, and recreation. The various instances are:

dogs => carnivorous mammal, animal

men => person => omnivorous mammal, animal

contestants => people, sport

frisbee => flying disc => sport, tool

archery => bows and arrow => weapon, sport, tool

Olympic arena => sport

city park => recreation, sport

The concept of "sports" is involved in both pictures, although the Olympic picture is more heavily weighted toward sports than the frisbee game with dogs. The concept of "animals" is not applicable to the Olympic picture except in the most general sense that humans are animals, but it certainly applies to dogs. Frisbee is not yet an Olympic sport, but both discus throw and frisbee toss can be viewed as sharing at least the concept of projecting flat round things into the air. The major difference is that only the frisbee toss involves humans or dogs attempting to catch them.

It can be determined from the above discussion that a good amount of work is required to set up such an indexing method. No doubt there is a high value in doing so, but only if the data is fairly static, and concept categories can be predetermined. Trying to automate such a method would involve quite sophisticated artificial intelligence. This problem is not limited to image database methods; it pervasively haunts computer science.

Format Information

The database might be variable in nature, so that structural formats are stored in the database along with the images, controls, and so on. Some syntax is used to describe the fields and their types, the storage locations or subsystems used, security issues, user preferences, etc.

```
RDBMS: Image_Database
CTRL TABLE: Image_Ctrl
CTRL FORM: Doc_num:n | Author:vs:80 | Date:d | Comment:vs:80
DATA TABLE: Image_Store
DATA FORM: Text Description:bigblob | Image Storage:bigblob
```

There are many brands of relational databases on the market, and at least as many methods of describing their interfaces and structures. The above example is meant only to show a typical description.

10.8 GEOMETRIC DESCRIPTION OBJECTS

Many indexing attempts are made to transform random photographic or line art images into geometric, caricaturistic, or mechanical drawing components. Political cartoons are good examples of the caricature method. Sometimes it is easier to recognize the caricature than the actual photographs of political figures. This is because a few essential qualities have been exaggerated and most of the commonest qualities have been eliminated.

Geometric descriptions are a form of caricature (see Figure 10.6). If one examines the blueprint of a house and then examines the actual finished house, it is apparent that there is almost no physical similarity. All the qualities of the house have been reduced to lines drawn on paper, which can be interpreted as an actual house only by someone who has learned all the symbolic meanings of the lines and can imagine the resulting whole.

Mechanical drawing is the mechanical engineer's program source code. By scribing outlines around the various spatial elements of an imaginary thing and determining the proper measurements and scale of the thing, it is possible for another person to blindly follow the prescribed functions that each symbolic description demands and produce the actual thing.

But how can computers automatically determine the symbolic description of an object which can only exist in the real world of molecules and energy? Computers can only determine the patterns of bits which result from the application of

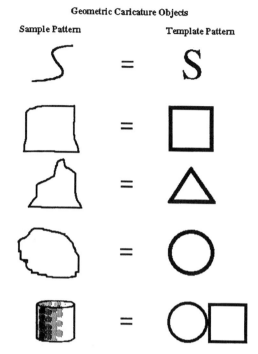

Figure 10.6 Idealized geometric on archetype symbols interpreted from source image objects to be used as indexing features

functions that are themselves composed of other patterns of bits. Any object characteristics must be mapped into various combinations of bits.

At least computers are good at measuring things. For example, if the computer is given a photograph and then asked to measure all the points of "interest" in the picture, one point of the computer's interest may be the actual centroid of the object; another may be a location where a sudden change of shade or edge direction occurs. The computer would then produce a strange, interconnected map of the mathematical properties of the object. Humans would probably find the resulting points of interest profoundly uninteresting.

You can divide trees up into tree parts—roots, trunk, branches, limbs, twigs, leaves, and so forth. Tree parts are made from even smaller and more numerous other tree parts, and those are made of yet more. But, if a list were made of all of the smallest elementary tree parts and several people were asked to describe the original tree purely by referencing the list, how many could? That is the computer's problem. It can memorize only the lists of elementary components or their hierarchies.

A simple example involves a ball. The ball is a round thing with some texture and some reflection. The computer would probably produce a circular outline of the ball and measure the radius of the ball. If the ball were an orange, then a texture of 2 of 5 possible points may be ascribed to it, but also 2 out of 5 of reflectivity. If the ball were a polished silver ball, then a texture of 0 and a reflectivity of 5 may be ascribed to it. At any rate, the descriptions thus generated are short and simple.

A more complicated example involves an elephant. Obviously, the elephant has far more geometric points than a ball; in fact, the points are so many and so seemingly nongeometric that the resulting drawing must be composed of hundreds or thousands of irregular line segments, not a regular polygon. Likewise, the assignment of textures and reflectivities depends on whether the ear or the eye is examined, so that localized measurements are necessary. The resulting mechanical drawing of the elephant would be quite difficult to read with so many lines and descriptions.

Instead, why not try to recognize subcomponents of the elephant from a library of other animal drawings? The ears of an elephant are rather unique in the animal world, but perhaps those of a bat or a mouse have rough similarity. The legs are quite thick, more so than most other animals, but at least they are cylindrical, like many other animals. Then there is the trunk: Most other animals with a long flexible prehensile tool are connected to it via the hindquarters instead of the head; or, if viewed as simply a long nose, there still are few other animals so endowed.

It is doubtful that an automatic way of making mechanical drawings from everyday objects can be very practical. Humans would have to help the computer do that or at least endow them with the most subtle of AI functions imaginable. Someday, a computer may be able to create and draw the blueprint of a house correctly, but it may always have difficulty in generating a satirical political caricature of the president.

There are, however, many existing engineering drawings that can be indexed according to their subcomponent drawings using the geometric caricature method.

10.9 OBJECT RECOGNITION SYSTEMS

Many of the indexing methods already discussed require that images be decomposed into recognized objects and relationships between objects. This is easier said than done, of course, but the state of the art is advancing steadily.

Image data can be broken into packages of components by various means. Segmenting an image by contrasts and edges is one way:

1. Images must be decompressed and/or translated to a form suitable for image processing.

2. Images may have to be enhanced so that noise or irregularities of lighting can be overcome. Edge detection, smoothing, median filters, histogram contrast conversions, and many other image processing functions are employed at this stage.

3. Cleaned images are then examined for their relative brightness values, which are divided into mountain tops and valleys. Each top has an X,Y coordinate and an H (height, or relative brightness). Valleys are just the residue caused by removing mountains higher than M from the image. Valleys are further

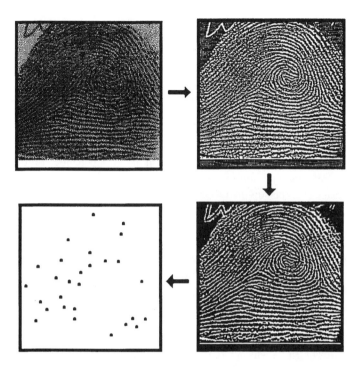

Figure 10.7   Successive stages of fingerprint analysis: original image → localized contrast enhancement → binarized by thresholding → feature points extracted

examined for mountains of height M/2, and so on, until no image remains. M is initially some arbitrary size. Eventually, all the mountains are described and output as AOIs (areas of interest).

4. The AOIs are described by their X,Y,H coordinates, the shape mask of the AOI, and the image bytes that fill that shape. Duplicate AOIs might be pruned out if they are frequent enough to impact memory or processing speeds.

5. AOIs can be recognized as template objects; i.e., an AOI that has the general shape of the letter "A" emits TOKEN_A, or a generally round and conical AOI emits TOKEN_CONE, etc. The tokens thus created can then be combined and converted to expert system truth values, indexing keys, relational database Boolean table items, etc., as needed to associate all necessary data about the object (see Figure 10.7 for an example of finger-print analysis).

6. An interactive user interface might allow adaptive learning of new AOI tokens as they are needed to define new shapes. Either actual patterns of new data can be learned, or combinations of existing connected tokens described as a single new token.

There are many ways to provide recognition capabilities, depending on the scope of the problem. OCR is a special case domain, where the set of all known characters in all known fonts is finite. At least it is smaller than the set of all known objects. The relatively small size allows humans to tinker and experiment until a solution is found by relentless trial and error.

For more immense numbers of patterns, or for especially unruly ones, the simplest (and usually slowest) way to match them is to directly compare all stored sample patterns with the unknown pattern, selecting the match with the lowest number of differences (the British museum method). Neural network methods can be applied instead and result in a more general and less pedantic solution, sometimes in an automatic learning mode.

Seed images can be supplied as the basis of larger macro images to be used as indexing keys. Elaborate geometric objects have been painstakingly designed and rendered for this purpose, but actually it is easier and probably less biased to simply generate them randomly. The software then examines arbitrary pieces of the source image and asks, "Which random seed image does this piece most look like?" Combinations of the results then form indexing keys referring to macro image objects, which then are used to form indexing keys to the whole image scene or video sequence.

Additionally, seed images may be designed to be position, size, and rotationally invariant, as in the case of optical Fourier Transform interference patterns. Actually, they are not truly invariant, only "less variant," so that otherwise "brute force" methods are optimized within a smaller domain of variation. Techniques such as these may involve immense computation, expensive or inconvenient hardware such as lasers or special cameras, or special image preparation, and therefore are not universally applicable.

A list of possible object recognition approaches includes:

- Gestalt silhouette recognition: Objects are reduced to black-and-white BLObs and compared with predefined templates.

- Combinations of gestalts: Clusters of black-and-white templates are identified by grouping recognized subcomponent templates.

- Simple contrast-oriented object segregation: BLObs contain shades or lines that may be important for distinguishing otherwise similar objects.

- Flow contrast object segregation: Use changes in line direction rather than shades to describe object boundaries. Useful for fingerprints, wood grain, cloth textures, etc.

- Major differentials: Observing the rate of changes in image elements such as line direction, contrast, and color. The geometric relationships between the locations produce distinguishing features.

- Random graph transforms: Images are compared to randomly generated images to produce correlation graphs to produce distinguishing features.

- Frequency transform correlation: Histograms or power spectrum correlation maps are used to reduce effects of noise, position, or rotation. Can be used alone or in combination with other methods.

- Expert system analysis: True or false statements about features of images gained with other methods guide Boolean logic analysis of the objects.

- Neural networks: Learn by "example" how to distinguish or identify objects or even groups of objects automatically by emulating the methods that higher animals use. Multiple levels of neural nets can be used in combination with any other methods for optimization.

11

Database Structure for Document Image Retrieval

Jeff Berger
Motorola

Oren Sreebny
BRS

Editor's Notes

Databases are essential to the management of any collection of organized objects, regardless of their medium and format. A large number of databases are maintained in any computer-based system, most of them dedicated to the operation of the system itself and hidden from the end user. The only "visible" database is the one that is used for information storage and retrieval; through a "database engine" it interprets user queries to locate relevant documents.

There are different types of database engines, each corresponding to a design trade-off made to reach the optimal compromise between various operational factors, such as speed of access and use of computer resources to support a given application.

Consequently, while all "reasonable" database engines could probably be used in any application, some are better suited to one simply because they are more efficient in that given environment. For instance, a Standard Query Language (SQL) engine can well serve applications represented by sequential files; however, such engines would not be as efficient as a simple indexed database engine. By the same token, optimal information retrieval solutions for heterogenous data formats and arrangements, as for imaging systems, are based on more complex database engines.

Imaging inserts large blocks of nonmachine-readable data into what may be an otherwise fully searchable database; therefore, the structure of the database used for image and data retrieval must be selected with great care so that it can be tailored to the application. In particular, the database structure must at least be able to accommodate retrieval of document images and related indexing data, and must be compatible with the database supporting the network operating system. To ensure such a compatibility with the minimum amount of programming, most modern database engines provide application programming interfaces (APIs), which are specifications for their interface with the outside world. In that way, a queried database must respond only in the appropriate API format, without concern for the mechanics of the data processing activities beyond its interface. At the same time, the application—such as the software driving a jukebox to retrieve a particular record—will only need to be programmed to understand the interface commands, and not have to be concerned with algorithms used in the database to provide the proper identification of suitable records.

This chapter discusses the various elements that enter into the construction of an imaging system database and how they relate to a network windowed environment. In particular, it discusses some of the issues involved in integrating document retrieval with other applications in a multitasking environment. It will be shown that construction involves considerations that are common to the design of the overall system, such as legacies and organizational policies. Some of the material given here may repeat segments of information in other chapters, but this redundancy has been kept to ensure complete treatment of the subject matter.

11.1   ELEMENTS OF THE IMAGING (OBJECT) DATABASE

Introduction

The fact that large blocks of stored data carry with them no extrinsic information sets this kind of system apart from traditional data environments. To allow the cataloging and finding of these binary "dumb" objects, it is necessary either to identify external data elements or specifically create them. In other words, the difference between a text and image database is that the image (information) does not usually contain searchable data elements; external data elements must be added and linked to the image to provide contents that contain both the image and information about it and its location. This creates what is sometimes called meta-data elements, with the image portion making up the single largest element of an image database.

Another difference is that traditional databases, while often made user friendly by a graphical user interface (GUI), do not necessarily require more than a simple ASCII terminal. This is not true in an image-based environment where not only may the user interface be graphical, but the data itself is graphical and demands an inherently graphical environment. Also, file systems are naturally larger in an image-based system; a page of ASCII text is about 2KB in size, and a Group IV compressed image of the same page takes approximately 30KB of storage. Whether optical storage systems are required over a more traditional magnetic media will be discussed later. Finally, as will be discussed here and elsewhere in the book, the demands on the network environment are greater with images than in more traditional databases due to two factors: The nature of the data and the traffic associated with both host environments and client-servers place high demands on the network; second, and perhaps equally significant, is the desire of the system developers to expand the imaging system to a user base not normally associated with a traditional system, or at least not the with the same system. The addition of purchasing, material quality, manufacturing, sales, engineering, and even management expand the scope and hence, the network demands of an image-based system.

Database Models for Imaging Applications

The dominant conceptual model in current database technology is the relational model. However, to accommodate the differences in information contents between machine-readable data and images, it is often necessary to modify that model. The following compares a traditional relational model and one that has been enhanced for images.

Relational Database Model Overview

Relational database systems can be described in terms of two rules:

1. The data is perceived by the user as tables (and nothing but tables).
2. The operators at the user's disposal (e.g., for data retrieval) are operators that generate new tables from old.

One classic example of a relational database implementation is for tracking inventory and sales in a retail store. Items for sale are usually distinguished by an identifying item number, while customers are referred to by a customer number. We could construct tables for inventory, customers, and items as shown in Tables 11.1–11.3.

It is easy to construct a query to retrieve a list of names, addresses, and items for delivery of sales. The query could look something like:

Table 11.1   Item relational database

Item#	ItemName	StockQuantity
001	Dining room chair	5
002	Dining room table	2
003	Double bed	4
004	Baby crib	1

Table 11.2   Customer relational database

Customer#	CustomerName	CustomerAddress
001	John Martin	80 Westpark Dr
002	Peter Philip	1301 Circle Rd
003	Jack Smith	455 Manor Rd

Table 11.3   Inventory relational database

Sale#	Customer#	Item#	SaleQuantity
001	002	004	1
002	001	001	3

Table 11.4   Query result

CustomerName	CustomerAddress	ItemName
Peter Philip	1301 Circle Rd	Baby crib
John Martin	80 Westpark Dr	Dining room chair

```
SELECT
    Customer.CustomerName
    Customer.CustomerAddress
    Item.ItemName
FORALL Sales
```

The table resulting from our query would look like that shown in Table 11.4.

This very simple example serves to illustrate some of the attractive features of a relational database system. It offers a tremendous amount of flexibility to the user of the system. Tables can be combined at will, based on key elements (like Item# and Customer# in our example). In addition, the complete descriptive data for each data element, such as the customer's name and address, needs to be stored in only one place in the system. In addition to saving storage, this makes maintenance of the system considerably easier.

It is important to remember that relational databases are optimized for flexibility, and, as such, have potentially significant shortcomings. The relational model typically requires a high degree of structure in the data it stores. While this works well for many commercial applications, it is not so advantageous when structuring the data in a document-based store. Retrieving elements from a relational database can be time-consuming because, typically, the items within a relational table are not ordered. To retrieve a specified item then, it is necessary to step through the entire table one row at a time, comparing each value to the specified search attribute. It *is* possible to set up indices for columns in relational tables, but this is not commonly done for all data elements.

Document Retrieval Database Properties

In a relational database system, retrieval is a one-step process, generating a new table that represents the results that satisfy the query. In a document retrieval database this is a two-step process: In a search operation, the user enters queries into the system, which then identifies a set of documents that satisfy the query; the retrieve operation is then issued against the identified set of documents, which are then presented to the user.

The types of documents that may be stored in a document retrieval database vary widely. Document retrieval applications might include storing technical documentation, procedures manuals, memoranda and correspondence, legal depositions and briefs, published journals, and library catalogs. Some of these document types may be highly structured. Memoranda, for instance, typically contain an opening section where the addressee, sender, date, subject, and distribution list are specified. Similarly, manuals usually contain hierarchically organized chapter, subchapter, and paragraph headings. What is common in these and most documents is that the actual body of the text is made up of unstructured prose (although we should not assume that document retrieval databases are limited to prose; see, for example, Dartmouth University's Dante and Shakespeare databases). This text is not only of variable structure, but is usually variable in length as well. The storage and retrieval of these documents is the goal of the document retrieval database.

What are the properties of a database system for retrieving this wide variety of documents? As with the previous definition of a relational database, we can specify two rules that define a document retrieval database:

1. The data is perceived by the user as documents.
2. The operators at the user's disposal (e.g., for data retrieval) are operators that identify and retrieve a qualified subset of the entire document store.

This definition implies a basic feature of document retrieval databases—that the elemental unit of retrieval is a single document. This means that the results obtained from a query of the document database are entire documents, even though in a particular situation we may choose to display only certain portions of the document to the user.

The definition of what constitutes a single document may differ from one database to another, even if the databases contain similar material. One database containing published journals, for instance, may be structured with a single journal article as a single document, while another database may be designed with an entire issue of a journal as a single document.

Database Structure for Document Retrieval

As already noted, the elemental unit of retrieval within a document database is the individual document itself. But what are the logical file structures used to obtain this retrieval? While the standard (relational) database is composed of records and tables, the image database is composed of an additional element: the image object. Even though an image object can be found in a form such as a Computer Graphics Metafile (CGM), which allows direct inquiry of the object, most imaging systems must be designed to allow for pure bitmapped or raster data. To the database, these are completely "dumb" objects.

To represent that variety of information objects, the most common data model for document retrieval databases is the inverted index structure. The inverted index model, developed in the 1960s for the maintenance of large indices to scientific and commercial literature, is used in most of the large commercial information retrieval services, such as BRS, Dialog, Mead Data Central, and the National Library of Medicine's Medlars service. And while they are widely available in many commercial document retrieval software systems, inverted index database models, which are highly effective in the retrieval of unstructured information, are not optimized for flexibility. Indeed, the structure of these systems frequently requires complete reconstruction of the indices with each database update. The inverted file structure, however, does offer extremely rapid database searching that is not very sensitive to the size of the database. This allows the construction of powerful mixed-format databases that contain millions of documents in both image and machine-readable format.

Archival, On-Line Reference, and Transactional Applications

Database structure is strongly influenced by the purpose of the information system. Most systems are optimized for a particular type of application, such as archival, on-line reference, or transactional. Because imaging applications will span the life cycle of business records, enterprise-wide databases may need to be segmented into local databases, optimized to provide the best response to a given set of operational circumstances.

Indexing Methodology

Another decision to be made in the selection of a database structure is how to index information for document retrieval, a subject that has kept librarians and classification specialists in business for hundreds of years. The advent of computerized information systems has provided very powerful tools for enhancing the capabilities of document retrieval systems. It is still true in retrieval system design, however, as in most computer systems work, that a little thought and effort in the design stage can save untold amounts of work and hardship in the implementation.

Language and Indexing

In a document imaging system the actual retrieved document will be, by definition, an image. This may be an image of a textual document or it may be a graphic image. Whatever the actual image represents, in almost all cases the method used to describe this image for retrieval will be the written language. We do not, for example, describe a photograph by drawing a picture of the photograph, but by describing its content, color, and/or shape ("a large red balloon"). It is the job of a document imaging system to match the user's linguistic request against an index of linguistic descriptions of documents to produce a document image.

Imprecision of Language The use of language is notoriously imprecise, and terminology shifts among nationalities (the English auto's "boot" is the American car's "trunk"), over time (the "trash collector" becomes the "sanitation engineer"), and between different professions (the word "program" has very different meanings to computer professionals and television executives). In addition, the proliferation of nonunique acronyms (is the NEA the National Education Association or the National Endowment for the Arts or both?) and shifting usage make linguistic information retrieval a mine field of problems for the system designer. Even seemingly simple data elements like personal names can pose problems: Are memos addressed to Bob Briggs and Joseph Robert Briggs to the same person? In addition to the natural imprecision of varied living uses of language, well-written documents are not necessarily well suited for retrieval applications. When we write prose we are taught to vary the ways in which we refer to things; we are instructed not to express concepts in the same terms over and over again. In document retrieval, however, we would prefer to have the same terminology used consistently in every instance so that we may retrieve all documents that refer to a given concept with assurance.

Tools for Dealing with Linguistic Problems There are tools available to help the database designer cope with this linguistic morass. The most rigorous method is to design and enforce the use of a thesaurus to control the indexing vocabulary. In a thesaurus the database designer decides upon the approved term for each concept to be represented in the index. These approved terms (known as the "preferred terms") are the only representations for these concepts that will be allowed to appear in the index. The thesaurus designer then lists all other terms used to represent each concept and builds pointers from these "entry" terms to the preferred term. The use of this thesaurus file can be automated to normalize data upon input as well as to map search terms at retrieval time. Other tools for coping with linguistic variations make use of word stemming, automatic pluralization, and phonetic algorithms.

Full-Text Searching

Most current document retrieval systems support the indexing of all of the text in a document. These are referred to as "full-text" retrieval systems. The power realized from having each word in a piece of text indexed is immediately apparent. In order to support full-text searching, document retrieval systems allow the user to specify sophisticated contextual relationships between multiple query items, such as requiring that terms co-occur within the same sentence or paragraph of text. The database designer must decide to what extent the complete text of documents will be indexed. There are costs involved in making the full-text searchable, including the cost of converting document text into searchable form and the additional cost of storing the extra indexing. In addition, the written text of most documents is exactly the type of material most prone to the linguistic retrieval problems discussed above. Full-text indexing usually implies that the material being indexed was not written and composed for the purpose of enhancing information retrieval. Because of this the user may end up retrieving documents that are only tangentially relevant to his or her query (because the query terms are concepts mentioned only in passing in the document) or miss relevant documents altogether (because the document author used different terminology).

Controlled Indexing

The system designer can alleviate the problems inherent in full-text indexing by either utilizing the existing document structure or by adding structured elements to documents. If, for example, the database is to consist of business memoranda, the database designer can place the DATE, FROM, TO, and SUBJECT data in separate search fields from the body of the text. This then allows for greater specificity when constructing queries. In addition, the system architect can choose to design query structures that weigh terms that occur in certain fields, such as the SUBJECT field. The database designer may decide that a given document base does not possess enough structure to make efficient retrieval possible. In this case, the addition of descriptive indexing to the original data may be warranted. The terminology used in such descriptive indexing should be controlled as much as possible to ensure consistent retrieval. The designer may be able to use existing lists of terminology from database publishers such as the National Library of Medicine's Medical Subject Headings or the Institute of Electrical and Electronics Engineers' IN-SPEC index.

Indexing for Image Retrieval

While it is common for an image to represent text, it is important to remember the difference between actual text (as represented by ASCII character codes) and the image of text (this distinction is analogous to Magritte's famous surrealist painting of a pipe with the legend, "This is not a pipe"). This distinction may seem obvious to computer professionals, but it is one of the most common points of real confusion in system users. The advent of GUIs and compound document architectures may serve to further cloud this distinction in the minds of system users. Since the image is not made up of text, it follows that the actual data being searched is not the image. In other words, while the data that is indexed may have been derived originally from the document image, the image itself is not searchable. In most imaging systems the ultimate view of the document presented to the user is an image of a document instead of an ASCII text version of the document. This means that the indexing must lead the system to the relevant image when a display is requested by the user. The image data may be stored within the actual document retrieval database itself, or it may reside external to the database in separate image files. If the image data is stored in separate files, the document retrieval database must store pointers to the locations of these files. Since the system administrator will want to remain flexible in choosing file locations, the system designer should be able to place an additional level into the database design, so that absolute file names and locations will not need to be stored in the actual database.

11.2 DESIGN REQUIREMENTS OF THE IMAGING DATABASE

Experience has shown that a well-designed document imaging database requires consideration of the four main system elements: document capture, control/indexing, file system, and document display. Other elements can be added such as OCR, and fundamental system issues such as backup and account management cannot be ignored, but those four elements are the cornerstones of any imaging system.

When laid against an emerging set of requirements, these four elements can help to crystallize a focus for the design of the system database. When broken down from all the bells and whistles, there are some very simple and fundamental items to be considered.

Overall Considerations

Document Capture

What is the source of the documents: paper (via scanning) or electronic (direct conversion of an existing electronic form)? Will an existing archive be converted, or does the system proceed from the day of initiation? Will the system scan or convert at a central location or multiple centers, or will all users be able to enter documents? What are the control points and checking associated with entering documents, and what are the criteria for saying they are accurately converted and indexed? Who signs off in that approval process? If a process view of the entire imaging system is used as a check against proposed requirements, flaws in the thought process are revealed, and often, more importantly, overdesign of the system can be avoided. We will come back to overdesign later.

Control/Indexing

What is the minimum indexing needed? What cost in time, hardware, and software is required to achieve that level? How much training is the organization willing to pay for both users and administrators? Can the indexing scheme be modified easily and at what cost? What is the expendability of that scheme? Does a new workflow need to be established, or can the system achieve payback goals by merely getting out the paper?

File System

How much information is reasonably going to be generated? How long does data need to be kept on line? What amount of backfile conversion must be accomplished? What response time is required for document access, both recent and historical? Can the data be maintained on magnetic media without optical storage? What network access must be maintained? Does the backup strategy meet with corporate and project requirements for frequency and off-site storage, particularly in the case of optical-based systems? This category is a great place to meet head-on with the issue of overdesign and out-of-control costs.

Document Display

The selection of a display system or viewer is key to user acceptance of the imaging system; it must match the function performed. The world's best-in-class viewer for check-clearing applications may be totally inappropriate for engineering drawings. Questions to pose include: How many hours a day will the user be in front of the system? Will the average user be performing other functions on the computer? What is the time to invoke vs. the average length of session? Are hardware accelerators needed to meet productivity goals? Is this system used in a workflow or documentation application where annotation is required? As above, what cost in training is the organization willing to expend per user? What is the user turnover and the related impact on training? What level of expertise and time is required to administer the end user software? How is it licensed and maintained, and what impact does that have on long-term cost of ownership? The temptation to allow all possible combinations and permutations of options just does not stand up to the real world in the way of the source and number of documents and the skill level and training of the people using and maintaining the system. The 80/20 rule must be applied in avoiding system overdesign. A system that meets 100 percent of the initial system requirements 100 percent of the time probably is not affordable or practical.

Other Considerations: Cultural Elements of Systems Design

Because the imaging system will so dramatically change the business, the system, and, consequently, its database, it cannot be designed without external consideration of the information process itself. In particular, the design and installation of an image management system and its underlying database involve not only technical but also cultural decisions. Integrating system analysis, process reengineering, organization mapping, and hardware and software selection is a significant technical challenge. However, the success of the imaging system in solving a business problem and achieving productivity improvement is only partially impacted by those technology-oriented decisions. To repeat the prime directive of imaging systems: Putting images into a document management system has no payback whatever; only retrieving images from such a system results in productivity. The point in this case: Users must perceive an improvement in their job function before they will use it. Until someone uses a system it will not be productive and will provide no payback. Thus, managing the user's perception of the document management system is probably the major element in successful implementation. Successfully managing the user's perception of the system will make the most cumbersome, archaic system a success in their eyes and, hence, in that of management. Simply turning users loose without sufficient support will sink the most elegant solution absolutely.

Books have been written on managing organizational change,[1] and an extensive treatment of the subject is outside the scope of this work. Nevertheless, some key elements of managing the cultural aspects of imaging system installation as they directly or indirectly affect the success of an imaging system must be discussed.

Involvement

Users must be involved in the entire process of developing an imaging system, from selection of projects to concept definition to final sign-off. If, as in many cases of imaging system design, a committee is making decisions, users (end users, not administrators or support staff) must be the key contributors to the process. If they do not understand the problems, then they must be educated first.

Ownership

Very similar to involvement, but beyond mere participation, users must be made to feel responsible for the outcome of the project. Involved users who don't feel a sense of pride and responsibility in the effort will have little motivation to reach deep and explore the possibilities of the new system. Lack of ownership will result in responses to the pilot phase of a project such as, "I know I told you that's how we do our work, but what really happens is. . . ." This kind of organizational behavior can turn a four-month project into an eighteen-month project before you can say, "Where's the schedule?" An almost infinite number of three-day and seven-day delays crop up out of nowhere. Anyone currently managing an out-of-control project who can't really pinpoint a specific problem would be well advised to look at the organization and its involvement and ownership, not of the developers, but of the end users. The symptoms are: a constant stream of changes, requirements well beyond any that your system or imaging supplier has ever run into, constant refocusing of the project, and routine turnover of "dedicated" resources from the end user community.

User Perception of Management Commitment

The subtle difference between managing the user's system and managing the user's perception of the system cannot be overemphasized. Peters and Waterman in *In Search of Excellence*[2] clarify that the difference between the delivered quality and the user's perception of quality is the final differentiation in reaching the highest attainable system quality. At first, this may sound like a way to deliver a less than high-quality system and "sell it" as quality, but it is not. No amount of selling will convince an end user that he or she is receiving a quality product if it does not perform. After delivering a quality system, it is time to begin managing the user's perceptions: Is it well supported? Is it available? Was I trained adequately? Can I see the payback? Is my life better? Are my customers better served? When the user answers these kinds of questions in the affirmative, a good system has been delivered. In the list of key elements above, the user's perception of management support hits directly on this issue. If users perceive that management believes the project is critical to success, they will be encouraged to contribute to that success. If management is committed but the users don't know it, either through lack of communication or visibly inadequate support, the project will suffer. If management truly does not support the project, why is it happening?

11.3 PREPARING THE IMAGING DATABASE— PRELIMINARY QUESTIONS

Once the overall structure of the database has been selected, the next priority is to refine the imaging system design by supplying answers to the following questions.

What Information Is to Be Stored as Images?

Choosing to store information as an image can be a complex decision. If information is mostly text with few embedded graphics, cost-effectiveness may drive a decision to file away the graphics and rely on the text alone. The wisdom of this depends on the impact of not having easy access to the graphics, the time and distances involved in recovering a copy of the original paper, the desire to get rid of paper completely, etc. In essence, ask what is the difference between the cost of making a wrong decision by having access only to the text of a document and the cost of storing sparse graphics in an otherwise text-only database? If access to source electronic documents is possible, conversion to a vector/ASCII form such as CGM may be ideal. A high content base of paper archival, inbound paper, and CAD-based documents (where non-CAD users need access) indicates image forms should be incorporated.

Textual Information

There is little reason why text should ever be stored as image (raster) since most image viewers can also view text. However, the capture of text data requires some thought as does the format of the text itself. Unformatted text, formatted text, and various forms of propriety text such as Interleaf ASCII, Encapsulated PostScript, and CGM are all possible ways that text information may arrive. Retention of descriptive data (font types and sizes, tab widths, underlines, etc.), conversion before storage to a common form, or conversion upon retrieval are all options that will place points on the cost/performance curve. Should you choose to retain descriptive information, the impact on a viewer that handles all of the above may be more costly from a purchase price and training standpoint than converting everything to a formatted ASCII for storage and viewing.

Graphics

The kind of graphics that will be stored is another of those areas where the 80/20 rule needs to be carefully evaluated. The decision that everything from CAD drawings to PowerPoint to full-color photographs must be stored can be the most expensive one any system buyer can make. The cost in conversion utilities, hardware, disk storage, and viewers can send an image system budget ballistic. A key to successful implementation is in narrowing the focus to one that satisfies a current, well-defined need and is expandable to meet future real or imagined requirements. This point cannot be overstressed: Meeting a current need is the key to initial user and management buy-in to an imaging project. Systems can be determined to be expandable in several ways:

1. Existing capability: The system being purchased already can perform the functions required in planned expansion phases.
2. Future capability: The system vendor can credibly show that the system purchased will have the future functionality to meet expected growth.
3. Conformance to standards: The system installed conforms to sufficient standards for image format, storage, and indexing methodology so that merging new functionality would require minimum energy.

How Is the Information Currently Stored?

There are several areas from which the image and indexing information can be extracted. System design must zero in on the top hitters for efficient movement between environments.

Paper

The elimination of paper accounts for only 25 percent of imaging system installations according to a recent Delphi Consulting Group survey as opposed to cost cutting and competitive advantage. Still, if that is the user's goal, decisions about back converting (capture of existing documents) and handling of new work must be made (see above), and the process of rooting out and eliminating paper must be addressed. Management of paper-based documents during conversion must be carefully handled as well, as changes occurring to documents during scanning can cause obsolete information to populate the database. The document management system, either a new one or a modified existing system, must be capable of managing the transition period while both paper and electronic media exist. In some cases where the cultural barriers are particularly high, it may be advantageous to run both systems in parallel and let users migrate gradually to the new system. Initially, the "techies" will switch, taking the role of early adopters, and they will provide encouragement and training for the less willing. Gradually, management must increase pressure to change over until the final day of cord cutting. This dual system is easier to maintain in a document distribution environment such as an engineering printroom more so than in a transactional system such as insurance claim processing.

Electronic

When the source of a document is an existing electronic form, other issues need to be addressed in formulating an effective strategy for image management. The foremost is perhaps, "Does this need imaging in the first place?" Department-level organizations or centrally managed enterprises must discover whether documents can be managed and shared using a common software platform, such as converting all to Word, Excel, or MacDraw. Since most departmental users require some or all of those tools anyway, document sharing and management can be done with simple file management functions from a product such as SoftSolution, rather than a complex electronic image management system and associated conversion tools.

Word Processing　The conversion of word processing documents into an image format can be easily accomplished. There are converters for PostScript output into a variety of raster and CGM formats. There is little case for the conversion of unformatted ASCII text to an image format. An analysis of where the documents will be used, how they are transmitted, and the volume will help determine whether the documents should be stored in the native WP format, include computer graphics metafile (CGM), or down to raster images. The mix of this kind of document vs.

others such as large-format engineering will determine the image viewer required to complete the system.

Spreadsheets Spreadsheet data is a special case of the above in that most users will have a spreadsheet program of their own available, obviating the need for imaging. In the instance where the data is to be distributed but not in modifiable form, conversion to image may be desirable, but as in the following case it may require a viewer that supports documents larger than the standard legal size.

Project Schedules The distribution of project schedules via image to large-format viewers with annotation capability can be a key way to implement a two-way, documented discussion of project management issues. In this way, a "frozen" version of a schedule can be released to a large class of project personnel, other impacted individuals, and management for review and markup without requiring that everyone purchase and be trained on the scheduling tool. The conversion to image means that users can be contacted via e-mail or other electronic means, which makes it possible for distant locations such as vendors and remote manufacturing sites in one application or co-counsel attorneys in other applications to be kept "in the loop" on project changes when paper would be slow at best. Large projects rarely fit on an 8.5" × 11" page, so that form of contact is even more cumbersome. Conversion through capture of a print spool file can be an easy way to configure and convert such large-format documents.

Databases The use of imaging to distribute database reports would seem to be of little use when, as mentioned above, most image viewers can display text and some even support the graphical annotation of text files, such as Motorola's WaveSoft.

Graphics The distribution of graphics via imaging systems, whether stand-alone or embedded in another document, is what we are all here for. The selection of viewers, conversion methodologies, and compression and decompression techniques all must center around the type of graphical objects and the end user of such documents.

How Much Information Is to Be Stored?

When the sources of data are so numerous and those sources have the ability to generate unprecedented quantities of data, the system designer must carefully evaluate what to save and what to let go. The primary issue is cost: the cost to capture or convert images, the cost of magnetic or optical file storage, and the cost of ownership such as backups and maintenance. Other factors are also significant in this decision, but honesty with oneself and the users is probably most important. It's important to ascertain what the chances are that anyone will ever use the information inscribed vs. the cost of storing or recreating the information through other means.

We have seen manufacturing environments that were entirely paper-based convert to imaging. The simple choice would have been to save all versions of the drawings on line. But examining the current system revealed that when paper was the master document, the original vanished when the pencil lines were erased and the new version was created; thus, the current version was the only one easily accessible, and everyone was used to that. No quality or end customer factors could be found to justify making the on-line system larger to accommodate old versions. Therefore, the urge to save everything on line was repressed, and the system functions very well with off-line storage of old versions. Of further impact on the decision to store only the current version was that magnetic storage was sufficient to hold the information, thus cutting substantially the cost of the file system over the optical system proposed. Additional ripple effects in the maintenance cost, ease of backup, and access time made a further positive impact on system performance and user acceptance. As discussed in the next section, it is possible to put more information in an image system than is practical to index unambiguously. The indexing capability selected should be evaluated when deciding how much to put into an imaging system. System developers must be honest about how items will be found, as well as if anybody really wants it.

What Kind of Retrieval Is Needed?

The design of a retrieval system should be based upon the actual user requirements of the particular situation. The system designer must take a careful look at what types of retrieval are necessary for a given document store in order to design the database to perform adequately at an acceptable cost.

Recall and Precision

The effectiveness of textual retrieval is often measured in terms of recall and precision. Recall measures the proportion of relevant documents retrieved by means of a query to the relevant documents not retrieved by the same query. Because of the difficulty in calculating the absolute number of relevant documents within a large production database, recall measures are usually performed on controlled test collections with controlled queries. Precision is the measure of *relevant* documents retrieved out of *all* of the documents retrieved. Because precision is calculated on just the retrieved set of documents, it is not necessary to limit its measurement to a test collection. Precision and recall are often portrayed as being inversely proportional: If measures are taken to increase recall, decreased precision will result. While this is often true, there are measures that can be taken that increase both precision and recall, such as improvement in the consistency of indexing or by overall improvement in the structure of a query. The absolute measures of precision and recall are entirely dependent on the contents of both the database and the query. These absolute measures are seldom important outside of laboratory settings. In a given design situation, however, it can be helpful to conceive of the system as emphasizing high recall (for instance, in patent searching applications where missing a single document can be crucial) or high precision (as in a library setting where students are likely to be looking for a "few good references").

Keyed Retrieval

In some situations, a unique document identifier may be the only search key necessary for image retrieval. This may apply, for example, in parts inventory systems where the only search criterion needed is the part number. The attractions to limiting to this type of retrieval are its simplicity and low cost. The disadvantages are in its relative lack of flexibility and power.

Descriptive Information

The next step in retrieval complexity and power is to add descriptive information to the document retrieval index. As mentioned before, the more the descriptive information can be normalized in a consistent manner, the greater the usefulness. Even in the simple example of the parts inventory system mentioned above, a phrase with the part name and one describing the part can greatly enhance the power of the system.

Keyword Retrieval

Keyword retrieval is the indexing of each separate word of a body of text. This body of text can be simply descriptive information or the entire text of a document. The power of keyword searching is harnessed by indexing the location information of the keyword, allowing the use of positional operations such as word adjacency or nearness. The ability to specify terms occurring in the same sentence or paragraph are other common positional operators.

Full-Text Searching

Full-text searching is the most complex and powerful method of document indexing. In full-text searching every word of a document is indexed for searching, with the usual exception of some words that occur so frequently as to render their informational content null (such as "the" or "and"). As mentioned above, full-text indexing is the most costly and the most complicated type of indexing to prepare. There are, nevertheless, situations where no other type of indexing will do, or where the effort of full-text indexing is easier than going through the rigors of preparing methods of controlled document descriptions.

11.4 PREPARING THE IMAGING DATABASE— OPERATIONAL QUESTIONS

The imaging database design is also influenced by the conditions under which the system is going to operate and the record life cycle. The following questions need to be answered before a design can be finalized.

How Will the Images Be Captured?

In developing the environment for document capture, the two key questions to investigate and decide upon are: "what" and "who." The "what" is answered by paper or film, electronic, and both. Existing bitmapped documents such as paper and microfilm have few choices for conversion and those revolve around the choice of scanners and whether to develop an in-house scanning capability or go to a service bureau. Scanners fall into two classes by price: those that require some amount of adjustment to get a good image and those that are compensated for more or less automatically. The newcomer is faced with this dilemma: A desktop scanner in the $500–$1,500 range can scan at up to 600 dpi (dots per inch) and has a sheet feeder. So why pay $10,000 and up for a scanner with the same capabilities? The user will discover that unless all the documents come off a laser printer and go directly to the scanner, the inexpensive system will require multiple scans of each page to get the brightness and contrast settings to a point where the scan quality is acceptable. We have visited sites where scanner configuration files have in excess of 400 presets to choose from for everything from fax to invoices to laser prints. These represent a tremendous investment in time and user frustration. Contrast that with the more expensive scanners that have compensation built into the scanner and produce high-quality scans over a much wider range of originals. The higher price of the scanner gets washed out when more than even a few scans a day are going to be made.

The decision about whether to go to a service bureau or not has a pretty straightforward cost analysis: the cost of equipment purchase and direct labor costs vs. the cost per page of scanning by an outside agency. Often, factors such as document security or continuous accessibility will prevent a service bureau from being used. Still, a hybrid approach can be adopted where new documents are done in-house while back-conversion of existing documents is done outside. In such an approach, however, care must be taken that indexing and file naming conventions are well understood and executed so that the two sets of images play nicely together. The last time we calculated an exact costs break-even, it was about 8,000 documents per year. Above that, it was more cost-efficient to go in-house. But, recent reductions in scanner prices and innovative new methods on the part of service bureaus have, no doubt, changed that point.

The type of document also can influence the decision. We were once back-converting engineering drawings for an organization, which had about a decade earlier, decided that the "boilerplate" section of the drawing should be updated. A 4" × 6" note was pasted over the old wording on about 1,000 drawings. As the papers sat in large flat files, the cement oozed out around the edges of the add-on sheet. When these were scanned, the cement gummed up the scanner rollers so badly that finally all the masters had to be photocopied before scanning. Too late we learned of a service bureau that filmed originals with a camera and then scanned aperture cards rather than scan the paper. Such a noncontact method is ideal for worn or valuable masters.

The other half of the "what" question answer is electronic. Access to the electronic form of documents greatly reduces the operational problems of creating image data elements. Those data elements can either be left in the native form or converted to a standard image format for consistency and lower training burdens on end users. Access to the electronic form also makes it very practical to incorporate indexing schemes such as full-text retrieval, where, rather than keywords, the entire text of the document is available for searching. In environments where both electronic conversion and scanning are used, there is very little synergy required to reduce duplication of effort.

Facsimiles (faxes) fall into that unusual limbo of being inherently electronic and almost always in paper form. Many good systems now exist for the electronic management of faxes, and businesses wishing to streamline workflows and integrate imaging systems should evaluate those with high priority.

The "who" question centers on whether a single individual or group does scanning and indexing, or whether a broadly spread community is allowed to scan and add documents to the system. As the volume of scanning builds, organizational pressure most often pushes scanning out to more and more user groups because "such a large group just does scanning!" is hard to look at on an organization chart. Whether this is the right decision is subjective, but there are more risks associated with widespread scanning due to bad scans, bad indices, and electronically misplaced images; security, audit trail, and training costs can also have negative effects on widespread scanning. In some cases, particularly when contributors are geographically distant, a good option is to submit scans and associated images to a central group of auditors who confirm quality and naming conventions and then submit the images to the on-line system.

How Will Data Be Extracted from the Images?

In order for a text retrieval system to function, it must have a body of text from which to build an index. If the document retrieval database is being built from images of documents, the images of text must somehow be converted into ASCII character representations of that text. This can be done manually by having the text keyed or by passing the images through some type of automated optical character recognition (OCR) process.

Manual Description and/or Rekeying

Manual keying of textual data has long been the primary method for transforming paper data into electronic form. The processes for data entry from paper are well understood, and there are many firms that specialize in contracting for data entry. These firms provide scheduling, facilities, coding, and quality control services. The costs for these services is based on the amount of data to be keyed and the desired level of quality. Charges typically are based on a per-kilocharacter amount; typical charges as of this writing start around 75 cents per thousand characters keyed. The advantage of manual keying is that it is an easy task to outsource with predictable costs and results.

OCR/ICR

The process of optical and/or intelligent character recognition (OCR/ICR) involves the automated recognition of ASCII character data from an electronic image. If the documents to be processed exist only on paper, then the first input step for OCR is to scan the documents to produce an image file. The OCR software then processes the image through pattern recognition algorithms, producing the ASCII output. It is much easier for OCR programs to decipher typed or printed text than it is to recognize human handwriting. Even in printed texts, the variability of type fonts, sizes, and backgrounds can have a deleterious effect on the accuracy of OCR processes, as can stylistic variations such as italic or outlined type. Very small print (generally 6 point type or smaller) is more difficult to recognize. The proper recognition of formatted tabular data is also a large consideration in many applications and is not equally supported in all software. Current programs can convert printed texts with an accuracy rate of approximately 95 percent. In most cases, the data produced by OCR will need to be proofread and edited before loading into the database. In some cases, it may turn out to be cheaper to have the data keyed manually than to begin with OCR processing. The system designer will have to decide for each application whether OCR can produce data at an acceptable error rate.

What Structure Will Be Applied to the Data?

The initial evolution of electronic document handling took place in an environment where documents always existed within the same piece of software, usually a word processing system. During the 1970s, the initial evolution of electronic publishing took place, which required publishers, usually those that indexed and abstracted journals, to distribute their data on tapes to vendors of on-line information systems. Most of these publishers created their own formats for distributing their data, requiring the information vendors to create custom conversion utilities for each vendor. As data exchange became more common, standardized distribution formats, such as MARC for library data, began to appear. With the current emergence of widely networked systems, along with the emphasis on open hardware and software systems, the use of standardized document interchange formats is assuming much greater importance.

Most document retrieval systems require that some amount of structure be applied to the text of documents that will be entered into the database. The system architect must be aware of three different levels of structure: the logical document content structure, the overall document architecture, and the physical document structure. The logical document content structure is a formalization of the content of the documents themselves. In a business letter, for instance, the standard elements include the sender's name and address, the addressee's name and address, the date, and the signature, as well as the body of text. Generally speaking, a single database is made up of documents that have a similar logical content structure. In some cases, the person responsible for database preparation will have to impose and ensure that structure upon the documents to be loaded. In all cases, the database designer will have to decide what elements are required for all documents, and a procedure for coping with missing values will need to be devised.

The overall document architecture is the application of some abstract syntax to the document content. Abstract syntax here means a way of "describing data types in a machine-independent fashion." In describing data to be added to a database, for instance, there must be some method for knowing when a given data field starts, and what the content of the data field signifies. This abstract syntax is different conceptually from the physical record format. It is possible for data to be formatted using the same abstract syntax in several different physical structures. It is also possible for systems designers to develop and implement their own abstract syntax for formatting and storing data. It is more common, however, to use typical abstract syntaxes that are imposed either by the system the data is produced in or by the document retrieval software.

The physical document structure refers to the way the bytes of electronic data are arranged on whatever medium is used to store the data. This can be referred to as the "concrete syntax." While a given document architecture will often imply the use of a corresponding physical structure, it is very helpful for the system designer to think of these as two different and separate items. This is especially true in environments where data will need to be transferred among different hardware and software architectures.

There are several competing document architecture standards currently being submitted by both vendors and standards bodies. As of this writing it is unclear which (if any) of these architectures will assume increasing importance and which will fall by the wayside. The competing architectures include: standardized generalized markup language, or SGML (ISO 8879), which is beginning to be widely used in the publishing industry; the Defense Department's Computer-Aided Acquisition and Logistics Support standard (CALS, MilStd-1840-B), which incorporates the use of SGML; the open document architecture (ODA) standard, which is an emerging ISO standard for document interchange (ISO 8613); and DEC's Compound Document Architecture (CDA) format. As more vendors begin to stress interoperability, it will be increasingly important for systems implementors to ensure that the systems they work with support data exchange in standardized formats.

Image Architecture Standards

There are as many ways to store bitmapped image data as there are ways to create it. An excellent reference book is *Graphics File Formats*.[3] This gives a detailed look at 24 common image formats and a brief description of 24 others. In general, there are two types: raster and vector. Raster data represents a bitmapped image in rows of image data. The resolution of the image is determined by how many bits of image data are represented per row and by how many rows there are. This information is either uncompressed or compressed via a number of lossless techniques such as CCITT Group IV or lossy techniques such as JPEG.

Where Will the Image Be Stored?

One of the more arguable decisions in the design of an imaging system is where to store the images.

Integrated Storage

One school subscribes to placing the image objects in the actual database schema. The argument is that this improves synchronization of the image and meta-data about the image. The argument against is potentially massive databases, with unknown impact on backups and access times.

Separate Storage

The other school argues that images should be stored separately from the database and use pointers to the image data. The advantage of reduced database size, however, is offset by the "double commit" process of updating image data separately from the associated meta-data. Another drawback of that method is a reduced robustness of the imaging system in case of system failure. Because pointers are on a separate medium, loss of these pointers or of synchronization with the image content will result in a total loss of access to the imaging data.

Media Selection

Most people considering imaging systems seem to assume automatically that optical storage, particularly jukeboxes, are the required storage media for imaging systems. This is far from true and may be the last thing an end user wants for his or her imaging system. Unless the image database is expected to grow beyond about 10GB, the system developer should strongly consider the option of using simple magnetic hard disk storage. Systems that have a high rate of change documents may want to push even larger magnetic options. Large disk farms are certainly manageable but issues of backup and recovery become greater concerns.

Before selecting WORM (Write Once Read Many) drives, the feasibility of erasable-optical (EO) and magneto-optical (MO) drives, both of which are erasable, should be considered. Highly static data and "forever" archive requirements will move the user toward WORM storage. Any choice for optical involves high media cost, potentially difficult backup and recovery strategies, and often closed system architectures. Disk swapping times in seconds to tens of seconds can impact system performance at the user level. Combination technologies, which mix magnetic and optical disk such as Epoch, can eliminate much of the system integration headaches of stand-alone optical storage systems and reduce or eliminate the user's negative perception of system latency.

11.5 QUALITY CONTROL

A last consideration in the design of the imaging system is adequateness of the database to support quality control procedures. One significant claim of image-based document management systems is that of "no lost documents." This claim is true in a well-administered system, but only if the document gets in correctly in the first place. The control of the capture, naming, and indexing processes is absolutely critical. Whereas misfiled paper can be found based on other documents that were in use, which drawers were opened, etc., incorrectly naming and indexing an electronic image can randomly place documents anywhere within millions and millions of pages, making them statistically lost forever. Or, incorrectly increment-ing an index at the beginning of the day can leave thousands of documents "off by one" at the end of the day. This, added to an optical storage environment, can be a time-consuming and costly mistake.

The most critical data is input using a double blind method with two operators: The first operator inputs the document ID, which is read from the first page, and the number of pages from the title bar. After scanning, a checker is presented with the image of the first and last pages of the document and the electronic page count. The quality of the scan is evaluated. The second operator checks the first and last page title bars to match page count and types in the document ID read from the image. The checking software matches the initial ID typed in during scanning with the ID read from the document. After these checks are passed, the document is available for release into the system. When batch scanning is taking place, care must be exercised that up-issues of documents are not mishandled while the current version is out for scanning. Chances are that the existing paper environment that is being replaced has a very formal, if not fast, method for controlling the release of changes to documents. Relaxing those standards with the advent of electronic imaging is probably not in the best interest of the organization. It does offer significant opportunity to gather statistics on usage and users and provide a framework for intelligent decision making in further modifying the workflow of a business or organization.

11.6 CONCLUSION: IMAGE ENABLING EXISTING INSTALLATIONS

Perhaps the single biggest challenge facing IS departments in the 1990s will be how to add imaging to existing systems. The "back up the truck" approach to conversion, where all the existing hardware and software is loaded up and driven away while all the new hardware and software is taken off and installed, is just not an option for most businesses. The cost in equipment, software, data conversion, and retraining is beyond budgetary limits in times of intense global competition and worldwide recessionary trends. This is true even in some cases where the payback in future cost avoidance and better cycle times is easy to see. Management has to allocate limited dollars to all areas of the business, and extraordinary expenses in IS often get cut proportionally with other business entities. So, the question remains, how does the IS manager, with perhaps half the money he or she needs for a totally new system, implement business-changing methods of handling critical information? While the answer varies from site to site, some general principles apply.

A first consideration for "the biggest bang for the smallest buck" item is usually in the area of networking. A principal benefit of imaging in the enterprise arena is that workers who previously had access to documents only through paper now have that access electronically. Network upgrades that allow fast, economical transfer of large binary objects to all areas of the business will have lasting payback. Connections that allow heterogeneous computer environments to share information, both text and binary, inside and outside the company, are the single most important aspect in creating a paradigm shift in the way companies design, manufacture, sell, and support products and services. (The topic of networking is treated elsewhere in this work.)

A second consideration in adding imaging to an existing environment is salvaging hardware, facilitated by the fact that the days of proprietary imaging workstations are at an end. The challenge now is to select software that will allow existing computers, often from different manufacturers with different operating systems, to access image data over the newly upgraded network. Two methods are used to address this: terminal emulation and multiplatform software. The first method involves adding terminal emulation software to existing DOS, Macintosh, UNIX, or other computer environments, with all users then actually running from one or more dedicated servers. The advantage is that all data and the "core" image processing is done centrally, where it can be better monitored and controlled. As the user base grows, however, that advantage also becomes the disadvantage, because all user functions, including pan/zoom/print are done on the image server, with a large amount of network traffic supporting the many users accessing that host.

The second method involves a more client-server approach where imaging viewing and manipulation software is installed on each user's computer and the image objects are sent in compressed form from the storage device to user, where decompression/pan/zoom/print are supported. Image meta-data, index, and retrieval information can either be located and accessed on the central server or distributed around the network as well. Some systems allow both methods to be implemented successfully, and the former approach is used for departmental data, where a limited, controlled number of users access image and indexing information on a UNIX workstation via X-emulation software from PCs and Macintoshes. The latter is the case for enterprise-wide applications. An example is in an electronic printroom shared among different organizational units. In a particular case, five regional "printroom" servers are accessed by over 3,000 user clients. Compressed image data is sent to the user where the decompression/viewing is done. A customizable API (application program interface) allows the same viewing software to be used for both applications.

Imaging enabling an existing system requires the addition of information about the images to a current database. As discussed above, image meta-data is fundamentally different from other data in the system. For the most part, it contains no information that is of primary interest to the end user. It fails the relational test given at the beginning of the chapter in that it is not perceived by the user as a table, and its function is not to generate another table. Once again, there is no "one size fits all" solution to adding the image meta-data to a database, but it should be a major area of interest in the design and implementation. The creation of the meta-data and its inclusion in the database should be as automated as possible. Ideally, all meta-data required to select an image exists in the current database, with the exception of where it is physically located in the file system. Information such as date, last access, revision level, document ID numbers, customer reference number, associated PO, or part numbers, which are already captured, are enough to narrow a search to a single image document or at least a set of image documents. Often, such information can be captured via selective OCR, or ICR as it is sometimes called, as part of the scanning process.

Once the network, hardware, software, and meta-data are in place, and the images are captured and indexed in a file system, the last element of image enabling is the design and implementation of the user interface to proceed from narrowing a search to identify a single image to the retrieval and viewing of the desired image. The simplest case, an archival or document distribution system, requires only that a single "button" be added with a descriptive title; "view image" leaps to mind. Transaction-oriented data, especially that where images are annotated as part of a review or sign-off process, require a more robust user interface and document control methodology.

NOTES

[1] Belasco, J., *Teaching the Elephant to Dance: Empowering Change in Your Organization* (New York: Crown Publishers), 1990.

[2] Peters, T., and R. Waterman, *In Search of Excellence: Lessons from America's Best-Run Companies* (New York: HarperCollins), 1982.

[3] Kay, D., and J. Levine, *Graphics File Formats* (Blue Ridge Summit, PA: Windcrest/McGraw-Hill), 1992.

12

Graphical User Interfaces and Imaging Systems

Jean-Marie Chauvet

Neuron Data

Editor's Notes

Early imaging systems had very simple graphical user interfaces (GUIs): a few command and status lines for interaction with the system and the rest of the screen to exhibit the raster image of a document on a monochrome screen. In those times, waiting several seconds to bring a full image to display was not really objectionable. And even when windowing was used to allow for instant simultaneous presentation of images and indexing information, the additional demands on computer resources from the "text" windows were relatively modest and did not significantly affect overall response time.

This "slow pace" has changed drastically over the past few years. First, imaging applications have moved into the mainstream of information transfer, and fast response is as much a matter of marketing and user acceptance as it is a necessity to free computer resources for other tasks. Second, with the appearance of graphical platforms, such as Microsoft Windows and OS/2 Presentation Manager, image display must now compete for resources with other graphical applications. Even on Apple systems, which always had a GUI, raster output requirements have a negative effect on response time. Third, graphical interface requirements have diversified, as the same screen is used to meet different operational requirements. Of particular concern are high-resolution monitors that are increasingly used in imaging systems and require a large amount of memory.

It is the purpose of this chapter to review the trade-offs that must be made in the design of a network imaging system when selecting a user interface.

233

12.1 STRUCTURE OF STANDARD GUIs

The ubiquitous desktop metaphor has quickly permeated the software industry after its early champions Xerox and Apple Computer first introduced hardware and system software to support desktop computing. The user interface quickly and rightly became the focal point of software development and delivery as more and more mission critical applications found their way to the "personal computing" environment.

As commercial products implementing and using GUI services were marketed, concepts, vocabulary, and practices were formalized. Mouse clicks and windows became familiar to the corporate worker on the personal computer or workstation. And despite the variety of GUIs currently available on different platforms, the underlying services offered by the system software layers are similar (see Figure 12.1).

At the bottom layer lies the operating system, primarily responsible for non-graphical tasks like process or memory management. The second layer consists of the "windowing system," responsible for low-level drawing and windowing primitives (clipping, and overlapping windows for instance), as well as window-related events (mouse clicks, joysticks, touch-screen, etc.). (Note that except for some operating systems that offer built-in network services, all layers are to be considered applications with respect to the standard OSI model.)

Writing an application that supports a GUI at the windowing system level represents a serious development effort, because even a simple graphical object like a push button involves fairly complex and tedious drawing and event management. So-called "graphical toolkits" were developed to alleviate the task of the programmer by creating templates of standard interface behavior like push buttons, check boxes, or scroll bars to populate windows (see Figure 12.2). These graphical templates, which, incidentally, were the subject of intense standardization and definition efforts by various vendors consortia over the past years, are called widgets or controls and encapsulate simple behaviors of the user interface. The application programmer is expected to choose the appropriate widgets for its GUI development and write code that makes direct use of the standard behaviors embedded in the toolkit widgets.

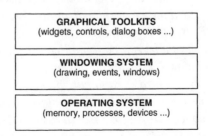

Figure 12.1   Standard system software layers in GUIs

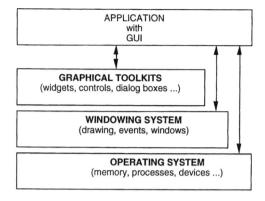

Figure 12.2   An application supporting a GUI

Although the previously described layered structure is fairly standard among various system software, a variety of incompatible operating systems designed for different processors and hardware architecture have evolved, thereby inducing an even wider variety of windowing systems and toolkits. Table 12.1 shows the various layers in the current state-of-the-art standards of the industry.

In addition to toolkits provided by hardware or system software vendors, higher-level toolkits became available from third-party commercial sources. The latter toolkits and products are often domain-specific, like dynamic graphic widgets for real-time, scientific, or CAD-CAM applications.

In an attempt to further formalize the desktop metaphor, vendors promoted their definition of the way a desktop should appear and behave when interacting with

Table 12.1   Standard operating systems and respective windowing systems and toolkits

Operating System	Windowing System	Toolkit
MacOS	MacOS : QuickDraw, Window Manager	MacOS Toolbox
DOS	MS Windows 3.xx: GDI	MS Windows Controls in Windows SDK
OS/2	Presentation Manager: GPI	PM SDK : complies to CUA'91
UNIX (various flavors)	X Windows v. 11, release 4 and 5	Xt XView NeWS Xt + Open Look Xt + Motif
VAX/VMS	DECWindows	OSF/Motif
NeXT (UNIX)	NeXTStep	NeXTStep

the user through formal and informal groups like OSF, UNIX International, or on an individual basis like Apple Computer, IBM, or Microsoft. These definitions are known as "look and feel" and are made public so that application developers can comply with them, and hence support and enforce homogeneous computing environment for users of their software applications.

12.2 AN OVERVIEW OF GUI SERVICES

The variety of GUI services provided to the application developer directly reflects the diversity of operating systems, windowing systems, and toolkits. It is important to understand both the quantity and the quality of the GUI features and services available to the application developer in the specific case of a network imaging system. The development—and at a later stage the maintenance efforts—for such applications, ultimately rely on the quantity, complexity, and quality of source code produced by the application developer. The availability of well-specified, widely published, well-understood tools and standards has a drastic influence on both the design and development maintenance process. On the other hand, user acceptance of the final application ultimately relies on the appropriate choice and organization of task-specific graphical objects on the desktop interface. Proper user interface design is still pretty much considered as craftsmanship, but is nonetheless critical for the success of imaging systems.

From the application developer's perspective, there are various technical dimensions to consider along which GUI services of various platforms can be organized and compared. The following discussion first emphasizes the *windowing model* dimension: Windows has become a ubiquitous word that defines different entities in different windowing systems. The second dimension of interest is the *metaphor* dimension for user interaction with the application: Form-based interfaces, iconic interfaces, and multimedia applications are all built on top of similar GUI services but support different metaphoric interactions with the end user.

Metaphors to Compute By

Metaphors invisibly permeate everyday speech and language; they act as a web of terms and associations that color the way we speak and think about a concept. As such it is no surprise to find that metaphors permeate in a very similar way human-machine communication through the user interface. They are a powerful and essential part of our thinking because they suggest models of reality. The interface metaphors exhibit the same properties: When an interface metaphor provides the user with realistic expectations about what will happen, system utility is enhanced; when one leads users astray or simply leads them nowhere, it fails.

Perhaps the most pervasive metaphor is the document-application distinction most interfaces impose on the user tasks. Regardless of how information is represented, it is generally agreed that users produce, input, edit, alter, and output documents with special-purpose applications. In this framework the computer can be seen as an information amplifier; the user operates on information like an electronic amplifier acts on electric sound signals.

The next layer metaphor is now well known as the desktop metaphor, which originated at Xerox PARC and was mass marketed by the Macintosh computer. The screen is a desktop on which documents and applications—tools to work on documents—are readily accessible through two input devices: the keyboard and the mouse. Documents and applications are represented as icons, and starting an application to operate on a document usually results in the document being presented within a window. Actions are available through menus and operations of the mouse. Of course, the screen does not behave exactly like a desktop, nor do the tools behave like their real counterparts. The overall and consistent use of icons, a mouse, windows, and menus, does, however, successfully implement the document and desktop metaphor within the bidimensional computer screen.

The field of interaction techniques is a wide open area of research culminating with what is now usually referred to as virtual reality. In these environments input devices like the dataglove or head-mounted displays like NASA Ames Virtual Workstation Environment are designed to closely mimic reality and offer a much larger array of interaction techniques to the user interface designer. Within a different framework, pen devices and the PenPoint operating system are interesting attempts at merging keyboard and pointing devices into a simpler device.

Eventually, new metaphors will appear to complement or replace the current ones. Two directions are quite promising: *reducing* the current desktop metaphor, in order to make it simpler to use interfaces; and *extending* current metaphors to cope with larger and larger volumes of more complex information. In the first class of metaphor shifts, the PenPoint operating system for pen-based notebooks is a prominent example. The screen is no longer a representation of a desktop but rather the representation of a folder that contains documents, still represented as icons or within windows. The whole interaction, however, is based on gestures rather than operations of conventional input devices like keyboards. All operations are executed through a restricted set of gestures with the pen, calling on the pen and paper metaphor directly rather than the desktop/document/tool metaphor previously mentioned.

Two critical illustrations of the extension of the desktop metaphor are the Information Visualizer from Xerox PARC and the NASA Ames Virtual Workstation Environment. They both try to tackle the problem of processing huge volumes of information by extending the desktop metaphor by making use of 3-D. In Information Visualizer, the screen is only a view on a particular room, and the user navigates through rooms and views according to tasks to be performed. Information Visualizer makes use of color and 3-D rendering with innovative widgets like 3-D Cam Trees and Perspective Walls and can be considered as the culminating development of hypertext concepts. On an even larger scale, the NASA Ames Virtual Workstation Environment relies on human body metaphors: for example, telepresence, a term coined for aerospace applications of user interfaces. The interface is the whole universe, and head-mounted screens linked to datagloves or special suits packed with mechanical sensors enable the user to actually move and act *within* the interface to perform tasks, pretty much like he or she would in actual reality.

Windowing Models

Although the term "windows" is used over and over in the GUI context, under closer scrutiny it seems to cover different entities in different operating systems. Each standard operating system in the industry, with its accompanying windowing environment, actually implements different windowing models. This section provides a quick survey of the various windowing models underlying these windowing systems.

The Window as a View to a Document

In all windowing systems, documents in the most general sense are displayed in windows. Documents can be text in a word processor, numbers in a spreadsheet, tables in a database, or images or graphics in a desktop publishing system. They are usually larger than the computer screen; therefore, a window displays only part of the document. At any given time, one or more windows displaying the same or different documents are floating on the computer screen, similar to a pile of papers lying on a desktop. This describes the basic desktop metaphor, where overlapping windows populate computer screens.

The basic desktop metaphor is usually coupled with an iconic representation, where nondisplayed documents and applications to produce them are displayed as icons on the screen/desktop. The mouse is used to operate on icons (documents and applications) using simple codified gestures like clicks, double-clicks, drag and drop, and so forth.

Windows are nothing more than containers for the representation of documents, which can be operated on in an icon-based visual environment. This metaphor is demonstrated in the Macintosh OS, MS Windows and upcoming NT, Presentation Manager on OS/2, and the numerous desktop products running with or on top of standards like Open Look or OSF/Motif.

The Window as a Graphical Object

In several windowing systems and toolkits, all visual elements cluttering the computer screen are actually windows. In this case, the latter visual object might look different on the screen but is implemented in the system software as a window. In such windowing systems, a button or a text field is implemented as windows, as are windows in the sense of the previous paragraph.

This use of the window as an implementation artifact for all graphical objects of the GUI provides a very homogeneous and compact implementation of system software layers in windowing systems, as it relies on a single data structure, which is reused to serve different purposes. This model is supported by MS Windows and NT as well as by Presentation Manager and the X library underlying Open Look and OSF/Motif.

The Window as a Resource

A further dimension of the window is unveiled in the unique client-server architecture of the X Windows model implemented in the X library, and accompanying Xt, Open Look, or OSF/Motif toolkits. In this model, the application and the GUI to the application might be running on different computers linked by a local TCP/IP network.

To the application, the display workstation is literally a display server allocating and deallocating window resources as needed by the remote application, which operates as its client. This model has several advantages in addition to providing the visual rendering of documents previously described: Any given application is easily displayed on physically distinct terminal workstations, perhaps supporting different characteristics or features (color, resolution, size, etc.). It simply requests the appropriate terminal to service its display over the network, without having to know the specificity of the addressed terminal. Further, adding new display terminals and workstations does not entail modifications to the existing applications, as the latter additions are handled by the X server, which is responsible for allocating and dispatching graphical resources requested by running applications. This model enforces a clear separation between the GUI layer, which is running with its own shared server, and the application back-end, which acts as a client to the X server.

The Window as a Process

The amalgam between the pure GUI concept of the window as a visual container of information and the operating system view of the window as a computing data structure is pushed even further in windowing systems like Presentation Manager and MS Windows. In the latter model, the window is also considered as an operating system process, which is actually scheduled by the operating system, competing for the computing resources (CPU time and memory).

In such models all graphical objects are windows, and all windows are processes with events flowing back and forth between windows as control moves from one program area to another in response to user actions and application operation. Each window is associated with a so-called "window procedure" in the source program that handles all incoming events to the window and is allowed to send or propagate events to other windows in the application.

This model also extends in NT to interapplication communication, where messages can be sent across applications using network services provided by the operating system. A somewhat equivalent interwindow communication service is provided by AppleEvents in the new Macintosh System 7 release, although in the Mac model there are graphical objects that are not windows, and windows cannot be considered as processes, strictly speaking.

The design and complexity of the underlying model has a direct influence on the difficulty of the implementation of network imaging systems. In addition, overall performance of the imaging system ultimately relies on features supported by the windowing system. In this respect, the GUI design methodology and tools are critical to the successful development and deployment of such systems.

Overview of Operating and Windowing Systems

This section surveys the various services offered by several industry standard operating and windowing systems: first, and by chronological order, MS-DOS, which supports command line interface for 80 columns by 25 lines, on nonbitmapped terminals. Several toolkits were developed after DOS was introduced to provide some level of window functionality. The latter toolkits are often referred to as "semi-graphic" libraries and provide limited windowing and mouse support.

The veteran of GUIs was first introduced in 1980 with Apple Lisa, then in 1984 for the Apple Macintosh. The Mac Toolbox burned in ROM actually contained a full-fledged operating system, windowing system, and toolkit. Based on pioneering research work at Xerox PARC, the Apple Macintosh was really the first mass-market personal computer to fully support the window-as-a-view model previously outlined. The GUI is the core of any Macintosh application, much more than on any other operating system or windowing system. A Macintosh application is event-driven and reacts to user interaction rather than performs a predefined hard-coded task. The Macintosh proprietary OS recently has been considerably enhanced by the introduction of System 7, which provides direct support for networked applications, file sharing, interprocess communications, and multimedia—including compressed real-time video, which makes it an attractive platform for network imaging systems.

The MS Windows environment was designed as a system software layer on top of and compatible with DOS. In its various versions, MS Windows fully supports mouse and window-based GUIs with extensive drawing and event-handling facilities. MS Windows supports the window-as-a-view windowing model, but also implements the graphical-object-as-window and window-as-process models. Each graphical object is actually implemented as a window, with its specific window procedure responsible for handling events sent both by user interactions and by other applications or system layers. In MS Windows, windows are visual representation for the GUI and also computational structures used by programmers to create software applications. Whereas the operating system remains the underlying DOS, MS Windows can use all CPU and memory resources; and from the application programmer point of view, its actual role is similar to an operating system, windowing system, and graphical toolkit.

The Windows NT environment generally provides the operating, windowing, and toolkit services supported by MS Windows on additional hardware platforms, whereas MS Windows is restricted to Intel processor-based machines. NT also incorporates network support at the operating system level.

It is worth mentioning that multimedia extensions, and more specifically video handling services, are becoming available for the Windows environment family. These usually involve additional hardware equipment: special video and sound boards and system software.

Based on the OS/2 operating system, which was designed as an alternative to UNIX without the DOS limitations for Intel processor-based machines, the Presentation Manager environment includes extensive drawing and event-handling capabilities, as well as mouse and window support. Presentation Manager is a critical component of the IBM extensive specification and definition of GUIs called CUA.

As operating systems, OS/2 and MS Windows differ in the way they support 32-bit addressing of recent Intel processors, both in the level of network support they provide, as well as the way they schedule processes and resources between running applications. From the windowing system and toolkit viewpoint, though, functionality is similar and several elements are common to both environments. In addition, OS/2 can run MS Windows and DOS applications, and MS Windows can run DOS applications.

UNIX is a full-fledged operating system supporting command-line interfaces, multiuser and multiprocess applications, and network applications. Windowing systems are a late addition to the UNIX operating system, and the X Windows model, originally developed at MIT, quickly became the de facto standard on UNIX-based platforms and some non-UNIX environments like Digital Equipment's VAX/VMS. X Windows implements the client-server windowing model outlined earlier, where windows are display resources requested by the application. There is a wide variety of GUI toolkits available on top of the X Windows system: Sun Microsystems has developed NeWS, and later Open Look, to specify the appearance of the GUI on their workstations. From other vendors, other specifications have emerged like OSF/Motif. Various toolkits are available on UNIX to conform to the GUI in various looks and feels: the X libraries, the X toolkit (Xt), the Motif toolkit, and even higher-level toolkits to generate Motif or Open Look specific code. The choice of a toolkit can critically impact on the overall performance of a network imaging system, especially in the case of the UNIX operating system.

Although a fairly recent introduction to the market, the NeXT workstations support innovative GUIs and development environment. The GUI presentation layer, called NeXTStep, allows the application developer literally to draw the GUI to the application and specify interactively the drawing and event handling. The whole environment is fully object-oriented, promoting reusability, modular development, and improved maintainability. NeXT also supports multimedia applications with built-in features like sound annotation—so called "lip service"—and Display PostScript imaging.

Table 12.2 recaps the various graphic dimensions by which to classify the standard windowing environments. Note that some features are dependent on the operating system itself, while others are provided with varying depths by the windowing systems or toolkits. The next section covers the development methods and available software tools to make the best use of these features when building imaging applications in heterogeneous network environments.

12.3 ISSUES IN GUI DEVELOPMENT

As outlined before, the world of the GUI is a heterogeneous universe of hardware platforms, system software layers, and toolkits. The previous discussion emphasized the fact that the various operating, windowing systems, and toolkits are incompatible. This heterogeneity is the critical issue to consider when developing and maintaining windows-based network imaging systems that are expected to run

Table 12.2   Relevant services offered by standard graphical environments for network imaging applications

	Windowing Model	Drawing	Fonts, Colors	Application Communication	Network Support	Locali-zation	Multimedia
DOS		semi-graphic	fixed				
Macintosh	window as view	Quick-Draw	bit-mapped, outline	Apple-Events, Edition Manager	PPC Toolbox	sort, format script keyboard	sound video (Quicktime)
MS Windows	object as window, window as process	GDI	bitmapped, outline	Dynamic Data Exchange, Object Linking and Embedding		format keyboard	additional hardware required
OS/2 PM	window as process, object as window	GPI	bitmapped	DDE support, Multithreads		format keyboard	
UNIX X-based GUIs	window as resource	X library	bitmapped	mailboxes, RPC	sockets, RPC		
MS Windows NT	object as window, window as process	GDI	bitmapped, outline	Dynamic Data Exchange, Object Linking and Embedding	network support	format keyboard	additional hardware required

in different environments while providing the same level of functionality. Recent studies by Carnegie-Mellon University and IBM Corporation have shown that on a survey of 74 software projects with a mean code length of 132,000 lines, an average of 48 percent of the code is devoted to the user interface, and even more so in imaging systems.

The second critical issue is extensibility of the graphical metaphor. Because mission critical applications rely on task-dependent functionality, specific user interfaces might be required that go beyond the standard services (widgets or controls) supported by standard native toolkits. The extensibility of the graphical toolkit is a major issue when considering user acceptance, successful deployment, and maintenance of the imaging applications. Again, the various platforms differ in their support for toolkit extensibility.

This section discusses the major issues to consider when embarking on a software project for an imaging system in a network environment and surveys some of the feasible methods and usable tools to assist the applications developer.

Portability for a Network Environment

Portability of the GUI is a critical issue as network applications ultimately will run from a heterogeneous set of workstations. Preserving the full functionality of the

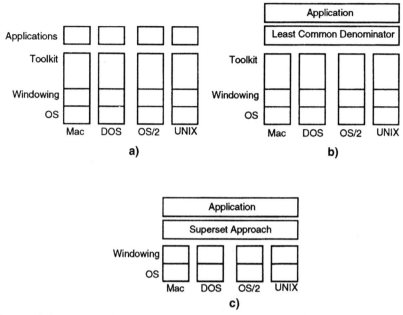

Figure 12.3   Three methods for developing portable GUIs

applications across various operating systems, windowing systems, and possibly different looks and feels requires a good understanding of the previously mentioned GUI features. Figure 12.3 shows three methods for developing portable GUIs. The method displayed on the top left makes use only of the native toolkits; the one on the top right shows the structure of "least common denominator" additional toolkits; and the one at the bottom displays the recommended "superset" combined extensible and portable approach.

Incidentally, the diversity of such GUI environments and their diverging set of features and services places additional burden on the programmers and developers of such applications. From the user standpoint, learning or relearning different environments when moving from one workstation to another can be a real barrier to the actual deployment and acceptance of imaging systems.

There are three ways to tackle the portability problem with various degrees of achievement. Figure 12.4 shows a native toolkit approach. It is characterized by duplicate developments and development teams, heavy learning costs, nonhomogeneous functionality, and high maintenance costs.

A first method is to use the native toolkit (see Figure 12.3a) on each platform supported by the imaging system. This approach is very costly in development and maintenance resources, because different programmers have to be trained on different toolkits and produce different source code for the application. In addition, the level of functionality reached by the different sources might be machine-dependent as the toolkits and windowing systems differ in their support for graphical objects.

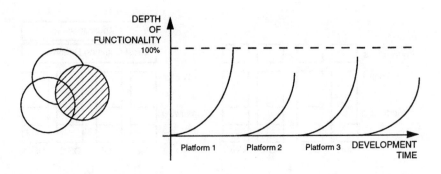

Figure 12.4   The native toolkit approach

A second method is to use additional software layers on top of the native toolkits, providing some limited support for common widgets among toolkits. This approach, known as "the least common denominator," works only for GUIs that restrict their use of widgets and controls to services that are common to all toolkits and windowing systems. This unduly restricts and constrains the functionality of the GUI, as the intersection of services is close to empty (see Figure 12.3b). Furthermore, as multimedia and upcoming extensions of the graphical metaphors are hitting the market, the common services are likely to be even more restricted. Finally, this approach does not support GUI extensibility, which was outlined as a major issue when building custom applications. New or innovative widgets and interfaces cannot be supported by the least common denominator approach, because, by definition, the latter widgets lie outside the area of common services.

Recently, though, a third approach combines portability and extensibility by not using the native toolkits, providing a superset of all widgets found in all toolkits, and portable extensions to the toolkits. This approach was made feasible following the introduction of advanced, open interface software tools for designing GUIs. The superset toolkit directly hooks into the windowing system layer rather than into the native toolkits, thus providing better performance at execution time and extensibility, as widgets are described and coded independently from the operating and windowing systems on which they ultimately will run. The applications developer writes less code and higher-level algorithms which can be extended as required without sacrificing portability of the application.

Figure 12.4 shows a native toolkit approach. It is characterized by duplicate developments and development teams, heavy learning costs, nonhomogeneous functionality, and high maintenance costs.

Figure 12.5 shows how the least common denominator approach constrains the applications developer to only the common widgets supported by the native toolkits, provides no extensibility, incurs heavy training and maintenance costs, and might involve redesign and rework when some platforms are incompletely supported.

Figure 12.6 shows how the superset approach reduces development and maintenance costs by providing combined portability and extensibility.

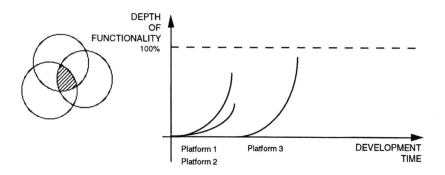

Figure 12.5   The least common denominator approach

Performance for Image Rendering

Image rendering performance depends on the hardware platform and its depth of support provided by the system software layers, as well as on how the native toolkits operate the underlying windowing system.

Drawing support is, in this respect, the essential feature; more specifically, attention must be paid to how the toolkit and windowing system handle display resolution, graphic devices, and time-consuming operations like painting, clipping, drawing off screen, and the like. While most toolkits—with the exception of native DOS—support bitmapped color displays and bitmapped and outline (TrueType) fonts and color definition, they still differ on several critical dimensions. X Windows, for instance, provides very low level support for graphical regions, clipping, and repainting events. On the other hand, its client-server architecture maps into network applications relatively easy. The latter operations are best supported in the Macintosh toolbox, which in addition has an efficient and fast implementation package (QuickDraw). High-resolution screens often require ad-

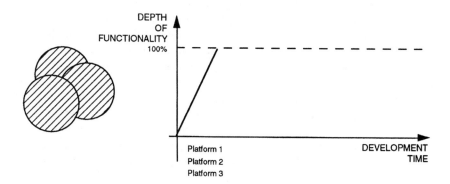

Figure 12.6   The superset approach

ditional hardware equipment and graphic device drives to MS Windows or Presentation Manager environments. The Macintosh supports multiple physical screens and displays, as well as off-screen painting. The NeXT environment works with Display PostScript, thereby eliminating screen resolution issues, for instance, and providing photographic quality displays.

To summarize, while most platforms support the basic drawing operations required for image rendering, the efficiency of implementation and overall performance of the applications differs widely according to the chosen platform.

Performance for Event Handling

The GUI imposes its event-driven flavor to the application architecture. User interactions are translated by the operating system into events that are passed up to the windowing system and toolkits. When supported, interapplication communication and network operations also translate into a discrete flow of events to the application. When considering GUI extensibility issues, the ability to create and use new user-defined events in the application is critical.

In the context of imaging systems, the granularity of supported events defines the interactivity of the application. While most GUI development environments offer some level of event handling for mouse or keyboard devices, toolkits define higher-level events that are specific to widgets they implement. A sequence of low-level events is transformed into a unique high-level event: For example, a mouse button down event, followed by a series of mouse movements, and a final mouse button up event are translated into a "button click" event to the widget, which is further processed by the toolkit to notify the application that a particular button has been clicked. Visual metaphors and interactivity of the application rely on this parsing of the flow of low-level events into significant functional events in the application. In most windowing systems and toolkits, this sequential filtering of events is supported, although there might be different implementations for the different levels of granularity, as is the case for the Macintosh, MS Windows, PM, and X Windows. This is not, however, the case for DOS, where the event-driven architecture is actually hidden from the developer and all programs are procedural in nature.

This event-driven flow of control finds its best expression in an environment like NeXTStep where it permeates not only the GUI, but the whole application. The object-oriented and coherent nature of both the operating and windowing systems breaks the flow of control of the entire application into messages sent back and forth between objects. In this object-oriented model, user-generated events are nothing but messages sent to the graphical objects of the GUI, which in turn react by possibly sending additional messages to application objects and so forth. Because imaging systems handle visual information at different levels of granularity, both in terms of representation and processing, the object model might ease the design and maintenance phases by providing a unique model for entities and data structures implementing the application.

Performance for Cooperative Processing

In network applications, besides the sheer hardware bandwidth of the links between workstations, the major critical criterion for selecting an architecture is the quality of dialog management between the GUI and the application's back-end: How is the work split between the clients and the servers, and what type of cooperative processing is being used in the application? In this respect, too, the various operating and windowing systems with their toolkits and design tools differ in service and performance.

Here the trade-off is between performance and complexity of the dialog management. Various windowing environments support different models; therefore, performance of some operations depends on design choices. X Windows or MS Windows insist on each graphical element being a window receiving a comprehensive set of messages from the user or from other parts of the system. This model requires that the dialog part of the GUI actually pay attention to messages that are potentially irrelevant to particular graphical objects; some overhead, therefore, exists in handling the latter messages. On the Macintosh, on the other hand, each graphical object supports its own application programming interface (API), which is different for each widget or control. This usually simplifies the dialog management at the additional cost of writing widget-specific code, even for similar processing.

This situation is made more complex when considering client-server services directly supported by the operating system of the windowing system itself. With NT network services between local area networks of PCs, they are directly supported by the operating system. APIs are defined for program-to-program interapplication communication, making it easy to split computational work between different applications running on different workstations. The Macintosh System 7 also supports its own form of interapplication communication at different levels: program-to-program or AppleEvents at a higher level. On stand-alone systems, DDE and OLE as defined by Microsoft for MS Windows environments offer similar high-level interapplication communication. On the UNIX-based platform, the existence of pipes or of remote procedure calls (RPC) allow low-level communication between processes, while the X Windows model relies on the client-server type of communications between the application and its GUI, which lends itself to cooperative processing design.

In imaging systems, when several tasks are clearly identified like scanning, storing, rendering, compressing, and decompressing, these tasks might be better implemented as a collection of communicating processes rather than as a bigger single unit. In a network application, the cooperative processing might help to balance the load of resources between different workstations at run time, thus offering smoother interfaces to the user and fewer delays between commands and their results.

The balance is a combination of hardware design choices (topology of the LAN and choice of a communication protocol) and software design choices (several clients single-server architecture vs. several clients distributed servers or fully cooperative processing between distributed processes).

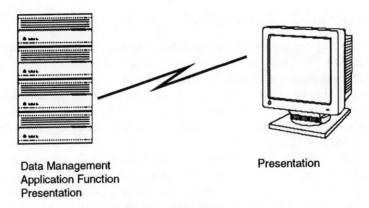

Data Management
Application Function
Presentation

Presentation

Figure 12.7   Frontware client-server model

Developers can choose from several application partitioning options. Frontware strategy, as shown in Figure 12.7, gives host applications a new look and feel; remote presentation maintains host control over presentation, a distributed database management system places single-data store on multiple processors, and distributed transaction enables applications to invoke one another. Figure 12.8 shows the remote presentation client-server model, Figure 12.9 displays the distributed DBMS client-server model, and Figure 12.10 shows the distributed transaction client-server model.

Localization

Localization is the process by which the application GUI can be adapted to support diverse national languages and representation formats; it is also referred to in the literature as internationalization. Needless to say, this issue could prove critical when considering applications targeted at global markets and different countries.

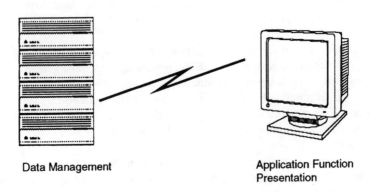

Data Management

Application Function
Presentation

Figure 12.8   Remote presentation client-server model

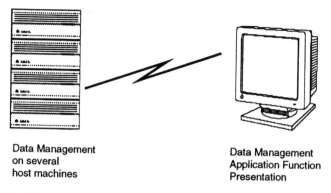

Data Management
on several
host machines

Data Management
Application Function
Presentation

Figure 12.9   Distributed DBMS client-server model

Localization issues are both hardware- and software-related: Different keyboards are physical devices handled by separate drivers, whereas scripting direction or different alphabets are supported by software drivers in the operating or windowing system.

One of the most comprehensive sets of internationalization services is provided by the Macintosh System 7. Along with keyboards and fonts, which can be customized to support national languages, the Script Manager provides additional flexible services to handle the direction of writing in text editors, for instance; or keyboard equivalents for often used commands; and font- and script-dependent text-size computations; as well as formatting utilities for dates, calendars, figures, and currencies. The resource management provided by the Script Manager shields the application developer from the idiosyncrasies of national language support.

Other operating systems and windowing environments usually support a limited set of internationalization services, mostly in character sets and keyboard definition. The selection of a deployment platform for an imaging system should take into account the international dimension as well.

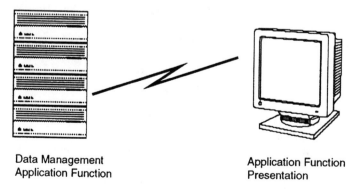

Data Management
Application Function

Application Function
Presentation

Figure 12.10   Distributed transaction client-server model

12.4 MULTIMEDIA AND METAPHOR SHIFTS

The current emphasis on multimedia also shows the limits and possible extensions of the desktop metaphor mentioned earlier. Pen-based systems are targeted at the "nomadic" user and usually present a form-based rather than desktop user interface to their users. Sound is being casually added to many commercial applications, including electronic mail. Video animation and films are provided within certain operating system extensions, in some cases without adjunction of specific hardware equipment. The trend is to disconnect the interface from the screen and relate it to the physical world.

The field of interaction techniques is a wide open area of research culminating with what is now usually referred to as virtual reality. In these environments, input devices like the DataGlove from VPL Research or head-mounted displays like NASA Ames Virtual Workstation Environment are designed to closely mimic reality and offer a much larger array of interaction techniques to the user interface designer. With a different framework, pen devices, and the PenPoint operating system from GO Corporation, are interesting attempts at merging keyboard and pointing devices into a simpler tool. As will be detailed later, both examples rely on extensions of the metaphors underlying the user interface. An active trend of theoretical research is also involved in trying to establish models of user behaviors and interactions: The User Action Notation, for instance, is a formal representation language to express asynchronous, direct manipulation interface designs.

Reaping the benefits of such multimedia extensions might involve a shift in the GUI metaphor, similar to the one that quickly brought dumb-terminal users to a mouse-based windowed universe. When sound and animated images are involved, the desktop metaphor might fall short as the reference GUI. Various research projects are already addressing these issues in laboratories; the "ROOMS" system developed at Xerox PARC and radio-linked networks of notebooks are only two examples of various extensions that can be foreseen for such systems. Still other systems keep the screen but change the feeling of the interaction: The ClearBoard system from NTT lets two users collaborate through screens that display overlaid images of computer-generated graphics, drawings made by either user and a video image of the other user. The Xerox Liveboard project is a computerized white board with a back-projected large screen. Users can write on Liveboard with markers that can also be used to pop up menus and make selections from projected text and graphics. As the discipline matures, the plausible evolution is not towards a unique GUI but rather to a proliferation of vertical, task-dependent or domain-dependent GUI metaphors that extend, or in some cases overcome, the limits of the desktop metaphor.

This maturation induces and is concurrent with a reengineering of the workflow within the organization. Today's efforts are too narrowly focused on one person interacting with one workstation; network imaging systems involve many people working with and through many machines. Interface design has gone from a craft to a discipline, and the coming years will see it as engineering.

12.5 CONCLUSION

This chapter shows that while the purpose of GUIs is to make user interaction more intuitive, their efficient and effective design is, in fact, a complex undertaking. Depending on the approach, impact on overall system performance may be significant for a given set of applications. Therefore, different operational objectives will dictate different designs, regardless of apparent similarities in functionalities or "look and feel." Whether the GUI is forced by an off-the-shelf package, or the result of a specific system development effort, its performance will likely be the result of design trade-offs, optimizing hardware platform, operating system, and overall system architecture.

Selecting the optimal set of trade-offs will require a thorough understanding of intended application and of the workflow in the reengineered environment.

Part III

Implementation

13

Image Management Development Software

Mary Ann Richardson
DATAPRO

Editor's Notes

Once images have been captured and indexed, they are ready for retrieval by end users, and traditional database management systems provide a direct access method to the documents. However, the data traffic of images retrieved at random, if left unmanaged, will result in poor network perform-ance due to contention for computing resources.

To reduce the wide swings in demands for resources, it is often necessary to use specialized management software, the role of which is to optimize data flow. Image management software can in fact be seen as a specialized database management system with limited search capabilities, tailored to meet workflow management functions. That type of software is especially valuable in predictable traffic environments, when workflow can be deter-mined by procedures based on the nature of the document itself.

Most commercially available packages are based on one of a few number of powerful engines. Consequently, a comparison between different pack-ages is a two-part process: one dealing with the basic engine, the other with the enhancements brought in by a particular vendor. This chapter is based on one of the DATAPRO reports on this topic.

13.1 INTRODUCTION

Image management development software provides program control over the input and output of images to a computer system. It provides the tools for adding the capability to handle images to any computer program. Off-the-shelf development software for image enabling existing applications or building new image-capable applications are now commonly available. These are often tailored by imaging vendors to develop custom systems or general-purpose imaging software to support user requirements on that vendor's platform.

One of the characteristics of image management development software is that it can run on a number of systems that users have previously installed or, in the case of original equipment manufacturers (OEM), are proprietary to the developer/vendor. Most image management development software packages are designed to run on open systems, i.e., those that run under popular operating system platforms such as UNIX and MS-DOS. A few systems have been designed to run on specific proprietary systems for which there is a large installed base.

Image management development software is usually sold as a set of modules, each of which provide a function (or service) required to handle images. In some cases, there is also a central processing module (sometimes called the central server) that controls how these functions work together. In others, imaging services are distributed peer-to-peer across a set of networked multivendor systems so that application functionality can be distributed to where it is required rather than "served" from a central server. In addition, these distributed services can be moved among different systems without changing the imaging application. Services include:

- Scanning services to convert paper documents into images for electronic handling and storage.
- Image manipulation to facilitate viewing and processing.
- OCR on scanned images.
- Printing, fax, and communications gateway services to distribute the images.

The central server software usually handles how images are stored on optical or magnetic media and how they are linked to their index names or values that are used to identify the image for retrieval.

While not all software has built-in functionality for more complex image management services (e.g., workflow, text retrieval, COLD, etc.), software interface tools should be flexible enough to allow external programs that perform these specialized functions to have access to the basic imaging services. Typically, runtime versions of the modules are sold under separate license from the applications development version of the software.

13.2 SELECTION CRITERIA

The most important strengths of image management development software as a product class are:

- Application flexibility.
- Ability to be ported across multiple vendors' systems.

- Savings in time and costs over development of image management functionality in-house.

The goal of image management development software is to help users develop the ability to use imaging to become more productive. Hence, it provides imaging services as well as the tools for interfacing applications programs to these services. Its ability to run on a number of systems already installed in-house enables users to add value to their previous computing investments. Because users don't have to build their own imaging services into their installed systems, they can access the benefits from their proprietary use of imaging more quickly and less expensively than if starting from scratch.

One limitation of most image management development software is that it often has to be integrated with the user system and therefore requires additional programming to develop and implement the application. This can be done either with in-house staff or through an outside source. Consequently, it is a good idea, especially when outsourcing for implementation expertise, to evaluate the quality of professional training and support that the imaging software vendor provides to its distribution channels. Will the vendor provide the VAR (value-added reseller) or consultant with specialized customization services (such as drivers to nonstandard devices) when the need arises? Will the software vendor work closely and cooperatively with the VAR to ensure the success of the implementation?

In addition, since image management development software usually is sold to run on previously installed hardware, users are also responsible for deciding whether or not their existing networks can actually handle image I/O efficiently. Users must also negotiate separate service and maintenance contracts for each system component. Finally, users will need to hire or obtain ongoing system integration expertise to diagnose which component is causing a problem before deciding whom to call to fix it.

With all of the above in mind, then, specific selection criteria should include:

- Ability to serve multiple server platform and peripherals.
- Vertical scalability.
- Image enabling and ability to build new applications on existing installed software.
- Built-in workflow processing.
- Ability to support multimedia document types.
- Database independence.
- Development tools.
- Choice of server platform, operating system, workstation platform, document formats, image indexing and classification methods, image-enable application types, and host application integration.
- LAN support.
- Imaging services provided, including application interface and systems administration facilities.
- Imaging hardware supported, including optical storage scanners and fax.

13.3 STRATEGIES FOR IMPLEMENTING IMAGE MANAGEMENT SOFTWARE

Once an organization has decided to image enable its work processes, it then must decide how it is going to do it. Today's imaging marketplace offers three alternatives:

1. Implement off-the-shelf or shrink-wrapped products.
2. Develop proprietary image I/O drivers and management programs from the bottom up for access by user applications.
3. Use image management development software for integrating image management functionality into specific business applications programs.

Off-the-shelf products may contain all the functionality that users need; often, however, they do not. Few turnkey systems can be used right out of the box without some type of customization. For those who are looking to develop a proprietary use of imaging software that provides new and different services to customers, only a custom solution will do.

Some organizations may find that their applications require more complex image I/O functionality than is provided by the available image applications development tools. Some may require specialized drivers to nonstandard imaging peripherals. These organizations will need to build their programs from scratch, developing proprietary drivers and interfaces for handling input and output of images by their application programs. Some may purchase packaged subsystem software to handle such functions as scanning or printing, then build their own central server software using in-house database programming tools. This alternative is the most time-consuming, and the user must weigh the benefits of "reinventing the wheel" against the high cost of development.

For those who would rather focus on developing a strategic business application rather than develop programs for image I/O, a better alternative is to find a software product that provides imaging functionality and concentrate in-house resources on developing the application that will access that functionality. While many off-the-shelf products can be used for this purpose, their application development tools are often limited in terms of flexibility and multivendor platform support. Image management development software is designed to give users the flexibility they need without the high cost of starting from scratch.

As users seek to downsize their organizations' information management systems and get more productivity out of their current computer infrastructure, the demand for document management software development tools for networked multivendor platforms will increase. Strategic applications for imaging are growing; users are realizing that unless their existing applications can handle images as well as text, data, and graphics, they will no longer stay competitive. In addition, users are finding that imaging allows them to develop new product services that could never have existed without imaging. These types of customers will want to be able to handle images in a proprietary manner. They will need the flexibility that image management development software affords them.

Many imaging software vendors offer applications development tools for image enabling networks, but whether they are flexible enough to meet an individual user's present and future needs must still be determined. Many vendors would rather sell their software off the shelf and offer limited external program access to imaging services. These vendors are usually out to sell complete turnkey imaging systems and services to end users, sometimes as a way to add value to their currently installed base of proprietary equipment. If these turnkey solutions meet an organization's applications requirements, then it is probably the most inexpensive way to go. It is important, however, that users look at the tools offered to ensure that the system will meet the organization's strategic goals as their needs expand.

Vendors who are strictly dedicated to offering image management development software usually sell their software to system integrators who, in turn, implement a proprietary solution for the end user. If it is decided that the system should be developed by a third-party integrator rather than by in-house staff, users must be sure to evaluate the system integrator's knowledge and experience with their individual business, as well as his or her background in image system implementation on client-server networks.

While there are many system integrators, the number of vendors who provide image management development software for client-server networks is small. Major competitors in this area include Plexus, Wang, Sigma, Metafile, Optika, ViewStar, and Sietec Open Systems. Plexus and Sietec compete in the market for image enabling UNIX-based client-server networks, while the rest provide software for image enabling PC-based LANs. Metafile provides software for image enabling PC/LANs as well as support for the IBM AS/400 as a central server repository for the PC workstation. Metafile and Plexus lead the group in installations, each with over 300 systems worldwide. Most of these vendors began image enabling networks around 1986; Wang and Sietec, however, introduced their open systems products in 1991.

13.4 IMPACT OF NETWORK COMPUTING DEVELOPMENTS

As images become just another data type, users will find that they will no longer have to add imaging services to their systems. One example of this movement toward built-in support for image I/O in mainstream software is Eastman Kodak's codevelopment efforts with Novell and Lotus to add imaging capabilities to PC networks. The Novell and Eastman Kodak team designed a range of image-enabling services that Novell will sell as optional extensions to NetWare version 3.2. Meanwhile, Lotus and Kodak released a companion product to Lotus Notes that can be used to add imaging capability to new or existing Lotus Notes applications. Such efforts will make imaging more a commodity item that can be applied easily to all business applications rather than being cost-prohibitive for all but the most high-level vertical applications.

13.5 COMPARING COMMERCIAL PRODUCTS

When comparing image management development software products, the main consideration should be the flexibility of their programming tools. What imaging services are already built in? What must be added? Remember: The more flexible the package, the more development effort is required.

Existing Platform Support

The most inexpensive way to build an imaging application is to use existing hardware. If an LAN is already operational, chances are it has already been optimized and tuned to the site's user requirements. It is recommended that imaging software be selected based on whether or not it runs on existing systems. Optimizing a network takes time and money; choosing imaging software that has been designed to run on an existing network will facilitate the image integration process.

Image Indexing and Classification Methods

Most systems support keyed data entry and provide application development tools for customizing index input screens. Some systems provide automatic indexing capabilities using bar codes or zone OCR. If automatic indexing is required, it is best to choose the software that already has these capabilities. Most systems use the electronic folder classification scheme; if this is not suitable, then software that does not incorporate electronic folders should be used. Sietec EMS, for example, is designed to support different document types (single-page, multipage, engineering drawings, medical images, etc.) comprised of image, text, and binary (voice or special devices) data. Data independence allows for custom indexing methods, including those provided by any conventional RDBMS.

Database Independence

Some systems require the developer to use one type of database for indexing images. This is the case with Plexus, which uses Informix; it was specifically designed to handle images. As more database software becomes image-enabled (e.g., DataEase and BasisPlus can handle images), users will want to develop and access databases using existing database application toolkits. Optika, Sietec, and Wang provide database independence.

Document Formats

All the imaging software products should support all major imaging formats such as tagged image file format (TIFF) and ASCII; and standard compression algorithms, including CCITT Group 3 and Group 4. It is important that the chosen system support standard formats, because these can be accessed from other programming platforms. (ViewStar is the only product covered in this report that supports CALS, an important standard for government defense applications.)

LAN Support

Another factor to consider when evaluating imaging software is whether or not it runs on existing LANs. Most of these packages have built-in capabilities for running over standard LANs. Sietec supports "any," meaning that although the product currently supports Ethernet and token-ring over TCP/IP, it is architecturally capable of supporting any communication mechanism, and Sietec will perform the necessary integration work to enable that support.

Host Application Integration

There are a number of methods for integrating images into a host application. For screen or terminal integration, a single-user terminal is used to interact with the imaging system and the application through separate windows. There is no program communication between the two windows; the host application is unaware of the imaging system and, hence, needs no modification. The imaging system looks at standard host screens to obtain index keywords for accessing the appropriate image. The keywords either may be physically entered by an operator typing the keyword into the imaging system window or entered automatically through program control. One drawback to this method is that the host application may have no control over user access to the images.

A second method allows the host application and the image system to communicate with each other and exchange information from a single terminal or between two terminals, such as through an LU 6.2 session or APPC, in which case the host application is modified. Because the application can recognize the existence of the images, it also has access control; for example, an image-enabled host application can turn off the Windows cut and paste feature, thus providing greater security. Wang's OPEN/image CICS and IMS, Sigma's OmniDesk, ViewStar, and Optika's Transaction Processing Module are examples of this type of integration. The highest level of image integration is characteristic of new image applications or those that have been revised to support imaging. In this case, the application and the image functionality are running off the same server. The imaging functionality is built into the applications to handle images via development toolkits (e.g., APIs or DLLs to and from existing applications).

Support for Existing Applications Programs

Each development software package image enables applications running on a certain set of programming platforms, such as those written in C or Windows. It is, therefore, important that any libraries, APIs, or DLLs can be called from within existing programs.

Image I/O Peripheral and Optical Storage Device Support

Although software vendors develop third-party relationships with the peripheral vendors whose devices they support, the user is ultimately responsible for device integration. Some packages offer a wide choice of scanning and storage devices; others are limited to one or two. Users must consider whether the supported devices are commonly used across all imaging vendors' software. These are the most likely to be supported and manufactured long after the less popular ones are withdrawn from the market.

Application Interfaces to Imaging Services

Users should determine exactly what imaging I/O services can be accessed from an application. If fax integration is needed, is it already there, or must it be developed? Does the software include support for OCR integration and print servers? In addition, can any of these functions be distributed to a dedicated server or workstation?

System Administration Facilities

A system without some sort of menu-driven or higher-level command language for system administration functions (such as configuration, backup and recovery, user setup, etc.) requires administrators to perform these functions through user-created macros or by physically editing internal files. This may be not only inefficient, but it may compromise system security (e.g., when users are added through internal file edits). It is important that these system administration tools be built into the system. Those that are not will need to be added by the developer.

13.6 SELECTED PRODUCT COMPARISON

Most of the systems available on the market today are based on one of the platforms discussed in this section.

XDP, from Plexus Software

XDP software is a set of design tools for building document-imaging applications. It allows graphical client applications to store scanned images and other multimedia information. XDP includes the following features:

- Interactive development tool for building user interfaces.
- Management of images on magnetic disks, optical disks, or both. The management module contains the relational database that indexes all images stored on magnetic or optical disk.

- Print server running a print spooler software.

- Fax server to provide fax support. Fax library routines link applications to the fax server.

- Library of image management functions that can be accessed directly or through a Windows-based 4GL. This library interfaces programs to all image-processing services. It includes functions for scanning, retrieving, and printing images.

- A component of the management module software that manages single-drive optical disk platters. It consists of a set of UNIX utilities for accessing and managing optical disks.

- Jukebox manager, which must be installed in addition to the single-drive manager for the management of jukeboxes, including such functions as import/export platters, move platters, etc.

- Relational database management system with extended SQL support for two types of data: BLObs (binary large objects), or arbitrary large binary objects (images, digitized voice, executable programs, etc.) and text data. Built-in workflow features include automated routing and user-defined document priority. Other features can be added using the 4GL development language.

- Application designer, including application builder; Windows-based 4GL programming language and report writer; debugger; Windows-4GL DDE library; and a utility that automates the generation of applications.

- Windows-based visual programming tool for building desktop forms processing applications. The software combines data capture and image processing tools and provides the capability of linking with various workflow managers, data access methods, and other application programs.

- Optional network service that allows the movement of work between applications or activities according to a user-defined workflow map.

EMS Imaging Development Toolkit, from Sietec Open Systems

EMS is a set of software tools, utilities, libraries, and services for building imaging applications. The kit provides the following imaging services:

- OCR

- Image manipulation including scaling, rotation, image negation, reflection, and smoothing.

- Printing services.

- Queuing services for directing information and processing flow across a network.

- Virtual device models to support peripherals such as scanners and printers.

- An information-processing model to display, move, print, and structure data.

- A communication model for transparent network operations.

- Debugging aids.

A separate product, Optical Archive Management System (OAMS), provides file management services for WORM and magneto-optical devices. This NFS-compliant archive server provides a UNIX file model interface that makes optical devices transparent to applications. Developers can use OAMS as a subsystem for their platforms or to provide archive services for imaging and nonimaging applications.

Workflow services are provided by Staffware, a procedure processing system that automates the execution and control of routine procedures. It automatically requests and passes the necessary documents and information among the individuals involved to ensure that a procedure is completed. Developers use Staffware to extend the document routing capabilities of simple step procedures inherent in EMS to accommodate large numbers of complex multistep procedures involving many people.

Dialog Builder is a graphical design tool for generating OSF Motif user interfaces. Because it is a complete user interface management system, application developers can design both the look and behavior of an interface with one tool, thoroughly test it in simulation mode, then generate the interface in C code or use it with a Dialog Builder runtime system. Either option can be linked to the processing part of an application.

Dialog Builder allows developers to prototype and simulate interfaces. It facilitates application modularity by separating the presentation and processing parts of an application. Further, user-defined widgets and libraries permit customization to accommodate corporate standard or application-specific and site-specific requirements.

OPEN/image from Wang Laboratories, Inc.

OPEN/image is a suite of application development tools for building LAN-based imaging applications or modifying existing applications to incorporate images running on the following platforms: MS-DOS/Windows, AIX, IBM CICS and IMS/DC, Macintosh, VAX VMS, and Wang VS.

OPEN/image Windows 3.0 provides developers with application programming interfaces for image enabling a PC or PC LAN-based applications. It provides tools for adding imaging capabilities to existing Windows applications without reprogramming those applications. Imaging capabilities include storing, retrieving, sharing, and printing image pages. Included is a collection of DLLs that provide image filing, viewing, editing, printing, and administrative services.

OPEN/image for NetWare provides tools for developing distributed imaging applications on Novell NetWare LANs. Imaging is tightly integrated with the network operating system as NetWare Loadable Modules (NLMs) that provide image services and large-volume storage to PC clients. Running on Novell's NetWare 386 Version 3.1 file server, the software consists of a set of NLMs divided into an image service subsystem and optical jukebox subsystem. Image management functions are provided by the image services subsystem. This subsystem consists of APIs for image file access, document management, and image printing, which are accessible to NLMs on the file server and to network-based clients on the workstation. The NLMs interface any MS-DOS, Windows, or NetWare 386 NLMs to the imaging services, including storage, retrieval, and printing of images.

OPEN/image Server for AIX provides tools for developing imaging applications on a WANG RISC series server. OPEN/image APIs for AIX and OPEN/image APIs for VMS provide application programming interfaces that enable existing RS/6000 AIX and VAX VMS applications to access imaging services from any one of Wang's OPEN/image server platforms, including Windows, NetWare, Wang RISC Series, and WIIS VS.

Wang's OPEN/image 3270 Windows enables Wang LAN servers to provide imaging services to mainframe applications. OPEN/image 3270 Windows supports Wang's OPEN/image-IMS/DC and OPEN/image-CICS. Under OPEN/image 3270 Windows, IMS/DC or CICS applications can control imaging functions (such as scan, display, copy, verify, and print) performed on a PC LAN server running Windows 3.0.

FilePower from Optika Imaging Systems, Inc.

Optika FilePower is a family of image and data management software modules that provides the ability to store, route, print, and access document images, faxes, and report pages on PCs. The product can be integrated to existing applications via ImageEngine, an object-oriented toolkit that may be accessed through an API or through batch processing. FilePower consists of the Windows-based modules listed below. The main module supports document processing and retrieval. Features include:

- Post-it notes capability allows text to be attached to images at any time.
- Support for Panasonic 7010 multifunction, rewritable drives.
- Image inversion on scanner settings used to convert white-on-black originals to black-on-white images.
- Print server software module performs the task of image retrieval to free the workstation for other work, while the print servers perform the retrieval and printing tasks.
- Fax server software.
- Support for Xionics and Kofax Controllers gives expanded support for high-end Xionics compression/decompression scanner and printer controllers.
- Color Windows for Images conforms to Microsoft standard desktop colors, allowing the background and foreground color to be selected for windows, including the image window.
- Double-sided scanning without operator intervention.

- Support for jukeboxes, internal database searching for nonindexed data, user security restrictions, and TrueType fonts.
- DataFile Import for import of computer-generated data from the host for storage on an optical disk (COLD).
- Data Finder for retrieving computer-generated reports from optical disk.

In addition, it offers:

- Signature image management system which provides for the capture, storage, retrieval, printing, and management of signature images.
- Multilevel electronic file folder software that allows a user to build an unlimited number of subfolders at each structural level.
- Image and information management tool designed for use by non-programmers for managing the flow of electronically captured documents and information.
- Microsoft Windows-based software package which provides for scanning, indexing, filing, and retrieving of images for viewing and printing.
- Servers for support of optical drive storage and jukebox.
- Server for managing network printing of images in conjunction with high-speed laser printer interface.
- Fax-server for fax distribution.
- Interfaces to host applications for data upload/download and image output requests.
- Services for remote requests for images via fax and off-line batch scanning.
- Import utilities for importing images and index information from other systems.

Metaview from Metafile Information Systems, Inc.

Metaview is a programming language and a set of related development tools for creating LAN-based applications that integrate data from PCs, IBM AS/400s, and IBM mainframes. It allows PC users to use AS/400 system services, such as IBM Workfolder Application Facility (WAF), which handles document routing and lets developers create PC front ends to existing AS/400 applications. The AS/400 serves as the central document repository for the PC LAN. Metaview language extensions provide for AS/400 5250 terminal emulation that allows a PC user to work with existing AS/400 applications without reprogramming. Metaview can also be used to build imaging applications for PC LAN or stand-alone PC environments. Metaview is available on a modular basis as follows:

- Development-enabling applications consisting of generic scan, store, retrieve, display, queue, print, and workflow modules customized and expanded to meet individual application requirements.

- High-level 4GL for building image applications.
- Metaview eXtended operating system or runtime version.
- Mainframe access program for accessing AS/400 and mainframe data and applications as if they resided on the PC.
- Terminal emulation language for building PC interfaces to 5250 or 3270 applications; controls up to five sessions under one Metaview image application.
- Image manipulation capabilities (pan, zoom, rotate) for VGA screens, 19", and high-resolution monitors.
- Writes document images to 5.25" or 12" optical disks and jukeboxes.
- Provides scanning services.
- Provides for printing of images merged with host data and PC text.

OmniDesk from Sigma Imaging Systems

OmniDesk provides imaging and workflow management and is designed to work with new and existing applications.

Image server software provides workflow management, image storage, and image retrieval services for OmniDesk workstations. High-volume archive and retrieval services are provided, as well as an enterprise-wide document catalog. Optional IBM OAM and MO:DCA storage support is also available. Image server supports direct attachment of the OmniDesk OCR subsystem and the fax server card. There is no set limit to the number of concurrent workstations supported by a single server. The actual number of workstations per server depends on the nature of the work being performed. Multiple server configurations are supported.

Workstation software, designed for both high-volume transaction processing and document management, provides for scanning, automatic document assembly, bar code and micrographics patch recognition, automatic or manual document indexing, data entry, document routing, and SQL-based query operations. Workstation functions can be distributed, and image and nonimage documents can be stored in flexible folder hierarchies. The software provides side-by-side display of image, text, application, and 3270 mainframe sessions in a windowed environment. Full DDE support allows integration with other Windows applications. Other capabilities include drop-out form and overlay processing and prefetching.

FormBuilder is an application development tool that allows nonprogrammers to design the user interface to the OmniDesk imaging services. FormBuilder defines a variety of forms, including input forms for extracting coded data and query forms for retrieving indexed documents. It supports all common form definitions features such as field types, range checking, value lists, ordering, and appearance. Signature fields can be specified. FormBuilder can also be used to define bar codes, OCR zones, and input definitions, as well as data entry zones. Field and data entry zones can be linked for image tracking. Built-in spreadsheet functions perform quality checks of calculated form data. In addition to defining indexing fields for retrieval and routing, FormBuilder is used to define field links to host emulators and other DDE-compatible applications.

RouteBuilder is a graphical software utility used to define the flow of work items from workstep to workstep. It allows the user to build a workflow by placing icons, representing worksteps, on the RouteBuilder window. Icons are connected by arrows, representing one or more logical conditions under which work moves from one workstep to the next. Routing rules are based on coded data captured in the FormBuilder design screen. Routing may be based on document age, priority, content, or other management criteria. User profiles specify the type of work that users are eligible to receive. Queue profiles determine the priority of work at each workstep; the image server then routes work to users based on defined rules and profiles. Rules based on document type, field values, or external events govern the transfer of documents between worksteps represented by the icons. These rules can involve constants, ranges, lists, or combinations of these. Workloads are automatically balanced and tracked. Local and remote printing, reporting, and fax are supported.

Workstation API, using dynamic data exchange (DDE), allows applications to request image and workflow services. Any application that can issue DDE messages can be used to control the OmniDesk workstation. These applications may be coded as traditional programs in C, developed in an interactive language such as Microsoft Visual Basic, or produced utilizing the scripting facilities of products such as Easel Corporation's EASEL and Microsoft's Excel. The workstation API provides high-level services for frequently needed functions, as well as a full set of low-level services that allow direct access to image data. For example, high-level services allow a program to search for a document, retrieve it, and display the first page with a few simple commands. The program need not be concerned with lower-level details such as image storage format and decompression. In response to a command to display a page, OmniDesk workstation software automatically opens a page viewer, then loads, decompresses, scales, and displays the image. All the standard page viewer functions, including image rotation, annotation, and magnification, are available to the user.

Server API permits the application to access the OmniDesk server SQL tables, data, and services. The server API is provided as a dynamic link library (DLL) function. The DLLs use standard OS/2 program linkage conventions and can be called by any program capable of issuing operating system calls. The server API can further automate processes by directly working with OmniDesk system services. For example, one program that uses the server API is the OmniDesk workflow loader, which is being used by one business to distribute externally generated transaction documents to customer service representatives. This program reads a flat file containing the transaction information and, using the server API, loads the data into forms. These forms are then automatically indexed and queued for OmniDesk workflow routing and processing.

APPC API, using advanced program-to-program communications formats and protocols, makes it possible for applications resident on different machines to communicate with each other. This API provides other systems with access to OmniDesk services such as document retrieval, forwarding, faxing, printing, and archiving.

ViewStar from ViewStar Corp.

ViewStar is an integrated software system that is comprised of four major classes of software, including system software, toolkit software, user software, and server software.

System software is an object-based system management and administration software that operates a layer above the network operating system to manage system resources and control document access, processing, and storage activities. ViewStar includes administration modules for document and data modeling, system security, access control, and resource management. The base ViewStar System is designed to support departmental applications of up to 50 interactive users. ViewStar Workgroup is designed for smaller departments or workgroups of up to ten interactive users. Customers wishing to configure larger systems can do so by licensing the Star Extender software, which offers support in increments of 50 interactive users.

Toolkit software consists of the following:

- DataScan, an integrated toolkit for the development and delivery of document workflow applications. It consists of the DataScan Admin software for workflow modeling, administration, and maintenance; as well as one copy of the workflow tracking server, one of the ViewStar workflow servers available for automation of workflow processing tasks. Also included are workflow script commands for system customization.

- Developer's toolkit, which is an advanced applications development environment that includes the script 4GL, program editing and debugging facilities, Windows DDE and foreign function interfaces, and a script compiler for delivery of production application code. The developer's toolkit includes one workbench developer license for program editing and debugging.

- D3270 toolkit, an administration software package for integrating the ViewStar system with host-based application programs that support 3270 terminal interfaces. It includes the 3270 Admin module for defining mappings between ViewStar data fields and 3270 script commands for system customization. ViewStar supports Attachmate Extra and Wall Data's Rumba for 3270 emulation.

Import toolkit is a class of software that encompasses a series of document import and conversion tools that support interactive and batch capture and integration of multiformat documents. Available toolkit extensions include:

- Import scan software for the interactive scanning and indexing of paper documents. Import scan must be licensed for every user performing scanning operations at a scan station.

- Import facsimile user, server, and administration software for capture and integration of facsimile documents through distributed fax servers. Includes Fax Admin system administration software and single licenses of the import fax application for interactive fax review and indexing and fax server software. Also includes fax script commands for system customization.

- Import ICR user, server, and administration software for performing ICR conversion and ICR-assisted data entry. Includes single licenses for the ICR zone editor and ICR server software. Also includes ICR script commands for system customization.

- Import Kodak user and administration software for interfacing Kodak ImageLink scanners and processing captured images to a DataScan workflow toolkit to enable operation.

- Import data application template that supports electronic importation of ASCII files from word processing and spreadsheet programs as well as data importation for form documents. Also includes import script commands for system customization.

- Import file application template that supports electronic importation of CCITT Group 3 and 4 images and conversion and import of AutoCAD DXF, Calcomp 906/907, and HPGL vector files. Also includes import script commands for system customization.

- Forms toolkit is an administration software that supports the definition and processing of form documents within the ViewStar system. It includes a single license of form editor software for form-backdrop selection and field-mapping definition as well as form script commands for system customization.

User software consists of the following:

- Retrieve is Windows-based software for the access, retrieval, display, and printing of documents managed by the ViewStar system.

- Workbench is Windows-based software that provides a workflow-enabled, document-processing environment for execution of applications defined through use of the developer's toolkit or other ViewStar toolkit software. Unlike Retrieve, Workbench is an extensible environment that supports the addition of user-customized functions and whose interface can be tailored.

- Workbench developer is a comprehensive programming environment for applications development and integration with ViewStar's script 4GL. One license of Workbench developer is included with the purchase of the developer's toolkit. This product is intended for customers who need to support additional application programmers.

Server software is a class of software consisting of the following:

- Database server, a distributed SQL database engine that supports key ViewStar database management functions. The database server software is required for every database server machine configured in the system. ViewStar provides the ability to define multiple database partitions based on chronology, by site, or by application. Because users can physically and logically subdivide the ViewStar database, they can distribute these database partitions over multiple servers to optimize image I/O over LANs and WANs.

- Workflow servers, which are system servers for automated processing of workflow tasks as required in high throughput and other advanced workflow application environments. The available workflow servers include the tracking server and process server. The tracking server provides dedicated server software for performance of document- and workpacket-tracking functions. One copy of the tracking server is provided with the DataScan workflow toolkit. Customers should order this product if their application requires multiple tracking services. The process server provides dedicated server software for performance of tracking as well as other workflow tasks and advanced routing functions.

- Archive server, a system server that interfaces to a variety of single-platter and jukebox optical storage subsystems. The specific software includes the Archive drive which provides interface to 5.25" and 12" optical disk drives; and the Archive autochanger, which provides autochanger robotics interface software for 5.25" and 12" optical jukeboxes with single or multiple drive configurations. Customers with optical jukeboxes must specify the archive autochanger software along with an appropriate number of archive drive licenses that corresponds to the number of drives in the jukebox.

Task server is a server software that supports the following tasks:

- Print/merge server supports distributed processing of print requests on laser printers and electrostatic plotters. Also supports image merge operations for merging of graphics layers with the base image prior to printing, plotting, or fax transmission.

- Fax server provides distributed fax import and export interface to the ViewStar system. Single license of the fax server is included with the purchase of the import facsimile toolkit. This product is intended for those customers who require multiple fax servers.

- ICR server supports conversion of image data into ASCII text for data entry purposes. Single license of the ICR server is included with the purchase of the Import ICR toolkit. This product is intended for customers who require multiple ICR servers.

13.7 CONCLUSION

This chapter shows the variety of tools and systems that are commercially available. Obviously, these tools are complex, and must be learned before they can deliver their benefits. It must be understood that the costs of adopting an off-the-shelf image management software are much lower, and the results are much more predictable, than for an in-house developed system.

14

Tools and Toolkits for Network Imaging and Workflow Systems

A. J. Wand
Plexus Corporation

Editor's Notes

The preceding chapter dealt with image management development software, seen from the perspective of image enabling an existing system. The focus in this chapter is on the application of such development tools in a context of downsizing, and it shows how the use of various commercially available tools can facilitate and reduce the costs of the integration of imaging in a redesigned workflow.

14.1 INTRODUCTION

You can still hear the cries of yesteryear reverberating through the data center: "What's good for the mainframe is good for the company." Host-based data processing was a powerful means of automating transactions in yesterday's paper-based world, allowing data to be managed and worked on in a central location. But as important as this on-line transaction processing was in making businesses more efficient, there was still a big issue relative to data processing: Some 95 percent of the corporation's data remained on paper, long after the mainframe transaction had been completed.

The downsizing movement has brought a number of options for processing corporate data in a local area network environment, and imaging is an enabling technology for companies that are automating work on vital business information.

The chief virtue of imaging is that it makes available on the desktop approximately 90 percent of the data that does not reside in the traditional data processing application, allowing people to work faster and more effectively. "Compound data processing" involves more than just alphanumeric data, allowing access to *all* the data relevant to the transaction, regardless if it is paper-based or audio-based.

14.2   THE NIWS DIFFERENCE

The Lay of the LAN—Open Client-Server Applications

A primary difference of network imaging and workflow systems (NIWS) is a distributed LAN-based architecture, which is new technological territory for many MIS organizations. Traditional host-based data processing systems were mono-lithic—the mainframe provided every element of the application. The system required little or no integration, and issues such as system compatibility and communication protocol were nonexistent.

Client-server applications represent a fundamental shift in MIS viewpoint; whereas mainframe applications are coded such that data storage, computation, and presentation occur in the same machine space, client-server applications require that the developer break the application into two pieces: The client handles the application logic and presentation of data queried from the server.

Today's LAN-based systems offer a lower-cost alternative to mainfame and minicomputer applications, distributing the overall computing workload across a variety of lower-cost (for both hardware and software) machines. The process of distributing applications is not, however, a free ride; there are costs associated with learning new architectures and allowing heterogeneous machinery to interact in enterprise applications.

Compound Data over the Network

Mainframe applications with terminal-based user interfaces traditionally do not manage compound data-like images. On-line transaction processing originated in a text-only environment, with host systems handling critical alphanumeric data that required state-of-the-art data management and security. These proprietary systems have a high cost-per-transaction, and some feel that mainframe cycles are wasted on image processing, and that smaller, cheaper LAN systems are better for imaging applications.

Local area networks, too, were originally designed to carry relatively small amounts of data (also typically alphanumeric) and not large bitmaps. Ethernet has a bandwidth of 10MBps, with a maximum theoretical throughput of approximately 3MBps. A distributed application using uncompressed 300 dpi images will quickly consume this bandwidth. LAN-based systems allow processing to be distributed, with local processing available to handle database querying, image decompression, and other local operations to boost the effective throughput of information. In addition, overall throughput of currently popular and affordable network topologies can be compensated for by using multiple networks to service workstations if volume is high. UNIX servers can handle a large number of networks simultaneously, in addition to storage devices and other peripherals required.

Sophisticated Work Processes

Older host-based applications inherently embedded all of the system facilities in a single environment, where the mainframe handles all aspects of the application user interface, data storage, communications, workflow routing, etc. All of these facilities are embedded in host systems, rather than a number of independent activities that communicate across networks and literally move work from one to the next. With client-server workflow applications, workflow is no longer deeply embedded in a monolithic application and difficult to change. Autonomous applications process information in a complex, orchestrated workflow that may be based originally on a manual paper workflow.

14.3 TECHNOLOGIES THAT MAKE A DIFFERENCE

Imaging as a Basic Technology for Work Process Automation (WPA)

Although once strictly the domain of specialized, high-cost systems, imaging technology has become a widely accepted commodity that is integrated with standard application functions. But imaging is no longer an end unto itself; it has evolved from "an application" (insurance claims processing, for instance) to a generalized application *service* that provides richer information in many applications. Imaging must be considered as a basic technology in the overall scheme of automating business processes, much like the windowing or network software on which the system is based.

Optical Storage

High capacity and low cost per gigabyte (compared to paper filing cabinets or mainframe DASD) make optical storage attractive. Assuming 6GB capacity platters and compressed images 60KB in size, each platter can store approximately 100,000 pages and provide much faster (on-line) access. Companies can literally replace buildings with optical jukeboxes, saving precious time and money in the process.

Another benefit of optical storage is endurance. When critical paper data is imaged, it needs to be available for a period much longer than the life of dismountable magnetic media (i.e., tape). Optical storage provides this durability, along with the security of a write-once medium.

Graphical Environments

GUIs provide the consistent and flexible interface required for dealing with richer data. Richer, more sophisticated data brings with it additional manipulation and management requirements that are not present in text-based applications, and current graphical software environments that support bitmapped displays, multitasking, sophisticated windowing, powerful interapplication communication, and other features are an obvious advantage in compound data applications. Not only are applications in this environment more effective for this type of processing, but the development tools available to build those applications are better as well.

Imaging and the Database

Many imaging systems store alphanumeric data and image data in separate facilities, requiring coordination of the two subsystems to maintain data integrity. The image server may consist of a standard relational (or proprietary) database to store the alphanumeric data and a proprietary image server manages the optical hardware devices. The servers communicate using remote procedure calls or network messages.

Although a loosely coupled approach allows more database independence, the system can experience integrity problems if it is not of robust design. For example, if an optical server fails, data records may be stored in the application database without the associated images written to optical if the system is unable to roll back this partial transaction. Keeping distributed systems "in synch" is of primary importance, as images stored on optical are a crucial portion of the application data.

Another approach is a tightly coupled one, where images are stored in a relational database itself. The capability to store BLObs (binary large objects) is becoming more prevalent among the major relational database management systems (RDBMS) vendors. These systems manage large data objects (e.g., images) as data that is as basic to the application as the alphanumeric information contained in a database record. Relational databases are designed to manage large amounts of related data and can provide all the integrity, concurrency, availability, and security for both image and other related alphanumeric data. In addition, allowing the DBMS to manage the archive and logging of images is significantly easier than developing the archive as a separate application service.

Character Recognition

Optical character recognition (OCR), long a boon to data entry operations, is an important technology in imaging, particularly for forms processing applications. OCR allows autoindexing, full-text search, and other capabilities that make it easier to manage and organize scanned data with less user interaction.

OCR is used in applications—both for data entry and indexing of forms, as well as text recognition—that often are used for full-text indexing the contents of documents. OCR's effectiveness depends on a variety of factors, including document quality, quality checking required for recognized characters, and the strengths of the specific character recognition product used.

Effectiveness is usually calculated in such a way that recognized characters that are guessed incorrectly carry a much greater penalty than characters that are unknown. This is to say that OCR provides a benefit only if a high percentage of characters can be recognized, and only if these characters are recognized correctly almost all of the time. Some implementers find that the cost of OCR is actually greater than a manual process, while some have "recognized" immense gains in productivity. Expertise with these specialized types of applications is important to making them successful.

14.4 WORK PROCESS AUTOMATION AND BUSINESS REENGINEERING

Ad Hoc vs. Structured

Workflow is the automatic routing of information between users so that they can process the data in some fashion and add value in performing business functions. This includes both the actual routing of the data, as well as the effective management of that process. Workflow can be divided into two broad categories: information-based and transaction-based.

Information-Based Workflow

Information-based workflow is the ad hoc routing of data between processing activities. This work process requires that the sender direct information explicitly to another user or activity, as in the case of electronic mail. In simple ad hoc workflow, users might process information on their desktops and route it as necessary using a basic technology such as e-mail. This type of workflow is essentially manual, where routing rules and decisions exist through the intelligence of the user and are not part of the automated system. The system simply provides the transport layer (how to send the data), but provides no other help in automating the *process* (when and to whom to send it). Information sharing systems (a.k.a. groupware) support work steps that are ad hoc in nature, but do not automate work processes. The term workflow in these systems is more loosely defined and ad hoc than other process-based systems, where work can follow predefined paths for processing. Transactions don't need to be monitored and recovered by the system, because the users interact and perform this function in the course of their work.

One example of ad hoc workflow (that is not groupware) looks like an extended storage-and-retrieval application, where routing is automated, but processes are not. Consider a medical records application where a doctor's initial retrieval of information may be triggered by a patient's arrival, a phone call, (e-)mail message, whim, etc. When the doctor is finished processing the patient information, he or she might determine that it needs to be routed to a certain specialist for more scrutiny. The routing is performed by the system and replaces a paper-based process where the doctor makes the same decision and routes the patient's paper files to another participant in the process. The doctor could alternatively send an electronic message to the specialist instructing him or her to retrieve the patient's information for processing.

In this example, transporting work electronically provides benefits for information sharing and communication, and to some extent flow management, though there may be no structured work process to be automated and evolved. All processing is essentially "exception processing" that is not predetermined. Workflow solutions can provide more functionality when there is a set of steps to be automated above and beyond the sheer physical routing.

In applications that involve a structured process, the flow of work can be automated beyond providing a transport mechanism, where both the routing and the work process are automated by the system. Structured processes provide an opportunity for transaction-based workflow and work process automation to add considerably more value, as computer systems are exceptionally good at automating tasks that are structured and repetitive.

Transaction-Based Workflow

Transaction-based workflow involves an active process of routing data, where rules and routes for the information flow are predefined. In this case, workflow should not only automate transactions, but should also make it possible to deal with exceptions and automate *them*, thereby providing the flexibility to adapt to exceptions that become the rule. This type of workflow is particularly effective when used in combination with imaging for compound data processing.

Transaction-based workflow requires an engine to monitor and manage workflow processes and information. Database management systems are good foundations for these sorts of tasks, where e-mail-based systems may not provide the appropriate transaction or state model for work process automation. E-mail may serve as a transport mechanism for data, where the state information is stored in a transaction-based system.

Work process automation systems provide another dimension to the solution in that they transport not only data, but allow organizations to automate and manage the underlying work process.

Interactive Workflow Management

Ideally, the rules for workflow routing are defined separately from the image processing applications in client workstations so that as the business environment changes, the procedures (i.e., routing rules) defined for processing information can be adapted with minimum effort. The embedded workflow found in image processing systems uses hard-coded routing instructions within desktop applications, requiring code changes in each and every desktop application that participates in the workflow.

Client-server workflow is a relative newcomer to the compound data processing scene and represents an important development in the integration of imaging with traditional applications. Clients in the workflow communicate with the workflow server according to an application programming interface (API), using callable libraries for the various workflow functions. So rather than a client application routing data to the next processing activity using explicit routing instructions, it simply "asks" the workflow server to route the data to the next process. The workflow server understands the routing rules and puts the data in the appropriate queue, where it waits until it is requested by the next application that needs to process it. When workflow is provided as a network service to desktop applications in this manner, users can easily reengineer their business processes for maximum efficiency and effectiveness and dramatically reduce the expense and complexity of adapting as a business evolves and work processes change.

Using Workflow to Integrate Compound Data

The power of the client-server workflow model can be applied to integrate existing applications with image. The workflow server communicates with various systems, and routes data to applications either by *reference* or by *value*. *Data by reference* means that the workflow client receives a message that points to the data's location, rather than the data itself. The client application must then be able to retrieve the data from the application/image server with its own access routines. *Data by value* is when the workflow server can fetch and route the application data (e.g., alphanumeric, image, other binary) directly to the client for processing. Note that image and workflow servers may or may not be on the same physical machine.

14.5 WPA TOOLS

Advances in computer technology, application software, and communications have contributed to the proliferation of PC-based workgroups within businesses. Workgroup members communicate and share information over local area networks; however, the actual workflow, the job of moving information from one processing step to the next, remains a task that is handled either manually or electronically by a complex computer program.

Choosing Your Weapons: The Pro-Am

Whether application development is provided by internal programmers (MIS or department) or by outside value-added resellers (VARs) and systems integrators, robust flexible tools are a requirement. Fourth-generation languages often provide the right combination of flexibility, power, and ease of use for the professional developer of work process automation systems. These development tools feature a comfortable combination of high-level functionality (user interface building, high-level language, integrated functions, etc.) with the flexibility to use lower-level facilities (e.g., granular control of application behavior, integration with C-level services) when necessary. The limitation is that applications and facilities developed using these tools can be changed only by the professional programmer.

Robust application development tools should allow the professional developer (e.g., MIS) to build a set of activities (applications) that allows a department to process its work. In a forms-based application, for example, the forms that are processed (and therefore the applications used to process them) will probably not be changed a great deal over short periods of time. The workflow between the steps, however, may need to change significantly. Once those individual applications are complete, the separation of the workflow from the work processing application allows the department to determine the proper workflow to connect those individual activities. Although MIS, for example, may provide basic application development, it is the department staff that understands, and therefore should be able to modify, the work processes.

Department-level "developers" require different tools that allow them to express and implement their knowledge of the business procedure without system-level programming. Today's graphical tools can provide such a facility for non-programmers to control work processes without modifying applications, provided that workflow is managed outside of the imaging application. Once the applications are developed for specific processing steps and activities, these tools typically provide an environment where "developers" manipulate icons that represent the processing activities (e.g., scan, approval) and control routing behavior by connecting the activities to form workflow paths. Activities may represent hundreds of workers all performing the same task. The developer can modify the rules that govern workflow routing decisions without modifying the processing applications themselves.

Criteria for Toolkits

Tools and toolkits come in many different flavors and colors, promoting different orientations, features, and styles for developing applications. Even with these differences, a number of the issues that toolkits help users to manage are universal ones: for example, providing ease-of-use without sufficient flexibility. The following are some of the basic features and capabilities to look for when selecting work process automation toolkits and systems.

Development Environment for Compound Data Applications

The toolkit should be integrated for the specific purpose of imaging and compound data management and should take advantage of operating environment-specific features as much as possible. Key features include graphical user interface builder and a fourth-generation language, preferably in an environment that was designed to build compound data-based programs. This type of integrated environment provides a more robust and efficient solution for sophisticated development than does cobbling together a solution with a raft of components.

Peripheral integration is a task that doesn't provide much value for application developers.

High-Level Interface to an RDBMS

SQL, for instance, is a standard language that provides the programmability to support any type of data model. Programming languages may use a folder construct, and although it provides a high-level interface, the data model is somewhat limited.

Transparent Support for Optical Storage

Access to and management of optical storage of application data should be integrated with the storage of alphanumeric data for maximum benefit.

Programmability and Flexibility

Applications should conform to the demands of the user, and not vice versa. Unfortunately, toolkit flexibility is often lost at the hands of ease-of-use, though this is not to say that these two objectives are incompatible. If a system does not provide configurability to fulfill the application's requirements, then the full value of computing systems may not be realized.

Changing Workflow

The capability to change the workflow "on the fly" without modifying or affecting applications allows the fastest and easiest possible alteration in business policies and procedures.

Control of Workflow

When users can monitor, analyze, and test changes to workflow, they can adapt to the ever-changing world as safely as possible.

Graphical Workflow Builder

Visual workflow programming is significantly easier than developing scripts in a 4GL, which allows nonprogrammer "experts" to modify systems. To be effective, such workflow builders should use a database as a robust workflow engine, because business processes imply transactions, and DBMSs are excellent at managing this sort of workflow meta-information. However, simplicity of use requires that such builders do not involve database coding to program a workflow; the database is simply an engine for the workflow management software. Consequently, workflow developers and administrators should only need to understand the work processes, not develop the underlying database code for managing workflow.

Workflow Management Tools

Workflow is not static; therefore, the benefits garnered from process redesign are only as good as the tools provided to implement and change the flow. Workflow redesign tools should provide benefits in several major areas concerning the development of workflow rules, and how, when, and by whom they can be changed.

Optimally, tools should make it easy for the "experts" to set up and modify workflow. In this case, "experts" refers to the organization that does the work and implements the workflow (e.g., department analysts), rather than the implementers of the base technology (e.g., MIS). If technical programmers are required to change the flow, the benefits of fast and flexible process redesign may be lost.

A methodology and validation for the workflow should also be provided so that "experts" can examine the effects of redesign. This includes feedback on system performance to help determine what adjustments should be made and a means to test the effects of a change to the flow.

Even though individual applications that perform work functions may not change very much after implementation, the processing flow will. Users will discover that they modeled existing (paper-based) workflow properly, but that the flow can benefit from modification. Ideally, workflow can be changed easily over time using the proper tools, without requiring the recoding of desktop applications. Users will likely find that adjusting workflow for maximum efficiency is an ongoing process (see Figure 14.1). Consequently, there will be a need for tools that provide easy ways to describe present requirements and address new ones.

Scripting vs. Graphical Tools

Workflow scripting is one common method that imaging vendors provide to flow enable imaging applications. Scripting provides a high-level way to define routing rules without having to understand the lower-level implementation of work queues,

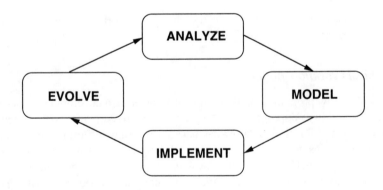

Figure 14.1   The process improvement cycle

transports, database access, etc. Scripting, however, is still like high-level programming; its syntax is strict, and some knowledge about transactions and queues (i.e., programming issues) is still required.

Ideally, work process automation tools allow user analysts to "draw" workflow maps in a graphical environment, where the different processing steps are represented by icons. The developer must understand only the work process steps and activities and need not concern himself or herself with structured programming or with the specific issues of underlying workflow data management. Once the new workflow is completed using a graphical tool, all database structures necessary to implement the workflow are automatically created without need for coding.

Another important capability of workflow tools allows administrators to change workflow easily and interactively. Workflow may be developed in various ways, usually using either a workflow script or a graphical tool. The key issue is that if routing rules are embedded in the desktop applications, then the workflow cannot be changed without changing each application that participates in the workflow.

Examples of Workflow Tool Capabilities

There are various types of tools on the market, with different capabilities. Choosing the best tool depends on the applications, the scope of the project, and the strength of the support staff. The most common characteristics are outlined below.

Interactive Tools

Interactive tools allow organizations to react quickly to procedure changes by modifying the workflow and adding new processing steps outside of the existing applications. Tools should allow changes to the flow while work is in progress, without disturbing users or the work flowing through the system. Once the new workflow is complete, whether by graphical tool or scripting, all database structures needed to implement the workflow should automatically be created without additional lower-level coding. In this way, an interactive workflow system can adapt to handle exceptions and accommodate changes in routine business operations without recoding, recompiling, or retesting individual applications that are already deployed.

Monitor Status of Processing Activities

Another useful workflow tool is one that displays the status of the work (e.g., number of users logged into the activity, the priority of the activity) that is flowing through the system for each work processing activity. Some information can be displayed graphically, rather than in a textual format, providing direct visual feedback about where the work is and how it is flowing. This type of tool can be helpful in monitoring and managing workflow performance, allowing managers to use real-time information to make decisions about day-to-day work processing.

Test Workflow before Going On-Line

Just as an automobile manufacturer might simulate the design and performance of a new sports car before putting the model into production, complex workflow requires a means to analyze system performance *before* it is put into use. Simulation tools provide a "sneak preview" of changes in workflow without processing real data, running a virtual model based on the rules and routing information defined in the system workflow map. Work processing activities are simulated by selecting and varying expected response parameters (such as delay time, output state of document, etc.), thereby modeling system performance before using live data. The system can then be adjusted off line to reach an optimal configuration before putting a new flow into practice.

Management Reports on Organizational Efficiency

Workflow management systems should also be able to track the history of work through the system for true management information. System data, including information about work items such as date and time of day, activities performed by users, etc., should be logged in a database. System administrators can then analyze an organization's efficiency by creating custom reports from the logged workflow meta-information using a standard DBMS report writer tool in much the same way these tools generate reports for application data.

Control and Integrity of Workflow Data

One of the issues of concern with workflow systems, as with other data management applications, is how and where the rules and state information are stored. Process integrity in transaction-based workflow requires that control and management of the workflow be from a single point, most likely using the services of a database management system. Work in the system may carry its own routing information, though a central workflow database is still needed to track the actual flow. If desktop-based scripts control the workflow, transactions and consistent flow are not assured, and control over the data is lost. Process integrity allows industrial strength applications with sophisticated workflows that interact with other complex systems beyond the scope of the local flow.

14.6 FACTORS IN DESIGNING WORKFLOW SYSTEMS

Because workflow represents a physical process, workflow design must follow specific rules that reflect practical constraints.

Processing Activities

The system designer(s) must decide how to divide the application work into different workflow activities to maintain overall application modularity. Existing applications should be divided into separate processing activities to allow flexible routing between different application steps. Newly developed custom activities would require only an interface to the workflow manager.

Input Devices

Inputs into the workflow system might include optical scanners, tape drives, gateways to and from another system, or keyed data entry input from a local application. Software applications associated with these input devices are written to process data and move it from the input device into the imaging and workflow system.

Depending on your requirement, you may choose either a centralized or decentralized approach to document image scanning. Some applications are best served by the "few plow horses" approach (high-speed scanner(s) attached to the server), while others are better suited to "hundreds of rabbits" (desktop scanners attached to a number of workstations) to perform the work in a more distributed fashion. The approach you take depends on how documents enter and are processed in the system, either through a central source (e.g., the mail room) or distributed across a number of scanning workstations.

Input/Output to Workflow Activities

An *input interface activity* takes data controlled by the workflow system and writes the data into a form usable by an existing activity and even executes a command known by the existing application to tell it about the new data.

An *output interface activity* either monitors the output data or is triggered by some command from the existing application. The activity retrieves the data from the existing application and prepares it for use by workflow activities downstream.

Data Access Considerations

Whether the workflow system can access data by reference and/or by value affects system attributes. If the system routes data by reference, then all access methods and drivers (e.g., database, file systems) must be present in and performed by the applications. The workflow manager tells the workstation where the data is located, and the software on the workstation retrieves the work. If the workflow manager can retrieve data for activities directly, then access methods for data need not be present in the workstation.

Multiple Server Considerations

When developing systems for future expansion, it is important to consider workflow management support distributed across multiple servers. In some non-distributed environments, gateways can manage the flow of information between single servers, though administration and data management must be handled at each server.

Processing Time for Each Activity

In planning the layout of workflow maps, it is important to calculate the duration of each activity. Appropriate numbers of users and resources must be available for each activity to prevent data flow bottlenecks, during which processing slows down to unacceptable levels. Bottlenecks also require more overall disk capacity for storage of the "slowed down" work; also, be sure that *destructor* activities that take work out of the system (for example, an archive activity) are present in the flow so that disk storage requirements are controllable.

Processing Hardware Requirements

The hardware requirements for a workflow manager are driven by the software environment and its system capacity requirements. Server hardware must be able to support the operating system activity, network communications, and the work-flow database. (Note that some databases use the CPU more intensively than others.) System memory requirements are mandated by performance, the number of applications running, and the number of users anticipated on the system. The available memory must be large enough to prevent system swapping during production. Minimum memory configurations for a small UNIX system may be 16MB, though a typical small production configuration might require at least 32MB. In high-performance environments, additional RAM for caching critical database indices could help.

Workflow Mapping Features

A map represents the procedures within an enterprise. It contains a graphical diagram of each step (or activity) in a procedure with connections between steps to show the possible routes between activities. Maps in work process automation tools have several features of interest.

Properties of Maps and Submaps

Maps (and submaps) allow the graphical workflow developer to put together small, easily tested maps and then use them in higher-level maps over and over again. Maps are like individual activities in that they have defined inputs and outputs, and once a map has been created to perform a function, it should not be necessary to recreate the map to perform the same function in a different context, even using a submap multiple times within the same map. Maps should also be able to reference themselves for recursive workflow.

Workflow systems should support a repository for all activities, including submaps, which have been created for the system and promote the reuse of processing activities and submaps.

Routing Behavior

Businesses have a number of procedures in place at any given time, and a workflow system must be able to accommodate new maps or procedures easily. Some procedures require that a processing step be repeated until reaching some (successful) conclusion. Another desirable feature is to associate a deadline with the event so that administrators are alerted if work "gets caught in a loop."

Some procedures occur over protracted periods of time, so maps should be able to change at any time while work is in process without disrupting work already in the flow. This guarantees that a procedure is followed when a user initiates the procedure, and that work follows the routes it was intended to follow. Users should be able to create maps, route work, and then modify the flow for a slightly different purpose, knowing that any work in progress will reach its intended destination.

Workflow systems should be able to route data based either on the "state" of the data leaving an application or using external "rule engines" which interpret user-defined rules after an application has completed its operations. Rules may be invoked as a result of a user's selection about the state of the work or based on a data value in the work itself.

Activities

Exception activities and global resource activities should not require explicit input routes. Exception activities do not execute automatically, but accept work that requires "hands-on" processing until a system administrator can take appropriate action.

Activities may be assigned a default priority, with the ability to change priority based on the amount of work queued for the activity. System administrators should also be able to change priorities.

Some activities need to participate in workflow in more than one map. These "global" activities (e.g., print, fax) may be referenced in several maps for different types of work and may need to run unattended.

Priorities of Work

Work is usually ordered in queues by priorities. The priority of a piece of work may need to be changed by a processing application, by a system administrator, or by the workflow system itself, based on factors such as the age of the work item, an irate phone caller, etc. In addition, users may need to bypass the normal work queue and explicitly select an item of work for accelerated processing.

Workflow systems may also allow users to set deadlines for completion of a procedure, elevating the work's priority as the deadline approaches to expedite the operation. Alarms should also be able to send a message back to a user or administrator as a deadline approaches.

14.7 WORKFLOW AUTOMATION AND IMAGING TOOLS

WPA is an integrating, not an isolating process, so the resulting architecture should be compatible with existing corporate computing architectures and open to embracing (nonimage) applications. Although very few people can predict the future, developers must try to plan systems that are both compatible today and extensible enough tomorrow to adapt to changing business and computing environments.

Flexibility and Ease-of-Use

Graphical tools (and to some extent, scripting languages) provide the facility for system users or administrators (i.e., not application programmers) to modify workflow for maximum efficiency. The developer in this case does not need to know the underlying programmatic concepts of queuing using a relational data model, what work information to track and how, and other lower-level concepts of workflow automation. Graphical tools allow workflow development at a higher level, so that the developer needs to understand only the work process (i.e., what needs to be accomplished), but not how to accomplish it programmatically. Therefore, applications can be developed faster, since application programmers will write code to handle the actual work process, and this code will be modularized using a workflow API. Department staff can then implement and change the flow without writing additional code.

Transparency

Imaging tools should allow developers to concern themselves with concepts and functionality at a sufficiently high level. An example of this is seen in the properties of SQL (Structured Query Language), a high-level language for managing relational databases that allows developers to declare *what* to do with the data, but not *how* to do it—the database "understands" the underlying mechanisms for sorting, retrieving, and manipulating the data. This concept can be extended to many (other) aspects of an imaging and workflow toolset, where the programmer is shielded from the system-level mechanisms required, and only needs to be concerned with the higher-level needs of the application.

Data manipulation, including interfaces to imaging peripherals, is one of the areas where tools should add value. Interfaces should be independent of specific hardware devices and data types, and image manipulation functions should allow the developer to concentrate on solving more abstract application requirements, rather than low-level technical ones.

Ideally, imaging tools make it easy to choose the right *data storage* medium for an application. Storage should be supported in a (relatively) transparent manner, so that developers don't have to understand all of the underlying mechanisms for managing storage on optical or other large-scale media.

The implementation of optical storage for image data is different from the magnetic-based one due to the unique characteristics of WORM optical storage, particularly of its write-once and dismountable nature. Any implementation that assumes the constant availability and random access characteristics of magnetic disks will collapse when applied to an optical environment because of the amount of time required to fault a platter, even in a jukebox environment. The overall architecture must allow for dismountability (i.e., the database data may not be available at the moment it is requested).

When an application references an image, say for retrieval, it should not need to determine the exact location of the data. If the optical platter holding the data is mounted in a drive, it is accessed, and the operation is completed. If the platter is in a jukebox but not mounted, the software determines if there is an available drive in the same jukebox. If a drive is available, robotic commands are issued to spin down and remove the platter in the desired drive, and then retrieve and spin up the needed platter. If a drive is not available, the request is queued, subject to time-out limits set by the application. If the required platter is not in a jukebox, similar results can be effected through interaction with an operator (i.e., a request to import the platter into the jukebox). The use of optical storage should be functionally transparent to the application, which need not be aware of the location of specific images nor manage the drives, issue mount requests, etc.

Imaging tools should also allow for appropriate media organization for optical storage. Applications do not have to understand the issues of two-sided removable media when only one side may be accessed at a time. In addition, optical must appear as an open-ended medium that can be extended indefinitely to take advantage of the large-scale storage. Since the time to exchange platters in an optical drive is high compared to the time to access the data, the organization of data across multiple platters is important. Data may be organized either sequentially or clustered. Sequential storage is straightforward: Data is added in order, much as on a tape device. Clustered organization is important when active data resides on many volumes. Optical clustering is a means for grouping logically related images so that related images can be retrieved together with a minimum of optical platter accesses. For example, typically a user will want to view all documents associated with a given entity together. If the images are spread over a number of volumes, the retrieval time could be several minutes. Even worse, the aggregate of multiple requests to the jukebox may swamp it, resulting in delays of tens of minutes, even hours. But if all the images are located on the same optical platter, there will be no more than one platter exchange and very reasonable response system-wide.

The dismountability and write-once (or erasable) nature of optical media introduces a number of issues for an imaging system that preferably are handled transparently. Optical disk volumes must be labeled and location tracked without requiring the user to do all of the management of the media. Optical disk volumes must be scheduled and mounted in drives for access as needed, including controlling the optical jukebox robotics. Platters may be moved into or out of jukeboxes with no effect on the application software.

Openness and Adherence to Standards

Today's corporate information systems are true technological melting pots, consisting of heterogeneous systems that must communicate to allow a diverse organization to function. Openness (usually) means that a wide range of custom and commercially available components can add value to the system as a whole at competitive prices. The solution is not bound to proprietary hardware and often supports a number of different vendors' hardware platforms, networks, peripheral devices, and the like.

Standards are necessary to ensure that systems will be interoperable and easy to maintain. Images stored in a standard format (e.g., CCITT Group 3 or 4 compressed TIFF file) promise access by diverse applications and ensure that data will be accessible in the long term. Other applications in the organization may be developed using different tools, though they nonetheless require access to the same data. Adherence to standards allows the melting pot to function using a common denominator, rather than isolating applications and requiring special treatment of data that should be widely available across the enterprise.

WPA cannot be a technology island with limited potential for growth and restrictions on interoperability. Openness is a key to evolution, both for hardware and software, that allows the use of best-of-breed components for specialized processing areas, such as database management systems, client application development, and workflow services.

System Architecture and Design

Workflow design impacts the selection of a system architecture to meet operational requirements.

Throughput/Performance/Response Time

CPU speed often is *not* the bottleneck in imaging server system design. Although processor speed is helpful when the image application requires a great deal of database activity (e.g., lots of SQL JOIN operations), it is network expandability that most often causes a problem for image servers. If the workflow server uses a DBMS and is running on the same hardware as the image server, then a fast CPU is probably a necessity to handle all the database activity.

Consider that in an on-line processing environment, where current 10- or 16MBps networking technology is capable of supporting only a small number of workstations, the server may need to support multiple networks to reach image throughput for a large, demanding application. Often, as applications grow, the architectural bottleneck is the server's maximum number of network interface cards and the expandability of magnetic storage, and not CPU processing power. Particularly on smaller servers, the network(s) may become saturated and the client applications unable to process work at maximum speed long before the server's processor starts bogging down with database requests.

Optical subsystem throughput is another bottleneck that is often reached before the limits of CPU or magnetic disk performance, again depending on the characteristics of the specific application. Optical drives provide an order of magnitude less throughput than magnetic disks, and the overhead of mounting optical platters and handling multiple read and write requests tends to lower overall throughput.

When considering the additional demands of workflow management (i.e., database operations), CPU performance becomes more important. Workflow managers that use database systems as a workflow engine demand more CPU performance. The ability for the workflow manager to run on a machine separate from the imaging server and other data storage software is a benefit as systems, processing volume, and performance demands grow.

Scalability/Portability/Robustness

Systems that grow over time can quickly extend beyond the capabilities of the initial hardware platform. Choosing a scalable architecture allows growth without reimplementing the application, and if the system is portable across a variety of hardware platforms, the cost of growth and change can be kept to a minimum.

The system architecture should support hardware with a range of performance that is appropriate for the variety of applications that the organization requires. Indeed, this might consist of a single hardware vendor's offering, but it is often desirable that imaging tools support different hardware and software platforms to serve different application needs, including both clients and servers.

Server platforms can span a range from single processor machines with relatively limited memory and disk storage expandability to mainframe-class servers with scalable multiprocessor architectures and vast amounts of storage. The requirements for a workgroup or pilot application will differ greatly from a larger production application, though it may be desirable to be able to use the same tools for larger applications or even to deploy the small pilot application on much larger machines. This makes it desirable that the image system architecture and resulting applications are scalable across servers with a variety of capabilities and capacities.

Reliability/Availability/Security

Other modern techniques of system reliability, data availability, and security are equally applicable to imaging and workflow applications. These include systems that support mirroring, disk striping, redundancy, and other fault-tolerant features that keep critical systems available. Imaging and workflow platforms that are based on standard components and architectures should take advantage of these system services and provide all the same benefits as "traditional" data processing systems.

Application Database Management Considerations

Imaging applications require the same administrative facilities as those enjoyed by "standard" data processing applications, as they are essentially DBMS applications that manage extended data types in a similar type of database environment.

Data Organization

Imaging systems generally use relational database technology to organize and manage data. The full power of the relational database allows a wide variety of data models for an imaging application using the same inherent facilities as for non-imaging applications.

The most common data organization scheme for imaging is the folder/document/page model, but all folders are not created equal. Applications have varying requirements for managing information, and the definition of a folder can vary widely among implementations. For example, folders can contain documents and/or other folders, where documents can be single or multiple pages; or, folders can contain folders, documents, and pages simultaneously; and, folders can contain objects other than images (e.g., word processing documents, spreadsheets).

Imaging systems should provide a data model that allows for the flexible organization of data as is appropriate for the application. Although many data processing applications appropriately manage documents for each account as a folder, some applications are not best served using the folder model. For example, an application that handles ticket reservations might not benefit from using folders to manage the items, if each ticket/owner combination is referenced uniquely.

Archive and Recovery

The diversity of data types and storage media can present a considerable challenge to system backup in network imaging systems. Images on optical need to be archived along with the related alphanumeric data, sometimes requiring a sophisticated coordination effort. Sometimes the sheer volume of data causes problems with a window of opportunity to complete the archive while maintaining adequate performance; for example, if the application must run 24 hours-a-day/7 days-a-week.

Optically based data can be archived to either optical or magnetic media, but the longevity requirements must be considered. If a primary advantage of optical storage is durability, then the archive technique must not compromise the security of the data by relying on magnetic storage as a fail-safe backup. Incremental archives usually use magnetic tape backup, as these are short-term revolving backups. Many systems make copies of optical platters once they are full, although this can be done incrementally, as well. If images are clustered on optical platters, the application can write a sequential copy of each image on a separate platter as they come into the system.

Availability

Database techniques for data availability, such as disk mirroring, striping, and other fault-tolerant features, are equally applicable to imaging systems based on DBMSs. In addition, imaging services at the application layer can take advantage of system-level services that are available to other applications running on that platform.

Database Reports

Data in imaging systems is often similar to nonimage systems with the exception of rich (and large) data. Reports consisting of alphanumeric data are still required, possibly with the extended need for reports with images as well. Report writers for these systems should allow reports that mix alphanumeric and image data with the usual formatting capabilities.

14.8 IMPLICATIONS FOR OPTICAL STORAGE

For all its benefits, optical storage does not offer the performance and access of magnetic disk, so image storage systems offer a number of techniques to speed up optical retrievals and overall performance. All these methods require planning in both software design and sufficient hardware resources (i.e., magnetic storage).

Caching

Optical caching on the image server helps to speed up image insertion and retrieval to/from optical by writing images to magnetic during the operation. On insertion, workstations need not wait for images to be written to optical (particularly useful if there is a queue or the optical platter is not mounted) before continuing with the next operation. Upon retrieval, all the images in a folder can be written to magnetic disk as an intermediate step before being sent down to the workstation. This allows much faster retrieval of subsequent items in the folder, as they will be available from faster magnetic disk.

Prefetching

Workstations can *prefetch* images and cache them locally to speed up the *flip rate*. For example, when a user wants to browse the first page of a document, the workstation application could automatically retrieve pages 1 through 10 into local workstation memory on the assumption that the user will want to view successive pages of the document. When the user flips the page, another database/optical access is not required to retrieve the image, and it can be displayed almost instantaneously.

Staging

Some applications benefit from *staging* work (images) for more efficient operation. If the processing of work items (images) is predictable, the application can automatically prefetch them from optical overnight and store them temporarily on fast magnetic disk. Note, however, that applications in which access to data is random usually cannot benefit from this technique.

Another straightforward method that can benefit application performance is to maintain images on magnetic media (possibly in addition to optical) during periods of high activity, for example, at the beginning of a processing cycle. This explicit implementation of caching allows images to be retrieved from much higher performance storage for fast access. Images need not be stored on optical during these active periods, though they could be for purposes of archival security.

14.9 ENABLING EXTANT (LEGACY) SYSTEMS

Dilemma: Rest or Recreation

Imaging brings a wealth of data to the desktop, but what about the mass of data in existing systems? Image enabling through the use of imaging toolkits provides a powerful means of extending extant applications without recreating or duplicating existing data. If a major benefit of imaging is that it "brings the rest of the transaction to the desktop" (the information currently stored on pieces of paper), organizations will both want and need to apply the benefits of imaging to existing applications and systems to make maximum use of imaging technology.

In this light, open systems imaging and downsizing does not mean scrap the mainframe, but rather, deploy networked systems as an adjunct to existing host-based or other custom applications (even existing client-server applications). Rather than relocating all the corporate data that has accumulated over time in extant applications, network imaging systems can leverage that information and provide essential services for automating and improving data processing.

Host-Based Applications: A Terminal Condition

Open systems-based imaging can be extremely valuable as a service to a host-based application, though one potentially thorny issue is the requirement to change existing mainframe application code. Mainframe code is generally complex and, for older applications, the original developers are often long gone. One powerful attribute of network imaging toolkits can be the ability to image enable host applications without changing mainframe application code by allowing imaging applications to run in a window side by side with the extant application (terminal emulation) on a workstation with a single display.

One application area that frequently benefits from image enabling is the ubiquitous mainframe-based application running on IBM 3270 terminals. While these

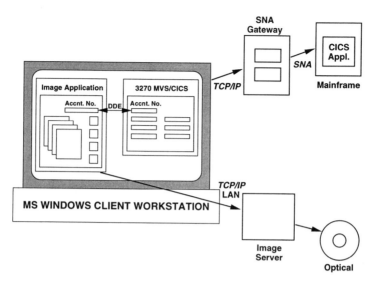

Figure 14.2   Diagram of a 3270 emulation configuration

applications run in the IBM SNA world, client-server open systems imaging integration can replace 3270 terminals with client workstations that run terminal emulation software and communicate with the mainframe via communications gateways. The appropriate tools can image enable existing mainframe applications with relative ease and moderate cost (see Figure 14.2). The 3270 terminal emulation sessions on the workstation run as separate applications from the image-enabling application, and the two must exchange data to interact.

For the purposes of this example, assume that the application being image enabled is a 3270-based MVS/CICS application used for traditional on-line transaction processing (alphanumeric data) for customer service. The imaging application consists of Microsoft Windows client applications running on a local area network. The imaging application uses the TCP/IP protocol to communicate with a UNIX-based image server that allows the storage of both alphanumeric and image data, in addition to image storage on optical disk. This application uses the client-server model, where the Windows client formulates queries and requests data and services from the image server across the LAN, and the image server is responsible for processing queries, managing data, and returning results to the clients.

Data Exchange

The imaging client application is a separate application from the 3270 terminal emulation session, and the imaging toolkit provides a means to transfer data between applications running in the client workstation. In the Microsoft Windows environment, for example, a primary facility for sharing data is DDE, which allows Windows applications to exchange information automatically.

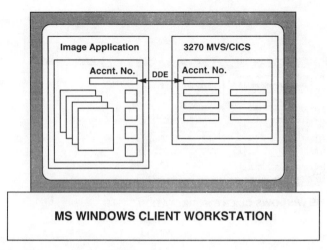

Figure 14.3　Diagram of a DDE screen

Microsoft Windows dynamic data exchange (DDE) is one method of transferring data and image-enabling extant applications. Dynamic data exchange is a protocol defined by Microsoft through which interprocess communications are used to exchange data between applications, either synchronously or asynchronously. DDE involves a *conversation* between a DDE client application and DDE server application, meaning that a data link has been established between the two applications, and linked data will be updated automatically. The link may be either *hot* (DDE server immediately sends changed data to the DDE client) or *warm* (DDE server notifies the DDE client that the data has changed).

In the customer service application example, historical customer account data is managed by the MVS/CICS application. When a customer phones in to inquire about an account, the service representative enters the appropriate customer information into the 3270 screen and retrieves the customer's records from the CICS application. The customer account number is sent from a field in the 3270 session to the imaging application via Windows DDE, and the imaging application uses the account number as a key to retrieve the associated billing document images from the image server automatically (see Figure 14.3).

By storing both alphanumeric and image (or other binary) data, the image server may serve to enhance the existing host-based application even further. In any case, no change is made to the mainframe application to implement the imaging solution; the sharing of data occurs strictly within the client workstation environment using mechanisms provided by the imaging toolkit.

Workflow Gateways with Heterogeneous Systems

Even though workflow routing can allow heterogeneous systems to participate in the same data processing workflow, some data translation might be needed. A workflow gateway retrieves routing data (either by reference or value) from the workflow server on behalf of its client system, converts the data into an acceptable format, and handles any necessary batching of the data. The workflow gateway can also act as a communications gateway to allow systems that don't use the same network protocols to communicate and participate in the workflow. This requires an appropriate set of communications APIs, in addition to the workflow APIs.

Using CASE with Imaging Application Tools

If imaging is really a complex form of client-server (database) application that requires a few additional technologies for handling sophisticated data types, then computer-aided software engineering principles should be applicable in the development process. Open imaging toolkits allow developers to apply various CASE (and other) methodologies when designing applications, because the same basic application development needs exist for applications that include the image data type. For example, data access, application flow control, calculation, and data presentation are functions common to both alphanumeric and image-based programs and require the same considerations for software development. Work process automation consists of a series of work steps that together comprise a larger meta-application. CASE methods must be adaptable to this form of distributed application in which a large number of executables perform an aggregate work processing function.

14.10 WORKFLOW SYSTEM APPLICATION DEVELOPMENT METHODOLOGY

Structured Methodology as Language

The system development process is one of iterative communication. The buyer (end user) needs something built; the builder (integrator or user development team) is charged with constructing that something. The builder is more likely to deliver exactly what the buyer wants if both agree on what that something is, what it is to look like, what function it is to serve, and when it is needed. The builder will be successful if he or she and his or her staff agree on what materials are needed, the tasks and procedures for using those materials in the construction of the goal, and the methods for determining that things are going according to plan. Failure to reach informed agreement (i.e., when both sides share a common conception of what is being agreed upon) will almost certainly guarantee subsequent problems.

A sound methodology should provide terms and symbols to convey system concepts and a "grammar" (or structure) that links these into a coherent description of the system requirements and its solution. The methodology and its components should be understood by both buyer and builder and should not be susceptible to misunderstanding or misinterpretation. Such a methodology is a language, facilitating communication among all parties involved in the project.

Document-Driven Method

Documents Record Work Accomplished and Track the Project   Documents not only record the work accomplished throughout a project's phases, but they also launch phases. The major documents generated during a complete system life cycle might include the following:

- Imaging/work process automation opportunities assessment
- Application profile
- System requirements definition (including essential model and behavioral model)
- External design specification (including user implementation model)
- Internal design specification (including processor model)
- Integration test plan and test script
- Acceptance test plan and test script
- User documentation

Milestones to Kick-Off Phases   The system development cycle consists of a series of phases, each punctuated by one or more milestones. At each milestone, progress should be assessed, with work reviewed and accepted; plans for future phases can be reviewed, and perhaps altered, in light of the experience to date.

At each major milestone, designated team members gather to review what was built and/or accomplished during the preceding phase or subphase. For most of the milestones (e.g., requirements definition, external design), a document is reviewed; for the others (such as installation or acceptance testing), a previously reviewed and accepted document should support the assessment process directly.

System Development Phases

Every new system passes through a number of stages, from initial conception through installation and production (and beyond). An analysis and development team will not necessarily have input to all phases; in some cases (and not infrequently), management will have already decided that the solution to the business problem is an imaging/work process automation system; the major requirements for the new system may also have been defined.

Nonetheless, the development team must be prepared to address the definition and design of the new system from the outset and take it through all phases. The chronological evolution of a development project occurs in four stages or phases: feasibility, definition, design, and implementation. A fifth "phase," project management, actually spans the life of the project, yet is so distinct in its activities and deliverable products that it merits separate treatment.

Feasibility   Prior to authorizing analysis of a new imaging system, management must determine that the work process automation and document image processing technologies have applicability in the work environment, that is, an initial determination that the new technologies are likely to solve the business problem.

Opportunities Analysis: The first step in such a determination is the identification of areas within the current business that are suitable for improvement by introducing imaging/work process automation. This procedure is conducted primarily via interviews with several levels of management, as well as through gathering information about the current system(s) using questionnaires and worksheets. An optional study is one that determines financial costs and benefits for each work area. Following the interviews and data analysis, the development team produces an opportunities assessment.

Application Profile: From the opportunities assessment, management selects one (or possibly two) application(s) of interest. The selection criteria usually takes into consideration factors such as risk, visibility, payback, and window of opportunity.

The development team should prepare an application profile for each application of interest. The profile describes in very general terms the business problem(s) to be solved, briefly describes the current system (manual and/or automated), and lists the reasons why it is unsatisfactory as well as goals for the new system; finally, it describes the benefits that will be derived from the new system, amplifying the benefits list that appeared in the opportunities assessment.

The application profile will likely be a relatively short document. It is, nonetheless, essential that care and time be taken in reaching agreement with the users on each section, since this document is the first to set expectations for the resultant system.

System Definition   During system definition, users state new system requirements by telling the analysts what the new system must do, how it must behave, what it must deliver, and how it must interact with existing systems (or those systems as they will be modified in the light of the requirements). Once the boundaries of the new system are established and the interface data transfers are defined, the development teams can model the new system as it will appear to the users.

Essential Model: Emphasis in this phase of development must be on securing user agreement on the functions of the new system and on how the user will interact with the system to activate these functions. The analyst teams interview the new system users to determine functional requirements (that is, how the system must respond when the user does something: add information, request the output of information, request the transformation of data, and so on). These user-initiated events usually make up the majority of the functional requirements. The system may also respond to temporal events (the passage of a specified amount of time) and conjunctions (the satisfaction of a number of prerequisites, such as the arrival into the system of all the documents required to complete a process).

Three documents comprise an essential model of the new system. An events list is the sum of all the identified events of the above three types, from which is derived the context diagram, which graphically depicts the boundaries of the new system and its interfaces with existing systems and other external entities (e.g., other departments, customers, suppliers). The team should also document the organization of the system data to create a preliminary data model.

The behavioral model follows; it is the first view of the new system as it will behave in response to the specified events. From the events list, the analyst team creates a preliminary dataflow diagram and group system processes in a partitioned function diagram. The processes in this diagram are in turn decomposed into lower-level dataflow diagrams, whose supporting documentation includes business process specifications and a preliminary data dictionary.

System Requirements: The analyst team packages the essential and behavioral models with a statement of requirements for performance, training, documentation, hardware and software, backup/recovery, and data conversion, and presents these to management for review and approval as the system requirements definition.

User Implementation Model: Following agreement on system functional requirements, the user analysts depict the new system as it will look to the user in the user implementation model, which builds on the work already done. The process is highly iterative, and the "look and feel" of the system should be developed with a great deal of input from those who will use it. This model should contain workstation screen displays for each set of activities to be performed by the users, as well as report layouts, as appropriate. The analysts develop a set of state transition diagrams to depict the stimulus/response associations for each discrete user activity (e.g., system response when user selects an object, such as an "Update" button on the workstation screen). The database schema builds on the work done earlier in creating the data model.

External Design Specification: The user implementation model is packaged with statements of business constraints, technical constraints, and design constraints that serve as guidelines in implementing the desired "look and feel." The user implementation model, together with the constraints sections, form the external design specification.

System Design   Whereas the audience for the document deliverables issuing from the system definition phase is primarily the user community, documents developed during application design are for the most part intended for the system design and development team.

Internal Design Specification: There are several components of this specification, which the developers use to actually build the application specified:

Processor model   This model partitions the processes defined in the lower-level dataflow diagrams (behavioral model) into groups according to the responsible processing activities (e.g., mainframe, data server, workstation, human).

Control level dataflow diagrams   These depict those user-interactive processes that have been assigned to client or user workstation processors on the processor model. They are used as the basis for high-level structure charts.

Module level dataflow diagrams   These are analogous to control level dataflow diagrams, but are for noninteractive (e.g., server-based) processes. They also form the basis for the derivation of high-level structure charts for server processes.

Module specifications   These provide a detailed narrative on what will occur in each of the processes in the control level and module level dataflow diagrams.

High-level structure charts   These depict the relationships between the control and functional modules that appear on the module level and control level dataflow diagrams.

System Implementation   Once the internal design specification has been approved, the development team proceeds with application coding and testing. The development method encompasses the following activities during application implementation:

- Design module structure charts
- Develop unit test plans
- Develop string test plans
- Develop integration test plan and test script
- Develop acceptance test plan and test script
- Create commented source code; test and rework
- Perform unit, integration, and acceptance tests based on the plans and scripts

Project Management—An Ongoing "Phase"   Project management is a critical set of activities that will ensure successful execution of the above phases. Some of the project management tasks include:

- Develop a work breakdown structure
- Develop a task GANTT chart
- Assign system resources
- Create subsidiary project plans: training, documentation, installation, etc.
- Track the project
- Develop acceptance test plan
- Install and test the system hardware
- Install the system and application software
- Perform acceptance test

14.11 CONCLUSIONS

Imaging is not a cure-all. Darwin probably said it best: "Change or die." Businesses in the 1990s are facing ever fiercer competition to survive and thrive, and the successful ones have found that an effective way of serving external customers better is to improve how they work on the inside. Traditional business applications model paper and data flows that already existed in the organization and, as a result, business processes are often tightly integrated in the software design. And because the whole mode of operation is bound tightly to these monolithic applications, business processes often have to adapt to existing applications, not vice versa.

Converting from paper to imaged documents often boosts efficiency and cost effectiveness of an operation by as much as 50 percent simply by automating an existing process to provide better response time, lower information storage cost, etc. Imaging as a basic technological capability provides the *means* to route, store, and manage data more efficiently. Imaging alone, however, cannot tackle the totality of the problem of helping an organization, be it workgroup, department, or enterprise, deal with change.

Just *having* workflow isn't good enough either, especially if it's coupled tightly with the applications involved; it's too difficult to change. The key is being able to analyze the model and change the work process in a natural, interactive way, and be able to adapt the workflow to a changing business environment with minimal effort. This can happen only when an organization can separate business process workflow management from the applications involved and focus on solving the real business problems without having to recode existing applications just because the *flow* changed. In this way, work process automation allows an organization to improve its efficiency vastly more than using imaging alone.

Work process automation (WPA) is the coordination of people, tasks, and data to improve the efficiency, flexibility, and effectiveness of an organization. A combination of tools and technologies, including database management systems, graphical user interfaces, optical storage, imaging, and workflow provide the necessary pieces of the puzzle. In concert, these technologies can be used to build flexible systems that allow users and organizations to adapt.

WPA represents a fundamental change in the way an organization does business, and adaptation is an ongoing process. Companies can evaluate and reengineer the way they work, carefully and constantly reviewing the relationships and activities within the enterprise. Process change need not be revolutionary; instead, processes should evolve with minimal trauma to best serve the goals and objectives of the organization. The easier this process of process evolution is, the faster a company can address costly changes in the business environment.

WPA is *true* management information, not only about data, but about business processes, as well. MIS has traditionally provided access to and analysis of crucial business information; for example, financial data about revenue and costs, manufacturing yields, and the like. But the "data about the data" provides higher-level information about the organizational processes in place and allows companies to analyze not only *what* they are doing, but *how* they are doing it, as well.

303

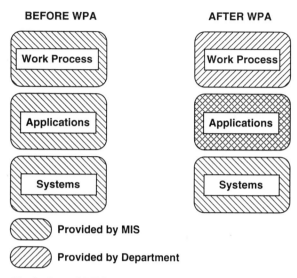

BEFORE WPA   AFTER WPA

Work Process

Applications

Systems

Provided by MIS

Provided by Department

Figure 14.4   Evolution of MIS responsibilities

The role of central MIS may be very different in a work process automation environment than in a traditional centralized data processing model. Rather than providing *everything* required to implement work (data) processing systems, from application development to designing and embedding workflows, MIS may specify and/or provide the basic systems and architectures (e.g, hardware platforms, networking architecture, DBMSs) and possibly the work processing applications as well (see Figure 14.4).

This paradigm for distributed contribution will allow central MIS and department organizations to contribute most efficiently to the computing environment within the corporation. MIS might manage the basic technology of the information systems used for work process automation, and department organizations have the ability to change how they work without requiring services from MIS.

Once an organization has embarked down this path, it will find it difficult to return to the ways of the past. The freedom of decentralized computing means that organizations contribute to the system in ways that allow them to add the optimum value. Technology infrastructure and technical/integration expertise are provided by one group, either at the corporate or smaller organizational level, while the department can define the application user interfaces, work processes, and other procedural elements according to the business practices that make sense.

Imaging and workflow are effective means for sharing the wealth of data throughout an enterprise, and they allow the scope of the data in a transaction to go far beyond that of yesteryear's transaction. The mainframe may remain a requirement for much of the data processing in the world, but open systems imaging and workflow can augment its efficiency without causing upheaval—change it without touching it. This means that as application requirements grow (to imaging and beyond), organizations can add to the imaging applications rather than the mainframe. Client-server applications can also benefit from an imaging add-on: The heart of the application is unaffected by the implementation of imaging or workflow; it is unaware of the means required to participate in this enabling technology.

The key to enabling with client-server image and workflow is the flexibility to create, change, and add to these "heterogeneous applications" that allow host-based, network, and local applications to interoperate for maximum leverage. And as the world turns away from the monolithic and towards open, synergistic, object-based environments, we will begin to see things (what we used to call applications) as providers of services to the real applications—ourselves.

15

Integrated Workgroup Image-Enabled Productivity Software

William A. Gelfand

Lotus Consulting Services Group

Editor's Note

One of the rapidly emerging business support strategies made possible by the capabilities of modern workstations is in the area of workgroup computing, where files and applications are shared between individuals working on the same project, regardless of geographical or organizational boundaries. These workgroups can benefit from the integration of imaging with the other document formats that are available through the network, including word processing, spreadsheets, electronic mail, voice, and, in a not so distant future, full multimedia and video conferencing.

This chapter describes some of the design issues that must be considered when trying to integrate an image document system with the rest of the business applications necessary to support the workgroup. Although the discussion is limited to a DOS/Windows/OS/2 environment, many of the issues are applicable to UNIX-capable networks.

Consequently, from a user point of view, deciding on the "best" workgroup productivity software may well be the result of two highly personal considerations:

*   *Familiarity with an existing battery of tools supporting the user's business*

- *Perceived need for "better" tool*

If the "better" tools are from a familiar family, user acceptance will likely be higher than if they are from a different product line, requiring learning new ways of doing business.

15.1 DEFINITION

Although the local area network (LAN) as we know it has been around for some time, the benefits a business derives from running its main activities on one have been inconsistent. On the one hand, if a PC application program existed to serve a particular business, more times than not, it was developed with a single user in mind. The advent of the LAN made it possible to "stretch" this program so it could be used by many people, but the program's single-user heritage always seemed to show up like an uninvited relative. And although the stretched version of the program was able to perform most tasks well, some operations, which performed flawlessly in the single-user version, turned into nightmares when attempted by multiple users on an LAN.

Eventually, programs were developed with the network in mind. These programs could be used on a single machine, but their main benefit was intended for groups of workers. Many mainframe application programs, which businesses had been struggling with for years, were laid to rest, and new programs were written and implemented using the benefits and cost-effectiveness of the PC/LAN environment.

During this time, document imaging systems, which resided on midsize or, more commonly, mainframe computers, had price tags that were almost as high as the long-term costs of maintaining them. Due to the significant processing and storage needs a document imaging system requires, these were the only platforms able to support business programs of this type. In fact, if a business could afford them, these systems did their job very well. They had relatively fast response times, excellent data storage and archive, and usually a large company to service and support them.

The PC/LAN market was speeding along, though. New and faster systems were being introduced weekly, and the storage capabilities of these computers increased dramatically. With the advent of optical storage devices that could store almost a billion bytes on one removable disk cartridge and still reside inside the PC, the reign of high-cost document imaging systems was coming to an end.

It became possible to purchase a document imaging system that would fit well within a budget and cost relatively little to maintain. Any organization could scan documents into the computer, store these images in folders and files, index and retrieve them in a matter of seconds. The time-consuming, and hated, manual process of searching the company archives for old files was exchanged for entering information on a computer screen and watching the results pop up. For any organization needing quick and painless access to their old records where the image can be defined as the application, this was and still is a very cost-effective solution.

15.2 THE IMAGE AS THE APPLICATION

For example, a law firm is preparing a case for its client. The client, a large chemical company, is the defendant in a lawsuit that claims it failed to follow the appropriate guidelines when handling hazardous chemicals. Since this type of lawsuit usually puts the defendant at risk for millions, even billions, of dollars, much effort and expense will be exhausted in order to produce, if not a victory, at least a reduction of damages. Recommendations for a document imaging system by the law firm will be taken seriously by the client even if the life expectancy of the system extends to only this one case.

In lawsuits of this type, the volume of documentation and paperwork is astounding. In one actual case, the defendant had to dust off files and documents from the early part of this century, and these were just some of the two million pieces of paper that conceivably could have been used by either party in the lawsuit. Obviously, this amount of paperwork is beyond the ability of even a team of lawyers and paralegals to deal with in a manual fashion. Even if all these documents were read by the legal team, they would find it impossible to precisely and fully cross-reference the information within these documents for the company's day in court.

In this situation, an automated document imaging filing and retrieval system makes a lot of practical and economic sense. It is practical, due to the volume of information, the need to cross-reference and index all of it, and the need to provide a fast retrieval method. It is economical, because in relation to the company's risk (potentially a billion dollars), spending half a million to two million dollars on an imaging system is minor. Even if this system is never used again, the cost can be justified. If the defense immediately fails to catch and rebut any significant statement made by the prosecution due to its inability to find contradictory information from literally roomfuls of legal documents, it could translate into many millions of dollars.

The above situation demonstrates the image as the application; that is, if it weren't for the need to automate the handling and referencing of the mountain of documentation, there would be no need for a computer system. The defendant's purchase of a computer system is not motivated by its desire for automated billing, word processing, or sending electronic mail to company employees. Its purpose is singular and will not be augmented, extended, or connected to other systems in this organization. As noted, it may never be used again.

15.3 THE IMAGE AS A COMPONENT OF THE APPLICATION

Imaging products that presume the image is the application generally do their job well. However, what if the image is not the application, but only a component of it? What if needs require the organization of all information related to a particular client? In one "folder" must be word processing documents, cost analysis from spreadsheets, market research from the database, and, last but not least, images of client correspondence: pictures, graphics, or any other documentation critical to this client.

What if you want to put together a subset of these components for a presentation without ever leaving the computer you are working on? What if all these components must be living documents; that is, when one component is altered, changes to the data will be reflected in the presentation finished last week? And what if various workers each have a role in producing or reviewing these components? Here, the software environment, not just the application software, as in the previous case, offers groups of people the ability to produce a presentation with the image as a single, albeit important, component of the final product.

For example, the purchasing arm of a large company requires the submittal of a number of signed documents by employees requesting a major purchase. This documentation must include financial justification (spreadsheets), usage or need justification (word processing, graphics, and/or spreadsheets), and technical details (drawings, schematics). In addition, the purchasing agents may need to route this documentation to various executives for review and signature. When all this is complete and the request is approved and purchased, tracking details, such as purchase orders, purchase invoices, shipping invoices, memos, warranties, and other documentation need to be retained for equipment servicing or warranty reasons.

If, in this example, an integrated program was used throughout the request and purchasing process to track and record all relevant documentation, company personnel would be able at any time in the future to collect complete and consistent information on any aspect of the purchasing process. This information may be a memo from the word processor or the shipping invoice from the image processing component; the specific type of document is unimportant. The fact that all components of the purchasing process coexist in one location and can be retrieved and analyzed in the future makes this invaluable to any organization, especially those with complex workflows.

The use of the image as only a component of the application is what integrated workgroup image-enabled productivity software (IWIPS) is all about. It is a software program or suite of programs that together allow people connected by an operational process to increase their productivity both during the process and after it when needing to research historical information.

The following sections detail how to decide if IWIPS is right for you and your business, the basic building blocks to an IWIPS system, and some add-on components to enhance and increase the efficiency of a standard system. Two products are presented as examples of the image as a component of the application to illustrate the strengths and weaknesses of various imaging systems. And finally, a number of key issues pertinent to the success of an IWIPS are discussed.

15.4   DESIGN CONSIDERATIONS FOR AN IWIPS

Before any consideration is given to which document imaging system is right for your organization, these questions must be answered: "What do I want to accomplish with this system?" and "How, within my budget confines, do I accomplish this?" The first is a complex question. Besides the obvious answer—to increase the efficiency and reliability of some manual or partially manual process—consideration must be given to what gains your organization will garner, what new functionality the system will provide, how it will affect employees, and what will be relinquished.

If you have simple goals, like organizing personal files, then the answers to these two questions will not be as rigorous for the person chartered with the responsibility of automating the organization's paper flow; saving money; and providing a safe, realistic, economical, and workable document retrieval and backup scheme.

Define Business Operation

The first step is to map out what groups in the organization are affected by the current process. Sit down with those responsible for both the data (i.e., nonimage) portion of the business and the documents; understand the current work process: how paper and data flow into the operation, how it is manipulated, how it flows out to other groups, and how it will be used historically. If your job is to automate an existing process, this workflow detailing may produce curious inconsistencies and questions as to why the process has taken on its current form. Many times you will discover that the evolution of this process has produced some very queer beasts which you somehow must unravel and understand.

If, due to your exceptional foresight with new technologies, you are proposing a beneficial new process, hopefully, you will have equal providence as to how it will affect both human and machine. This new method must be both workable for those using it, economically realistic for those paying for it, and technically feasible for those installing it on the computers you currently own. More times than not, your proposal will include additional hardware and software requirements on each user's computer, in addition to at least one central site hardware configuration. Be aware that the installation of a workgroup document image processing system may change the way people use their computers even during nondocument image tasks.

In either case, it is critical after this workflow analysis that serious thought be given to improving the process and not just replacing it. More times than not, simply replacing one system with another translates into doing the same job faster. Faster is nice, but a simple translation of a manual workflow to an automated workflow has the undesirable effect of moving warts and scars from one process to another. Just because it's being done now doesn't mean it makes sense in the future. You need to define system goals, understand the current process and all its inconsistencies, strip out as many inconsistencies as possible while retaining functionality, and finally design the system based on these facts. You are in the unique position of understanding both the current workflow and the potentials of a future automated operation. No one else has this knowledge: Use it wisely.

There are many different points to consider before investing in any document imaging system, and all of them are not detailed here; however, make sure you address at least these points listed below before investing your organization's money and operations in any product. First, understand the workflow of documents in your present operations:

- How do documents presently enter, reside, and exit your business process?
- Do these documents need to be saved? For how long?
- Who needs to access these documents? From where? When? How frequently?
- Do these documents need to be saved and grouped in a file with other types of documents?
- How much paper enters the process each day: 50, 500, 50,000 pages?
- Is the scanner you have budgeted for hardy enough for the type of documents you intend to enter into this system and the workflow you have planned for it?
- What are the bottlenecks and potential points of failure of the current system?

Second, after analyzing the workflow, determine what enhancements to the process you would like:

- Integrate these documents with a company-wide database?
- Extract the text from these documents (OCR)?
- Send and receive faxes directly into this system?
- Integrate this system with your company-wide e-mail system?
- What are the bottlenecks and potential points of failure of the new system and how can you design them out of the process?

Windows Workgroup Imaging System Architecture

Connection to a network of some kind is a given these days for people who work together. This network may be local or wide area, or it may mean communicating with fellow workers through a central hub as in mainframes and minicomputers. In either case, information is passed from one person to the next.

In the MS Windows and OS/2 environments, the choices for types of networks usually involves Novell NetWare, Banyan Vines, Microsoft LAN Manager, or NetBIOS. Any of these network choices allow for a fully functional document imaging system. Below, the most common requirements for Windows-based document imaging systems are detailed. Be aware though, that each imaging product has its own requirements, so before purchasing, it's a good idea to thoroughly check and make sure your organization's network infrastructure can support the system you have selected.

Client-Server Computing

Connecting to a company network today is not as simple as it used to be. Not so long ago a standard local area network consisted of workstations that were connected via cable to a central network server that handled file storage, communications, and printing. It was true to its name; it was local. Today, the guts of the network you connect to may very well exist in location far from where you are. Be it from a laptop computer over a standard phone line, a wide area connection over high-speed phone lines, or across the street over a dedicated fiber optic link, the local area network has outgrown its name.

From the point of view of the user, the imperceptible interaction of the document imaging system and the network, whether local or wide area, is critical to the success of the system as a whole. When the network speed is appropriate for the task, when the imaging software efficiently uses the network tool set, and when the design of the system as a whole is a result of a detailed understanding of the organization's goals and workflow needs, then, and only then, will the user feel that this is a tool that increases efficiencies and in the long run saves money. In other words, the network must not get in the way; it should be conspicuous by its absence.

The client-server model is used today both by workgroup document imaging products as well as by mainstream document imaging products, due to its inherent ability to separate processes best done on the server from those best done on the workstation. The server facilities provided by most imaging systems are: image server, fax server, OCR server, and, in some cases, a variation of a scanning server; these are in addition to the network operating system's server facilities. For example, the image server stores document images, receives requests for images, and responds to the requests by transmitting images to the requesting workstations. The workstations, on the other hand, run the programs that request, display, and print the image.

Server processes can be combined where it makes sense. For instance, the image server can be one and the same as the network file server (NFS). In such a case, the document image software manufacturer develops a special program that is placed on the NFS to manage the storage and retrieval of images and data files for the document image software. As of this writing, Novell and Kodak are jointly developing software that will enable the NetWare network operating system to efficiently manage image files, something it can't do very well today. It is hoped that the product that emerges from this effort will provide many benefits to the NetWare user, not the least of which is a more centralized storage and backup facility for all types of files. The various servers available for a document imaging environment are detailed in the next section.

The Image Server

The most common feature of a workgroup document imaging system is its image server. It is used to separate the image file storage from the NFS, thereby increasing the flexibility of image storage management and significantly reducing the file access delay nonimage users incur when both images and data files exist in the same storage environment. An image server manages the storage of all network-based image files and works in concert with the requesting agent, the workstation. It is also specially designed to handle extremely large storage capacities and the wide variety of storage media available today. Besides magnetic media, image servers can manage WORM optical drives (write-once read-many), RW optical drives (read/write), jukeboxes containing these media, and archive systems—most commonly tapes.

How is this done? The image server receives requests from the workstations and processes these requests by locating the desired documents and sending them to the requester. That sounds simple, and it is, except for the part about locating the documents. The main task of the image server is document management. At all times it must know the whereabouts of all documents put into its trust. In an environment where everything exists on a magnetic drive and doesn't move until it's deleted by the user, that's simple: Look up the name of the file in the internal file directory and get the file. However, when there are a number of drive types on a system (magnetic, WORM, RW optical, tape), and file locations are not stagnant (an unused file may be automatically moved to a slower media), the image server can't just pluck a file off its disk. It must know which media type it is on, how to access it, if that device is available, and where it is on that device. And it must have the ability to signal to both the requester and computer operator that a file was requested but its media is not on line. Luckily for the user, this is all handled by the software itself.

Although this method of image storage requires the purchase of a separate and dedicated computer, it is currently the best solution for image file management. As mentioned, work is being done on some network platforms that will allow the NFS to handle this task, thus eliminating the need for an additional computer, and thereby reducing the price of the complete imaging system.

The Fax Server

It is quite common today to send and receive documents via fax. However, if you have ever tried to scan a paper fax, you have noticed a degradation in image quality in the resulting image document. If you then tried to OCR this document, the result was no doubt less than pleasing. Enter the fax server, a computer that manages and routes inbound and outbound faxes. Inbound, it stores the fax as an image file so that the quality of the stored image is greatly increased over the method just mentioned. As for outbound faxes, any network user can fax data or stored images or can scan and send an image directly to the fax server, usually with increased resolution over standard fax machines.

Like the image server, the fax server may be a machine dedicated to its particular task, but most products do not require this. If the volume of faxes is not significant enough, the fax hardware and software may exist on a workstation, or it may share a server with another process (e.g., fax/OCR server). It is up to the system designer to determine if, in fact, the volume of faxes sent and received vs. the needs of the sister process warrants a dedicated machine.

The OCR Server

The process that converts images into text, known as optical character recognition, is important only in those document imaging systems that need to manipulate or search through the text of documents. Similar to the other server tasks mentioned, the OCR server acts as a common point of processing for all users who need its services. If your needs are simply to manage images, this option can be eliminated.

The OCR server can be set up through a hardware and software configuration or simply through software. With the advent of faster computers and cheaper memory, the trend today is toward software processing. This has an added benefit in multitasking environments like IBM OS/2 and Microsoft Windows, since multiple OCR tasks can be spawned off either from a single request or from multiple OCR requests.

In the single request scenario, the controlling OCR software analyzes an image of text and separates it into usable pieces. Each piece is sent to the OCR engine for processing; thus, each section becomes an OCR subtask. When all subtasks are completed, the controlling process can stitch together all the pieces into one text file. This method is extremely efficient in that it uses the operating system to speed the conversion from image to text. Similarly, with multiple requests, the controlling OCR procedure can process a number of requests at once without significant delays due to backlog.

Although OCR has come a long way since its introduction, it is still the only process discussed here that cannot always be counted on. In concept, its potential is great: automatic conversion of images into computer-processable text; in reality, it is highly dependent on the quality of the image it is given. Good image quality yields high translation accuracy. Low image quality yields poor translation accuracy, which therefore results in an inability to be considered seriously for anything but ad hoc needs. In the case of fax documents, the problem is compounded by the low resolution of the fax scanning process. In time, as machines get smarter and faster, and faxes get clearer, this will be less of a problem, and the OCR process can be counted on to a greater degree.

The Scanning Station

In order to enter your documents into an imaging system, you probably will have to scan them in, and, given the proper hardware, this can be done at any workstation. However, a few questions should be asked before you bankrupt your organization and start buying scanners for all network users: What type of documents will they be scanning? Will you need special paper handling for these documents? Will you need bulk scanning? How many people will be scanning documents? Will you need to index a folder of documents at scanning time or can it be done at a later time? There are more questions that are beyond the scope of this chapter, but the point to take home is that a good-quality scanner still accounts for a significant portion of the total imaging system cost, so it is critical to fully understand the "who" and "how" of the scanning process as it relates to your organization.

Unlike the image, fax, and OCR servers, most document image management systems (DIMS) recommend placing scanners on the workstations of those people doing the bulk of the scanning. The server concept does not exist here since a scanner is a device requiring, at minimum, some human interaction on each usage.

There does exist one product, detailed below, that comes closer than anything else to the concept of a scanning server. It allows the system administrator to configure the scanner on a dedicated computer and, when given the name of the person whose documents are to be scanned, scans the images and routes them to that person's desktop. This doesn't remove the manual step of scanning, but it comes closer than anything else to providing an economical scanner for workgroups.

Scanner Placement Considerations

In an operation with a significant amount of scanning, the placement of the main scanning station relative to the storage device is important. For example, suppose a workgroup currently has its desktop computers connected to an LAN. Performance is not a big issue since small data files are the most common form of network traffic. Since they need to keep track of client correspondence, a simple workgroup DIMS is recommended and installed onto the existing LAN, complete with an image server, a workstation scanner, and software. The DIMS runs through the pilot with flying colors and the company decides to go "live" with this system. "Live" meaning that instead of scanning 20 documents a day, as they did in the pilot, 500 documents are now scanned. All of a sudden, network performance is down to a crawl. Why? Well, one reason could be that the design of this system did not take into account the effect that large image files transmitted from the scanner through the network to the image server would have on network performance. Whereas before, small data files were the main network traffic, now large beefy image files are moving through the wire using up significant network bandwidth.

There are a few simple solutions to this problem that can be defined as inexpensive and efficient. The inexpensive solution would require the scanner to be physically connected to the image server; that is, instead of the image server receiving images through the LAN, it would get them directly from the scanner. This would decrease network traffic on scanned images to zero and also speed up the storage of images on the server.

This poses other problems, though. Merging these two components would mean that either Mohammed would have to come to the mountain, or the mountain would have to go to Mohammed. Having the mountain move is fine for Old Mo', but the person responsible for the security of the images might not like the image server out in the open. On the other hand, Old Mo' might not like being dislocated from his desk and moved to the image server's secure location. Although this is a management issue, its significance to the successful system deployment should not be taken lightly.

The efficient solution would not require any movement of people or resources, but would require that a second network "ring" connected to the main "ring" be installed. The image server, the scanning workstation, and a connection to the main network ring would be the sole components on this new "mini-LAN." All users still could access images, with the benefit that the network resources on the main ring would not be used during the transmission's intensive scanning process. Users would not even know that scanning and storage were occurring. This method does, however, have its costs in hardware, network software, and rewiring the scanning station.

Workstation Client

This is where the action is. The workstation in a client-server environment initiates almost all image storage and retrieval functions. It is the requester of image documents for display, printing, and faxing, as well as the main conduit of images that have been scanned or faxed into the system. The workstation must present a clear, easy-to-use, and consistent interface to all applications needed by the user. Therefore, for workgroup-type applications that correspond to this discussion, it is quite common for developers to use an operating environment like the Macintosh, Windows for PCs, or X-Windows for UNIX.

By definition, this discussion requires that all components of workgroup software be "integrated." Applications written specifically for each of these user-integrated interfaces must look and operate according to certain guidelines which, when held to, provide to the user both a smooth transition from one application to the next, as well as behind-the-scenes communication among applications and data. In the case of Microsoft Windows, one might make the assumption that it is possible to use software developed for Windows in tandem with software developed for DOS. But this cannot be called fully integrated due to the lack of both a consistent user interface and a background mechanism that all applications adhere to.

Features for Integrated Workgroup Software

Besides the consistent look of the software, what other features are important when deciding on the suite of integrated workgroup software?

Mobility of Images and Data

The operating environment must allow the free exchange of any type of data between different applications. For example, data and images residing in a customer file created by "Bob" can be included in a report or presentation created by "Betty." Bob and Betty may be using completely different software, but each can use the other's data to complete his or her own task.

Ability to Display and Operate Multiple Applications Concurrently

Since this discussion deals with software that increases a workgroup's productivity, these workgroups must use a variety of software products to complete their tasks. Many times, the user must work on a database in conjunction with image display software. It is imperative that the screen "real estate," that is, the usable area of the screen, be maximized. If not, users will be flipping between overlapping windows or resizing less frequently used windows in order to clearly view what they are working on. This has the undesirable effect of actually decreasing productivity due to the constant housekeeping on the windowed desktop.

In the PC world, maximizing display real estate means enhancing two components: the video display card and the display monitor. The standard PC comes with a VGA display card and a 14" monitor sufficient for the DOS or basic Windows applications. If, however, you want to simultaneously operate using multiple windows, then increasing both the resolution of the display card and the size of the monitor allows you to concurrently view multiple applications, each in full-screen mode. Inefficiently flipping between applications has been eliminated.

Ability to Perform DDE

Any application used in this environment should be able to perform an operation called DDE, or dynamic data exchange. This operation allows links to be established between data files of different origin but common relation, thereby allowing multiple data files to automatically reflect a single common change.

An example of this is the linking of the data from a spreadsheet with the text of a word processor. After the initial number crunching is done in the spreadsheet, the remainder of the work most likely will be done in the word processor. If, however, changes need to be made to the numbers, it would be very convenient if (instead of having to exit the word processor, enter the spreadsheet, make the changes, save the changes, exit the spreadsheet, enter the word processor, and finally copy the changes back into the text) you could modify the numbers directly in the word processor, which would automatically update the spreadsheet with the changes.

Object Linking and Embedding (OLE)

As recent as three years ago, a computer-based customer file could be defined as any text-based information that could be entered into the company's database. This was fine as long as the work did not involve receiving paper-based documents, producing any spreadsheets, or creating any graphics.

Today, however, what makes up a customer file includes such things as graphics, images, and spreadsheet data, in addition to the standard text-based information. Each of these data elements calls a different place home, but they all meet in a primary location when the user wants them to. This primary location, or data hub, can be defined as an application with the ability to reference and invoke any other application so that when a secondary application appears, it shows a screen displaying the information that is directly relevant to the current task.

Let's say you work in the human resources department of a large company and maintain a database of all people who have sent you résumés. Currently, you receive a résumé and enter some of its information into your database and then put the résumé into a folder. Let's also assume that all hiring managers can access your database to view the new prospects. When a particular prospect looks good for the job, the hiring manager calls you to get the résumé. You then go to your file, and, assuming you refiled it correctly after the last request, pull it out, photocopy it, and send it off to the requester. If you put it through interoffice mail, the hiring manager will finally see it half a day to a day later.

Let's say, instead, you had a database with integrated image capabilities that all hiring managers could view. Now, when you receive a résumé, you enter a few pieces of information and then scan the résumé into the database so that it becomes just another piece of information in this applicant's file. When a hiring manager selects a prospect, he or she can view or print the résumé immediately. You are free from the paper-pushing task detailed above and no longer need to think of yourself as a clerk. This example can be applied to almost any office function where a bottleneck is created when those who need information must request it from those who have it.

Printing Document Images

Now that a decent laser printer is affordable for most workgroups, it would seem that printing documents from a document imaging system would be fast and simple. Well simple it is, but fast . . . sorry, that's not the case. That peppy laser printer that a workgroup uses to print text-based documents will become a silent monster when asked to print images. Instead of measuring performance in pages per minute, sit back, relax, and measure minutes per page. The standard office laser printer was designed to efficiently print text, not pictures or images. This is not to say it can't do it; it can, with enough memory and patience.

For those people who always are pulling that partially printed page from the laser printer, there are products on the market that recognize this as a problem and do in fact speed up the printing process. These products require you to purchase an expansion card for your printer (only a few of the most popular printer models are supported), which essentially replaces the printer's parallel connector in the DOS and OS/2 environments. Print data is sent to the card, which formats the data, be it images or text, and directs the printer to print it, bypassing most of the printer's built-in processing. Although this may cause some irregularities with normal text printing, it is a definite improvement over the printer's internal image processing for those workgroups that need it. Images now can be printed at speeds close to the printer's maximum throughput.

Some software products require full printing engines to facilitate fast laser printing of images. Although the software manufacturer must develop its product around these components, they provide printing speeds up to the printer's advertised specifications as well as an integrated printing solution. The standard configuration includes expansion cards in both the printer and the computer to which the printer is connected, bypassing the parallel ports on both machines. One configuration even goes so far as to include the scanner in this loop, which allows immediate printing of scanned documents, making it a kind of high-tech copier. A downside to this type of software-printer integration is the imaging system's inability to use the shared print queues provided by the network software, thus delivering the above benefits only to the person whose workstation is connected to the printer.

Selection Criteria for Integrated Workgroup Software

Many software manufacturers will soon be jumping aboard the integrated workgroup software bandwagon. Some might even claim to support document imaging. To be sure that their claims are accurate, ask the following questions:

1. Can you envision their product as the hub application used by all your network users?

2. Can you link this product with the specific applications you need?

3. What is the software developer's idea of integrated workgroup software? Is it fully developed and simple to use out of the box, or must it be customized through supplied or third-party development tools?

4. Other than scanners, does this product require the purchase of expensive workstation hardware? Considering the number of users on your network, is this figure within your budget?

5. Does the product support the use of a common image file by multiple users?

6. Does the product include image management and archiving features?

7. Is integrated workflow document routing important to you?

These are not all the questions you need to ask, but this list can be a general starting point for your investigation.

15.5 SOME FINAL POINTS TO CONSIDER

The implementation of any successful workgroup process requires an understanding of the way it's done now. How does information flow through the workgroup? How and where is the information changed or manipulated? What positive aspects of the current workflow will you retain, and what negative aspects will you remove, replace, or redesign? Where are the cracks and bottlenecks in the process into which both information and money vanish? What is missing or what just doesn't work in the current process from the point of view of both management as well as workers? Should the image lead the integration process, or is the image just another, albeit more complex, piece of data?

Next, it's important to understand the way it can be done with an IWIPS. How can your organization efficiently and effectively use all the new tools available in a Windows environment with existing image-enabled workgroup systems? Where can manual, oftentimes clerical steps be eliminated and replaced with a system's innate ability to sort, process, and notify you of changing information? How can the cracks you identified be removed, and how can you guard against others from forming? How quickly can a working system be implemented? Can you use your new workgroup tool out of the box, or will you need to spend time tailoring it to your needs? And do you or your client have the time?

It is critical that management and the eventual users understand and buy into the workgroup concept. They must understand that a properly designed IWIPS is a productivity enhancing process and not just a replacement for the file cabinet. The system should not be designed just to mimic an old process but to create a new, more efficient and simpler one. Its function and role within the workgroup should be well-defined and explained, with special emphasis placed on the added value of the image store. Too many times, those using a system with image capabilities perceive it as fun and alluring ("Wow, pictures on my screen!"), only to wake up to the realization that it was a very expensive one-night stand. The perception of this system, both within the workgroup and without, needs to be managed closely.

In many cases, the selection of an integrated workgroup software may well be dependent upon a strategic design decision as to the long term need for maintainability of the imaging application. For instance, the choice may be between using an inherently tightly integrated environment and an integratable architecture. In the first case, the development path may be easier because of the uniformity of interface, but its flexibility may be constrained by the capabilities of the underlying engine. A good example of this approach is Lotus Notes:Document Imaging, which requires a Lotus Notes server, but has built-in image embedding features, which make an image part of an existing Notes document. In the second case, the developer may want to use a wider range of options, but will need to asses the cost of integration. An example of a product that supports such an approach is Keyfile, which, as a Windows-based package, offers the flexibility associated with that environment. In that approach, the development of image embedding features requires additional effort. Whether that feature is valuable to an imaging application depends upon a variety of factors, including the number of times an image must be retrieved vs. the number of times textual information is sufficient.

One of the greatest benefits of integrated workgroup image-enabled products is not so much what they provide in their box, but the potential they offer through their use of the Windows and OS/2 environments. With the current ability of many new or updated programs written for these environments to share data with other similarly configured programs, or to be the launching pad for an organization's workflow, the line between single function programs and workgroup programs is becoming less clear. Today, the mark of a full-function product is not how much it can do, but how well it can integrate with other products. In the near future you will not purchase a program hoping it works well with other programs, but assuming it will.

16

Combining Microforms and Optical Disks

Marc R. D'Alleyrand, Ph.D.

16.1 INTRODUCTION

Regardless of the nature and architecture of the information network, there are instances when, for operational, legal, or other reasons, electronic imaging comes in competition with conventional and computer output microform-based systems.

Because of the delays associated with microform production, most microform usage is found in either look-up or archival applications. In contrast, optical disk systems provide immediacy of access, making it possible to extend the use of imaging to transaction and other on-line applications.

There are two different options for capturing and retrieving documents when microforms are involved, and each has its advantages over the other. Everything else being equal, when requirements are for immediacy and speedy communication, there is a strong argument in favor of optical disk installations; when archiving is a major consideration, a good case can be made for the use of microforms.

In many cases, however, an analysis of information retrieval requirements throughout the life cycle of a document often shows that both are desirable to support the business objectives of an organization. For instance:

- In financial applications, optical disks allow the design of integrated information systems, where data extracted from digitized paper records are processed in a cost-effective manner. The dissemination of reports generated as a result of this processing may be more cost-effective on microform than if retrieved through network imaging stations.

- In legal areas, optical disks allow efficient information retrieval. However, the cost of storing inactive files may favor the use of microforms for long-term retention.

- In sales and marketing activities, optical disk systems can provide quick access to information in support of the organization. But, because the need for instant retrieval begins to fade, microforms provide an inexpensive storage medium for archival data.

Clearly, optical disks and microforms can often be seen either as complementary or competitive rather than exclusive media (see Figure 16.1), and many organizations actually use both. There are essentially three ways to generate and use images from documents. Figure 16.2 shows that documents, once captured, can either be printed on paper, displayed on a computer screen, or printed on film. Operationally, these different methods are not equivalent.

The difference in information usage reflects different organizational responsibilities; therefore, it is not unusual that documents are captured independently on both optical disks and microform. This results in a substantial duplication of effort in preparation, indexing, and quality control. A better solution is to replace this dual image capture procedure by a process that combines recording in one medium, either on film or on optical disk, followed by an automatic conversion to disk or to microform. An alternative method, concurrent image capture, uses specialized equipment that contains both a scanner and a microfilm camera. Whatever the approach, the result is the creation of interdependent microform/digital image sets (MDIS). This chapter compares these three methods from both an operational and financial perspective.

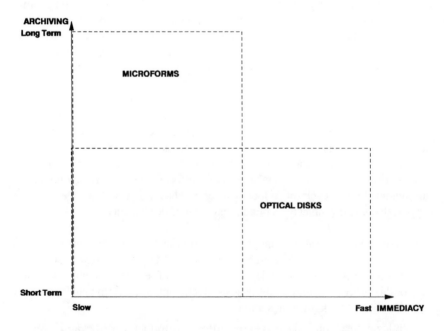

Figure 16.1   Comparison between application areas for optical disk and microforms

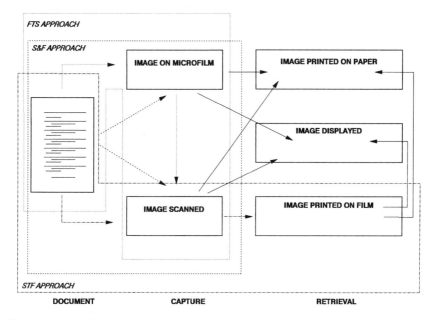

Figure 16.2   Paths for document retrieval

16.2 GENERATING MDIS

Three MDI generation methods have developed to meet diverging business requirements. Organizations that have an initial inventory of microforms and want to take
advantage of the operational benefits of digitized images may choose to use a
"film-then-scan" (FTS) approach. Operations that require a chronological audit
trail and will generate simultaneous recordings on disk and microforms probably
will use a "scan-and-film" (S&F) technique. Finally, organizations that need
accurate backup files on microforms may want to use a "scan-then-film" (STF)
methodology (see Figure 16.3).

Traditional Method: Film-Then-Scan

The film-then-scan method is often found in organizations that have geographical
or institutional obstacles that separate direct interaction between microfilming and
optical disk areas. This method is also used in situations where there is a substantial
inventory of filed material that needs to be converted to a digital format. As such,
its implementation does not require changes in microfilm or scanning procedures,
because these two processes can proceed independently. Manufacturers of film
scanners for such a method include Meckel and Sunrise for roll film and fiche and
TDC for fiche formats.

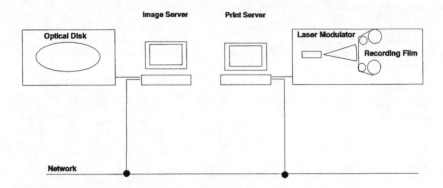

Figure 16.3   Principle of a film recorder

Approach

In the film-then-scan approach, microforms that have been generated elsewhere are processed by a microform scanner (see Figure 16.4). Standard workflow can be described as follows: Documents are recorded on a conventional rotary or planetary camera. The resulting film is processed and inspected, and any filming errors are corrected in retakes. Once the film has been accepted, it is sometimes duplicated for safety and then sent for scanning. The scanned images finally are submitted to quality control and indexing procedures to ensure retrievability of the individual images.

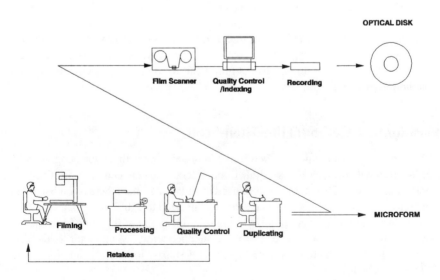

Figure 16.4   Principle of film-then-scan approach

Advantages

Advantages of the film-then-scan method are: It does not disrupt existing operations, and it provides an efficient method to digitize manual files. Assuming that the contents of the film meet accepted quality standards, the conversion of the files to a digitized format can be done in an unattended mode, which saves on operator's expense. In addition, if the microforms are part of a computer-aided retrieval (CAR) system, the conversion may be facilitated by importing the index already used for the CAR system into the digitized environment. Even if the film quality is below standard, most film scanners can be equipped with an image enhancer so that marginal images, such as records of multipart forms, can be brought back to a level where they can be used.

Drawbacks

The major drawback of the film-then-scan method is the same as that associated with microfilming in general—namely, the inability to detect filming errors as they occur. These errors include missed pages or overlapping images; poor document registration; and poor-quality originals, such as receipts printed with dried-out ribbons and multipart forms. Such errors are often objectionable, and it may be necessary to refilm the rejected material at significant additional expense. The total unit cost of such a retake, including searching for the originals and inserting the corrected images in the filmed record, either by splicing or through indexing, may be an order of magnitude larger than the cost of image capture alone. In addition, indexing is often a dual operation, as microform indices seldom meet the precision required for the retrieval of images on optical disks, thus requiring a second indexing activity at time of scanning.

Concurrent Method: Scan-and-Film

While film-then-scan methods can be implemented in separate sites, scan-and-film techniques require the use of dual-purpose equipment, containing a scanner and a microfilming camera. These devices, most of which are of recent design, are manufactured by a variety of vendors, including Kodak, Bell & Howell, and Photomatrix for roll film, and TDC and Staude for microfiche.

Approach

In the scan-and-film method, the image of a document is captured on film and scanned at the same time. Figure 16.5 outlines two different uses for this approach. Because there is no control on the quality of the microform that is produced during scanning, there may be rare conditions where the microform copy must be of acceptable quality, requiring a separate optional quality control and retake. Depending on the design of the document system, quality control of the recording may be done on the fly by looking at a monitor attached to the scanner or at a later time.

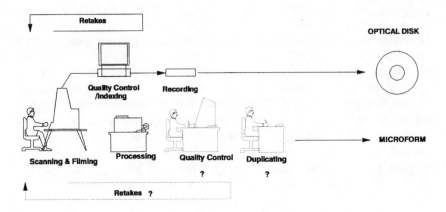

Figure 16.5   Diagram of concurrent scanning and filming approach

Because of the linkage between the scanner and the microfilm camera, any errors requiring rescanning result in a duplicate image on film.

Advantages

The major advantage of this technique is that it is possible to identify document capture errors, such as skew and other misfeeds, as they occur. This allows immediate correction of the scanned image, and, depending on the economics of the correction process, may reduce the volume of refilming that would be required under the film-then-scan approach. Furthermore, it is possible under certain circumstances to calibrate the scanner so that it emulates the microfilm camera within a given range of exposure. Finally, because filming is a sequential operation, the resulting microform can be used as an audit trail.

Drawbacks

Because each scanned image, acceptable or not, generates a microfilm record on a scan-and-film device, it is not possible to prevent unacceptable images from being recorded on film. The significance of this depends on the purpose for the film copy. For instance, when the film is created only for audit trail purposes, duplicate frames recorded as the result of retakes are of little consequence. However, if the film is to be used as the official copy of record, there may be a need to cross-reference images on disk with their microfilm duplicate frames. Under these conditions, it may be necessary to develop and reconcile two different indices. Last but not least, scan-and-film devices are in the high end of scanning equipment prices. Therefore, the use of multiple scan-and-film devices may prove to be more expensive than other imaging equipment.

Advanced Method: Scan-Then-Film

Scan-then-film (STF) methods convert digitized images to film without the drawbacks associated with conventional microfilming. They use laser-driven devices called microform printers or film recorders. These devices are produced by manufacturers specializing in computer output equipment, such as iBase and Anacomp for black-and-white imaging. For color output, it is possible to use more expensive equipment by Dicomed and III, which use a cathode ray tube (CRT) instead of a laser source, at a significant reduction in recording speed.

Approach

Scan-then-film methods, depicted in Figure 16.6, capture digitized images of documents on an appropriate medium, such as optical disk or DAT, and use that medium as input to a printer specifically designed to record digital signals onto film.

At the present time, there are three types of recorders on the market, using lasers, CRTs, and electron beam recording (EBR). Most commercial recorders for document systems are laser-based machines. CRT and EBR systems, which are much more expensive to acquire and run, are used for specialized applications, such as high-end monochrome or color publishing. Because current laser-based installations operate in a binary mode, they are not well adapted to the reproduction of continuous tone materials. CRT- and EBR-based machines may be appropriate for that purpose, but their speed may be too slow for a given application, and their operating costs are substantial.

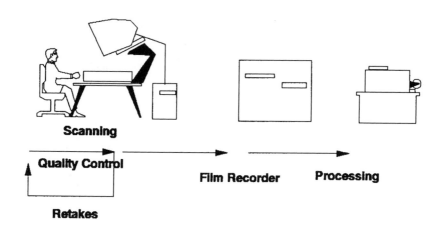

Figure 16.6   Diagram of a scan-then-film operation

Advantages

The advantages of scan-then-film methods are derived from the superior quality of digitized images, which are typically electronically enhanced by the document scanner before being recorded on the digital medium. In addition, because the disk contains only valid images, the copy to film will be comprised only of relevant frames. This reduces the need for film quality control mentioned for the scan-and-film method. Furthermore, because the digitized images are fully indexed, there is no additional work required to generate an index to scan-then-film films. Finally, because the transfer is done under computer control, it is possible to merge data from different sources on the same film, including sequential numbers, electronic logos, title frames, and other machine-readable data. This provides the flexibility necessary for the production of composite documents for various applications such as desktop and workgroup publishing and reports on microform for distribution purposes.

Drawbacks

Film recorder resolution is determined by the number of addressable spots, thus limiting the maximum resolution for a given image size. At the present time, most film recorders use bimodal monochrome lasers, which, because they are either on or off, require special dithering drivers to emulate the continuous tone capabilities of conventional microfilm. Speed is also an issue when using CRT-based devices.

16.3 COMPARISON BETWEEN THE THREE METHODS

Depending on the situation, there may be overriding organizational considerations that dictate one or the other method. For instance, institutions such as libraries, which already have extensive microform collections that they make available to the public, would use the film-then-scan technique; an operation with a high volume of transactions would benefit from a scan-and-film approach; and a micropublishing house might need a scan-then-film installation. However, everything else being equal, the three methods present different technical attributes. One of the major elements of comparison between the three methods is in the area of image sharpness as it is presented to the user.

The industry uses different measures to quantify image sharpness. This reflects the fact that while maximum original size and optical quality of the image capture device are determined by the image capture system, the size of the displayed or printed document depends on the display or printing device. Therefore, an objective comparison between the three methods requires a precise qualification of the output image. This issue is discussed below in more detail.

Quality

Due to the difference in recording processes, the quality of digitized and non-digitized images varies with the image capture technique. For instance, film-then-scan methods usually provide lower-quality digital images than scan-then-film because the digital images are generated from film (i.e., is an additional generation) rather than from the originals. At the same time, the quality of images generated through scan-and-film may not be as good as either, because the microfilm camera in a scan-and-film device is usually of a rotary type, which yields a lower resolution.

The comparison criteria for the three methods focus on the quality of both the digitized image and the microform produced. This includes image sharpness, contrast, and integrity of the imaging record.

Image Sharpness and Resolution

The method for measuring image sharpness depends on the medium and recording process. For microforms recorded with a conventional camera, image sharpness is usually expressed in terms of line pairs per millimeter (lp/mm) and refers to the number of standard black-and-white lines that can be comfortably distinguished with an appropriate microscope. For scanned images, it is expressed in terms of dots per inch (dpi) and describes the number of picture elements per unit length that can be differentiated on the original or the number of separately addressable picture elements that can be printed or displayed per unit length. These two methods of measure are diagrammed in Figure 16.7.

A good resolution value for office documents on microforms is 140 lp/mm for images captured at a linear reduction ratio of 24 (noted 24X). This corresponds numerically to an approximate scanning density of 300 dpi for an 8.5" × 11"

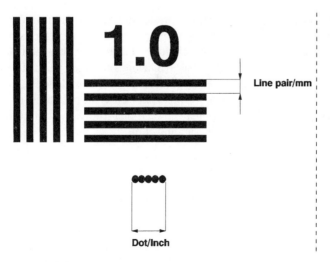

Figure 16.7   Defining image sharpness

document. However, differences in image characteristics require a scanning density of 400 dpi to match the resolution of a 140 lp/mm.

With film-then-scan and scan-and-film techniques, sharpness is determined by the quality of the microfilming camera. Two types of cameras are used most often to generate the film. Rotary cameras, generally less expensive to operate, also inherently have a lower resolution. Planetary cameras yield film at a higher-resolution recording, but at a higher cost than rotary filming. A third type of camera, called step-and-repeat, uses planetary film transports.

For applications that require image processing, such as OCR, only film generated on planetary cameras should be considered, and its resolution should be at least 140 lp/mm at 24X. However, one should be aware of the economics of OCR techniques; correcting recognition errors may be more expensive than direct key entry, and this may eliminate the film medium altogether. Even if the type of document is such that film processing can be cost-effective, scan-and-film solutions may not be acceptable, due to the fact that currently, scan-and-film devices on the market use rotary cameras, yielding film of lower resolution than if generated by a planetary camera or with a high-resolution film recorder.

For microforms generated by the scan-then-film method, resolution also depends on the recording process. CRT-based recorders are limited by the imaging screen definition. Resolution of laser recorders is limited by the size of the recording spot. A quick calculation shows that a recording at a reduction ratio of 24X, yielding an image sharpness equivalent to a 300 dpi scanning density, requires a spot of 3.5 micron, which is well within the capabilities of commercially available laser recordings. The same image recorded at a 96X reduction would require submicron spot size.

Contrast

The ability to record different shades, one of the strong advantages of microforms, is not a primary consideration for most present digital applications. Without special treatment, grayscale reproduction is potentially better on microforms generated by film-then-scan and scan-and-film techniques than by scan-then-film methods. For scan-then-film applications, CRT-based machines are better adapted because electronic imaging is essentially a binary recording. The use of dithering techniques to simulate shades of gray on a laser recorder, as well as the possibility of modulating a laser beam, should give laser-generated scan-then-film film similar tone rendition capabilities as film-then-scan or scan-and-film.

Recording Integrity

By necessity, correction of conventional microfilming errors requires refilming of correction frames and their insertion (splicing) in the appropriate place on the microform record. Error correction on microfiche requires the refilming of entire cards. The resulting loss of physical integrity of the film has significant importance when film is used for archival purposes, because the strength of most splices decays over time, yielding disconnected strips of film. The presence of splices may also raise issues of authenticity of the corrected frames and weakens the argument for using microforms as archival evidence. Recording integrity can be preserved in the scan-and-film technique if the film is used only as an audit trail, and not as an active retrieval tool, thus eliminating the need for splices.

In contrast, scan-then-film methods provide the ability to generate splice-free microfilm, because film recording is performed only after the image capture process has been completed and verified.

Operational Considerations

In many applications requiring the production of microforms, quality criteria are overshadowed by operational issues related to workflow and efficiency. The following discusses some of the major factors that influence the selection of one method over the others.

Indexing

Retrieval of digitized documents requires a precise directory of the recorded electronic document; therefore, indexing designed for microform applications is often not detailed enough for digitized images. Consequently, if documents have to be stored both on film and digital media, indexing first for the digital media and then extracting the data required for the microform application will eliminate the need for two different indexing activities.

For that reason, scan-then-film methods have a cost advantage over the other techniques. The automatic extraction of microform index data from the digital image base can be performed automatically, so the creation of that index is practically "free," requiring only that the extraction process replace the address of digital images with the location of the corresponding microform. This replacement is, by nature, automatic with the scan-then-film method. This is not the case in a scan-and-film system, because occasional insertion of correction frames in microform distorts the one-on-one relationship between the digitized image and film. This distortion must be manually identified and corrected in the index, causing additional costs to ensure accurate retrieval.

A second cost benefit of the scan-then-film and of the electronic portion of the scan-and-film technique is that it allows "heads-up" indexing, where the process is done from the digital image as it is displayed on a computer screen. This process has been reported to be 30 percent faster than the more traditional "heads-down" indexing from original paper documents. In the case of a film-then-scan approach, this benefit cannot, obviously, offset the cost of initial microform indexing.

Quality Control

Quality control is probably the second largest expense in microfilm production. As such, the scan-then-film method is the most effective, as it ensures that the recorded image is of an acceptable quality before it is committed to film. The immediacy of the image display facilitates a concurrent quality control, which, in the case of film-then-scan methods, is not possible.

Such concurrent quality control is possible to some extent with scan-and-film systems, and some errors can be caught immediately. However, practice shows that some errors will be caught only during indexing, which usually does not occur during the scanning process. Such errors require the creation of new frames that will be physically located on a different piece of film.

Titling

Microform standards require that they be identified by eye-readable title frames. In the film-then-scan approach, these are created by printing large-size targets, which are interfiled manually with the documents being filmed. In the scan-and-film and scan-then-film methods, these targets can be generated directly on the computer that is driving the scanning device, thereby reducing the production cost of the digitized record. However, unless the scan-and-film device has electronic titling capability, these targets still need to be inserted in the workflow.

Format

Microforms are used in different formats, including standard roll film, microfiche, and aperture cards. Depending on the application, one format will be preferred to another. For instance, office applications use mostly 16mm roll film, micropublishing mostly microfiche, and engineering drawings either aperture cards, microfiche, or 35mm roll microfilm.

In the film-then-scan approach, the creation of the microform requires a different type of camera, and the resulting microform can usually be fed to the same microform scanner by simple mechanical change of film transport. In the scan-and-film case, recording devices are, by construction, single-format machines, for either roll film, microfiche, or aperture cards.

In contrast, film recorders used for scan-then-film methods are multiformat, allowing the generation of film, microfiche, and aperture cards by simple substitution of film transport.

Management

The management of a document capture process requires keeping track of the status of the various processes involved, from document preparation to duplication and distribution. While the film-then-scan method can be automated as well as the other two, the scan-then-film method is the most effective of all, because the film is created only when the document capture cycle, including indexing and quality control, has been completed, thus simplifying management of the overall workflow.

In addition, because all data in a scan-then-film installation are kept in a digital form until final output, they can be routed electronically under workflow control. This makes it possible to reach higher throughput than with the two other methods, corresponding to lower personnel costs for delivered images (i.e., initial capture and retake).

Finally, from a production backup standpoint, it is much easier to back up a film-then-scan or scan-then-film operation than a scan-and-film installation. In the first two cases, failure affecting document capture can be backed up at a relatively low cost by standby units, and failures of microform scanners or film recorders can usually be repaired before backlog from document capture becomes objectionable. In the scan-and-film method, deficiency in either type of recording results in the disruption of the total workflow, unless expensive standby equipment is available.

16.4 COST COMPARISON BETWEEN THE VARIOUS METHODS

Equipment

From an equipment standpoint, both film-then-scan and scan-then-film techniques can operate in a cluster mode, using groups of input devices (microform cameras and scanners) to feed their output into one conversion device (microform scanner or film recorder). These techniques can therefore be adapted to large production installations with centralized or decentralized scanning. In contrast, scan-and-film methods that use camera-scanning assemblies operate best in a centralized scanning environment.

Consequently, the share of the conversion device (microform scanner or film recorder) in the overall cost for scan-then-film and film-then-scan techniques will likely be lower than for scan-and-film methods as soon as production levels require more than one scanning workstation.

Personnel Costs

From a staffing standpoint, all three methods require document preparation, the cost of which is approximately the same for all. Indexing is more expensive for film-then-scan methods than for the other two, due to the need for a dual index for both the film and later for the digitized image.

Cost comparison between the three methods involves quantification of the different operations in the entire workflow, from document preparation to final delivery of film, including chemical processing, quality control, and equipment depreciation. This quantification is strongly application-dependent. While its precise determination may require a thorough cost analysis by a consultant familiar with both microfilm and electronic imaging workflows, it can be shown that in most instances, there is a level of production above which lower personnel costs resulting from a higher throughput of scan-then-film equipment more than offsets the higher equipment costs, thus making that method the most cost-effective of the three. This is demonstrated in Figure 16.8 where, using the production figures corresponding to labor-intensive document capture and conservative microfilm

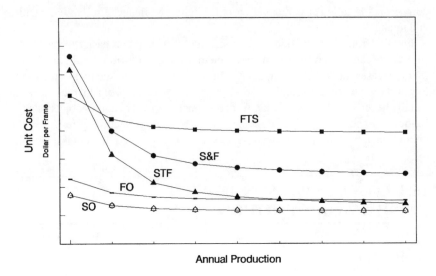

Figure 16.8   Cost comparison between microform and digitized production methods

equipment costs shown in Figure 16.9, the cost per frame for scan-then-film, initially higher than all other techniques except for the scan-and-film, eventually drops below the cost of conventional microfilming (FO) due to the higher staff productivity. To provide a balanced comparison, Figure 16.8 also provides a comparison with scan-and-film, film-then-scan, and scan only (SO).

16.5 OTHER CONSIDERATIONS

Regardless of cost advantage, the identification of the best method depends on application requirements, which will need to be weighed. A method for selecting the best technique may be to weigh the various characteristics for a particular operation, using a ranking similar to the one provided in Table 16.1.

Here again, because the choice of selection criteria and their relative weight must reflect business priorities, it may be necessary to secure the help of an experienced consultant. Some of the most common selection criteria are given in the next section.

Equipment Sharing

The model used in Figure 16.9 assumes a one-on-one relationship between film and scanners, which may overestimate the equipment costs of film-then-scan and scan-then-film methods for higher production volumes. Often, an issue will be raised as to the value of shared equipment.

WORKFLOW ASSUMPTIONS		
Preparation		
Unstapling	150	Documents/hr
Marking	100	Documents/hr
Batching	100	Documents/hr
Indexing	150	Documents/hr
Preparation Duplicates	25,000	Images/hr
Filming	500	Pages/hr
Scanning	2,000	Images/hr
Processing	10,000	Images/hr
Duplicating	25,000	Images/hr
Quality Control Film	1,500	Images/hr
Quality Control Duplicate	30,000	Images/hr
Quality Control Scan/Indexing	100	Documents/hr
Retake Film	100	Documents/hr
Recording	2,500	Images/hr
Packaging/Shipping	25,000	Images/hr
Hourly Rate (with fringes)	$18.00	
Document Assumptions	5	Pages/document
	5%	Error rate
Equipment Costs	Capital Cost ($)	
Microfilm Camera	10,000	
Film Processor	10,000	
Camera/Scanner	100,000	
Scanner	15,000	
Film Recorder	1,250,000	

Figure 16.9   Hypothetical production assumption for cost comparison

Only scan-then-film techniques can offer the benefits of true network document capture installations, as scan-and-film equipment cannot share its microform portion. In the case of scan-then-film installations, it can be shown that they can yield lower overall cost per image than the use of stand-alone techniques. Furthermore, network installations make it possible to rearrange workflow to accommodate operational requirements, especially in case of equipment breakdown.

Database Reconciliation

Another cost element that further increases the cost advantage of the scan-then-film technique is the cost of matching microform and digital databases. This reconcili-

Table 16.1   Summary of features of microform and digitized image production methods

Features	Rank		
	FTS	S&F	STF
IMAGE QUALITY			
Resolution	1	3	2
Contrast	2	3	1
Recording Integrity	2	3	1
OPERATIONAL CONSIDERATIONS			
Indexing	3	2	1
Quality Control	3	2	1
Electronic Titling	3	2	1
Formats	2	3	1
Management	3	2	1
Costs—Low Volume	1	2	3
Costs—High Volume	2	3	1
OTHER CONSIDERATIONS			
Data Extraction	3	2	1
Database Reconciliation	2	3	1
Records Management and Archiving	3	2	1
Document Composition	3	2	1

ation cost is nonexistent in the scan-then-film method because the film and its index are generated from the digital database itself. Reconciliation is an added cost for the two other methods, and, for large databases, that cost can be quite substantial.

Records and Archive Management

Because microforms generated in a scan-then-film mode can be produced to represent the most recent version of a document file, that technique is appropriate for file consolidation for archiving, using the digital database index to eliminate automatically unnecessary documents and generate archival records on film and produce the appropriate index at no additional cost.

In addition, film recorders produce high-resolution images; therefore, the archived files can be scanned back into a digitized system and produce images with acceptable quality. Furthermore, if the index has been preserved in a machine-readable form, this rescanning can be done with minimal intervention.

Data Extraction

In many applications, data contained in captured images must be extracted, usually by optical character recognition, for future processing. Unless the microform has been generated specifically with that requirement in mind, image quality often will not be sufficient to ensure acceptable levels of accuracy. Therefore, only the digital recording of a scan-and-film device and scan-then-film installations will be acceptable. As already mentioned, economic consideration of the relative costs of OCR error correction and keyboarding may be a determining factor for this selection criterion.

Document Composition

In applications involving heavy document editing and final output to film, scan-then-film equipment offers a unique advantage over the other two. In publishing in particular, it is often necessary to merge documents from different sources and reformat them. The resulting document, such as an updated technical manual, is then reproduced for mass distribution.

Because scan-then-film is mostly an electronic process, it allows the use of desktop and workgroup publishing techniques to create final documents, which can then be output in an appropriate format for micropublishing or photocomposition.

Selection of Best Method

From this discussion, it is apparent that the selection of an appropriate method for creating microform/digitized image sets is a complex process, in which operational and other benefits must be carefully weighed. In particular, one must be aware that the potential cost advantage of one method must be fully assessed over an entire product cycle, not just during the production of the set. For instance, in publishing applications, the flexibility offered by electronic editing far outweighs, beyond a certain production level, the higher initial equipment cost of scan-then-film systems. Using the same data as those used for the model depicted in Figure 16.9, it can be shown that scan-then-film techniques can become competitive for production levels approaching 50,000 pages per month when operational criteria, such as quality, flexibility, and management of the workflow, are added to pure cost-per-frame considerations.

16.6 APPLICATION TO COLD TECHNOLOGIES

Computer-output-to-laser-disk (COLD) technologies are the computer data equivalent to source microfilm, intended for the storage and retrieval of computer reports. In COLD systems, computer reports that traditionally would have been output to microform through computer output microform (COM) technologies are directly recorded on optical disk. As such, it is vastly superior to earlier inefficient and low-quality digitizing methods in which computer printouts were scanned so that their electronic images could be searchable.

When compared to computer output microform, COLD technologies benefit from the same medium advantage that optical disk has over source microfilm. Cost justification of a COLD installation, based on a comparison between cost-per-output pages, is a straightforward operation.

Currently, there are several COLD packages on the market and, depending on their features, they can provide intelligent information retrieval. In fact, COLD software are database management systems bundled with optical disk drivers designed to read input computer data submitted in a report format and to display them in a variety of ways, including traditional tabular layouts. As such, they can be found in a multiplicity of configurations, for either direct computer input or for batch processing from magnetic tape, the traditional input medium for COM recording.

There is, however, in spite of its technological similarities, a major difference between COLD and document imaging. In contrast with scanned images, COLD data are received and stored in a machine-readable form. Any graphical attributes, such as logos and forms, are added through external merge. Because of this difference, file formats between COLD and scanned documents are different, and the dissimilarity in retrieval patterns makes it rarely reasonable to store both types of data together.

16.7 CONCLUSION

As it has been shown, there is no fundamental reason why microforms may not be part of a full imaging system. As a backup, it offers the possibility of low-cost emergency support. However, it must be understood that such a backup mechanism must be designed with consideration for recovery. Under these conditions, the design of the imaging system must take into account the processes that will be necessary to "reload" the central system, once the emergency has passed.

17

Deploying an Imaging Network

Mark Roy
Bitex Corporation

Editor's Note

As the acceptance of an imaging system becomes a fait accompli, it becomes necessary to plan for integration of the imaging network with the rest of the organization's communication system. Two considerations, internetworking and interoperability, are at the heart of such an integration.

Internetworking relates to the combination of local area networks and wide area networks. Interoperability refers to the ability of users of an internetwork to exchange data in a transparent manner, without consideration of intermediary hardware and network systems and protocols. At the present time, the only reliable methodology for designing interoperable systems is to use the ISO seven-layer model, described in Chapter 3.

Most important for interoperability in local area networks are the services offered by layer 3 (network) and layer 4 (transport) protocols. These services will often be bundled with software that control higher levels, such as Xerox Network Service (XNS), which roughly spans between layers 3, 4, 5, and 7, or TCP/IP, which covers all layers from 3 to 7.

Ensuring interoperability with mainframe-based networks requires special handling, depending on their architectures, as explained in Chapter 9. Successful interoperability depends on two different considerations:

1. *Ability of two different protocols to coexist on the same network.*
2. *Ability of two different implementations of the same protocol to interact.*

There is no general methodology to ensure such interoperability besides a systematic compliance testing, using all possible combinations of software available on the networks. Such testing will be greatly facilitated by (in fact, will often require) the use of powerful network and protocol analysis tools.

This chapter addresses some of the issues that must be considered when combining LANs and WANs, using the example of an insurance claims processing application to do so. Its perspective can be used for many enterprise-wide implementations.

17.1 GENERAL SYSTEMS DEPLOYMENT CONSIDERATIONS

Among the myriad considerations necessary for the successful deployment of an imaging system is the impact that imaging will have on existing platforms. Regardless that LAN technologies may currently exist in an environment, it's likely that the increased demands of imaging will require major changes in platforms and the infrastructure. The technologic criteria notwithstanding, close attention to the details of personnel ergonomics and the process enhanced or replaced by imaging must be analyzed. In many cases, as stated throughout this book, imaging technology dramatically changes the means by which a company conducts its business. In the discussion that follows, examples of an insurance company dental claims processing application will illustrate the impact of the various decisions that must be made when using imaging systems. From this example, applications for other industries like banking, brokerage, service, and manufacturing can be extrapolated.

The criteria for the dental claims application are based on some simple factors:

- Ninety percent of imaging retrieval will occur within thirty days of initial input.
- That same 90 percent must be available within twenty seconds of request.
- All data must be stored for up to three years.

Before delving deeply into the specifics of each criterion, a brief overview of the critical components will provide a good starting point.

Data Storage Considerations

The imaging system you choose will probably use a combination of storage technologies including disk, tape, and optical media. The choice of one, many, or all of these technologies will determine the capacity and environmental criteria for the system. In general, imaging systems will use a combination of magnetic and optical storage for regular image access. Specific process requirements will determine the need for local or near-line storage.

Using the criteria list for the dental claims application, the high-speed access afforded by magnetic disk storage will provide the responsiveness required for this application. The baseline for disk sizing includes the size of the image to be stored as a factor of the image storage format chosen (TIFF, DDIF, IOCA, etc.), whether or not the images include high-resolution grayscale or color (X-ray and photographic support documentation), and the volume of claims to be processed within a thirty-day period. As will be discussed later, disk sizing will also be affected by the decision for centralized vs. distributed system implementation. All this notwithstanding, the sizing of magnetic disk storage is a major decision, as imaging systems quickly consume gigabytes of disk space.

Optical storage and retrieval (OSAR) systems provide economical storage of data for archive and long-term retrieval and analysis. Optical disk systems typically perform more poorly than magnetic storage based on the highly mechanical "jukebox" methods used for disk selection and mounting. Optical systems have the unique advantage of data integrity over extended time frames. Unlike magnetic storage, once an optical disk is encoded with data, the data will not be deleted. Even highly secured magnetic storage degrades over time as the ability of the media to reliably hold a magnetic charge wanes.

Retrieval Times Impact

Not all issues regarding retrieval are limited to the magnetic and optical subsystems; the overall implementation must be carefully considered. However, a combination of well-meshed technologies is critical to optimal performance. A complete analysis of workstation, network, and storage is necessary to fine-tune the system for maximum responsiveness. Once all components in the system have been integrated, the weak link in the chain is generally the optical subsystem.

Optimized Use of Resources

The most reliable implementations of imaging use this powerful combination of magnetic media for high-speed, short-term storage and optical disk for long-term data management. Many smaller systems can be used on existing LAN systems. Add-on optical subsystems to a variety of servers running an equally wide variety of network operating systems can provide an economical means to provide magnetic, optical, or combo storage systems. Depending upon the demands of your implementation, you may choose to use existing LAN servers for one of many magnetic storage requirements for imaging. These include, but are not limited to, scanning, indexing, and short-term retention.

Centralized vs. Distributed Criteria

The nature of a business has a major impact on the choice to centralize or distribute the system. Obviously, a single-location real estate office will centralize. In the dental claims application, it may or may not be advantageous to distribute certain portions of the system to regional sites. Once again, the complexity of maximizing performance coupled with the need to economize where possible will be greatly impacted by this decision.

Legacy Systems Integration

If your company is like most, you'll not have the luxury to start with a clean slate. Legacy systems from small PC LANs to large global networks will have already been built. Equally large and politically complex fiefdoms to support these systems will provide a variety of supporters and detractors to the use of imaging technology. In most cases, linkage with these legacy systems is necessary to avoid duplication of data already managed and maintained. Although not all components of legacy systems are reusable for imaging, it is generally possible to integrate the absolutely necessary parts through gateways or front-end applications.

17.2 INTEGRATION WITH CURRENT SYSTEMS

PCs, Minis, Mainframes

Integration with legacy systems is a major challenge. Successful installations use the dynamics of the graphical user interface (GUI) on the PC to build interfaces to mini and mainframe applications. Front ends using GUI application generators buffer the user from the text-based application while concurrently capturing and submitting the entered data and communicating to other applications in the GUI environment. For maximum capability, systems larger than PCs should be LAN attached. Application software for async and 3270 terminal emulation over LANs is readily available. Although not absolutely necessary, LAN access to larger systems provides a more easily installed and maintained physical infrastructure, although nothing precludes individually wired async or sync connections.

In the dental claims application, a claimant requesting information provides a group claim number and social security number for identification. The customer service rep enters this data into a GUI dialog box. Iconized on the GUI desktop is a 3270 emulation application that sends the info to a CICS application on the mainframe. The returned data from the mainframe is captured and displayed graphically, with option buttons providing a variety of choices. In this instance, the claimant requests a copy of the original claim form for submission to a secondary insurance carrier. The customer service rep clicks a button, which initiates the address; then other claim information is loaded into a boilerplate cover letter. An image of a claim form is populated with the claim information, and the whole package is sent to an outbound fax server for transmission to the claimant.

SNA Wide Area Networks

In general, traditional SNA wide area networks (WANs) are not capable of holding up under the rigors of image traffic; nor were SNA networks designed for imaging. This does not mean that the entire SNA network must be abandoned. Many companies with large-scale SNA WANs have also implemented private backbones of 56KB, fractional T1, full T1, and even T3 links. The more traditional portions of this network infrastructure, low-speed multidrop lines, will not be replaceable. The portion that is capable of reuse in an LAN backbone, however, can be reused for imaging.

Token-Ring and Ethernet

Traditionally, image systems require a high bandwidth for reasonable response time and input traffic. Even with the bandwidth available in Ethernet (10MB) and token-ring (4MB and 16MB), portions of the image system providing high-volume services like scanning and indexing will be designed into small segments with only a few workstations.

It is advisable that the LAN infrastructure include both token-ring and Ethernet capability for maximum connectivity. With this philosophy, image components with preference for one media type or another can be included in your mix. The ability for workstations on one media to communicate with servers or services on the other will be supported by routers providing the physical translation services and relying upon the upper-layer protocols of the ISO OSI model for communication.

17.3 NETWORK INFRASTRUCTURE

The previous section opened the discussion on the issues of network infrastructure capacity and pointed out that, in many cases, portions of that system may need replacement or be abandoned. How does one decide what to save and what to discard? And from that which is saved, must it be rearchitected for the new environment? Beginning with the low-speed SNA or async networks, these architectures will be examined, and a migration path towards the more robust networks needed for large-scale imaging will be suggested.

Low-Speed Network Overhaul

As stated earlier, low-speed networks lack sufficient bandwidth to support the volume of data generated by imaging systems. Low-speed networks, designed for ASCII data or SNA 3270 block mode data streams, are optimized for short bursts of text information, with even shorter acknowledgments. In contrast, an image containing both sides of a personal check at 300 dpi resolution could be as large as 50,000 bytes. Low-speed multidrop SNA networks, or async networks with statistical multiplexors, must be abandoned and rearchitected for imaging traffic. Likewise, the terminal equipment used for the interface with the systems must also be replaced with a workstation capable of providing the rich graphic displays necessary for imaging. The restructuring of the end user facilities will usually carry the largest budgetary balance. The geographic dispersion of your system and the choice to build a centralized vs. distributed system will also factor into the cost of telecommunications in your network.

Meshed Architecture

Since imaging will be highly reliant upon an LAN/WAN system, a sufficient degree of redundancy and bandwidth availability is necessary in the successful implementation. A meshed architecture will provide maximum capacity. Figure 17.1 represents a traditional SNA network system using modern multiport DSUs on 56KB multidrop lines. How could this network be redesigned for imaging?

Since the mainframe is no longer an integral part of the connectivity, it is removed along with the 3 × 74 cluster controllers at the two remote sites. In addition, since LANs cannot be multidropped, the two remote offices will receive private links from the network. This means an additional central site DSU must be employed. The redesigned network looks like that shown in Figure 17.2.

- Much of the SNA WAN has been preserved and used as the new infrastructure for the LAN/WAN needed for imaging.

- Many management systems have also been preserved, thereby reducing training to support the new network.

- Meshing can be accomplished in two ways, as diagrammed in Figure 17.3. One (Figure 17.3a) continues to use T1 nodal processors and channel banks for low-speed LAN/WAN links, and the other (Figure 17.3b) provides direct connectivity into the routers. In either case, the scenario and effect is the same.

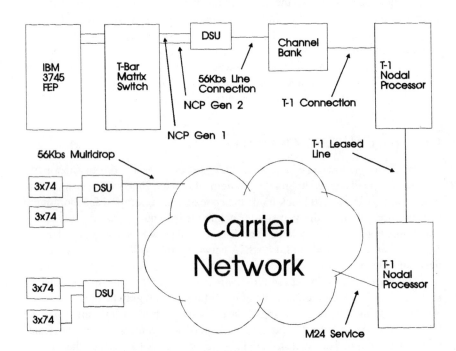

Figure 17.1   Traditional representation of an SNA network

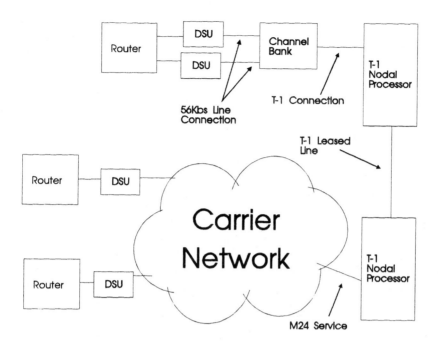

Figure 17.2   Example of a redesigned network

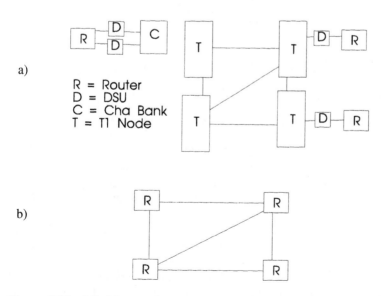

Figure 17.3   Meshing options: a) meshed T1 network; b) meshed router network

The power of this design comes from the ability to recover from the loss of a major leased line. In the meshed nodal processor design, the loss of a single T1 does not disrupt the network as the nodes allocate and redirect channels over the remaining links. The limitation of this design is its lack of bandwidth load sharing, which is performed dynamically in the meshed router design. All bandwidth in the network is in use continuously until a line loss is detected. Then, redirection of data occurs like a meshed T1 nodal system. Many system designs incorporate a combination of both designs in the network. The meshed T1 design allows for the continuation of older systems which may not have outlived their usefulness.

Advanced Bridges and Routers

Since the base method for connectivity for imaging systems is local area networks, a decision must be made as to the use of bridges or routers. Using the classic definition, a bridge is a device used to link like networks and a router used for unlike networks. In addition, a router can consolidate multiple simultaneous interfaces, while a bridge is a two-interface device linking LAN A to LAN B. The ability of modern routers to provide all the functions of bridging while also providing interface consolidation and translation between network types makes the choice of routers easy to make.

What brand of router you choose will be based entirely on the complexity of the network implementation. If you are not already familiar with the concepts of TCP/IP and internetwork routing, a considerable learning curve must be accomplished. The power of routing systems allows LAN capabilities to be dispersed in powerful high-speed networks in local geographic areas (campus network) at speeds of 100MB or more and over the WAN at speeds of 1.5MB and up. As WAN technology and the communications infrastructure improves over time, the differences in capacity will diminish.

Network Management

Like all network resources, the ability to manage the image system components is critical. Tools to analyze capacity and performance, and manage administration and security will typically come directly from the manufacturer. In many cases, software agents that can provide an interface with SNMP-based management systems will provide a reasonable means to provide fault and alarm monitoring. As more advanced management systems based upon ISO or OSF/DME models emerge, a more rich and heterogeneous management environment will be available. Under these conditions, a performance alarm event may cause the automatic gathering of statistics for analysis and subsequent action by the network designer. Or a capacity trigger may initiate the order for a magnetic or optical subsystem upgrade. Regardless of the mechanism used, an imaging system and its network infrastructure must be manageable to maintain the desired levels of performance and administer to the ongoing capacity needs of the system.

High-Speed Transports

As imaging capabilities begin to permeate a network, the demands for greater bandwidth will be inevitable. Although high-speed networks for LANs exist today (Ethernet, token-ring, FDDI), the same is not necessarily true for the WAN. Currently, the most economical communications link is the T1, operating at 1.544MB. T1s are not necessarily inexpensive, but compared to the next level of WAN link operating at 45MB (a T3 line), T1s are the level of connectivity that most companies can afford. Although a company can build a meshed network as described earlier, all the work necessary to manage the data relies on the capabilities of the router. Many companies building LAN/WAN systems are looking to the communications carriers for better WAN capacity. By doing this, the routers can limit themselves to the functions of interface and protocol management, while the WAN handles the high-speed transport of the data.

The carriers are currently developing, and in some cases have limited deployment of, certain high-speed systems which will see greater usage shortly. One of these is frame relay, diagrammed in Figure 17.4.

In a frame relay network, the address of each private node attached to the communications cloud is also known to the carrier system. In this way, an addressing function similar to that used on the LAN is used by the carrier to route traffic. In this system, the private and public networks work cooperatively to manage the data and assure accurate, efficient delivery. A frame relay system operates very similar to an X.25 network with a few exceptions. Frame relay

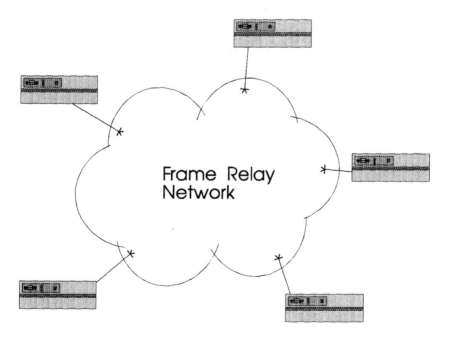

Figure 17.4   Diagram of a frame relay

operates over very high speed office channel (OC) links running at speeds beginning at T3s 45MB and upwards. This is not to say that X.25 networks cannot operate at these speeds, but the error correction employed by the X.25 network imposes a performance overhead not needed in a modern fiber optics–based system. Frame relay employs the reliability of this fiber network to impose no management overhead. Instead, the integrity of the data must be verified by the private nodes.

Once again, the cooperative nature between the LAN and WAN systems allows high-volume systems like imaging to effectively incorporate a distributed architecture with minimal impact on system operation.

Traffic Modeling

Many companies employ tools for traffic modeling to optimize performance. This is very prevalent in SNA networks. Note that older modeling tools may not be upgradable to LAN modeling. However, several good modeling tools can perform LAN, SNA, sync, and async analysis. As with SNA tools, the ability to accumulate accurate traffic data is key. Look for tools that allow the importation of traffic captured by protocol analyzers. Most analyzers provide a utility to export captured data and statistics to an ASCII file. It is necessary to capture data over time and provide the tool with statistically accurate data for good modeling to occur. Without an import feature, your tool is nearly useless, because the data upon which its calculations will be based are raw estimates. An import feature also relieves you from entering pages of statistical data.

17.4 PERSONNEL ERGONOMICS

There's no getting around it: Even the most sophisticated imaging system needs operators to perform key functions. Although the workflow software and process by which the work is done may have changed, the impact on the operators must be taken into account for a successful implementation. This includes not just the ergonomics of the workstation, critical of course, but also the psyche of the operators themselves. In some situations, the radical change brought on by imaging requires adjustments in how people measure their success, and how *they* are measured.

Workstation Platforms

An obvious necessity for imaging is a workstation with sufficient power and facilities to generate the visual presentation of the data and applications. Questions quickly arise regarding the sizing and scalability of the workstation. Serious consideration must be invested in the workstation decision, as this line item generally represents a large percentage of the image system cost.

For maximum functionality, the chosen platform should be scalable in terms of memory, graphics, and storage. Likewise, the operating system and GUI should allow upward use of the same application software. These decisions will eliminate the need for expensive platform replacement as requirements change and eliminate the need for costly retraining on new software systems.

Low Performance

Low-performance workstations should be given only to the most casual users. These people generally perform intermittent access of images and are under no response-time constraints. Researchers and analysts may fall into this category. These workstations may contain Motorola 68020 or Intel 80286 or 386sx processor types. They may or may not use a software compression application to display the images. Good resolution monitors of VGA level will suffice, although color may not be required. Baseline RAM and hard disk subsystems and minimal network connectivity are provided. These workstations provide the best economy for a wide group of users. Because of the smaller low-resolution monitors, a good zoom facility is necessary to obtain better image readability.

Midrange Performance

Midrange systems apply to those persons with regular access needs who are not in a customer service or highly visible position. Administrators and application developers may fall into this category. Midrange systems typically have Motorola 68030, Intel 80386, Sun SPARC, or Mips R4000 processors and higher. These workstations have high-resolution monitors, often color, at or about the 17" range, better RAM and hard disk facilities, and use software-based compression for faster image display. Although not of the highest resolution, good zooming and access to other peripherals like modem and fax pools are generally available.

High Performance

These systems are used in areas where maximum performance is needed when imaging is highly visible or customer service is in operation. They generally are based on RISC platforms like Sun SPARC, Mips R4000, DEC Alpha, HP9000, IBM RS6000, and others. High-resolution 20" monitors with hardware-based graphics accelerators provide quick display of image graphics. The speed of the processors supports rapid interaction between applications. Due to the size and resolution of the monitors, zooming is not as necessary as with other platforms because the image will be clearly displayed and should be easily read. The personnel impact of using even slightly lower resolution screens when high volume is required should be considered. The result may be frequent breaks for users due to eyestrain and other related symptoms.

Compression Methods

The method used to display images may be based on the use of software compression and decompression. The decision to use these drivers should be based largely on both the capacity of the workstations and subsystems. It is necessary to work closely with the image system vendor to deploy such systems.

The use of software compression impacts an LAN/WAN system as well as the workstations. At the workstation level, additional CPU and memory resources are needed to generate and present the display. This in turn impacts overall workstation performance and degradation as image retrieval and density increases. Compression has exactly the opposite effect on the network infrastructure. Since the compressed image represents a smaller data record, the network can transport compressed images faster as the amount of data is diminished. In addition, images that are stored as compressed files on the magnetic or optical subsystems consume expensive resources at a lower pace.

In a utopia, images would be compressed at all points in the underlying infrastructure until reaching the workstation, where decompression would occur. As major vendors work to resolve this problem, the ability for "smart images" to traverse the system will become more of a reality. At this stage, however, it is necessary to carefully assess the ability of your chosen vendor's product to work with a variety of software- and hardware-based compression and acceleration at the workstation and storage points.

17.5 SYSTEM STRUCTURE

One of the greatest decisions you will face in your design is that regarding the centralized or distributed structure of your system. Much of this decision will be based upon your company location(s) and political structure. A small one-location installation will have limited cause for concern; a large insurance company with two or more data centers and regional offices will have a larger task with which to grapple. There are many pros and cons to each approach. Again, a careful examination of your criteria for performance, access, and telecommunications must be made before making this determination.

Distributed Theory

The choice to distribute an imaging system should be based on a business need for fast response time, optimal network utilization, maximum regional mail service, high disaster recovery, and ability through workflow design to distribute post-scanning activity around the system.

In the dental claims example, a distributed system would provide a means for regional collection of claim information either by mail or fax. Mailed claim forms would be scanned and entered into a queue for indexing and further adjudication. In the pros and cons sections that follow, a discussion of the salient points should help you determine if a distributed system would apply to your plan.

Distributed Approach—Cons

Distributing an imaging system is a more costly implementation. This factor will permeate the distributed system at every level, which is not to say that a distributed system is a poor design, but that the bottom line costs will be greater.

Higher Systems Cost Although all components of the distributed system need not be duplicated at each site, many systems components like local magnetic storage will be necessary. It may also be the case that a fully distributed system will have multiple scanning, indexing, and optical storage components. This equipment and the staff necessary to perform the various functions will need office housing as well. Even though you may place these users in low-rent suburban office space, the duplication of that office space has a direct real dollar cost.

Dislocation of Staff Presuming your infrastructure may currently be centralized, you may experience a dislocation of staff while converting to a distributed system. Even if currently distributed, it may be necessary to dislocate highly trained personnel to various locations during the implementation for local training and installation oversight. Finding personnel to perform this function may require additional staff or using consultants for successful deployment.

Cost Center Allocation Many companies are divided by profit and cost centers. The major components of an image system will be expensive and require knowl-edgeable management. Typically, these support functions will be handled by a centralized information systems group, the cost center of which is likely to differ with the regional locale. Allocation of environmental and other expenses will require negotiation with internal groups.

Cultural and Political Perturbations One of the key reasons for distributing a large-scale application like claims forms processing is the ability to distribute the workload among a wide geographic group based on time zones or cost of personnel. The ability to effectively manage important issues among these disparate groups is more difficult. Credit for work done on nonlocal accounts must be included as part of the overall reward structure to assure continuity of service to customers.

Distributed Approach—Pros

The issues that make a distributed system attractive are the high performance and resilience to regional problems or issues. Local databases on magnetic storage will respond rapidly to requests. Since optical storage is typically slow, retrieval across the WAN to a centrally located OSAR will provide reasonable response time. A blizzard in the Northeast does not preclude the claims in their work queue from being distributed to locations in the South.

Smaller Databases Since the databases are small and contain only the minimal amount of data needed locally, response times are maximized. LANs run at high speed to make quick work of scanning and indexing functions, database backup, and image retrieval.

Disaster Recovery Even though local backup of data will occur, nothing precludes the duplication of the database to a central repository. With this mechanism in place, the loss of a site to disaster allows an alternate site to assume its data and function. A distributed system provides the highest level of system availability.

Lower Occupancy Rates Granted, there will be more locations to support, but it's likely that the distribution of the imaging system is in line with a solid business case for distributed sites to sustain your business. For this reason, smaller suburban sites in regional locations will probably reduce site and environmental costs.

Best Customer Service Since the database and personnel managing the data are geographically close to the customer, normal business hours for support will apply locally, and data entry problems can be quickly resolved. In general, service to the customer is faster due to the close proximity.

Mailing Zone Optimization In those instances where the use of the postal system for original documentation gathering is necessary, short transit times to regional locations will assure that critical data are entered into the system in a timely manner.

Centralized Theory

The centralized method for design minimizes overall cost. Collocation of expensive resources, skilled staff, and the necessary environment allow the construction of a system with large capacity. Political and cost center problems are moot, as are issues regarding system management and maintenance. A centralized system represents a single point of failure for the entire network. Alternate network routing, equipment, personnel, off-site storage of backup data, and a strong disaster recovery plan must be considered.

Centralized Approach—Cons

Disaster Recovery The negatives of a centralized approach to the construction of an imaging system are not unlike that for any large data system. Should a major system component fail, or the environment housing the imaging system become unusable, the ability to convert to a backup system will include considerable downtime. As an environment becomes increasingly more complex, the cost of disaster recovery services becomes more expensive.

Delayed Data Entry Since all input to the system will be performed in a central site, the problems with mail delay will be pervasive. Regardless of where in the world you locate your data center, there will always be a band of mail zones that emanate outward to the fringes of the customer base. Subsequently, customers living on the fringe areas will always be subjected to a delay in service because of the added time to get their input data processed and/or returned. This assumes there is no inbound fax capacity; if input supported by fax is available, then a centralized system has no impact.

Staffing Needs A centralized staff may at first seem to be a plus since you will reduce headcount and eliminate redundant training and personnel overhead. But further analysis shows that processing of documents for the business will begin and cease with the daily working hours of the personnel in the data center locale. Thus, a continental U.S. West Coast operation would open for business three hours after the start of business in the East and discontinue operations two hours prior to the end of business in Hawaii. Even with extended hours and additional personnel, there will always be dead periods when service is curtailed.

Data Error Resolution Needless to say, humans will occasionally make data entry mistakes. Either the submitter has incorrectly populated a field or the keypunch operator has fat-fingered the keyboard. In any event, the ability to quickly reach the party who made the mistake and correct it will generally be exacerbated by the geographic separation of the parties.

Centralized Approach—Pros

High Productivity Since all submissions will converge on a central location, productivity will reflect the high degree of experience of the operators in the business process and methods used to operate the equipment. Expensive high-speed systems can also be purchased to further improve performance and productivity.

Lowest Hardware Cost Only the equipment that is required to populate the workers' desktops and provide short-term magnetic storage and optical service need be purchased. The system can be fine-tuned and easily managed due to the tight correlation between system use and capacity. Unlike the distributed approach, each component is used to maximum advantage with little wasted capacity.

Lowest Telecommunications Costs There may in fact be no telecommunications cost for a centralized image system unless fax input is promoted by supplying an incoming 800 number. Since the network infrastructure supporting the system is local to the office or campus, telecommunications costs will be minimized. To leverage image capacity, some telecom cost may be incurred for linkage with large customers or suppliers. Even here, agreements that share costs or quid pro quo for storage on a system can limit leased line expenses.

Central Storage of Originals Because all originals are stored centrally, retrieval time, even for paper backup is reduced to the minimum. A high degree of customer service is assured by centralized storage and processing. It is necessary to include a secure environment for backups and paper documentation. If the documents are legal in nature, there may be no choice but to keep the paper originals; if this is necessary, it is best to use a nearby storage facility.

Redundancy Eliminated   Any redundancies that are necessary for even the most rudimentary distributed system are eliminated when using the centralized approach. As with any large-scale centralized system, maximum efficiencies and benefits of scale will inure to your benefit. All areas of your implementation will be affected including facilities, systems, and personnel. In many cases, after initial implementation, headcounts are further reduced as the conversion process wanes. The personnel needed to maintain the business process established by the image system is generally about 50 percent of the startup staff. This does not include the staff needed for the infrastructure system.

Improved Management   Collocation of the image system with other large systems and the support network allows for a tight integration of real-time management and the logistics to provide ongoing maintenance and repair. This will manifest itself in a high degree of system availability and performance.

17.6   CONCLUSION: THE CHOKE POINTS

Throughout this discussion, the pros and cons of each approach, and the highlights and traps of each decision are biased by the general need for performance that meets or exceeds the need to support the business process. It's difficult to be specific regarding the impact of each component decision, because each implementation is unique. The personality of the system you build will be affected by your legacy systems, political perturbations, and a less than optimal budget. But, a few general rules apply to any system.

In real estate, the mantra is "location, location, location." In this endeavor, "planning, planning, planning" will determine how well your implementation performs. Although it's difficult, analyze as best you can the volume of images that may be entering the system, multiplied by the density of the image format you will process. For example, a personal check measuring 2" × 6" comprises 12 square inches. At a resolution of 200 dots per inch, each square inch needs 40,000 bits ($200 \times 200 = 40,000$) of storage, or 5,000 bytes (40,000/8 bits per byte). Thus, a single side of a personal check will require 60,000 bytes or 58.59KB per side. Assuming that 10,000 checks per day may be processed, a thirty-day magnetic storage system of 18GB will be needed. And that's only to store the images of the front side of checks!!

Likewise, examine closely the throughput of your network system. Carefully analyze the true performance of Ethernet, ArcNet, token-ring, and/or FDDI systems. The combination of physical system performance and protocol will impact the ability to process the maximum number of images. If this data also flows over a wide area network, make realistic assumptions about the throughput of a WAN link. In general, the greater the bandwidth, the better. Although expensive, be prepared to purchase the fastest links you can afford, and then adjust your application to take best advantage of what you've got. Few companies can afford T3s between sites. But even with a T1 or multiple T1s your decision to use data compression to improve price/performance of the workstations will also help to reduce the demands on the network infrastructure. Capacity-planning tools should be used and programmed to assume the latency delays associated with each component in the network.

If sufficient forethought is exercised, and informed decisions are made about the process to be converted and the methods used to support that process, you will find your implementation of an image system both rewarding and profitable.

Index